eBay®

10th Edition

by Marsha Collier

A Wiley Brand

eBay® For Dummies®, 10th Edition

Published by: **John Wiley & Sons, Inc.,** 111 River Street, Hoboken, NJ 07030-5774, www.wiley.com

Copyright © 2020 by John Wiley & Sons, Inc., Hoboken, New Jersey

Published simultaneously in Canada

For general information on our other products and services, please contact our Customer Care Department within the U.S. at 877-762-2974, outside the U.S. at 317-572-3993, or fax 317-572-4002. For technical support, please visit https://hub.wiley.com/community/support/dummies.

Wiley publishes in a variety of print and electronic formats and by print-on-demand. Some material included with standard print versions of this book may not be included in e-books or in print-on-demand. If this book refers to media such as a CD or DVD that is not included in the version you purchased, you may download this material at http://booksupport.wiley.com. For more information about Wiley products, visit www.wiley.com.

Library of Congress Control Number: 2019953324

ISBN 978-1-119-61774-7; ISBN 978-1-119-61784-6 (ePub); ISBN 978-1-119-61783-9 (ePDF)

Manufactured in the United States of America

V10015415_110719

Contents at a Glance

Table of Contents

Introduction

These days you have a lot of choices when you want to sell online. There are some apps/platforms that may seem easier than eBay . . . but . . . there's only one eBay. You have the opportunity to sell your items to a worldwide audience who may be looking for the things you choose to sell.

Selling on eBay is profitable and empowering if you follow the basics rules. The beginning steps are outlined in this book and can take you to easily bring in $60,000 a year. You don't need any more to start out than what you read in the pages of this book. After you've mastered the basics, you're on your way to your own part- or full-time e-commerce empire.

This is the *tenth* edition of *eBay For Dummies*. When I wrote the original edition in 1999, eBay had just gone public, and the gross merchandise sales by sellers on the site was estimated at a staggering $2.8 billion. There has been little change in Internet transactions since eBay pioneered the collaborative economy. In 2018, eBay enabled almost $95 billion of gross merchandise volume with person-to-person transactions. I had no idea that eBay would become the worldwide marketplace it has — and that this book would become the top-selling book for those wanting to learn about eBay. (Pretty cool, though.)

Literally millions of people have learned how to succeed at an eBay business by reading my books. In your hand you have the book that will get *you* on the road to your own online business. Heed my words and you'll be getting the no-nonsense facts about eBay from an active user who was selling on eBay almost from day one.

I'm a longtime eBay shopper as well as a Top Rated Seller. My original career was in retail marketing, and since launching my eBay adventure, I've been making money on the site. (I even put my daughter through college on my profits!) I work from home and apply my background successfully to all facets of the site.

My enthusiasm and excitement for shopping and selling on the eBay Marketplace seems to have spread to so many corners of the world. eBay users (like you and me) currently total 182 million active users worldwide — that's quite a community. (In 1999 there were only 10 million registered users.)

It's a community of buyers who enjoy shopping with mom-and-pop businesses (along with many famous celebrities and brand names) worldwide — and of sellers who forage for items to sell online and make a few dollars (or a full-time living). The best part is that eBay is available to anyone who wants to take the time to learn how it works.

The venue is constantly evolving; familiar links may move, but the basics are there. It isn't too hard to master, but just as with any tool, once you know the ins and outs, you're ahead of the game. You can then get the deals when you shop, and make the most money when you sell. You've come to the right place to find out all about eBay. This book is designed to help you understand the basics about buying and selling on eBay, the world's most successful e-commerce community.

You need a firm grasp of the basics before you can succeed in any endeavor. Here are all the tools you need to get moving on eBay, whether you're new to the Internet or a seasoned veteran. You see how to turn your everyday household clutter into cold, hard cash — and how to look for items that you can sell on eBay.

If you're an online shopper, I show you how to figure out how much you should spend and how to get great deals. How much money you earn (or spend) depends entirely on how *often* and how *smartly* you conduct your eBay transactions. *You* decide how often you want to sell items and place bids; I'm here to help with the *smart* part by sharing tips (along with the rules) drawn from my years of experience on eBay.

A website as complex as eBay has many nooks and crannies that may confuse new users. Think of this book as a detailed road map that can help you navigate eBay, getting just as much or as little as you want from it. If there's a specific question you want answered, try looking it up in the index. I bet you'll find a reference that will help.

As you figure out the nuts and bolts, you can start buying and selling stuff. This book is full of terrific strategies that help you get the most out of your transactions. With this book and a little focused effort, you can join the ranks of the millions of people who use the Internet to make a profit. When you get the hang of eBay and feel that it's time to graduate (no cap and gown required) from this book, look for my *eBay Business All-In-One For Dummies* — it'll take you to the next plateau.

MARSHA SAYS

Remember one thing. The more items you list for sale, the more profits you make. "Thinking" about listing items brings in no profit; trust me, I've been there. Action = profits.

About This Book

Remember those open-book tests that teachers sprang on you in high school? Well, sometimes you may feel like eBay pop-quizzes you while you're on the site. Think of *eBay For Dummies*, 10th Edition, as your open-book-test cheat sheet with all the answers. You don't have to memorize anything; just keep this book handy to help you get over the confusing parts of eBay. Over the years, some of the top sellers and buyers on the eBay site have visited with me when I'm at a book signing or teaching a seminar just to show me their dog-eared, highlighted, marred copy of an earlier edition of *eBay For Dummies* that got them started. This book will do the same for you.

With all that in mind, I've divided this book into pertinent sections to help you find your answers fast. I'll show you how to

>> Get online and register on eBay.

>> Navigate eBay to do just about anything you can think of — search for items for sale, set up listings, monitor your transactions, and join the social media fun.

>> Bid on and *win* eBay auctions and find low prices at fixed-price sales.

>> Choose an item to sell, pick the right time for your listing, market it so that a bunch of people see it, and make a nice profit.

>> Handle problems with finesse, should they crop up.

>> Become a part of a unique community of people who like to collect, buy, and sell items of just about every type!

REMEMBER

Do not adjust your eyes. To protect the privacy of eBay users, screen images (commonly called *screen shots*) in this book blur user IDs to protect the innocent (or not-so . . .).

Foolish Assumptions

You may have picked up this book because you heard that people are making huge money selling online and you want to find out what's going on. Or you heard about the brand-name bargains and wacky stuff you can find in the world's largest shopping emporium. If either of these assumptions is true, this is the right book for you.

Here are some other foolish assumptions I've made about you:

>> You have, or would like to have, access to the Internet so you can do business on eBay.

>> You have an interest in collecting, selling, or buying, and you want to find out more about doing that online.

>> You want tips and strategies that can save you money when you buy and make you money when you sell. (You too? I can relate. We already have a lot in common.)

>> You're concerned about maintaining your privacy and staying away from people who try to ruin everyone's good time.

Icons Used in This Book

The icons that appear from time to time in the left margin serve some special purposes. I try to throw them in where appropriate to draw your attention to specifics. Here's a rundown of what they mean.

TIP

These are facts that you just *have* to know! Just picture me jumping up and down, just waiting to interrupt your reading with a little extra bonus tidbit. Time is money on eBay. When you see this shortcut or timesaver come your way, read the information and think about all the greenbacks you just saved.

REMEMBER

Think of this icon as a sticky note for your brain. If you forget one of the pearls of wisdom, you can go back and reread it. If you *still* can't remember something here, go ahead and bookmark the page — I won't tell. Even better: Use a yellow highlighter on the print edition.

WARNING

Don't feel my pain. I've done plenty of things wrong on eBay — and really want to save you from my mistakes. I put these warnings out there bright and bold so that you don't have a bad experience. Don't skip these warnings unless you're enthusiastic about masochism.

MARSHA SAYS

When you see this icon, you know you're in for the real deal. This icon will give you my personal tips as well as war stories and successes I've heard from eBay veterans. They can help you strategize, make money, and avoid the perils faced by others. ("Learn from others' mistakes" is my motto.)

You also see a sidebar now and then — text on a gray background to make the topic stand out. Sometimes these decorative items have important short facts that I want you to know, or they contain an interesting aside.

Beyond the Book

Like everything else in the world, eBay changes. Some of the screen grabs in this edition may look slightly different from what you see on your device. That's just eBay tweaking and improving things on the site. My job is to arm you with everything you need to know to begin conducting transactions. Keep in mind that the table of contents or index of this book is your friend. In this book I either help you solve your problems or let you know where to go for some expert advice.

Although eBay makes its complex website as easy to navigate as possible, you may still need to refer to this book for help. Don't get frustrated if you have to keep reviewing topics before you feel completely comfortable trading on eBay.

After all, Albert Einstein once said, "Don't commit to memory something you can look up." (Although I forget when he said that . . . .)

In addition to what you're reading right now, this product also comes with a free access-anywhere Cheat Sheet that covers eBay buying terms. To get this Cheat Sheet, simply go to `www.dummies.com` and search for "eBay Cheat Sheet" in the Search box.

Where to Go from Here

It's time to open the book and dive in. For updates on this book and to contact me, visit my website:

`www.coolebaytools.com`

You'll find articles about things going on at eBay, online business, and social media. For small business and technology posts, I also have a blog at

`http://mcollier.blogspot.com`

If you'd like to ask me questions through social media, you can find me on the following networks (I am on more, but a girl only has so much time):

- **Twitter:** @MarshaCollier

  `http://twitter.com/MarshaCollier`

- **Facebook:** Marsha Collier

  `www.facebook.com/MarshaCollierFanPage`

- **Instagram:** MarshaCollier

  My family, garden, pet, and work pictures

  `www.instagram.com/marshacollier`

- **YouTube:** DealingDiva (Don't judge my ID — I opened that account a long time ago.)

  I often post videos to answer questions I receive.

  `www.youtube.com/user/dealingdiva`

You can email me directly from the Contact page on my website. I read all emails and try to answer as many as I can. But please remember that I'm just me. No giant staff, no big office. I write books, research new products to help online citizens, consult with people just like you, run an eBay business, and take time to enjoy my family.

You can also send me tech questions to answer on my podcast. Every Saturday, from noon to 1 p.m. Pacific time, I cohost the *Computer and Technology Show* (#techradio on Twitter) with Marc Cohen. The show is also archived online at `www.computerandtechnologyradio.com` and on IHEARTRadio (`www.iheart.com/podcast/263-computer-and-technol-28119131`), Tunein (`https://tunein.com/podcasts/Technology-Podcasts/Computer-and-Technology-Radio-p29078`), Stitcher (`www.stitcher.com/podcast/wsradio/computer-and-technology-radio`), and iTunes (`http://itunes.apple.com/us/podcast/computer-technology-radio/id575805424`).

Thank you for buying this book. Please give me a shout out and let me know about your eBay successes.

1
Getting a Feel for eBay

» Learning about eBay

» Figuring out your buying and selling options

» Selling stuff for cash

» Researching items to buy or sell

» Knowing how eBay is protecting you

» Using features and fun stuff

Chapter **1**

Why Being on eBay Is Fun on So Many Levels

e Bay emerged as *the* marketplace of the 21st century. Way back in 2003, *Wired* magazine predicted that eBay's promise was that "retailing will become the national pastime." Promise fulfilled: In 2018, worldwide online e-commerce sales topped $2.86 trillion. The founder had a pretty great idea back in 1995 (read about some eBay history in the "eBay's humble beginnings" sidebar, later in this chapter), and the world has taken to shopping and selling online. eBay is a safe and fun place to shop for everything from collectibles to brand-new clothing and tech gadgets, all from the comfort of your home.

Once referred to as an "online garage sale," eBay is now also a marketplace for new merchandise. It's no longer just the destination for locating unusual collectibles and hard-to-find china patterns. These days major brands have signed up; you can purchase new and useful items, such as alarm systems, tablets, lightbulbs, clothing, cars, homes — just about anything you can think of.

Take a look around your house. Nice shoes (that you never wore). Spiffy artwork (that you're bored with). Great-looking clock (souvenir that doesn't match your décor). Not to mention all the other cool stuff you own. All these great fashions, household appliances, and collectibles are fabulous to own, but when was the last time your clock turned a profit? When you connect to eBay, your PC or mobile device can magically turn into a money machine. Just visit eBay and marvel at all the items that are just a few mouse clicks away from being bought and sold.

In this chapter, I tell you what eBay is and how it works. eBay is today's gas-free alternative to driving and spending hours wandering through boutiques, big-box stores, or outlet malls looking for the perfect bargain or tchotchke. The site can also be your personal shopper for gifts and day-to-day items.

Not only can you buy and sell stuff in the privacy of your home, but through your connections on eBay, you can also meet people who share your interests. Those who use the eBay site are a friendly bunch, and soon you'll be buying, selling, swapping stories, and trading advice with your newfound friends via various social media outlets.

To get to eBay, you need to access the Internet. To access the Internet, you need a Windows PC, a Mac, a tablet with the eBay Mobile app, or simply a smartphone. (Inexpensive brand name Chromebooks can be found for under $200.)

What Is eBay, and How Does It Work?

The Internet spawned all kinds of online retail marketplaces (known as *e-commerce sites* to Wall Street types), and eBay is the superstar as the people's marketplace. The reason it remains a leader is simple: It's where buyers look to do business with both big brands and small homespun family businesses. It's also where a quick look at the listings can give you a ballpark figure on how much an item is "going for" these days.

REMEMBER

eBay itself *doesn't* sell a thing. Instead, the site is a platform for selling and does what all good markets do: It creates a safe environment that brings together buyers and sellers. You can think of eBay as the person who set you up on your last blind date — except the results are often a lot better. Your matchmaking friend doesn't perform a marriage ceremony but does get you in the same room with your potential soulmate. eBay puts buyers and sellers in an e-commerce environment and lets them conduct their business within the rules that eBay has established.

All you need to do to join eBay is fill out a few forms online and click. Congratulations — you're a member, with no fees or secret handshakes needed (you don't pay a fee until you sell something). After you register, you can buy and sell anything that falls within the eBay rules and regulations. (Chapter 2 eases you through the registration process.)

The eBay home page, shown in Figure 1-1, is your first step to finding all the kick-ass stuff you can see and do on eBay. You can conduct searches, learn about current promotions, and get an instant link to the My eBay page, which helps you keep track of every item you have up for sale or have a bid on. You can read more about the eBay home page in Chapter 3 and find out more about My eBay in Chapter 4.

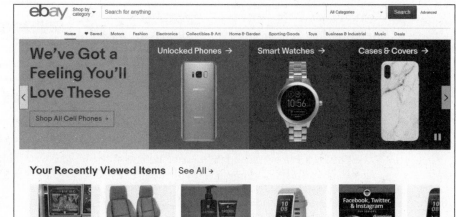

FIGURE 1-1:
The eBay home page, your starting point for bargains and for making some serious cash.

Yikes! What happened? The eBay home page on your computer looks nothing like the one in Figure 1-1? Don't rub your eyes — even squinting hard won't help; eBay has a different version of the home page for those who have never registered on eBay — and customizes the page even if you're not signed in. If *you* have never registered on eBay, someone else who uses the computer may have done so already. Know that whatever version of the eBay home page you view, it has the same basic elements.

eBAY'S HUMBLE BEGINNINGS

The long-standing urban legend says eBay all started with a Pez dispenser. But as romantic as the story is (of the young man who designed the site for his fiancée to trade Pez dispensers), the story is, sadly, public-relations spin. The founder, Pierre Omidyar, had the right vision at the right time, and the first item he sold on the site (which was originally named AuctionWeb) was a broken laser pointer. Day by day, new people were drawn to the site from Internet chatter, including me in 1996. The site eventually grew (hosting 2 million auctions in January 1997) until it began to strain Pierre's ISP server. The ISP charged him more, so he started charging a small listing fee for sellers, just so he could break even. Legend has it that the day $10,000 in fees arrived in Pierre's mailbox, he quit his day job and embarked on building an Internet legend.

(continued)

(continued)

eBay's forerunner, AuctionWeb, was born on Labor Day 1995. The name eBay is taken from Echo Bay, the name Pierre originally wanted for his company. Upon checking with the State of California, he found that the name was taken by another company, so he shortened the name to eBay — and the rest, as they say, is history.

All About Auctions

When it comes to auctions, the value of an item is determined by how much someone is willing to spend to buy it. That's what makes auctions exciting. eBay offers several varieties of auctions, but for the most part, they all work the same way. An *auction* is a unique sales event where the final selling price of the item for sale is not known. As a result, an element of surprise is involved — not only for the bidder (who may end up with a great deal) both from a seller's perspective and a bidder's perspective:

» **Seller:** A seller may pay a fee, fill out an electronic form, and set up the auction, listing a *minimum bid* he or she is willing to accept for the item. Think of an auctioneer at Sotheby's saying, "The bidding for this diamond necklace begins at $5,000." You might *want* to bid $4,000, but the bid won't be accepted. Sellers can also set a *reserve price* — sort of a financial safety net that protects them from losing money on the deal. I explain how all this works later in this section.

» **Bidder:** Bidders in auctions duke it out over a period of time (the minimum is one day, but most auctions last five days, a week, or even longer) until one comes out victorious. Usually the highest bidder wins. The tricky thing about participating in an auction (and the most exciting aspect) is that no one knows the final price an item goes for until the last second — when, often, the most action occurs.

eBay auctions

Unlike "traditional" live auctions that end with the familiar phrase "Going once, going twice, sold!" eBay auctions are controlled by the clock. The seller lists the item on the site for a predetermined period of time; the highest bidder when the clock runs out takes home the prize.

Reserve-price auctions

Unlike a minimum bid, which is required in any eBay auction, a *reserve price* protects sellers from having to sell an item for less than the minimum amount they want for it. You may be surprised to see a brand-new Tesla up for auction on eBay with a minimum bid of only a dollar. It's a fair bet that the seller has put a (much higher) reserve price on this car to protect himself from losing money. The reserve price allows sellers to set lower minimum bids, and lower minimum bids attract bidders. Unfortunately, if a seller makes the reserve price too high and it isn't met by the end of the auction, no one wins.

eBay charges a fee for sellers to run this type of auction. Nobody knows (except the seller and the eBay servers) what the reserve price is until the reserve is met, but you *can* tell from the auction page whether you're dealing with a reserve-price auction. Reserve-price auctions are in the listings alongside the other items, so you have to click to find out whether it has a reserve. If bids have been made on an item, a message also appears on the page telling you if the reserve price hasn't been met. You can find out more about bidding on reserve-price auctions in Chapter 6 and setting up a reserve-price auction in Chapter 9.

Restricted-access adult auctions

If you're over 18 years of age and interested in bidding on items of an adult nature, eBay has an Adult-Only category, which has restricted access. In an effort to respect site visitors, eBay gates the Adult-Only area so members can make a decision as to whether they want to view these kinds of items. Although you can peruse all the other eBay categories without having to submit credit card information, you must have a credit card number on file on eBay to view and bid on items in this category. Restricted-access adult auctions are run like the typical timed auctions. To visit the adult items category, first you need to agree to the conditions listed on a terms-of-use page after you enter your User ID and password. That page pops up automatically when you attempt to access this category. The Adult Only category also hosts fixed-price sale listings.

CHARITY SALES: ALL FOR A GOOD CAUSE

A *charity sale* is a fund-raising auction promoted by eBay for Charity and PayPal Giving Fund, where the proceeds go to a selected charity. Most people don't wake up in the morning wanting to own the shoes that Ron Howard wore when he put his footprints in cement at Mann's Chinese Theater in Hollywood, but one-of-a-kind items like that often are auctioned off in charity auctions from approved 501 3(c) organizations. (In fact, someone did want those shoes badly enough to buy them for a lot of money on eBay.) Charity auctions became popular after the NBC *Today Show* sold an autographed jacket on eBay for over $11,000 with the proceeds going to Toys for Tots. Charity auctions are run like most other auctions on eBay, but because they're immensely popular, bidding can be fierce, and the dollar amounts can go sky-high.

Many ultrafamous celebrities use eBay to help out their favorite charities. Billionaire Warren Buffett, for example, has auctioned a private lunch yearly — for the past 16 years — to support one of his favorite charities, the Glide Foundation. In 2015, lunch with the Berkshire Hathaway chairman went for $2.35 million; the record high winning bid occurred in 2012, for $3,456,789. I suggest that you visit these auctions and bid whenever you can. Charity auctions are a win-win situation for everyone. (You can read more about celebrity auctions in Chapter 18.)

REMEMBER

If you aren't interested in seeing or bidding on items of an adult nature, or if you're worried that your children may be able to gain access to graphic adult material, eBay has solved that problem by excluding adult–content items from easily accessible areas. Children under the age of 18 aren't allowed to register on eBay anyway and should be under an adult's supervision if they do wander onto any part of the site — especially when they log in under an adult's account.

Private (shhh-it's-a-secret) listings

Some sellers choose to hold *private listings* (whether auctions or fixed–price sales) because they know that some buyers may be embarrassed to be seen bidding on a box of racy neckties in front of the rest of the eBay community. Others may go the private route because they're selling big–ticket items and don't want to disclose their bidders' financial status.

Private auctions are run like typical timed auctions, except during and after the sale, each bidder's identity is kept secret.

"Buy It Now" on eBay

You don't have to participate in an auction on eBay to buy something. If you want to make a purchase — if it's something you *must* have — you can usually find the item and buy it immediately. Of course, using *Buy It Now* (*BIN* in eBay-speak) doesn't come with the thrill of an auction, but purchasing an item at a fraction of the retail price — without leaving your chair or waiting for an auction to end — has its own warm and fuzzy kind of excitement. If you seek this kind of instant gratification on eBay, click the Buy It Now tab when browsing categories or performing searches.

PREFER TO SHOP ON A MOBILE DEVICE? IT'S YOUR CHOICE

When it comes to buying or selling on eBay, you can choose how you transact your business, whether from your desktop or on the go. If you're addicted to your tablet or smartphone (who, me?), you can easily download the eBay App from the app store for your mobile operating system. Just type **eBay** into the search bar and you should see an icon for the eBay Mobile App in the results.

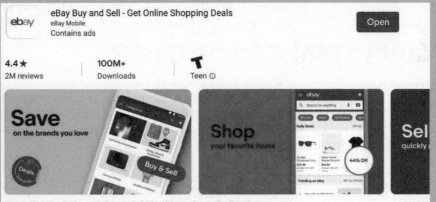

Online shopping deals on clothes, tech, DIY, and more. Buy and sell on the go.

Know that I recommend that you still use a laptop or desktop computer with some regularity. As you work more with the eBay platform, you'll see that there are some functionalities that work best on a big screen.

You may visit an eBay item only to see an option to Buy It Now. It's not an error! The seller has decided on a price at which to sell the item outright. By clicking Buy It Now, you can do an end run around the auction process and buy the item outright. If you bid on an auction that shows the Buy It Now option, the Buy it Now option will disappear unless the seller has placed a reserve price that hasn't been met.

eBay Stores

Visiting eBay Stores is as easy as clicking the *Visit Store* link on any item page. Thousands of eBay sellers have set up these online stores with merchandise meant for you to Buy It Now — and when you find a seller you like, you can visit the store with a click of your mouse. Sellers who open an eBay Store have to meet a certain level of experience on eBay, and when you buy from an eBay Store, you're protected by the same eBay Money Back Guarantee that covers you in any eBay transaction.

Buy It Now and fixed-price sales

More and more sellers are selling items with a Buy It Now option or at a fixed price. These features enable you to buy an item as soon as you see one at a price that suits you. (For more on how these sales work, check out Chapter 6.)

Want to Make Some Cash?

If you're a seller, creating a listing page on eBay is as simple as filling out an online form. You type the name of your item and a short description, add a crisp picture, set your price, and voilà — it's selling time. (Okay, it's a tad more involved than that, but not much.)

eBay allows any seller without an eBay Store to post 50 free auction or fixed-price listings per calendar month (store owners get 100–100,000 free listings per month). Once you exceed the number of free listings, you are charged a fee of $0.30 (less when you have a store) for the privilege of listing an item for sale. You don't pay an additional penny unless your item sells. You'll find more details on eBay Stores in Chapter 11.

When you list your item, millions of people (eBay has over 162 million active users) from all over the world can take a gander at it and place bids or buy. With a little luck, a bidding war may break out in your auction and drive the bids up high enough for you to turn a nice profit. After the auction, the buyer sends you the payment either through a payment service or PayPal. Then you ship the item. Abracadabra! You just turned your item (everyday clutter, no doubt) into cash. You can run as many listings as you want (no duplicates, please), all at the same time. To get info on deciding what to sell and when, leaf through Chapter 9; to find out how to set up an auction, jump to Chapter 10 — and when you're ready to go pro, check out the appendix.

Get a Deal and Get It Fast!

If you're a collector or you just like to shop for bargains on everyday goods, you can browse 24 hours a day through the items up for sale in eBay's tens of thousands of categories, which range from Antiques to Writing Instruments. Find the item you want, do a little research on what you're buying and who's selling it, place your bid, and keep an eye on it until the auction closes. When I write or update any of my eBay titles (like this one or *eBay Business All-In-One For Dummies*), I have a great time browsing the different categories and buying a little something here and there — it's amazing just how varied the selection is. I've even bought a refurbished hair dryer from the Dyson store!

Take a look at Chapter 5 for the 411 on searching for items on which to bid. When you see an item you like, you can set up a bidding strategy and let the games begin. Chapter 6 gives you bidding strategies that can make you the winner. After you win your first auction, look in Chapter 8 for expert advice about completing the transaction.

REMEMBER

You can bid as many times as you want on an item, and you can bid on as many auctions as you want. Just keep in mind that each bid is a binding contract and that *you are required to pay should you win.*

Research for Fun and Profit

eBay's awesome search engine allows you to browse through countless *categories* and items up for sale. As a buyer, you can do lots of comparison shopping to research that special something you just can't live without — or just browse around until something catches your eye. If you're a seller, the search engine allows you to keep your eye on the competition and get an idea of how hot your item is. That way you can set a competitive price. To find out more about using search options and categories, check out Chapters 3 and 5.

The search engine also lets you find out what other people are bidding on. From there, you can read up on a seller's *feedback ratings* (eBay's ingenious reputation system) to get a sense of the seller's reliability — *before* you deal with him or her.

eBay's Role in the Action

Throughout the process, eBay's servers keep tabs on what's going on. When an auction or sale is over, eBay takes a small percentage of the final selling price and instructs the buyer to make payment through email. At this point, eBay's job is pretty much over, and eBay steps aside unless a problem arises.

Most of the time, everything works great, everybody's happy, and eBay never has to step back into the picture. But if you happen to run into trouble in paradise, eBay can help you settle the problem, whether you're the buyer or the seller.

eBay regulates members with a detailed system of checks and balances known as *feedback,* which is described in Chapter 4. The grand plan is that the community polices itself. Don't get me wrong — eBay does jump in when shady activity comes to light. But the people who do the most to keep eBay safe are the community members, the buyers and sellers who have a common stake in conducting business honestly and fairly. Every time you sell something or buy an item, eBay members have a chance to leave a comment about you. You should do the same for them. If they're happy, the feedback for the seller is positive; otherwise, the feedback is negative. Either way, your feedback sticks to you like glue.

Building a great reputation with positive feedback ensures a long and profitable eBay career. Negative feedback has an effect like multiple convictions for grand theft auto — it's a real turnoff for most folks and can make it hard to do future business on eBay.

WARNING

If your feedback rating becomes a −4 (negative 4), eBay may suspend your buying and selling privileges. You can find out more about how eBay protects you as a buyer or a seller in Chapter 16.

TIP

Buyers can leave positive or negative feedback for a seller, but sellers can only click "positive." Sellers still do have the option to leave a descriptive comment, however, so problematic buyers don't get off scot-free.

Features and Fun Stuff

So eBay is all about making money, right? Not exactly. The folks at eBay aren't kidding when they call it a community — a place where people with similar interests can compare notes, argue, buy, sell, and meet each other. Yes, people have married after meeting on eBay. (Take a guess how their friends bought the wedding gifts!)

The Security Center is the catchall resource for information and services about making deals on eBay safer — and for information on what to do if something goes sour. I don't like to think about it, but sometimes — despite your best efforts to be a good eBay member — buyers or sellers don't keep their word. In a very small percentage of cases, unscrupulous louts try to pull scams. You may buy an item that isn't as it was described, or the winner of your auction may not send payment. Sometimes even honest members get into disputes. The Security Center is a good resource when you need questions answered or you need a professional to come in and handle an out-of-hand situation. Chapter 16 tells you all about the Security Center.

Extra Apps You're Gonna Want

At some point in your eBay career, you'll find you've become comfortable with all the computer-related hoops you have to jump through to make the eBay magic happen. At that time, you may be ready to invest in a few extra apps or devices that can make your eBay experience even better. Digital cameras and online free apps can help make your time on eBay a more lucrative and fun adventure. You find out how to use all that lovely tech for your sales in Chapter 18.

Chapter **2**

Let's Do It! Signing Up on eBay

Y ou've no doubt figured out that you sign in to eBay electronically, which means that you don't *really* sign on the dotted line. Nowadays, the art of scrawling your signature has become as outdated as CRT monitors (although you can still get these old-school monitors on eBay if you're feeling nostalgic).

Compared to finding a parking space during the holidays, signing up for eBay is easy-peasy. The toughest thing you have to do is type your email address correctly (and if you're like me, that can sometimes be a challenge).

In this chapter, you find out everything you need to know about registering on eBay. You get tips on what information you have to disclose and what you should keep to yourself. Don't worry — this is an open-book test. You don't need to memorize state capitals, the periodic table, or even multiplication tables. (Whew.)

Registering on eBay

You won't have to wear your name on a lanyard sign after you sign in, but eBay does need to know some things about you before it grants you membership. You and millions of other folks will be roaming around eBay's online treasure trove; eBay needs to know who's who. So, keeping that in mind, sign in, please!

The only hard-and-fast rule on eBay is that you must be 18 years of age or older. Don't worry, the Age Police won't come to your house to card you; they have other ways to discreetly ensure that you're at least 18 years old. (*Hint:* Credit cards do more than satisfy account charges.) Head to the eBay home page and register. The entire process takes only a few minutes.

Registering Is Free

Before you can sign up for buying and selling on eBay, you have to be connected to the Internet. So fire up your computer or mobile device and tap the browser. After you open your browser, you're ready to sign up.

Now type `www.ebay.com` in the address box of your browser and press Enter; this will take you to the eBay home page. Right there, in the upper left corner, is the Register link (look for a button or link indicating Register somewhere on the page). Click Register and let the sign-up process begin. Figure 2-1 shows you the resulting page where you get started.

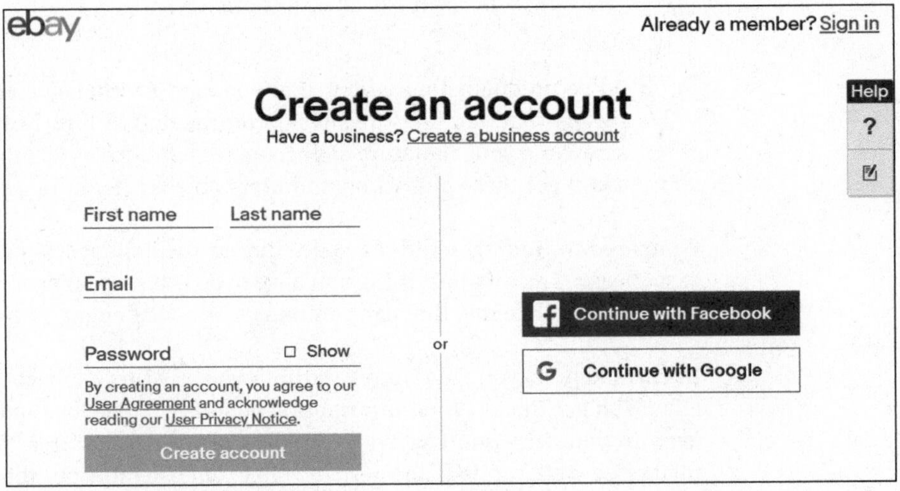

FIGURE 2-1: Click the Create account button, and soon you'll be dealing online like a pro!

> **eBay**
> Already a member? Sign in
>
> ## Create an account
> Have a business? Create a business account
>
> Help
> ?
>
> First name   Last name
>
> Email
>
> Password   ☐ Show
>
> By creating an account, you agree to our User Agreement and acknowledge reading our User Privacy Notice.
>
> Create account
>
> or
>
> f Continue with Facebook
>
> G Continue with Google

MARSHA SAYS

Just to keep things interesting, the eBay home page changes occasionally. If you don't see a Register link, look around the page — a Register button or link will be there somewhere.

WARNING

You will see the option here to create your account by clicking a link to register through Facebook or Google. This means that your data will be taken from the other platforms and used by eBay. If you've ever read my books before, you know that I try not to give away too much personal information on the Internet. Almost all platforms sell data about you. This is a truth that is impossible to escape. I've read that there are in excess of 3,000 data points documented on every person on the Internet. By linking accounts with another site, you are sharing your personal data, not just at the time of linking, but forever. Sure, it's easier to just click "Sign In with Facebook," but generally, this practice makes your data reciprocal. Protect as much of your privacy as you can. Let Facebook know what they know about you . . . and let eBay have their own data. Why make sharing your data easier?

Here's an overview of how easy it is to register:

1. **Enter the basic required info.**

2. **Read and accept the User Agreement and Privacy Policy.**

3. **Confirm your email address.**

4. **Breeze through (or past) any optional information.**

The following sections fill you in on all the details.

Thanks to modern technology, you access the Registration pages securely, through an encrypted *SSL* (Secure Sockets Layer) connection to eBay. You can tell you're on an SSL connection because the normal *http* at the beginning of the web address (also called the URL) is now *https*. I could tell you how SSL works, but instead I'll just give you the bottom line: It *does* work. The more precautions eBay (and you) take, the harder it is for someone to access your data.

When you're at the Registration form, you go through a four-step process.

TIP

You can also sign up on your mobile device (tablet or smartphone) after downloading the eBay app from the App Store or the Play store.

Follow these steps to register on your mobile device:

1. **Tap on the Register button (see Figure 2-2).**

2. **Tap Sign In on the menu that appears.**

3. **On the resulting screen, click the Register button.**

4. **Fill out the form and tap Register.**

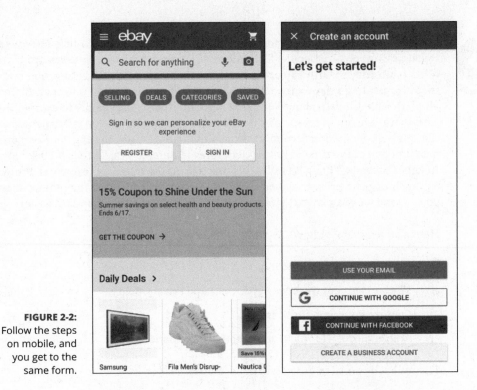

FIGURE 2-2:
Follow the steps on mobile, and you get to the same form.

Filling in required information

After you click the Register (or Create Account) button, you're taken to the heart of the eBay registration pages. You may register as a business or as an individual; I registered as an individual (you can change your registration to a business on eBay later). So if you don't quite have a business up and running, register simply as an individual. To get started, follow these steps:

1. **At the top of the first registration page, after eBay shows the steps of the registration process, fill in some required information.**

   Here's what eBay wants to know about you:

   - Your full name (eBay keeps this information on file in case the company or a member who is a transaction partner needs to contact you).

   - Your mobile number.

   - Your password. Choose a password and enter it in the Password text box. If asked, type it again in the text box to confirm its accuracy.

     For more information on choosing a password, see "A Quick Word about Passwords," later in this chapter.

   - Your email address (yourname@myISP.com).

TIP

If you have an existing business and you want to register on eBay with your business name, it's a good idea to click the link that says *Register for a business account,* as shown in Figure 2-1. That way you start out on the right foot with a legitimate business registration. eBay will still need your personal information because you represent your business on eBay, so fill out the form shown in Figure 2-3.

After you input your personal information and click Register (again), you're ready to create your eBay persona.

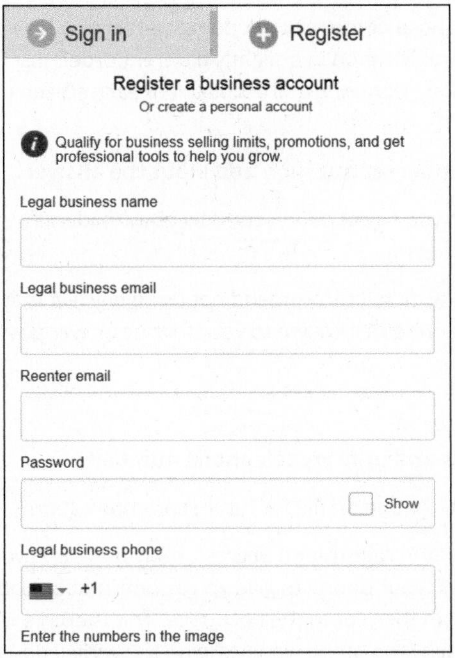

FIGURE 2-3:
Register as a business account, rather than a personal one, if your business is already set up and ready to go.

MARSHA SAYS

2. **On the next page, select your new eBay User ID.**

See "A Not-So-Quick Word about Choosing a User ID," later in this chapter, for some tips on selecting your User ID.

Because many of the "good" User IDs are taken, eBay checks the availability of your preferred ID. (Figure 2-4 shows eBay's suggestions when a User ID is already taken.) If your preferred name is taken, try again. (Lather, rinse, repeat.) Finding an awesome User ID can be as difficult as finding an untaken vanity plate at the California DMV. See more information on User IDs later in this chapter.

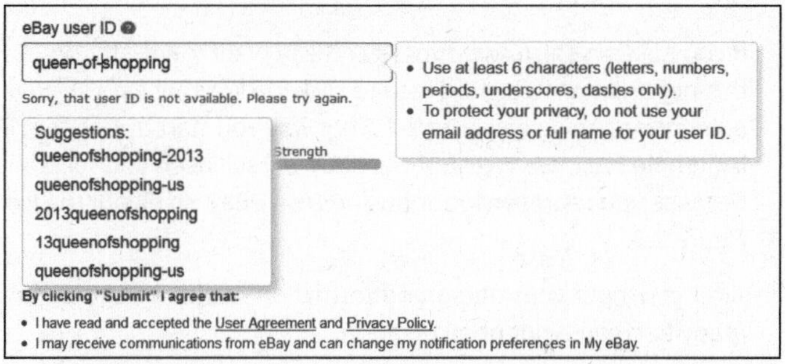

eBay user ID ⊘

```
queen-of-shopping
```
Sorry, that user ID is not available. Please try again.

• Use at least 6 characters (letters, numbers, periods, underscores, dashes only).
• To protect your privacy, do not use your email address or full name for your user ID.

Suggestions:
queenofshopping-2013
queenofshopping-us
2013queenofshopping
13queenofshopping
queenofshopping-us

~~~~~~Strength~~~~~~

By clicking "Submit" I agree that:
• I have read and accepted the User Agreement and Privacy Policy.
• I may receive communications from eBay and can change my notification preferences in My eBay.

FIGURE 2-4:
Type your proposed User ID and check whether it's available.

TIP

Depending on the phase of the moon (kidding!), eBay may have the questions in this step-by-step registration in a slightly different order. Just follow these steps and keep clicking Continue at the bottom of each screen until you're finished.

3. Create your unique secret question and input the answer.

The secret question you select here is used by eBay to identify you if you ever have problems signing in.

TIP

When choosing a question, I recommend not using *any* fact that is generally known about you — whether known to your friends or *ever* posted in social media.

4. Click Continue.

5. Input your address and primary telephone number.

eBay keeps this information on file for future communication.

REMEMBER

At different points in the registration process, eBay may send you an email or send a text to (or call) your phone to give you a confirmation code. Just type the code you receive from them onto the next page. This is eBay's way of verifying your information each step of the way. More on the verification process further on.

6. If eBay requires your credit card information (for identification that confirms you're a real person), it asks on the next screen.

7. Type your date of birth.

TIP

If eBay finds a glitch in your registration, such as an incorrect area code or zip code, you see a warning message. This is one of eBay's security measures that ward off fraudulent registrations. Use the Back button to correct the information. If you put in a wrong email address, for example, eBay has no way of contacting you — so you don't hear a peep from eBay regarding your registration until you go through the entire process all over again.

8. **Click the Continue button and check your email!**

eBay sends you an email containing a clickable link. Clicking the link from the email opens a window in your Internet browser. Ba-da-boom! You're registered!

9. **Sign up for a payment processor.**

To transact business on eBay, you will need a payment processor. You will be presented with a link to sign up. If you don't have one, now is the time to sign up. I've used PayPal for years and I'm convinced they are safe, and all your information is kept confidentially — with the same level of safety you expect from a reputable financial organization. Payments on eBay are in a bit of a flux right now. Check my blog (`www.coolebaytools.com/blog`) for updates and advice.

Do you solemnly swear to . . . ?

During the registration process, you'll be asked to check the boxes that say you agree to the eBay User Agreement and Privacy Policy. At this point, you essentially take an oath to keep eBay safe for democracy and commerce. You promise to play well with others, not to cheat, and to follow the Golden Rule. No, you're not auditioning for a superhero club, but don't ever forget that eBay takes this stuff very seriously — and most eBay members do, too. You can be kicked off eBay, or worse, if you play fast and loose with these principles. (Can you say "federal investigation"?)

Be sure to read the User Agreement thoroughly when you register. So that you don't have to put down this riveting book to read the legalese right this minute, I provide the nuts and bolts here:

>> You understand that every transaction is a legally binding contract. (Click the User Agreement link next to the copyright notice at the bottom of any eBay page for the current eBay Rules and Regulations.)

>> You agree that you can pay for the items you buy and the eBay fees that you incur. (Chapter 8 fills you in on how eBay takes its cut of the action.)

>> You understand that you're responsible for paying any taxes.

>> You're aware that if you sell prohibited items, eBay can forward your personal information to law enforcement for further investigation. (Chapter 9 explains what you can and can't sell on eBay — and what eBay does to sellers of prohibited items.)

>> eBay makes clear that it is just a *venue,* which means it's a place where people with similar interests can meet, greet, and do business.

When everything goes well, the eBay website is like a school gym that opens for Saturday swap meets. At the gym, if you don't play by the rules, you can get tossed out. But if you don't play by the rules on eBay, the venue gets un-gymlike in a hurry. eBay has the right to get state and federal officials to track you down and prosecute you.

If you're a stickler for fine print, click the links provided on the Registration page for all the *Ps* and *Qs* of the latest policies. The User Agreement is vital to your success on eBay.

By registering, you indicate that you really, *really* understand what it means to be an eBay user. Because I know that you, as a law-abiding eBay member, will have no problem following the rules, go ahead and confirm your account. You're almost done.

It must be true if you have it in writing

After you accept the User Agreement and Privacy Policy, eBay takes less than a minute to email you an activation notice. When you receive the eBay registration confirmation email, don't delete it.

With your confirmation code from the email in hand, head back to the secure eBay Registration page by clicking the link supplied in your email. If your email doesn't support links, go to this address:

```
https://scgi.ebay.com/ws/eBayISAPI.dll?RegisterConfirmCode&Register
ConfirmCode&registerconfirmcode=
```

A LITTLE ABOUT USER AGREEMENTS AND PRIVACY POLICIES

As you spend more and more time on the Internet, you'll be required to click many boxes that say you agree to a User Agreement or Terms of Service. These documents can be many pages long — and involve a lot of making sure that you agree to do the right thing. The bottom line is, if you don't agree, you can't use the site (or the app).

Privacy Policies are a bit more important. You should always know how much of the information you give will be kept confidential — and how much of that info can be given away. Many sites share your personal data — and you often have the option of "opting out" of data sharing. I always recommend reading the privacy provisions carefully before clicking.

After you reconnect with eBay and it knows your email address is genuine, you'll be heartily congratulated with an eBay email. It's time to start shopping!

TIP

If you don't receive your eBay registration confirmation email within 24 hours, there was most likely an error in your email address. At this point, the customer support folks can help you complete the registration process. Try visiting the Contact Us area from the Customer Support link at the top of the page and indicate that you're a guest.

REMEMBER

If, for some reason (even a late-night watching of the *Breaking Bad* marathon is a perfectly acceptable excuse), you incorrectly type the wrong email address, you have to start the registration process all over again with a different User ID (eBay holds the previous ID for 30 days).

Uh-oh, you made a mistake?

If you run into a snag, you can go to the Help and Contact link at the top of the page. It will ask for your password, but if you're just starting on eBay, don't worry; just follow the steps below:

1. **If you haven't registered, click the box that indicates you're new to eBay or need help signing in.**

    You're brought to the Contact Us page.

2. **Click the box to indicate that your problem is with your account.**

3. **Click the link to indicate that your problem is with registration, and then click the option labeled *Register for a new account*.**

    Some suggestions will pop up, but the most important will be the Call Us button (it has a telephone icon).

Click that phone icon any time, Monday through Sunday from 5:00 a.m. to 10:00 p.m., Pacific Time, and you will get a phone number so you can talk to someone at eBay.

WARNING

If somebody you're in a transaction with requests your info from eBay, you get an email from eBay giving you the name, phone number, city, and state of the person making the request. Keep your own information up to date. If you don't, you risk penalties. See Chapter 15 for details.

A Quick Word about Passwords

Choosing a good password is not as easy (but is twice as important) as it may seem. Whoever has your password can (in effect) "be you" on eBay — running sales, bidding on auctions, and leaving possibly litigious feedback for others. Basically, such an impostor can ruin your eBay career and possibly cause you serious financial grief.

REMEMBER

As with any online password, you should follow these rules to protect your privacy:

>> Don't choose an obvious password, such as your birthday, your first name, or (especially!) your Social Security number. (**Hint:** If it's too easy to remember, it's probably easy to crack.)

>> Make things tough on bad actors — combine numbers and letters (use uppercase and lowercase) or create nonsensical words.

>> Don't give out your password to anyone — it's like giving away the keys to the front door of your house.

>> If you ever suspect that someone has your password, immediately change it by going to the following address:

`https://scgi.ebay.com/ws/eBayISAPI.dll?FYPShow`

>> Change your password every few months just to be on the safe side.

>> Definitely *don't* use the same password for eBay and PayPal.

A Not-So-Quick Word about Choosing a User ID

eBay gives you the option of picking your User ID. Making up a User ID is my favorite part. If you've never liked your real name (or never had a nickname), here's your chance to correct that situation. Have fun. Consider choosing an ID that tells a little about you. Of course, if your interests change, you may regret having too narrow a User ID.

You can call yourself just about anything; you can be silly or creative or boring. But remember, this ID is how other eBay users will know you. So here are some common-sense rules:

>> Don't use a name that would embarrass your mother.

>> Don't use a name with a negative connotation.

>> Don't use a name that's too weird. If people don't trust you, they won't buy from you.

>> eBay doesn't allow spaces in User IDs, so make sure that the ID makes sense when putting two or more words together.

TIP

If you're dying to have several short words as your User ID, you can use underscores or hyphens to separate them, as in *super-shop-a-holic*. If you sign in to eBay once a day on your computer, typing underscores or dashes won't slow you down.

REMEMBER

You can change your User ID once every 30 days if you want to, but I don't recommend it. People come to know you by your User ID. If you change your ID, your past does play tagalong and attaches itself to the new ID.

Nevertheless, to change your User ID, click the My eBay link at the top of most eBay pages. From your My eBay login page, click the Account tab, then scroll to the Personal Information link. Click the Edit link next to User ID under Account Information. Follow essentially the same steps you used when selecting your initial ID — and you have a new eBay identity.

eBay also has some User ID rules to live by:

>> No offensive names (like &*#@@guy).

>> No names with *eBay* in them. (It makes you look like you work for eBay, and eBay takes a dim view of that.)

>> No names with & (even if you *do* have both looks&brains).

>> No names with @ (like @Aboy).

>> No symbols such as the greater-than or less-than symbols (> <) or consecutive underscores _ _.

>> No emojis.

>> No IDs that begin with an *e* followed by numbers, an underscore, a dash, a period, or a dot.

>> No names of one letter (such as Q).

THE CRAZE THAT BEGAN WITH AW

Back in 1994, when eBay founder Pierre Omidyar had the idea to start a web auction, he named his first venture AuctionWeb. The following figure shows a vintage AuctionWeb Internet auction that I won in February 1997. There were some great deals even in those days!

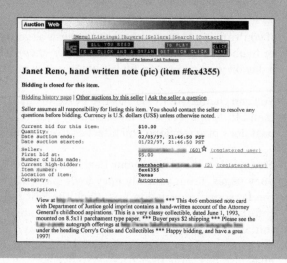

TIP

When you choose your User ID, make sure that it isn't a good clue for your password. For example, if you use *Natasha* as your User ID, don't choose *Boris* as your password. Even Bullwinkle could figure that one out.

Your License to Deal (Almost)

You are now officially a *newbie,* or eBay rookie. The only problem is that you're still at the window-shopping level. If you're ready to go from window-shopper to item-seller, just zip through a few more forms, and before you know it, you can start running your own sales on eBay.

Chapter **3**

Finding Your Way Around eBay

The famous writer Thomas Wolfe *was* wrong; you *can* go home again. At least on eBay — to the home page. Try to visit the eBay home page on a regular basis; it's a place to keep up with eBay's newest offerings. Day after day, month after month, millions of people (just like us) land on eBay's home page without wearing out the welcome mat (probably because they're wearing their robes and slippers). The eBay home page is the front door to the most popular marketplace on the Internet.

Everything you need to know about navigating eBay begins right here. In this chapter, I give you the grand tour of the areas you can reach right from the home page with the help of links.

What Is the Home Page?

The desktop eBay *home page* is shown in Figure 3-1. When you're visiting the site on a mobile device, you will have a completely different experience. So I suggest firing up your computer so as to fully understand what's to be found here. The main home page includes the following key areas:

>> A ribbon at the top of the page provides seven eBay links that can direct you straight to important eBay areas. These links repeat on every page.

>> A search box helps you find items by title keywords and offers a link to eBay's Advanced Search page.

>> Top-level categories offer more detail when you put your mouse pointer over the names.

>> A drop-down list under each category offers links to the lower levels of the product-listing categories.

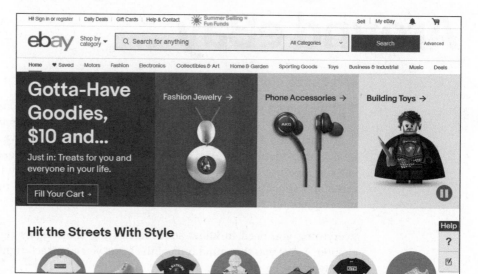

FIGURE 3-1:
The home page — starting point for fun, profit, and values.

REMEMBER

Do not adjust your computer monitor. You're not going crazy. Today you may notice that a link that was on the eBay home page a minute ago is gone. That's normal. The links on the eBay home page change often to reflect what's going on — not just on the site, but in the world as well.

Sign In, Please

Sign In is possibly the most powerful of all the links on the eBay pages, and it will be your first stop if you plan to do business on the site. Click the Sign In link in the upper left corner of the home page, and you arrive at the official Sign In page (shown in Figure 3-2).

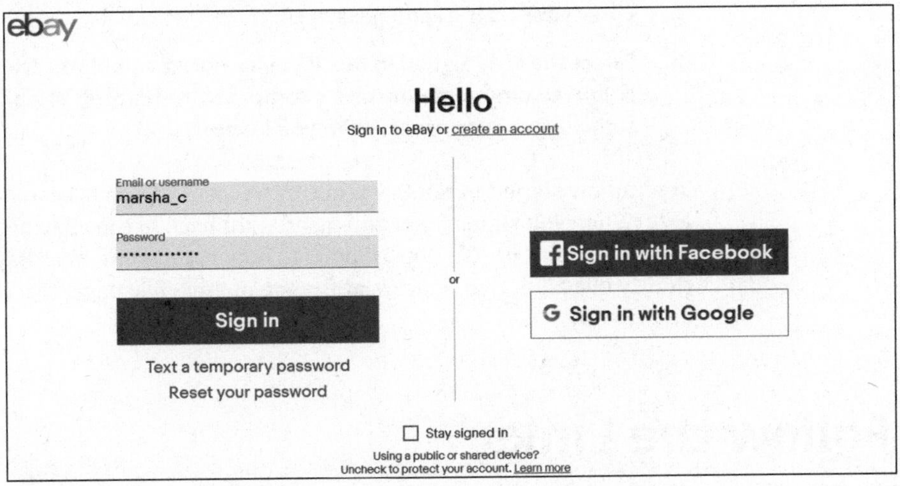

eb**a**y

Hello
Sign in to eBay or create an account

Email or username
marsha_c

Password
•••••••••••••

Sign in

Text a temporary password
Reset your password

or

f Sign in with Facebook

G Sign in with Google

☐ Stay signed in
Using a public or shared device?
Uncheck to protect your account. Learn more

FIGURE 3-2:
The eBay
Sign In page.

When you go to the Sign In page and then sign in, you don't have to enter your User ID again that day. You can set your preferences to take you directly to your My eBay Summary page. This little timesaver is essential for every eBay user. (See Chapter 4 for info on My eBay.)

TIP

You can shop for items on eBay as a "Guest" user without becoming a registered member, but what fun is that? Registering on the site opens up lots of extra benefits. The most important is that your purchases will show up in a Purchase history on the site. Things just run a bit smoother if you're all set up. You can pay with eBay's current approved payment processors, such as PayPal, credit card, debit card, Apple Pay, or Google Pay. As a guest, you're still covered by eBay's Money Back Guarantee. If you're the only one who uses your computer, be sure to select the box that says *Stay Signed In*. That way you're always signed in to eBay within the browser every time you go to the site. The Sign In process places a *cookie* (a technical thingy — see Chapter 15 for details) on your computer that remains a part of your computer for the rest of the day. If you don't select the box, you'll be signed in to eBay just for this session.

After you've registered and have done some business on the site, eBay will prompt you to sign in before you proceed to anywhere on the site. If (say) you're on a friend's computer, or have just updated your browser, here's how to get to the eBay Sign In page and sign in:

1. **Click the Sign In link on the eBay home page.**

   In the address bar, you'll notice the URL of the new page that appears is a Secure Sign In page. The change from http to https indicates that your personal information is secure. (See Chapter 2 for details about SSL.)

2. **Enter your User ID and password.**

3. **Select the Stay Signed In box if you're not at a public or friend's computer. If you're using someone else's computer, remember to sign out in the same upper left corner when you leave.**

You're now signed in to eBay and can transact and save searches on the site with ease. When you sign in, you will be brought back to the eBay home page and you'll see your name on the top ribbon. If not, enter your My eBay page by clicking the My eBay link that appears at the top of any eBay page. (See Chapter 4 for more on My eBay.)

Follow the Links

As mentioned, the *navigation links* at the top of the eBay home page list seven top-level eBay links that take you directly to different eBay areas through drop-down menus. You can also click the Cart link at the far right to view your cart and check out. Using the navigation area is like having a one-stop click zone. You can find this ribbon at the top of every page you visit on eBay. No matter where you are on the site, you go straight to a related page when you click one of the seven navigation links.

TIP

Think of links as expressways to specific destinations. Click a link just once, and the next thing you know, you're right where you want to be. You don't even have to answer that proverbial annoying question, "When are we gonna get there?" from the noisy kids in the backseat.

Here, without further ado, are the seven upper-level navigation links and where they take you:

» **Sign In or Register:** When you're signed in to eBay, you'll see a greeting (mine says "Hi Marsha!"). Click the down arrow next to your name to sign in or out, or go to your Account Settings page. If you haven't registered on eBay, turn to Chapter 2 to get the quick and painless facts about the easy eBay registration process.

>> **Daily Deals:** Items and deals that are featured each day in many categories.

>> **Gift Cards:** Send someone an eBay gift card for any special occasion. eBay will send your gift to any address you provide. The gift certificate is good for any item on the site for the value you specify, and you pay for it immediately with PayPal. They never expire and have no additional fees. More details on eBay Gift cards can be found in Chapter 18.

>> **Help & Contact:** A quick and intuitive Customer Service page appears when you click the Help & Contact link. Here you can find answers to many of your questions, as well as keep apprised of any changes in eBay's rules and regulations that govern trading on the site. You'll also find a link to the Resolution Center where you can solve most problems that may emerge with trading partners. I explain its uses in Chapter 4.

>> **Sell:** Takes you to the start of the Sell Your Item form, which you must fill out to start your sale. I explain how to navigate this form in Chapter 10.

>> **My eBay:** Clicking the top-level link, My eBay, may bring you to different places depending on how long you've been a member of the site. You'll see a drop-down menu with many links to important places on the site. If you're new to the site, it will bring you to your personal Summary transactions page. This is where you keep track of all your buying and selling activities and account information. Figure 3-3 shows a My eBay Summary page.

If you've been selling on the site for a while, you will probably go to the Seller Hub; clicking the links below will take you to these pages: (The complete details on this area can be found in Chapter 4.)

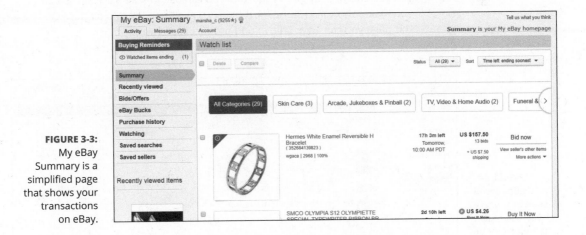

FIGURE 3-3:
My eBay Summary is a simplified page that shows your transactions on eBay.

By mousing over (and not clicking) the links on the drop-down menu appear as follows:

- **Summary:** Clicking here takes you to your eBay Summary page. It's basically a hub for your eBay shopping. When you scroll to the very bottom of the page, you can click your All Selling summary page.

- **Recently Viewed:** In case you lose track of what you view on the site, this page shows you the last items you've viewed from most recent to last. Very handy when you are shopping.

- **Bids/Offers:** Clicking here takes you to a page that tracks any bids you've placed on items up for auction. It also shows any listing for which you've placed an offer. (Find how to make an offer on a fixed-price item in Chapter 7.)

- **Watch list:** A link to watch an item appears on every eBay item. It gives you an opportunity to bookmark an item for possible future purchase or to keep an eye on bidding in an auction. Any item you've marked as such is listed on this page. (More on your Watch list in Chapter 4.)

- **Purchase History:** If you've been buying items on eBay, the site has kept an online record of every purchase you've made. There's also a record of your returns and canceled items.

- **Selling:** Click here and if you are a seller, you will land on the Seller Hub with stats and information on your sales and account. There's also a useful bunch of links to almost any action you might need when it comes to selling.

- **Saved Searches (and Sellers):** If (like me) you have many different things you search for, eBay gives you a tool you can use to save a certain search you make, shown in Figure 3-4. (Chapter 5 gives you the info on this.) On this page you can view, edit, or add product searches.

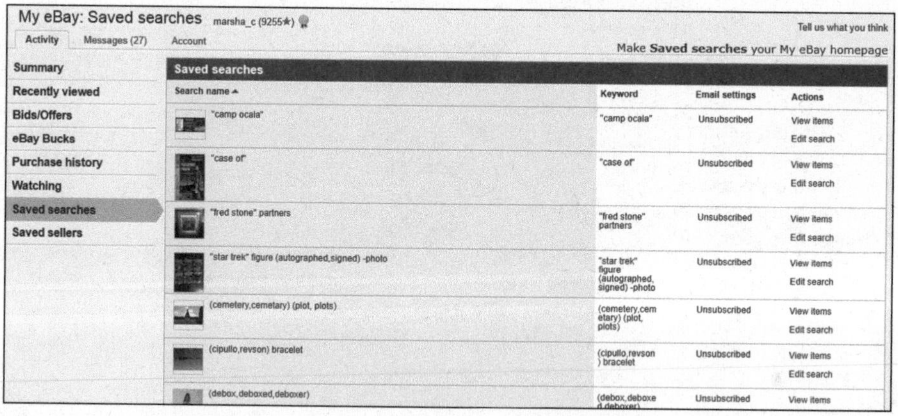

FIGURE 3-4: eBay Saved Searches, where you can repeat the search or be notified when a particular item goes up for sale.

- **Messages:** Click this link and you'll be brought to the eBay message area (also accessible from the tabs at the top of your My eBay page). When someone wants to contact you regarding an eBay item, their messages appear here. You'll also find messages from eBay — which it also sends to your registered eBay email address. Archiving questions and answers between you and another party in a transaction can be very useful should an issue crop up.

REMEMBER

This is eBay's private email system, where you reply without exposing your personal email address. The only time email addresses are exchanged is during a transaction.

>> **Notification Bell:** If you have eBay messages or notifications from eBay, you'll see them here.

>> **eBay Logo:** Click the eBay logo and it takes you right back to the home page. Use this link from any other page when you need to get back to the home page right away.

Exploring Your Home Page Search Options

An ancient expression says, "Every journey begins with the first eBay search." Okay, I updated the quote just a tad, but they are wise words nonetheless. You can start a search from the home page in one of two ways:

>> **Use the search box.** It's right there at the top of the home page, with the Search button next to it. It's a fast way of finding item listings.

>> **Use the Advanced link next to the search box on the home page.** This link takes you to the Advanced Search page, where you can do all kinds of specialized searches.

Both options can give you the same results. The instructions I offer in the next two sections about using these search methods are just the tip of the eBay iceberg. For the inside track on how to finesse the eBay search engine to root out just what you're looking for, visit Chapter 5.

Seeking items through the search box

To launch a title search from the home page, follow these steps:

1. **In the search box, type no more than a few keywords that describe the item you're looking for.**

   Refer to Figure 3-1 to see the search box.

2. **Click the Search button.**

   The results of your search appear onscreen in a matter of seconds.

You can type just about anything in this box and get some information. Say you're looking for *Star Trek* memorabilia. If so, you're not alone. The television show (now known as *Star Trek: The Original Series*) premiered on September 8, 1966, and even though it was canceled in 1969 because of low ratings, *Star Trek* became one of the most successful science-fiction franchises in history! If you like *Star Trek* as much as I do, you can use the search box on the eBay home page to find all sorts of *Star Trek* stuff. I just ran a search and found 538,733 items — in hundreds of categories — with *Star Trek* in their titles (your results will probably vary).

To be fair, these days *Star Wars* is far more popular, and it seems there are many more products to purchase. My search for *Star Wars* netted 2,120,441 items. Whew. Fortunately the eBay universe is big enough for all of it.

Luckily, when you do a search as broad as this one, you can look to the left side of the page and click on a category that will bring you closer to what you're looking for. Figure 3-5 shows you how this works.

FIGURE 3-5: Look for the item categories on the left side of the page.

To find an item that sold on eBay in the past, perform your search from the search box. On the left side of the results page, you have the ability to refine your search. Under the Show Only heading, you can select Completed Items, which shows all the items that have gone through the sales cycle and have expired unbought or have been purchased. Select the Sold Items box to see a list of items of this type that have been sold in the last 90 (or so) days, as well as what they sold for. You can use this type of search to strategize your asking price before you put an item up for sale (or to determine how much you'll have to pay to purchase an item).

Try the Advanced link next to the search box to narrow your search. This link takes you to the Advanced Search: Find Items page, which is explained in the following section.

When you search for popular items on eBay (and a classic example is *Star Wars* memorabilia), you may get inundated with thousands of listings that match your search criteria. Even if you're traveling at hyperspeed, you could spend hours checking each auction individually (even if the force is with you!). If you're pressed for time like the rest of us, eBay has not-so-mysterious ways to narrow your search, so finding a specific item is much more manageable. Turn to Chapter 5 for insider techniques that can help you slim those searches and beef up those results.

Going where the Advanced Search box takes you

One of the most important buttons on the eBay page is the Advanced link next to the search box. When you click here, you're whisked away to the Advanced Search: Find Items page, which promptly presents you with several search options. Each option enables you to search for information in a different way. Here's how the search options on the menu can work for you:

>> **Find Items:** Search by keywords, item number, in eBay Motors, or by an individual seller or bidder. Type the keywords that describe an item (for example, **Superman lunch box** or **antique pocket watch**) and click Search, and you can see how many are available on eBay. The site gives you the option to search by one of the main categories — but to get the largest number of items, use All Categories and then narrow your search from the results.

Sellers on eBay are notorious for listing items in the wrong category (especially when they're rushed and upload lots of listings quickly). A search for all matching keywords will bring some of those hidden nuggets to the surface. Just peruse the pictures on the Search Results page.

Another handy way to search is by *item number*. Every item that's up for sale on eBay is assigned an item number, which is displayed at the top right of the Description box. To find an item by number, just type the number in the box, click Search, and away you go. (To find out more about how individual sales pages work on eBay, spin through Chapter 6.)

» **Advanced Search drop-down menu:** By clicking this link, you can define your search. It works pretty much the same as the basic Search method, but you can exclude more features from your search.

You can also search by location to find items for sale in and around your neighborhood. Figure 3-6 shows some of the Advanced Search options.

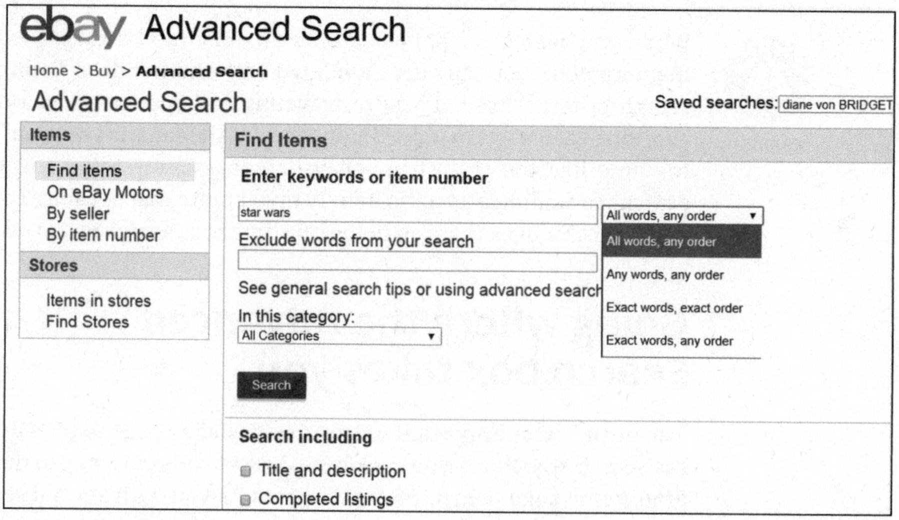

eBay Advanced Search

Home > Buy > **Advanced Search**

Advanced Search

Saved searches: diane von BRIDGET

| Items |
| Find items |
| On eBay Motors |
| By seller |
| By item number |
| **Stores** |
| Items in stores |
| Find Stores |

Find Items

Enter keywords or item number

star wars

All words, any order ▾

Exclude words from your search

See general search tips or using advanced search

In this category:

All Categories ▾

Search

| All words, any order |
| Any words, any order |
| Exact words, exact order |
| Exact words, any order |

Search including

☐ Title and description
☐ Completed listings

FIGURE 3-6:
The Advanced
Search page and
its options.

TIP

The In This Category search filter is a snappy function that helps you figure out which subcategories have the item you want — or, if you want to sell, helps you decide where to list your item for sale. What you get is not only a regular search in a selected category, but also a column on the left side of the page that tells you which subcategories (within the top-level category you selected) list your item — as well as how many of the item you'll see listed in each subcategory.

Although Chapter 5 tells you all you need to know about searching eBay, the following list explains some other searches you can perform from the Advanced Search page. In a nutshell, here's what they do:

- » **eBay Motors:** Clicking this link brings you to a page where you can type in specifics for motorized vehicles, RVs, and boats to find exactly the type of vehicle (or part) you want.

- » **By Seller:** Every person on eBay has a personal User ID (the name you use to conduct transactions). Use a By Seller search if you liked the merchandise from a seller's auction and want to see what else the seller has for sale. Type the seller's User ID, and you get a list of every item that person has up for sale.

- » **By Item Number:** Every item has a number (you can find it just below the Description tab on the item page) that uniquely identifies a listing. You can type in an item number you've saved there. (You can also type in an item number in the regular search box to find a listing as well.)

- » **Items in Stores:** Here's something I bet you didn't know. When you use eBay's advanced search, it searches eBay Stores for matching items. Since eBay Store items show up in the regular search, I can't imagine why you'd need to use this option.

- » **Find Stores:** If you're looking for a particular eBay Store, eBay provides a search box that allows you to search for a store by name (or by part of the name).

Home Links, the Next Generation

If you look carefully, you can see that the home page has several other links that give you express service to key parts of the site after you've registered. These results are based on your searching history, what you've bought, and what eBay might think you're interested in.

If you've been browsing around the site and then return to the home page, you see several boxes with images of items you've looked at in past history. You'll see items you have indicated that you want to watch on your My eBay page, your recently viewed items, and your recent searches.

eBay also gives you recommendations on popular products similar to things you've searched for. There's also information on what items are *trending* (growing in popularity) on the site.

TIP

You may notice that some graphic links on the home page change from day to day — or even hour to hour.

Maneuvering through Categories

So how does eBay keep track of the millions of items up for sale at any given moment? The brilliant folks who developed this system decided to group items into a nice, neat little storage system called *categories.* The home page lists most of the main (top-level) categories, but currently eBay must list tens of thousands of subcategories — ranging from Antiques to Writing Instruments. And don't ask how many sub-subcategories (categories within categories) eBay has — I can't count that high. I downloaded eBay's category list and found that as of June 2019, there are 19,954.

Well, okay, I *could* list all the categories and subcategories currently available on eBay — if you wouldn't mind squinting at a dozen pages of really small, eye-burning text. If you'd like to download the list for yourself, you can find a PDF at `https://pics.ebaystatic.com/aw/pics/catchanges/US_New_Structure_Jun2019.pdf` and a CSV file (for Excel or Google Sheets) at `https://pics.ebaystatic.com/aw/pics/catchanges/US_Category_Changes_(Jun2019).csv`.

But a category browse is an adventure that's unique for each individual, and I wouldn't think of depriving you of it. Suffice it to say that if you like to hunt for that perfect *something*, you're in browsing heaven now.

Here's how to navigate around the categories:

1. **Click the category that interests you, such as Collectibles & Art.**

   You're transported to the category's page. You see categories and subcategories listed next to each heading. Happy hunting.

   TIP

   On some of the main category pages, you see a link in the left column for Live Auctions. These are pages where traditional (going, going, gone) auction houses share their live auctions on eBay in real time. There's nothing more exciting than bidding live.

   If you really and truly want to see a list of all the categories and subcategories after you've clicked through to the top category, click the arrow to the right of the left-hand subcategories to view sub-subcategories in the drop-down menu, as shown in Figure 3-7.

   TIP

   To see all the eBay categories, click the link to All Categories at the bottom of the *Shop by category* drop-down menu. Alternatively, you can go to `www.ebay.com/sch/allcategories/all-categories`. If you're looking for a particular brand, you'll find a link to All Brands at the bottom of that menu. There you'll find an alphabetic list of all the brands and their pages on eBay.

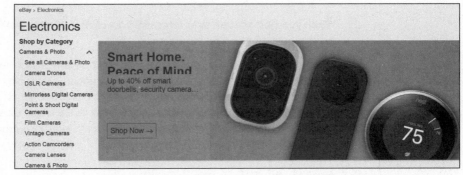

eBay › Electronics

Electronics

Shop by Category

Cameras & Photo

  See all Cameras & Photo

  Camera Drones

  DSLR Cameras

  Mirrorless Digital Cameras

  Point & Shoot Digital Cameras

  Film Cameras

  Vintage Cameras

  Action Camcorders

  Camera Lenses

  Camera & Photo

Smart Home. Peace of Mind
Up to 40% off smart doorbells, security camera...

Shop Now →

FIGURE 3-7: Delving deeper into eBay's subcategories.

2. **When you mouse over the major categories at the top of the promotion box, a flyout menu appears, showing top categories that may interest you. Click a subcategory, and keep digging through the sub-subcategories until you find what you want.**

    For example, if you're looking for items honoring your favorite TV show, click the Collectibles and Art category on the home page, and on the resulting page, select Entertainment Memorabilia. Additional categories appear. Then, when you click, you arrive at a page similar to Figure 3-8. On the left of the page, even more subcategories appear.

    If you click the TV Memorabilia subcategory, a page shows up with links to various sub-subcategories that include Ads, Flyers, Clippings, Merchandise & Promotional, Photographs, Posters, Press Kits, Props, Scripts, Wardrobe, Price Guides, and Other. In the center of the page, you also find links to the most popular searches in the category.

    Click any link here to see the listings in the categories. From the listings page (among other things), you can click the boxes at the top to narrow your search to Auctions or Buy It Now items.

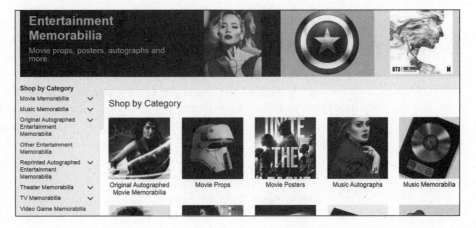

FIGURE 3-8: Landing on the Entertainment Memorabilia main category page.

3. **When you find an item that interests you, click the item, and the full listings page pops up on your screen.**

Congratulations — you've just navigated through several million items to find that one TV-collectible item that caught your attention. (Pardon me while I bid on that *Big Bang Theory*/Johnny Galecki–signed picture for my husband.) You can instantly return to the home page by clicking its link at the top of the page (or return to the listings page by repeatedly clicking the Back button at the top of your browser).

Near the bottom of every Search Results page, you see a line of numbers. The numbers are page numbers, and you can use them to fast-forward through all the items in that subcategory (next to the numbers, you can also select how many items you want to see on the pages). So, if you feel like browsing around page 8 without going through eight pages individually, just click number 8: You're presented with the items on that page (their listings, actually). Happy browsing.

If you're a bargain hunter by habit, you may find some pretty weird stuff while browsing the categories and subcategories of items on eBay — some of it supercheap and some of it (maybe) just cheap. There's even a Weird Stuff category that breaks down into subcategories of Slightly Unusual, Totally Bizarre, and Really Weird (accessible through the site map only)! I just checked that category and saw quite a few sales for the contents of people's junk drawers. But I'm moving along. I have enough of my own junk around without importing fresh stuff.

WARNING

Remember that (as with any marketplace) you're responsible for finding out as much as possible about an item before you buy — and definitely before you bid. So, if you're the type who sometimes can't resist a good deal, ask yourself what you plan to *do* with the pile of garbage you can get for 15 cents — and ask yourself *now*, before it arrives on your doorstep. Chapters 6 and 7 offer more information on savvy bidding.

Bottoming Out

At the very bottom of the home page is a group of eBay-centric links. Clicking these takes you to an unassuming group of very valuable links that provide more ways to get to some seriously handy pages. I list some of my favorites in this section:

>> **Tools & apps:** Several links are important here.

Mobile Apps: Click here to download eBay's mobile app.

Security Center: This link takes you to a page where concerns about fraud and safety are addressed. It's such an important eBay tool that I dedicate an entire chapter to this program. Before buying or selling, it's a good idea to check out Chapter 16.

Site Map: My favorite way to find what I want on eBay, using this very handy road map of links.

Developers: So are you a geek too? If you are, you can enter eBay's Developer program and get access to the eBay API for fun and profit.

>> **About eBay:** Click this link to find out about eBay, the company, and to get its press releases, company overview, and stock information. You can even apply for a job at eBay.

Policies: This is a good place to visit to brush up on the site's policies and guidelines.

Government Relations: Here's where your eBay membership can make a real difference. Join eBay's Main Street Member Program and become involved with important legislation that may affect your online future. If you sign up, you'll receive important updates.

>> **Community:** Visit the Announcements Board (linked here) when you want to know about any eBay-related, late-breaking news. Clicking the various options takes you to pages where you can ask questions of fellow sellers, have online discussions with the eBay community, try new features, and find out more about eBay. (Chapter 17 gives you ideas on how to use these resources.)

>> **eBay Sites:** Click United States, and a menu appears with links to eBay's international auction sites — 49 total, in addition to the United States. Click one of these links and you jet off (virtually) to eBay sites in these countries. The international sites are in the countries' native languages. It might be a good place to practice your third-year French — or maybe not!

REMEMBER

After you leave eBay USA, you're subject to the contractual and privacy laws of the country you're visiting.

Chapter **4**

Ground Central, Your Private, My eBay

It may seem that eBay is this huge company that doesn't even know you exist, but they do. They know all about you, and they give you a space to easily manage all your eBay business. eBay's My eBay page is viewed only by you and is ground central for all your activities on eBay — sort of a "This is your eBay life." I think it's the most convenient organizational tool around, and I want to talk to somebody about getting one for organizing my life outside of eBay.

In this chapter, you find out how you can use the My eBay page to keep tabs on what you're buying and selling, find out how much money you've spent, and add categories to your personalized list so you can get to any favorite eBay place with just a click of your mouse. You gain knowledge of the ins and outs of feedback — what it is, why it can give you a secure feeling that you're in charge, and how to manage it so all that cyber-positive reinforcement doesn't go to your head.

TIP

I do want to preface this chapter by warning you that the My eBay page has become the hub for the zillions of features that eBay offers. As a beginner on the site, you'll be doing yourself a favor if you stick to the basics of the buying, selling, feedback, and account settings. eBay's offerings are helpful, but they can do a heck of a job confusing you when you're just starting out. Ease into the extra options slowly.

Getting to Your My eBay Pages

Using your My eBay makes keeping track of your eBay life a whole lot easier. And getting there is easy enough. After you enter eBay, sign in through the Sign In link (described in Chapter 3). After you sign in to eBay, you can access your My eBay page by clicking the My eBay link in the navigation area (see Figure 4-1) at the top of almost every eBay page. If you have registered as a business, this link will take you to the Seller Hub; in that case, you can still visit My eBay by clicking the Summary link below.

FIGURE 4-1:
The My eBay link in the navigation bar.

After you click the My eBay link, you arrive at your My eBay Summary page for shopping. As you can see by my page in Figure 4-2, you can access just about any information about your eBay shopping sprees right here. There are a couple of handy reminders on the top of this page. All pertinent buying reminders also show up here.

The My eBay menus in the navigation area on the left side of the page take you to the main areas of My eBay. Also, look at the tiny drop-down menu under Activity on the left side of the My eBay Summary page in Figure 4-2. That drop-down menu will also take you to pages that organize your selling activities. Another way to get to your selling information is to scroll to the bottom of the Summary page and click the link to All Selling. The Summary heading has several convenient links that take you to different areas of your eBay shopping.

Because eBay is always trying to improve things, you may notice at the top right of the page a link to see an alternate version of an existing page. Figure 4-3 shows you the current versions available of the My eBay ⇨ Selling page. Use the one that suits you best. You can always return to the other view.

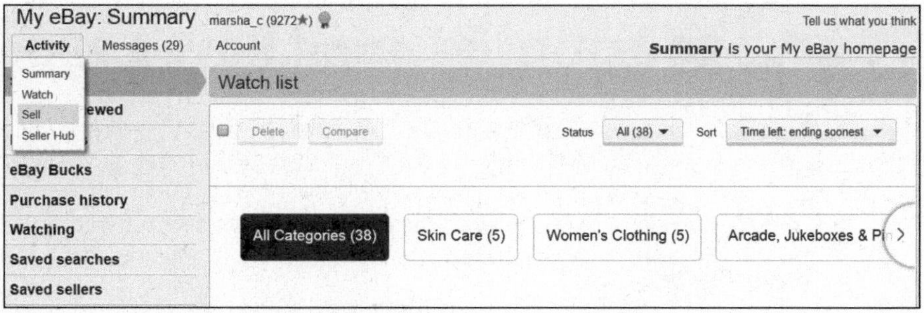

FIGURE 4-2:
Your My eBay Summary page, the hub for your eBay activities.

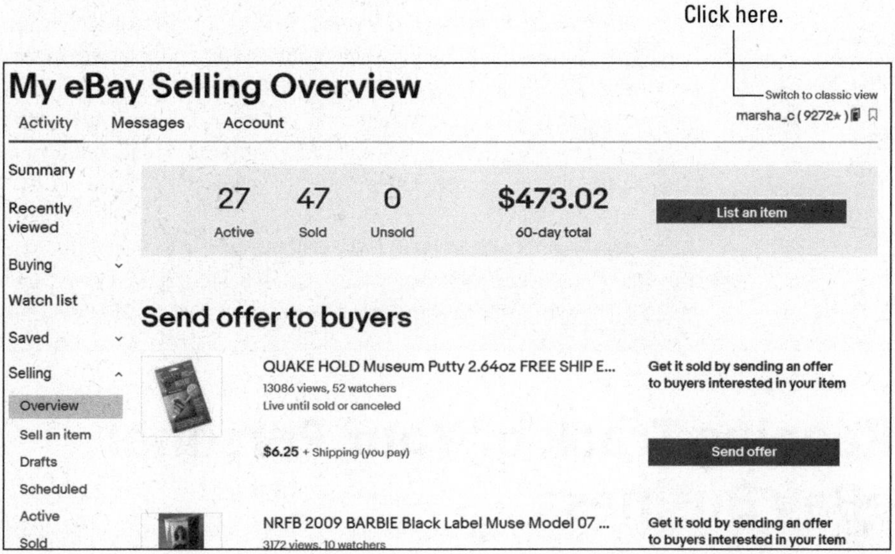

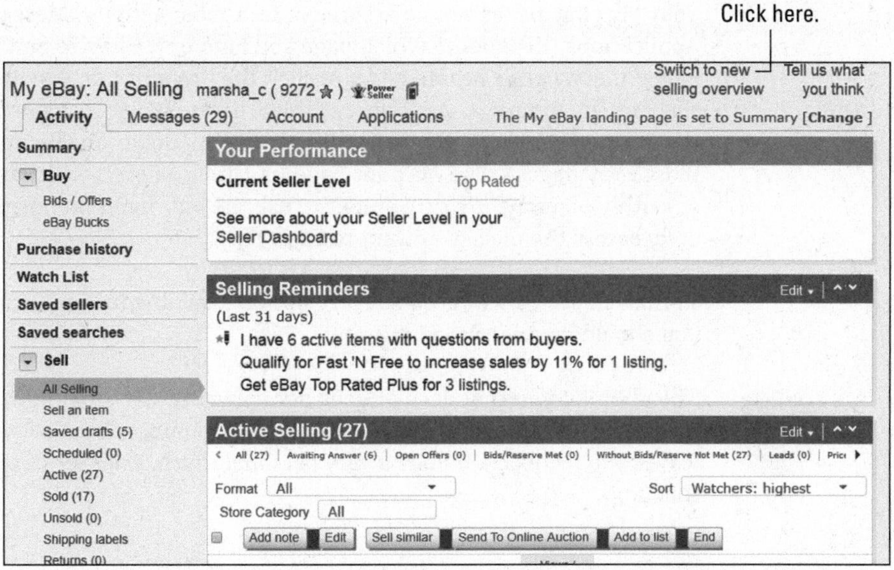

Click here.

Click here.

FIGURE 4-3:
Alternate views of My eBay ⇨ Selling.

MARSHA SAYS

HOUSTON, WE DON'T HAVE A PROBLEM

Here's an item I wish I'd bought: a very clean 8-x-10-inch color Neil Armstrong–signed official NASA portrait w/COA (Certificate of Authenticity). In his last years, Armstrong, the first human on the moon, was reclusive, and his autographs are difficult to obtain in any form. Many forgeries and reproductions are being offered, so buyer beware. This portrait came with a lifetime COA. The starting price was $10, and the portrait sold on eBay in 1999 for $520!

Many believe that Neil Armstrong's autograph will be among the most important of the 20th century. Just think about it. He was the first human to step onto another celestial body. This feat will never happen again, and the first people on other planets may not land there in our lifetimes. When I updated this book for the third edition, this same portrait was selling for $650. When I checked this out for the 4th edition in 2004, the picture sold for $1,925. A quick scan in 2005 showed that such a signed picture had just closed at $2,025, and for $3,500 in 2009.

Armstrong original signed photos are still selling (one — Best Offer Accepted — was just listed for $8,995), but you'll not find an authenticated, signed photo up for sale for less than $3,000. Why, oh why, didn't I follow my own advice and buy one in 1999?

Keeping Track of Your Personal eBay Business

Your My eBay pages can have three or four tabs: Activity, Messages, Account, and Applications (depending which page you land on). They're on the top of the page below the My eBay heading. If you click the Account tab, you arrive at a page like the one in Figure 4-4. (You can also access your Account page by clicking the Account Settings link beneath the Hi! dropdown on the upper left corner of most eBay pages). The Account page has links to each topic you need to operate smoothly on eBay. It's convenient to use the left-hand menu options to immediately access the place you want to explore.

In this chapter, I will not list every option available to you — only the ones I feel you should double-check at first.

TIP

The photo of you that does or does not appear in Hi! drop-down menu gets there when you fill out your eBay profile. It also appears on the page when a buyer leaves you feedback. It adds a very personal touch. Chapter 14 tells you how to set this up.

My eBay marsha_c (9272 ★) ⚜ ⓘ ⓜⓐ

| Activity | Messages | **Account** | Applications |

My eBay Views

My Account
- Personal Information
- Addresses
- Payment Options
- Communication Preferences
- Site Preferences
- Manage communications with buyers
- Seller Dashboard
- Feedback
- PayPal Account
- Seller Account
- Donation Account
- Subscriptions
- Resolution Center
- Advertisement Preferences
- Permissions

My Account   Close My Account

There will be a delay of 24 hours or more in updating your fee and account balance.

Account Summary   ⌃ ⌄

Latest invoice amount (Jul-31-19) :   US $⬛⬛⬛
New Activity applied to the latest invoice noted above: US $0.00

Amount due as of Aug-03-19:   US ⬛⬛⬛⬛
New activity not yet invoiced: US $2.10
Current Balance: US ⬛⬛⬛⬛

View: All account activity | Fees | Credits | Payments and refunds

Invoices

Select Invoice ▼ Go

You can set preferences to download your invoices periodically.

PayPal account information   ⌃ ⌄

We'll take you to PayPal to update your information.
- See your PayPal account summary

FIGURE 4-4: Access individual areas of your account in this menu.

Checking your account information

The Account page lists the most important parts of your eBay account. This is where you update your contact information. Initially, all this data comes from your registration. But it's policy on eBay that every user files his or her current contact information — so if you move or change phone numbers, email addresses, or banks, you need to input that information here.

It's also where you can change your User ID (if you ever decide that Charlie18907 doesn't properly reflect your personality). When you use the eBay mobile app, notifications will be sent directly to your smartphone. You can also change your password and all your other registered information in this area.

REMEMBER

On eBay you can change your User ID at any time (every 30 days), and your feedback rating will follow.

Choosing your communication preferences

Because we live in a world where everyone has his or her own way of doing business, eBay allows you to set a multitude of preferences for your eBay account. One of the links leads to the Communication Preferences page. The Preferences settings are all important to your eBay tasks. You have to decide which activities you want activated for your eBay account (you can always change these later).

The most convenient thing is to select all the options that make sense to you. You can set many Notification preferences:

» **Notification Delivery:** This is where you let eBay know which method of notification works best for you. You can also indicate whether you want HTML or text-based emails.

» **Buying Notifications:** Be careful here. If you indicate that you *want* all this email and you plan to be active on the site, prepare to be deluged. Select wisely, on this page there are 27 options! But remember, you can always make changes. Most important is to get real-time notifications on your shopping. Here are a few I recommend:

- Watch alert (also daily, weekly, or monthly) email
- Watched Item relisted by the seller
- Confirmations for your bids
- Emails when you're outbid in an auction
- Order Confirmations
- Returns started

As you can see, this is way too many emails, especially if you do a lot of buying and selling. eBay will send you emails for even more than I mention here. For sanity's sake, narrow your selections to the minimum, but please, go over this list carefully.

» **Selling Notifications:** If you're selling on the site, most of these notifications will be useful. There are 28 to choose from. You can indicate you want to receive the following emails (among others):

- Notification that you've saved a draft on the Sell an Item form
- Email confirmation each time you list an item for sale
- Yay! The end-of-listing email when your item has sold
- Boo. The email you get when your item doesn't sell
- Notification when your buyer performs Checkout
- Shipping label information
- Items received
- Returns started

These are all important, especially when you're a new seller. When you become more active as a seller, you might want to whittle these down a bit — but not too much! Information is power.

>> **Other Transactions and Notices:** Again, the choice is up to you. These can be overwhelming. eBay gives you the option to receive emails in the following areas:

- Member-to-member communications

- Receive Second Chance offers

- Reminders to leave feedback

- Account preference changes

- Resolution Center (if any transaction runs into trouble, you can get notices in real time)

Without enumerating everything else (I can see you're about to doze off), you can also opt into (or opt out of) eBay surveys, promotions, and automated phone messages from eBay.

Next on the Preferences hit parade are your *actual* site preferences — how you'd like to conduct business on the site. These are settings for the more-advanced seller. You can make most of these decisions on the Sell an Item page. If you have time, though, click through each of the individual links to show the options and be sure that the default settings work for you.

Your Feedback link

The menu also provides a convenient link to Feedback. In the Feedback area, you see all the items that need your feedback attention, and you can see the recent feedback that has been left for you. Save yourself a trip; you can leave feedback more conveniently from the item page, your Sell page, or your Buy page.

Account links

Not surprisingly, the Seller Account option leads you to more links for your PayPal and eBay Seller accounts. After you start selling, your Account pages become powerful. You can click links to view past or current invoices. You can also look up every detail of your account history, as well as make changes to your personal preferences (such as how and when you want to pay fees).

Before you jump into the money game, you may want to review the links that eBay gives you for managing your money:

>> **Seller Account:** Click here to get a complete explanation of your eBay account — charges, credits, and your current balance since your last invoice.

>> **View Invoices:** Click the drop-down menu to see your most recent invoice and details of the transactions. You can also arrange to download PDF copies of your invoices.

>> **PayPal Account:** A quick click here, and you're taken to the PayPal home page. Check out Chapter 6 for more on the PayPal payment service.

>> **Automatic Payment Method:** Although you need to post a credit card for ID purposes to sell on eBay, you can pay your eBay bill in one of three ways. They like to deduct it directly from your registered checking account, but I prefer the ways listed next. You can change your method of payment at any time. See Table 4-1 to find out when the different payments are charged to your account.

- **Credit Card on File:** You can place your credit card on file with eBay so that eBay can place your selling charges on your credit card each month. I've been using this format since I became an eBay user and find that it works out very well.

- **PayPal:** You can make single payments directly through your PayPal account. If you have a cash balance in your account, you can have it applied to your eBay bill; if not, you can pay the amount through the credit card you registered on PayPal.

TABLE 4-1   **eBay's Automatic Seller Fees Payments**

Billing Cycle	Payment Due By	Deducted from Checking Account	Credit Card Charged
15th of month	15th of next month	5th of next month	15 days after receipt of invoice
Last day of month	The last day of next month	20th of next month	15 days after receipt of invoice

Understanding Your Seller Dashboard

If you look on the left of your Account Summary page, you see a group of links called My eBay Views for quickly accessing specific areas of the site as well as navigating by using the drop-down menu at the top of the page. One of the most important is the link to the Seller Dashboard, which is where eBay calculates your ratings on the site. Chapter 8 contains an explanation of the Detailed Seller Ratings (DSRs). Figure 4-5 shows you a portion of my Seller Dashboard. This shows your progress to becoming a Top-Rated Seller (see Chapter 20 for the benefits).

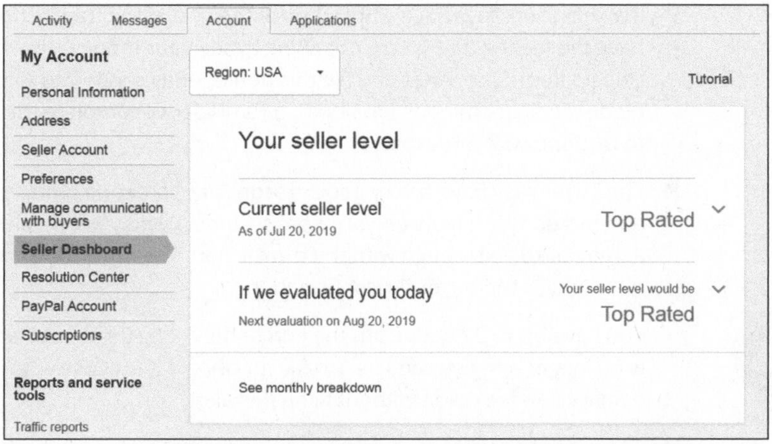

FIGURE 4-5:
Viewing my current Seller Dashboard.

This is an important place to go on a regular basis because eBay evaluates your status on the site daily. Your status affects your placement in searches and whether you get a discount on your fees (based on your customer satisfaction ratings) if you're a Top Rated Seller. Be sure to click the down-facing arrows on the right to give you in-depth data on how you're doing on the site.

MARSHA SAYS

When you scroll to the very bottom of the Dashboard, you can see the cumulative dollar amount of your total sales on eBay since you started selling.

Using the Resolution Center

If you sell an item and the buyer backs out (a rare but disheartening situation), you can at least get a refund on some of the fees that eBay charges you as a seller. These are the final value fees, and they're based on the selling price of the item. In the Resolution Center, you can keep track of the disputes in progress and send or receive messages from the other party regarding payment.

If you and the buyer mutually agree not to go through with the transaction (for any number of reasons), your final value fee will be refunded.

TIP

Before you can collect a final value fee refund, the following conditions must apply:

>> After your listing is over, you have to allow a buyer at least two business days to respond to you. If the buyer doesn't respond, you can send an email politely reminding him or her of the commitment that a buyer makes to buy.

>> If at least two days have elapsed since the end of the transaction and you have the feeling that you're not going to see your money, you *must* open an Unpaid Item Case. After you file this notice, eBay sends you a copy, and the bidder gets an ominous email with a reminder to complete the transaction or to respond with a reason.

>> The buyer may have a very good reason (say, someone didn't read this book and clicked Buy It Now on your item six times), and you are allowed to mutually agree not to go through with the transaction. The buyer must respond when eBay emails the buyer for confirmation.

WARNING

You have up to 32 days from the end of the listing (or immediately if the buyer is no longer a registered user) to file an Unpaid Item Case — and you can't get a final value fee credit without filing this alert.

>> The buyer has up to four days to send payment after you file the Unpaid Item Case, or contact you to "work out" payment arrangements. You should try to send a message through the Dispute Console to resolve the situation during this time.

>> If you do not receive a payment, you'll have to manually close the case to receive your credit. In this case, you must address the issue in the Resolution Center within 36 days or you're out of luck.

TIP

If you begin the process and file for a final value fee credit — but then manage to work things out with the buyer — eBay removes the complaint from the buyer's account after the buyer pays through eBay's approved payment methods. Buyers with too many of these warnings, however, can be suspended from using the eBay site.

Organizing Saved Sellers/Searches

Part of the fun of eBay is searching for stuff that you'd never in a million years think of looking for. Wacky stuff aside, most eBay users spend their time hunting for specific items — say, Barbie dolls, designer dresses, plumbing supplies, or smartphone accessories. That's why eBay came up with the Lists area of your My eBay page. Whenever you view your My eBay Saved Searches, you see a list of your watched items (through a left side link), saved searches, and saved sellers. But because eBay isn't psychic, you have to tell it what you want listed.

If you shop eBay at all like I do, you'll be looking for similar things and sellers over and over. The My eBay Saved Searches area allows you to make note of your favorite searches and sellers. You can repeat these searches and visit these sellers with a click of your mouse.

Searches you follow

You have the opportunity to list a bunch of searches here. When you want to repeat one of these searches, just click the Search name to search for the item. eBay will even email you your searches when new items are listed. (For more on that advanced function, check out Chapter 18.)

To add a search to your favorites, first perform the search. (For details on how to perform a search, see Chapter 5.) When the search appears on your screen, click the heart (♡) next to the word Save, as shown at the top of the Search Results in Figure 4-6. The search is now transported to your My eBay Saved Searches area for that particular search.

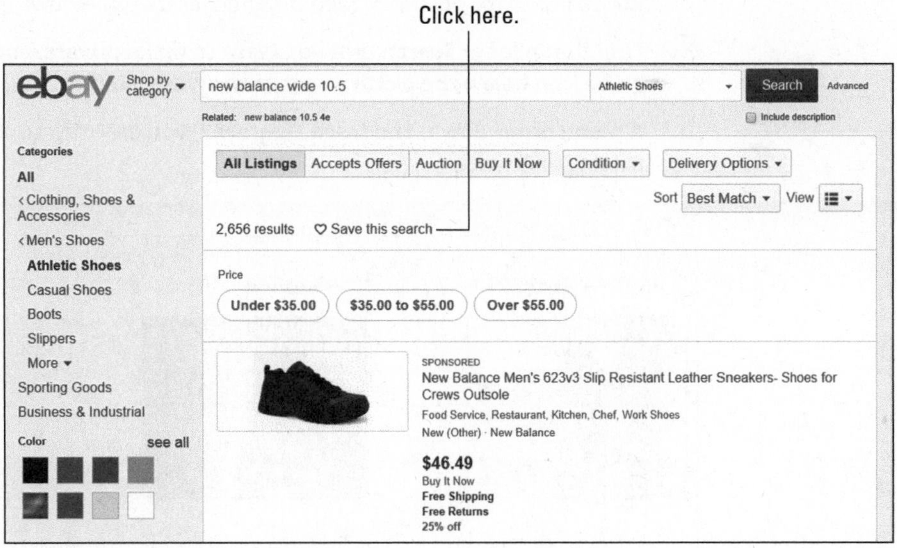

FIGURE 4-6:
Adding a Favorite
Search to your
Saved list.

If you change your mind and no longer want to follow the search, click the Following This Search link and a red X appears. Clicking there removes the search from your list.

Sellers you follow

When you find a seller whose merchandise and prices are right up your alley and you'd like to occasionally check out the seller's items for sale, you can list the seller in the Saved Sellers area.

When you've shopped eBay and found a seller that you're happy with (or just like their items), click the ♡ sign next to Save This Seller on the listing page. Voilà! The seller is saved to your Saved Sellers page and to your Profile page.

Keeping your follows on the "down low"

If you follow some sellers or searches because you source merchandise from them or use them for researching products (or you don't want the fact that you are following public), you can remedy the situation:

1. Go to your Profile page by clicking your eBay User ID on any page.

2. Scroll down to the Following section.

3. Click the cog icon on the right next to the word Settings.

    You are brought to a page where you can set Privacy settings for any Interests (for Searches You Follow) or Members (for Sellers You Follow).

4. Find the Seller or Search that you want to make private, and click the globe icon below the picture next to the word *public*.

5. A menu drops down, and (as in Figure 4-7) you can click to change your setting to Private.

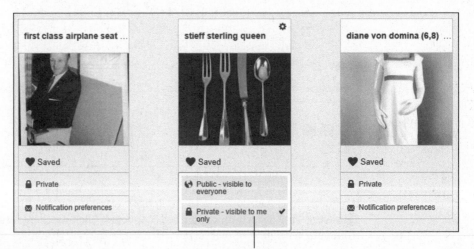

FIGURE 4-7:
Making your Follows private from your profile settings page.

Click here.

Once you've set a Follow to Private, folks can no longer see it on your profile page, but you can still reach it from your My eBay ⇨ Saved Sellers (or Searches) links.

Sleuthing with your Watching list

The Watch list may be the most active area of the My eBay page (see Figure 4-8). This is the place for you to work on your strategy for getting bargains without showing your hand by bidding. In this area, you can watch the auction evolve and decide if you want to bid on it. When you come across a fixed-price listing that you don't want to take advantage of just now, save it here for future reference. You also can list several auctions for the same item and watch them develop, and then bid on the one that can give you the best deal. You can track the progress of up to 100 items in your Watch list area.

FIGURE 4-8:
The Watch list area on the My eBay page.

Moving listings into the Watch area is easy. When you find an item that you want to keep track of, look for the Add to watch list link, which is located on the listing page. You can also add to your Watch list by clicking the Add to watch list link, as shown in Figure 4-9. Just click this link to transport the item to your Watch list area.

FIGURE 4-9:
The drop-down list in the bidding/ buying box gives you many options to save the listing for future reference.

Following the Action on Your Buying

I have the most fun on eBay when I'm shopping. Shopping on eBay is exciting, and I can find a zillion great bargains. Fortunately, eBay gives you a place to keep all your shopping information together: the Buying area.

Seeing the items you're buying

When you bid on an item, eBay automatically lists the item in the Summary ⇨ Bids/ Offers area of your My eBay page. If you're winning an auction, the price appears in green; if you're losing, it appears in red. After the auction's over, the listing moves to Purchase history (yea!). You can watch the progress of the auction from here and see the number of bids on the item, the high bid, and how much time is left until the end of the auction. All this information can help you decide whether you want to jump back in and make a bid.

eBay also keeps a total of all your active bids and buys to the left of your data in the Totals: Buying Total box — which I hope helps you stay within your spending limits.

Keeping track of your purchased items

When you win an auction or purchase an item with Buy It Now, the item appears in the Purchase history area. From this area, you can visit the listing to double-check it. From the links in the More Actions column, you can also pay for your item; if you've already paid, you can view the payment details. You can also click a Leave Feedback link here from the drop-down menu — after you've received the item and are satisfied with your purchase — to leave feedback. If you want to return the items to the seller, just click the Return This Item link to initiate a return.

**MARSHA
SAYS**

Maybe because I'm a stickler for politeness (or perhaps I believe in *Do unto others . . .*), but before I initiate a return on eBay, I message the seller and tell them why. Sometimes things can be solved between you both. Why turn this into an adversarial situation?

Surveying Your Sales on Your My eBay Selling Overview

Your My eBay page supplies you with the tools to keep track of items you're selling on eBay. The My eBay Selling page works much the same as the purchasing area, but this time you're making the money — not spending it! Your current auctions and fixed-price listings are listed in the Active area. The auctions with bids on them appear in green, and the ones without bids (or where the reserve hasn't been met) are in red. In the left column, you have a dollar total of the current bids on your auctions, items sold, and totals of payments received.

Your Selling page

As with the Buy section, the Selling area keeps track of your ongoing listings on eBay. You can observe the action in real time (or at least every time you refresh the page). You can see how many bids have been placed, when an auction closes, and the time left in an auction. If you want more information about what's going on (for example, how many people are watching or bidding), just peruse your listings in this area.

Your Sold page

When the sale is final, the items go into the Sold area (shown in Figure 4-10). Here's where you can keep track of the sale. You can check whether the buyer has paid with PayPal as well as the transaction status. The transaction will appear with an expected shipping date after the buyer has completed Checkout and paid. If they haven't, you can see the status of the transaction by the icons (shown in Figure 4-10). Be sure to click the drop-down menu arrow (shown in Figure 4-11) to see links to other actions. The actions may vary, based on the status of the transaction.

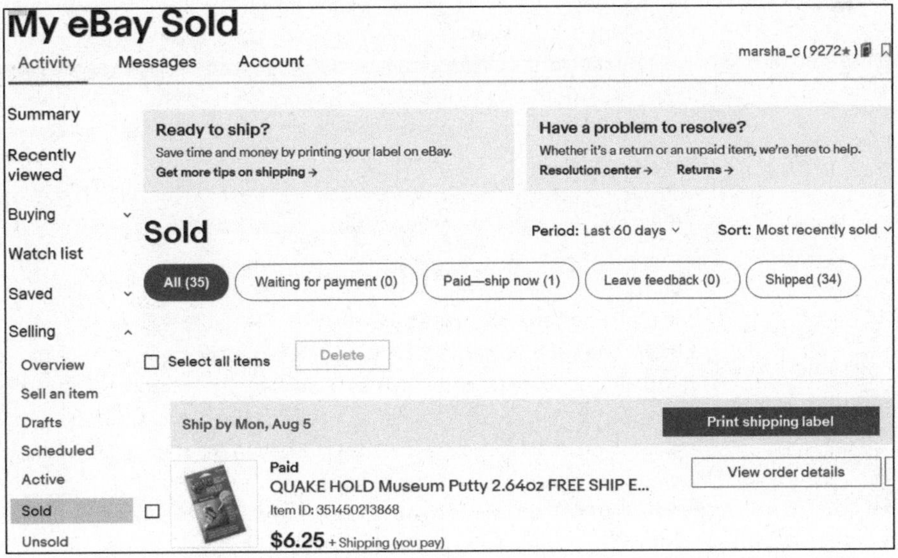

FIGURE 4-10: The My eBay Sold area.

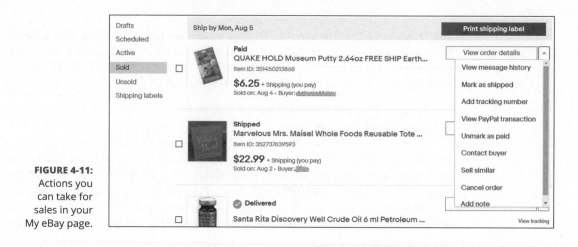

FIGURE 4-11:
Actions you can take for sales in your My eBay page.

After the transaction is complete (which means the item has arrived and the buyer is happy with his or her purchase), you can click the handy Leave Feedback link to leave feedback about the buyer.

You can also relist the item from a quick link or make a Second Chance offer to an underbidder if you have more than one of the item. See the nearby sidebar for more on the Second Chance feature.

YOUR SECRET SELLER TOOL — SECOND CHANCE!

The e-commerce experts at eBay have come up with another great selling tool. Say you have multiples of a single item (you *did* sell that set of Minton china one piece at a time, didn't you?) or the winning bidder backs out of the transaction without paying. The Second Chance offer gives you the opportunity to offer the item to one of the underbidders (okay, the losers) at their high bid price (gee, maybe they didn't lose after all). You can also create a Second Chance if you set a reserve that wasn't met before the auction ended. The Second Chance opportunity is available for up to 60 days after the sale ends.

You can offer the item to as many of the underbidders as you'd like (as long as you have the merchandise) and make this personal offer good for one to seven days. Each bidder receives an email regarding the offer and can access it on the site through a special link. It is only visible to you and the other bidder for the duration of the offer. The best part is that eBay doesn't charge any additional listing fees for this feature — but you are charged the final value fee after the transaction is complete. Chapter 13 has the details on how to use this little known feature too.

Keeping Track of Your Transactions

Yes, I bug you about saving stuff at the outset of your selling career because I care. The eBay transaction process can be daunting, and beginners can easily lose track. The best way to protect yourself is to keep good records on your own. This is your money, so keep a close eye on it.

Now don't become a packrat and overdo it. To help point you in the right direction, here's a list of important records that I think you might want to file whether you're a buyer or a beginning seller:

>> eBay invoices for your sales

>> PayPal statements indicating any payment you receive that doesn't clear

>> Insurance or escrow forms

>> Refund and credit requests

>> Receipts from purchases you make for items to sell on eBay

TIP

All messages between you and the buyer are saved in your Messages mail box. For more information about email from eBay and correspondence etiquette, see Chapters 8 and 12.

Why should you keep track of all this stuff? Here are some reasons:

>> Even if you're buying and selling just a few items a month on eBay, you need to keep track of who you owe and who owes you money.

>> Good correspondence is a learned art, but if you reference item numbers as you correspond, then your email and eBay messages are an instant record. If you put your dates in writing — and follow up — you have a nice, neat paper trail (even if the trail is digital).

>> Documenting the transaction through eBay Messages will come in handy if you ever end up in a dispute over the terms of the sale.

>> If you sell specialized items, you can keep track of trends and your frequent buyers.

>> Someday the IRS may come knocking on your door, especially if you buy stuff for the purpose of selling it on eBay. Scary, but true. For more on where you can get tax information, take a look at Chapter 9.

Getting and Giving Feedback

You know how they say you are what you eat? On eBay, you are only as good as your feedback says you are. Your feedback is made up of comments — good, bad, or neutral — that people leave about you (and you leave about others). In effect, people are commenting on your overall professionalism. (Even if you're an eBay hobbyist with no thought of using it professionally, a little business-like courtesy can ease your transactions with everyone.) These comments are the basis for your eBay reputation.

WARNING

Because feedback is so important to your reputation on eBay, you don't want others leaving feedback or making bad transactions under your name. The only way to ensure that this doesn't happen is to keep your password a secret — always. If you suspect somebody may know your password, change it before that person has a chance to sign in as you and ruin your reputation. (For more on selecting and protecting your level of privacy, see Chapters 1 and 15.)

When you get your first feedback, the number that appears next to your User ID is your feedback rating, which follows you everywhere you go on eBay, even if you change your User ID or email address. It sticks to you like glue. Click the number next to any User ID and get a complete look at the user's feedback profile. The thinking behind the feedback concept is that you wouldn't be caught dead in a store that has a lousy reputation, so why on earth would you want to do business on the Internet with someone who has a lousy reputation?

REMEMBER

You're not required to leave feedback, but because it's the benchmark by which all eBay users are judged, whether you're buying or selling, you should *always* leave feedback comments. Get in the frame of mind that every time you complete a transaction — the minute the package arrives safely to your buyer (if you're a seller) or an item you've bid on and won arrives — you should go to eBay and post your feedback.

Every time you get a positive comment from a user who hasn't commented on you before within the past week, you get a point. Every time you get a negative rating, this negative cancels out one of your positives. Neutral comments rate a 0 — they have no impact either way. eBay even has what it calls the Star Chart, shown in Figure 4-12, which rewards those with good-and-getting-higher feedback ratings.

Sellers are only allowed to leave positive feedback for buyers — I know this may not make sense, but that's the way it is. You can leave a "positive," but still be honest about your transaction in your words. eBay made this rule so sellers wouldn't leave retaliatory feedback to buyers who left them negative feedback.

Star	Color	Number of ratings
☆	Yellow	10 to 49
★	Blue	50 to 99
★	Turquoise	100 to 499
★	Purple	500 to 999
★	Red	1,000 to 4,999
★	Green	5,000 to 9,999
🌠	Yellow shooting star	10,000 to 24,999
🌠	Turquoise shooting star	25,000 to 49,999
🌠	Purple shooting star	50,000 to 99,999
🌠	Red shooting star	100,000 to 499,999
🌠	Green shooting star	500,000 to 999,999
🌠	Silver shooting star	1,000,000 or more (Wow!)

FIGURE 4-12:
The eBay feedback achievement Star rating.

Should a buyer who hasn't paid leave you a negative, eBay cooperates and removes the feedback, provided you've filed an Unpaid Item report.

TIP

If feedback is left individually and stretched out over several weeks (only one per calendar week of eBay Time), the person on the other end of the transaction will get a single feedback point each time you leave a positive. I do this for my buyers who buy multiple items from me (it's easy from the My eBay page). But most buyers don't seem to know this rule, so I'll get several positives — one after another — netting me only one positive. *Sigh*

REMEMBER

Remember, just because a user may have a 750 feedback rating, it doesn't hurt to click the number after the name to double-check the person's feedback page. Even if someone has a total of 1,000 feedback messages, 250 of them *could* be negative. *Always* note the feedback percentage.

TIP

You can get to your personal feedback profile page right from your My eBay page by clicking the number next to your User ID.

Feedback comes in three exciting flavors:

>> **Positive feedback:** Someone once said, "All you have is your reputation." Reputation is what makes eBay function. If the transaction works well, you get positive feedback; whenever it's warranted, you should give it right back.

>> **Negative feedback:** If there's a glitch (for example, it takes six months to get your *Charlie's Angels* lunch box, or the seller substitutes a rusty Thermos for the one you bid on or you never get the item), you have the right — some would say *obligation* — to leave negative feedback.

>> **Neutral feedback:** You can leave neutral feedback if you feel so-so about a specific transaction. It's the middle-of-the-road comment. Say you bought an item that had a little more wear and tear on it than the seller indicated, but you still like it and want to keep it.

How to get positive feedback

If you're selling, here's how to get a good reputation:

>> After you receive payment, send the item posthaste (see Chapter 12).

>> Make sure that the item you ship is exactly in the same condition as you described it (see Chapter 10).

>> Package the item carefully and ship it in an appropriate package (see Chapter 12).

>> React quickly and appropriately to problems — for example, the item's lost or damaged in the mail, or the buyer is slow in paying (see Chapter 12).

If you're buying, try these good-rep tips:

>> Send your payment fast (see Chapter 8).

>> Contact the seller through eBay Messages if a problem arises (see Chapter 8).

>> Work with the seller to resolve any problems in a courteous manner (see Chapters 8 and 12).

How to get negative feedback

Okay, this section can be read in one of two ways: (a) as what to do if you're a glutton for punishment, or (b) as a list of major blunders (with their antidotes). So here goes: If you're selling, here's what to do to tarnish your name big-time:

>> Tell a major untruth in the item description. (To defend truth, justice, and legitimate creative writing, see Chapter 10.)

>> Take the money but "forget" to ship the item. (Who did you say you are? See Chapter 16.)

>> Package the item poorly so that it ends up smashed, squashed, or vaporized during shipping. (To avoid this sad fate, see Chapter 12.)

If you're buying, you can't get official negative feedback, but the sellers still have their "say." If you want to make your eBay experience suck, here's how to make a serious mess of the feedback comments you get:

>> Bid on an item, win the auction, and never respond to the seller. (Remember your manners and see Chapter 6.)

>> Pick up the item in person and give the seller a personal check that bounces and never make good on the payment. (See Chapter 16 — and don't pass Go.)

>> Ask the seller for a refund because you just don't like the item. (Remember how to play fair and see Chapter 8.)

The Feedback page

When you click the feedback number next to a member's User ID, you'll see all the tools you need to gauge the member. Think of your feedback profile as your eBay report card. Your goal is to get straight *As* — in this case, all positive feedback. Unlike a real report card, you don't have to bring it home to be signed.

When someone clicks the feedback number next to your User ID, they see the following information (see Figure 4-13) and a few handy links:

>> **Your User ID:** Your eBay nickname appears, followed by a number in parentheses — the net number of the positive feedback comments you've received, minus any negative feedback comments you may have (but that wouldn't happen to you).

>> **Your Membership Information:** Listed here is the date you first signed up as a member of the eBay community. Below that is the country from which you're registered, your star rating (refer to Figure 4-12), and any icons leading to more areas related to you on eBay, such as your profile page (see Chapter 14). This area also notes whether you have an eBay Store.

>> **Detailed Seller Ratings:** This area sums up the ratings, from one to five, that buyers have left for you.

>> **Your Recent Feedback Ratings:** This area is a scorecard of your feedback for the last 12 months. At the bottom of the feedback tote board is a summary of your bid retractions in the past six months — the times you have retracted bids during an auction.

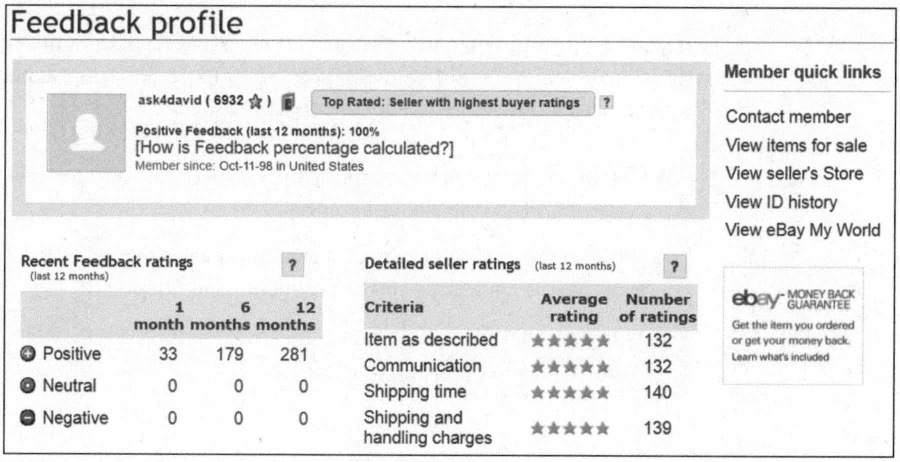

Feedback profile

ask4david (6932 ⭐) 📋 | Top Rated: Seller with highest buyer ratings | ❓

Positive Feedback (last 12 months): 100%
[How is Feedback percentage calculated?]
Member since: Oct-11-98 in United States

Member quick links

Contact member
View items for sale
View seller's Store
View ID history
View eBay My World

Recent Feedback ratings
(last 12 months) ❓

	1 month	6 months	12 months
⊕ Positive	33	179	281
◐ Neutral	0	0	0
⊖ Negative	0	0	0

Detailed seller ratings
(last 12 months) ❓

Criteria	Average rating	Number of ratings
Item as described	★★★★★	132
Communication	★★★★★	132
Shipping time	★★★★★	140
Shipping and handling charges	★★★★★	139

ebay MONEY BACK GUARANTEE
Get the item you ordered or get your money back.
Learn what's included

FIGURE 4-13:
One of my favorite seller's Feedback profile — there's one for every member.

TIP

To protect your eBay reputation, be careful when you retract a bid. All bids on eBay are binding, but under what eBay calls "exceptional circumstances," you may retract bids — very sparingly. Here are the circumstances in which it's okay to retract a bid:

>> If you mistakenly put in the wrong bid amount — say, $100 rather than $10

>> If the seller adds to his or her description after you place your bid, and the change considerably affects the item

>> If you can't contact the seller (your email continuously bounces back and the phone number doesn't work)

REMEMBER

You can't retract a bid just because you found the item elsewhere cheaper, or you changed your mind, or you decided that you really can't afford the item. If that's the case, message the seller directly and ask *the seller* to please remove your bid. See Chapter 6 for more information on retracting bids.

Reading your feedback

Your eBay reputation is at the mercy of the one-liners that buyers and sellers leave for you in the form of feedback comments. Each feedback contains these reputation-building (or reputation-trashing) ingredients:

>> The User ID of the person who sent the feedback. The number in parentheses next to the person's name is his or her own feedback rating.

>> The approximate time the feedback was posted.

>> The item number of the transaction that the feedback refers to.

>> Seller or Buyer (only in the All Feedback area) — indicating whether you were the seller or the buyer in the transaction.

>> Feedback bullets in different colors: praise (in green with a plus mark), negative (in red with a minus mark), or neutral (in gray with a white dot).

>> The feedback the person left about you.

You have the last word — responding to feedback

After reading feedback you receive from others, you may feel compelled to respond. If the feedback is negative, you may want to defend yourself. If it's positive, you may want to say thank you.

To respond to feedback, follow these steps:

1. **Click the Account tab on your My eBay page, click the Feedback link in the My eBay Views list on the left, and then click the Go to Feedback Forum link at the top of the page.**

   You're transported to the Feedback Forum, where you can reply to feedback comments left for you.

2. **Click the Reply to Feedback Received link on the right side of the page.**

   You will land on a page that lists all the feedback you have received.

3. **Find the feedback you want to respond to and click Reply.**

   You may now type your response.

If you want to follow up to feedback you've already left for someone, follow the preceding steps, but in Step 2, click the Follow Up to Feedback Left link on the Feedback Forum page.

WARNING

Do not confuse *replying* to feedback with *leaving* feedback. Replying does not change the other user's feedback rating; it merely adds a line below the feedback with your response.

Leaving feedback with finesse

Writing feedback well takes some practice. It isn't a matter of saying things; it's a matter of saying *only the appropriate things*. Think carefully about what you want to say because when you submit feedback, it stays with the person for the duration of his or her eBay career. I think you should always leave feedback, especially at the end of a transaction, although doing so isn't mandatory. Think of leaving feedback as voting in an election: If you don't leave feedback, you can't complain about lousy service.

eBay says to make feedback "factual and emotionless." You won't go wrong if you comment on the details (either good or bad) of the transaction. If you have any questions about what eBay says about feedback, click the Feedback link on your My eBay page, and then click the Go to Feedback Forum link.

In the Feedback Forum, you can perform six feedback-related tasks:

>> **See feedback about an eBay user.**

>> **Leave feedback for many items at the same time.** Here, you see all pending feedback for all transactions within the past 90 days. You are presented with a page of all your transactions for which you haven't left feedback. Fill them in, one at a time, and with one click you can leave as many as 25 feedback comments at once.

>> **Review and respond to existing feedback about you.**

>> **Review the feedback you have left for others.** Here you may also leave follow-up feedback after the initial feedback, should situations change.

>> **Report buyer problems.**

>> **Check the Feedback FAQ to review any changes in the feedback system.**

TIP

If you're angry, take a breather *before* you type your complaints and click the Feedback button. If you're convinced that negative feedback is necessary, try a cooling-off period before you send a comment. Wait an hour or a day and then see whether you feel the same. Nasty feedback based on emotion can make you look vindictive (even if what you're saying is true).

Safety tips for giving feedback

And speaking of safety features you should know about feedback, you may want to study up on these:

>> **Remember that feedback, whether good or bad, is *sticky.*** As a buyer, once you leave feedback, you have 30 days to change or remove it. After that, eBay won't remove your feedback if you change your mind later. Be sure of your facts, and carefully consider what you want to say.

>> **Before you leave feedback, see what other people had to say about that person.** Is your thinking in line with the comments others have left?

MINCING WORDS: GUIDE TO KEEPING FEEDBACK SHORT

Let's keep things simple. If you want to compliment, complain, or take the middle road, you have to do it in 80 characters or less. That means your comment needs to be short and sweet. If you have a lot to say but you're stumped about how to say it, here are a few examples for any occasion. String them together or mix and match!

Positive feedback:

- Very professional
- Quick email response
- Fast service
- A+++
- Good communication
- Exactly as described
- Highly recommended
- Smooth transaction
- Would deal with again
- An asset to eBay
- I'll be back!

Negative feedback:

- Never responded
- Never sent item
- Desperately slow shipping
- Beware track record
- Not as described

Neutral feedback:

- Slow to ship but item as described
- Item not as described but seller made good
- Poor communication but item came OK

>> **You can leave feedback as long as the transaction remains on the eBay server.** This is usually within 90 days of the end of the listing. After 90 days have passed, you must have the transaction number to leave feedback.

>> **Your comment can be a maximum of only 80 letters long, which is really short when you have a lot to say.** Before you start typing, organize your thoughts and use common abbreviations to save precious space.

>> **Before posting negative feedback, try to resolve the problem by email or telephone.** You may discover that your reaction to the transaction is based on a misunderstanding that can be easily resolved.

>> **eBay users generally want to make each other happy, so use negative feedback *only as a last resort*.** See Chapters 8 and 10 for more details on how to avoid negative feedback.

The ways to leave feedback

Several ways are available to leave feedback comments:

>> If you're on the user's Feedback page, click the Leave Feedback link; the Leave Feedback page appears.

>> In the Purchased Items area of your My eBay page, click the Leave Feedback link next to the listing.

>> Go to your listing and click the Leave Feedback icon.

>> In the Feedback Forum, click the Leave Feedback link to see a list of all your completed items from the last 90 days for which you haven't yet left feedback.

To leave feedback for a buyer, follow these steps:

1. **Enter the required information.**

    Note that your item number is usually filled in, but if you're placing feedback from the user's Feedback page, you need to have the number at hand.

2. **Type your comment.**

    Only positive feedback can be left for a buyer, so choose your words carefully.

3. **Click the Star ratings from one to five to rate the transaction.**

    I rarely give under four stars when the seller has fulfilled the transaction (see Figure 4-14).

4. **Click the Leave Feedback button.**

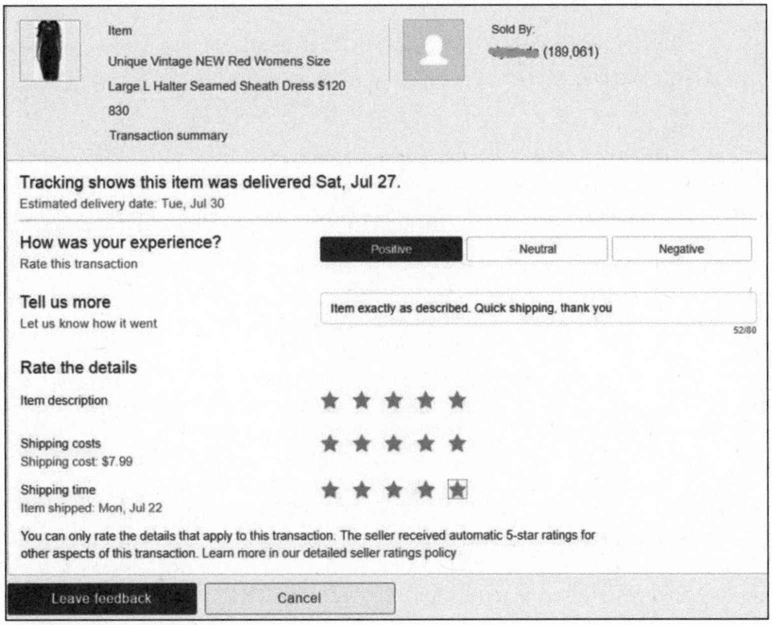

FIGURE 4-14:
Leaving Feedback is important and only takes a minute.

2
Buying Like an Expert

Chapter **5**

Deal or No Deal? Buying Hacks and Searching Tips

P icture all the stores you've ever seen in your life, located in one humungous mall. You walk in and try to find the single item you're looking for (not an easy proposition). Consider also walking into a store with thousands of aisles of shelves with tens of millions of items on them.

Browsing the categories of listings on eBay can be just as pleasantly mind-boggling, without the prospect of sore feet. Start surfing around the site, and you instantly understand the size and scope of what's for sale there. Everything. Without question, you'll feel overwhelmed at first, but eBay comes up with lots of ways to help you find exactly what you're looking for. As soon as you figure out how to find the items you want to bid on or buy on eBay, you can protect your investment-to-be by making sure that what you find is actually what you seek.

Of course, searching is easier if you have an idea of what you're looking for. In this chapter for collectors, I offer the first-time buyer some expert tips and tell you how to get expert advice from eBay and other sources. I also give you tips for using the eBay search from a buyer's perspective.

REMEMBER

The best advice you can follow as you explore any free-market system is *caveat emptor* — let the buyer beware. Although nobody can guarantee that every one of your transactions will be a great deal, research items thoroughly before you bid or buy so that you don't lose too much of your hard-earned money — or too much sleep.

Online Tips for Vintage Enthusiasts

If you're just starting out on eBay, chances are you like to shop and you also collect fun items that interest you. You'll find out pretty early in your eBay journey that a lot of people online know as much about collecting as they do about bidding — and some are serious contenders.

How can you compete? Well, in addition to having a well-planned buying strategy (covered in Chapter 7), knowing your stuff gives you a winning edge. I've gathered the opinions of two collecting experts to get the info you need about online collecting basics. (If you're already an expert collector but want help finding that perfect something on eBay so you can get ready to bid, you've got it. See "Looking to Find an Item? Start Your eBay Search," later in this chapter.) I also show you how one of those experts puts the information into practice, and I give you a crash course on how items for sale are (or should be) graded. I often purchase vintage 1950s/60s clothing on eBay and follow these tips.

TIP

Although these tips from the experts are targeted for collectors of vintage items, much of the information is sound advice for those involved in any transaction online.

The experts speak out

Bill Swoger closed his collectibles store in Burbank, California, and sold the balance of his G.I. Joe and Superman items on eBay. Lee Bernstein, a columnist who ran a collectibles business from her home base in Schererville, Indiana, was the author of eBay's now-defunct Collectibles "Inside Scoop." Lee still sells on eBay and sells artisan knitting projects in her Etsy store, Simply Heaven Knits. My favorite tips, along with Bill and Lee's, follow:

>> **Get all the facts before you put your money down.** Study the description carefully. It's your job to analyze the description and make your bidding decisions accordingly. Find out whether all original parts are included and whether the item has any flaws. If the description says that the Fred Flintstone

figurine has a cracked back, message the seller for more information on just how cracked Fred really is.

» **Don't get caught up in the emotional thrill of bidding.** First-time buyers (because they have fewer than ten transactions under their belts) tend to bid wildly, using emotions rather than brains. If you're new to eBay, you can get burned if you just bid for the thrill of victory without thinking about what you're doing.

WARNING

I can't stress how important it is to determine an item's value, whether vintage or new. But because item values are such flighty things (depending as they do on supply and demand, market trends, and all sorts of other variables), I recommend that you get a general idea of the item's value and use this ballpark figure to set a maximum amount of money you're willing to bid for that item. Then *stick to* your maximum and don't even think about bidding past it. If the bidding gets too hot, there's always another auction. To find out more about bidding strategies, Chapter 7 is just the ticket.

» **Know what the item should cost.** Those who buy collectibles used to depend on *price guides* — books on collectibles and their values — to help them bid. But price guides have become a thing of the past. Sure, you can find a guide that says an original-cast *Wicked* Broadway poster in excellent condition may have a book price in excess of $100, but if you do a search on eBay, you may see that they're actually selling for a fraction of that amount.

TIP

When your search on eBay turns up what you're looking for, average the current prices you find. Also check the sold listings. Doing so gives you a much better idea of what you need to spend than any price guide can.

» **Timing is everything, and being first costs.** If you're into movie posters, for example, consider this: If you can wait three to six months after a film is released, you can get the poster for 40 to 50 percent less. The same goes for many new releases of collectibles. Sometimes you're wiser to wait and save money.

» **Be careful of presale items.** Sometimes you may run across vendors selling items that they don't have in stock but that they'll ship to you later. For example, before *Star Wars Episode I: The Phantom Menace* came out, some vendors ran auctions on movie posters they didn't have yet. If you had bid and won, and for some reason the vendor had a problem getting the poster, you'd have been out of luck. Unless you are willing to roll the dice, don't bid on anything that can't be delivered as soon as you pay for the item. See some of eBay's presale rules later in this chapter.

» **Being too late can also cost.** Many collectibles become more difficult to find as time goes by. Generally, as scarcity increases, so does desirability and value. Common sense tells you that if two original and identical collectibles are offered side by side, with one in like-new condition and the other in used condition, the like-new item will have the higher value.

>> **Check out the seller.** Check the feedback rating (the number in parentheses next to the person's User ID) a seller has before you buy. There is also a positive feedback percentage to give extra insight. The higher the positive feedback percentage, the better your chances that this is a reputable seller. For more on feedback, see Chapter 4.

REMEMBER

Although eBay forbids side deals, an unsuccessful bidder may (at his or her own risk) contact a seller after an auction is over to see if the seller has more of the item in stock. If the seller is an experienced eBay user (a high feedback rating is usually a tipoff) and does have more of the item in stock, he or she may consider making a perfectly eBay-legal Second Chance offer. Don't ask to buy the item outside of eBay. Policy strictly prohibits using contact information to sell items off the site. If you conduct a side deal and are reported to eBay, you can be suspended. Not only that, but buyers who are ripped off by sellers in away-from-eBay transactions shouldn't look to eBay to bail them out; if you go that route, you're on your own. The way to purchase these items is by asking the seller to post another listing for you — or if you were an underbidder in the auction, send you a Second Chance offer. That way, you're also protected by eBay's Money Back Guarantee.

>> **If an item comes to you not as described, contact the seller to work it out.** Use eBay messages to let the seller know exactly what you received and how it differs from the description on the listing. Give the seller a chance to make good before you go nuclear and file a case against them. People can make honest mistakes; if their feedback rating is good, odds are they want to keep it that way. Chapter 6 provides pointers on dealing with transactions that go sour.

Following an expert on the hunt

I know that not many of you collect G.I. Joes, but by studying what an expert looks for in this specialty vintage item, you can get a good idea of what you should look for when purchasing whatever it is that you collect. All the tips below work the same for collectibles of all genres, even *Star Wars*. Bill looks for specific traits when he buys his very collectible G.I. Joe figures. Although his checklist is specific to the G.I. Joe from 1964 to 1969, the information here can help you determine how much you might be willing to pay for other collectibles (or whether an item is even *worth* bidding on) before an auction begins.

As you find out in Chapter 7, the more you know before you place a bid, the happier you're likely to be when you win. Bill's checklist can save you considerable hassle:

>> **Find out the item's overall condition.** For G.I. Joe, look at the painted hair and eyebrows. Expect some wear, but overall, a collectible worth bidding on should look good.

>> **Be sure that the item's working parts are indeed working.** Most G.I. Joe action figures from this period have cracks on the legs and arms, but the joints should move, and any cracks should not be so deep that the legs and arms fall apart easily.

>> **Ask whether the item has its original parts.** Because you can't really examine items in detail before buying, email the seller with specific questions relating to original or replacement parts. Many G.I. Joe action figures are rebuilt from parts that are not from 1964 to 1969. Sometimes the figures even have two left or right hands or feet! If you make it clear to the seller before you buy that you want a toy with only original parts, you'll be able to make a good case for a refund if the item arrives as rebuilt as the Six Million Dollar Man. Chapter 7 has plenty of tips on how to protect yourself before you bid, and Chapter 16 has tips on what to do if the deal goes bad.

>> **Ask whether the item has original accessories.** A G.I. Joe from 1964 to 1969 should have his original dog tags, boots, and uniform. If any of these items are missing, you will have to pay around $25 apiece to replace each missing item. If you're looking to bid on any other collectible, know in advance what accessories came as standard equipment with the item, or you'll be paying extra just to bring it back to its original version.

>> **Know an item's value before you bid.** A 1964 to 1969 vintage G.I. Joe in decent shape, with all its parts, can go for over $1,000 without its original box. (Mint-in-box Joes can sell for thousands of dollars.) If you're bidding on a G.I. Joe action figure on eBay and you're in this price range, you're okay. If you get the item for less than $250, congratulations — you've snagged a bargain.

>> **If you have any questions, ask *before* you bid by clicking the Contact Seller link on the right-hand side of the listing page.** Check collectors' websites, research similar auctions on eBay, and visit one of eBay's category discussion boards.

Grading vintage items

Welcome to my version of grade school without the baloney sandwich. One of the keys to establishing value is knowing an item's condition, typically referred to as an item's *grade*. Table 5-1 lists the most common grading categories that collectors use. The information in this table is used with permission from (and appreciation to) Lee Bernstein.

TABLE 5-1   **Collectibles Grading Categories**

Category (Also Known As)	Description	Example
Mint (M, Fine, Mint-In-Box [MIB], 10)	A never-used collectible in perfect condition with complete packaging (including instructions, original attachments, tags, and so on), identical to how it appeared on the shelf in the original box.	Grandma got a soup tureen as a wedding present, never opened it, and stuck it in her closet for the next 50 years.
Near Mint (NM, Near Fine, Like New, 9)	The collectible is perfect but no longer has the original packaging or the original packaging is less than perfect. Possibly used but must appear to be new.	Grandma used the soup tureen on her 25th anniversary, washed it gently, and then put it back in the closet.
Excellent (EX, 8)	Used, but barely. Excellent is just a small step under Near Mint, and many sellers mistakenly interchange the two, but "excellent" can have very minor signs of wear. The wear must be a normal, desirable part of aging or so minor that it's barely noticeable and visible only upon close inspection. Damage of any sort is "very minor." Wear or minor normal factory flaws should be noted. (Factory flaws are small blemishes common at the time of manufacture — a tiny air bubble under paint, for example.)	Grandma liked to ring in the New Year with a cup of soup for everyone.
Very Good (VG, 7)	Looks very good but has defects, such as a minor chip or light color fading.	If you weren't looking for it, you might miss that Grandma's tureen survived the '64 earthquake, as well as Uncle Bob's infamous ladle episode.
Good (G, 6)	Used with defects. More than a small amount of color loss, chips, cracks, tears, dents, abrasions, missing parts, and so on.	Grandma had the ladies in the neighborhood over for soup and bingo every month.
Poor (P or G-, 5)	Barely collectible, if at all. Severe damage or heavy use. Beyond repair.	Grandma ran a soup kitchen.

WARNING

Grading is subjective. Mint to one person may be Very Good to another. Always ask a seller to define the meaning of the terms used. Also, be aware that many amateur sellers may not really know the different definitions of grading and may arbitrarily add Mint or Excellent to their item descriptions.

Finding More Research Information

Experts have been buying, selling, and trading collectible items for years — and when they are selling on eBay, they tend to have high feedback ratings. But just because you're new to eBay doesn't mean you have to be a newbie for decades before you can start bartering with the collecting gods. I wouldn't leave you in the cold like that — and neither would eBay. You can get information on items you're interested in, as well as good collecting tips, right at the eBay website. Visit the category-specific discussion boards in the community area. You can also search the rest of the web or go the old-fashioned route and check the library (yes, libraries are still around).

TIP

Keep in mind that there are truly several prices for a collectible: *retail price* (also called *manufacturer's suggested retail price* — MSRP); *book value* (estimated value as listed in standard price guides for the item); *secondary market price* (the price charged by resellers when an item is unavailable on the primary retail market); and the *eBay selling price*. The only way to ascertain the price an item will go for on eBay is to research the listings of sold items. Later in this chapter, I give you the 411 on how to research successful sales.

Searching sites online

If you don't find the item you are searching for on eBay, don't go ballistic — just go elsewhere. Even a site as vast as eBay doesn't have a monopoly on information. The Internet is filled with websites that can give you price comparisons and information about items.

Just connect your browser to one of many fast-searching *search engines.* Remember, if something is out there and you need it, you can find it right from your home PC, tablet, or smartphone in a matter of seconds. Here are the addresses of some of the web's most highly regarded search engines or multi-search-engine sites:

>> Google (www.google.com)

>> Microsoft Bing (www.bing.com)

>> Shopzilla (www.shopzilla.com)

>> Yahoo! (www.yahoo.com)

GETTING REAL-TIME DATA FROM TERAPEAK RESEARCH

If you become an eBay fanatic someday, you may find yourself praising the genius of an amazing service offered by eBay and Terapeak. Although an eBay search can show you 90 days of sold listings and/or 30 days of unsold listings, Terapeak Research allows you to research pricing farther back. If you come across a special or very old item, and there are not many on the site, you can use this tool to find how much the item has sold for in the past few months.

A little further on in the chapter is some of the research I performed on a G.I. Joe Buzz Aldrin figure. Researching the price lets me know when the item is trending and getting the highest prices.

As with third-party applications, there is a charge to use the service. But the price is reasonable for collectors, and you can subscribe just for a month. Starting in 2019 (when eBay purchased the platform), eBay sellers in the U.S. with an active Basic, Premium, Anchor, or Enterprise eBay Store subscription will have access to Terapeak at no additional cost. There are several levels of search. I recommend using the 90-day search because in my (not so) humble opinion, 90 days is an eternity in Internet time — what sold well three months ago may be worth bupkis now. But if the item is truly rare, a 365-day search will give you a better idea of long-term value. You can search sales history by clicking the Research tab at the top of the Seller Hub page (as shown below) or https://www.ebay.com/sh/research. You can also visit the site at www.terapeak.com.

The basic process of getting information from an Internet search engine is pretty simple:

1. **Type the address of the search-engine site in the Address box of your web browser.**

   You're taken to the website's home page.

2. **Find the text box next to the button labeled Search (or something similar).**

3. **In the text box, type a few words indicating what interests you.**

   Be specific when typing search text. The more precise your entry (see "Shortcuts for a quick eBay search," later in this chapter), the better your chances of finding what you want. Look for tips, an Advanced Search option, or help pages on your search engine of choice for more information about how to narrow your search.

4. **Click the Search (or similar) button or press Enter on your keyboard.**

   The search engine presents you with a list of the Internet pages that feature the requested information. The list of links includes brief descriptions and links to the first group of pages. You'll find links to additional listings at the bottom if your search finds more listings than can fit on one page. (And if you ask for something popular, like *Harry Potter,* don't be surprised to get millions of hits.)

Always approach information on the web with caution. Not everyone is the expert he or she would like to be. Your best bet is to get lots of different opinions and then boil 'em down to what makes sense to you. And remember — *caveat emptor.* (Is there an echo in here?)

Many people out here on the West Coast buy cars on eBay. (Could it be because cars are way more expensive here? Or could it be that there's less rust?) If you're researching prices to buy a car on eBay, look in your local newspaper to get a good idea of prices in your community. Several good sites are on the Internet. My personal favorite is www.nadaguides.com. I've had many of my friends (and editors) visit the various sites, and we've settled on this one because it seems to give the most accurate and unbiased information.

Finding other sources of information

If you're interested in collecting a particular item, you can get a lot of insider collecting information without digging too deep:

>> **Go to other places on the Internet.** The Internet is full of insider info. Remember to take advice with caution, however, because sometimes the "competition" likes to keep the good nuggets of info for themselves.

TIP

» **Go to the library (or buy a book)!** Books and magazines still exist and are the best sources of authoritative info, especially out-of-print books. You'll no doubt find at least one book or one magazine specializing in your chosen item. For example, if old pottery is your thing, consider the 1999 edition (now on Amazon Kindle) of *Antiquing For Dummies,* by Ron Zoglin and Deborah Shouse, for evergreen content on what antiques collectors look for.

If you find an interesting specialty magazine at the library, try entering the title in your search engine of choice. You may just find that the magazine has also gone paperless and you can read it online.

» **Go to someone else who's in the know.** Friends, clubs, and organizations in your area can give you a lot of info. Ask your local antiques dealer about clubs you can join and see how much info you end up with.

Looking to Find an Item? Start Your eBay Search

The best part about shopping on eBay is that, aside from collectibles, you can find just about everything from that esoteric lithium battery to new designer dresses (with matching shoes) to pneumatic jackhammers. New or used, it's all here — if you can find it hiding in the millions of new daily listings. (According to Venture-Beat, 1.2 billion listings are on the site worldwide at any given time. That's a lot of virtual gavels banging!)

Finding the nuggets (deals) can be like searching for the proverbial needle in the haystack. The search secrets in this chapter will put you head and shoulders above your competition for the deals.

eBay has lots of ways for you to search for items (for a sample, see Chapter 3). Although eBay allows you to search by item number, let's be realistic here. Do you remember what I said a few paragraphs back about the number of active listings? I can't remember my own phone number, let alone an item number (and I never write them down correctly). Look for those numbers to get longer and longer as eBay continues to grow in popularity. These main options are the most useful for researching:

» Search Title Keywords (or Search Title and Description)

» Search Items by Seller or Bidder

» Search Items on eBay Motors

MARSHA SAYS

TESTING, TESTING . . . HOW LONG DOES A SEARCH TAKE ON EBAY?

Having a massive search engine is a matter of necessity on eBay — millions of items are up for auction at any given time — and often an easy, fast search makes all the difference between getting and not getting. After all, time is money, and eBay members tend to be movers and shakers who don't like standing still.

So how long do searches really take on eBay? I put it to the test. In the Search window of the eBay home page, I typed **1933 World's Fair Pennant** and let 'er rip.

The search engine went through the millions of general items and **World's Fair** items (860 of them in 1999; 1,200 items in 2003; 2,100 in 2006; 13,847 in 2010; 23,443 in 2012 — and today? An incredible 38,813!) and gave me my one specific item in a blink of an eye. (Now, if the wizards at eBay could only figure out a way to find that sock that always escapes from my clothes dryer, they'd really be on to something.)

Narrowing the search to the **1933 World's Fair Pennant**: In 1999, that slightly wrinkled felt pennant got four bids and sold for $17.50; in 2003, the aging pennant sold for $43.88 with eight bids. In 2009, one went for $14.99. Things must be looking up; in 2016, one sold for $27.00 (11 bids). Today, some pretty shabby ones sold for around $25, but an almost mint version (with a matching felt hat) is up for sale for $99! You can never take the temperature of the collectibles market once and for all. It can run either hot or cold!

You can access these additional search options by clicking the Advanced Search link to the right of the Search box at the top of any eBay page. Each search option can provide a different piece of information to help you find the right item from the right seller at the right price.

MARSHA SAYS

Clicking the arrow in the Saved Searches drop-down box at the top right of the search results page allows you to scroll through your My eBay Saved Searches. You can tell eBay about the items you're looking for, and it does automatic searches for you. You can also have eBay email you when auctions that match your descriptions crop up. (Chapter 18 gives you more info on how this works.)

Using the Advanced Search page

When you click the Advanced Search link to the right of the Search box, the Search page appears. It's the most basic of searches (with a few options) and the one you'll be using the most.

When you use any of the Search options on eBay, the search engine looks for every listing (auction or fixed-price) that has the words you're looking for in the title (and the description if you specify so). The title (as you may expect) is a group of *keywords* — words used to describe the item. For example, if you're looking for an antique sterling iced tea spoon, just type **sterling iced tea spoon** into the search window (see Figure 5-1). If someone is selling a sterling iced tea spoon and used exactly those words in his or her title or description, you're in hog heaven.

FIGURE 5-1:
Searching
(including
description) to
find sterling iced
tea spoons.

ebay Shop by category ▾ | sterling iced tea spoon | All Categories ▾ | Search Advanced
☑ Include description

Before you click the Search button, know you can narrow your search further. If you go to Advanced Search, you have the option of choosing how you want the search engine to interpret your search entry. You can have the search engine search the title and description for

>> All the words you type

>> Some of the words you type

>> The exact phrase in the word order you wrote

TIP

When you're familiar with the tips listed later in this chapter, you'll be able to get most of these fancy Search Results in one of the many search boxes you see littered around the eBay site.

In addition to the following, you can find other useful criteria on the Advanced Search page (more on this further on):

>> **What price range you want to see:** Type the price range you're looking for, and eBay searches the specific range between that low and high price. If money is no object, leave this box blank.

>> **Words to exclude:** If you want to find a sterling iced tea spoon, but you don't want it to be silver plated, use the drop-down menu to exclude the word *plated*.

>> **From sellers:** You can exclude (or include) particular sellers. If you like, you can just search sellers from your Saved Sellers list. (But why?)

>> **Within a category:** Use this option if you want to limit your search to a particular main (or *top-level*) category, for example, instead of searching all eBay categories. But why? eBay sellers are notorious for making listing

mistakes and selecting wrong categories. Wait till you see your results, and then decide whether you want to narrow things.

>> **The item location:** You can narrow your search to the United States only, North America, or worldwide. Depending on your item, this search criterion can help weed out the most esoteric items. If you're looking for hefty items (like an elliptical exercise machine that will probably end up as a place to hang clothes) that would cost much too much to ship, you can specify how many miles from your ZIP code (or any ZIP code) you will allow the search to extend.

>> **The order in which you want your results to appear:** If you indicate Time: ending soonest, the search engine gives you the results so that items closing soon appear first on the list. Best Match is the eBay default, but I recommend you select a sort that better fits your needs. Time: newly listed lists all the newly listed items. Price + Shipping: lowest first and Price + Shipping: highest first list them just that way. If you're looking for a large item that you'd want to pick up locally, select Distance: nearest first.

>> **Whether you want the search to check through item titles alone or check both item titles *and* item descriptions:** You'll get more hits on your search if you select the Include description check box, but you may also get too many items that are out of your search range. See "Shortcuts for a quick eBay search," later in this chapter, for some solid advice.

Okay, *now* click the Search button. In a few seconds, you see the fruits of all the work you've been doing (see Figure 5-2). (Wow, you're not even perspiring.)

Check this box to include the description.

Choose an option for sorting results.

FIGURE 5-2:
Use eBay's handy refined Search to uncover even more related listings.

ebay	Shop by category	sterling iced tea spoon		Flatware & Silverware	Search	Advanced
		Related: sterling iced tea spoon tiffany			☑ Include description	

Categories		All Listings	Accepts Offers	Auction	Buy It Now	Condition ▾	Delivery Options ▾	└ Sort	Best Match ▴	View ▦ ▾
All		5,917 results	♡ Save this search							g to: 91325 ▾
‹ Antiques								✓ Best Match		
‹ Silver								Time: ending soonest		
‹ Sterling Silver (.925)		Price						Time: newly listed		
Flatware & Silverware		Under $75.00	$75.00 to $150.00	Over $150.00				Price + Shipping: lowest first		
Other Antique Sterling Silver								Price + Shipping: highest first		
Tea/Coffee Pots & Sets			SPONSORED					Distance: nearest first		
Salt Cellars			International Trianon Sterling Silver Iced Tea Sp...							
More ▾			$34.99					⊡ FAST...		
Home & Garden			Buy It Now					Guaranteed by...		

TIP

You may notice that eBay has a way to refine your search to the left of your results. Be sure to click the related specifics here because eBay's search functions can often be a bit temperamental — and you don't want to miss any great deals.

MARSHA SAYS

Within the search listings you often see pictures, or *icons*. A tiny truck icon followed by the words *FAST AND FREE* means the seller will ship out the item within a day of payment and there is no charge for basic shipping. The gold seal with the words *Top Rated Plus* indicates an item is being sold by a seller who has been ranked as giving some of the best service on eBay.

TIP

An easy way to keep track of an item you're interested in is to click the Add to watchlist link at the bottom right of the price box on an item page. The listing then appears on your My eBay Watch list, and you can keep your eyes on the action or save to compare with other finds.

On the left side of the results page may be a list of categories that your search term is listed under, which is a great reference. Below that are further identifiers, and next to each is a number in parentheses that tells you how many times your search item appears in that category. Figure 5-3 shows a sample of the ways you can narrow a search. To view the items appearing only in a particular category, click that category (or subcategory) title.

FIGURE 5-3: Left column Search Results show the category breakdown on the left and others below.

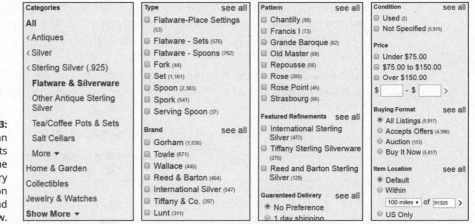

Finding Sold Items

To the left of the Search Results (if you scroll all the way down), you'll see options listed under Show Only so you can limit what you see to certain items. If you click Completed Items, you're presented with every expired item (whether or not it sold) that matches your keywords. A Completed Items search returns results of items that have already ended.

To get the real data on how much the item will sell for (other than using Terapeak), select the Sold Items box. This is my favorite search option because you can use it as a strategic bidding tool. How? If you're bidding on an item and want to know whether the prices are likely to go too high for your pocketbook, you can use this search option to compare the current price of the item to the selling price of similar items from items that have already sold.

You can use this tool also if you want to sell an item and are trying to determine what it's worth, the demand for it, and whether this is the right time to list the item. (Chapter 10 offers the nuts, bolts, and monkey wrenches you need to set up your auction.)

In this area, you can also refine your search to find only items sold by sellers who accept returns; simply select Returns accepted.

Type your keyword criteria, scroll down the page, and click the Sold Items box. Step by step, here's how to do a Sold Items Only search:

1. **In the title search field, type the title name or the keywords of the item you want to find.**

2. **Click the Search button.**

3. **On the Search Results page (Figure 5-4), select the Sold listings check box to see items that have sold (and how much they sold for) as far back as the eBay search engine will permit.**

   Currently, you can go back about four months.

4. **Once the sold listings appear, tell eBay how you want the results sorted.**

   In the Sort drop-down menu, choose one of the following options:

   - *Ended Recently:* Lists the most recently sold items first.

   - *Time: newly listed:* Shows items that were sold from the oldest listings to the newest.

   - *Price+Shipping: lowest first:* Lists items from the lowest price attained to the highest price paid for an item.

   - *Price+Shipping: highest first:* Lists completed items from highest to lowest price. (This is a very useful option when you're searching for a 1967 Camaro and you want to buy a car and not a Hot Wheels toy.)

   - *Distance: nearest first:* Unless you're looking to see how many of your item sold close to you, this is a pretty useless sort. You want pricing info!

   Your Search Results will refresh automatically.

Click for more details.

FIGURE 5-4:
The Show only
Sold Items box
on the results
page is followed
by links to
more specific
refinements.

An international search

On the Advanced Search page (you get there by clicking the word *Advanced* to the right of the Search box), you can select any country (from Afghanistan to Zimbabwe, no kidding!) or narrow your search to the United States or Canada, as shown in Figure 5-5. Don't forget that you have to pay for shipping, so if you don't want to pay to ship a heavy, Victorian-style fainting sofa from Hungary to Hoboken, New Jersey, stick close to home. By the same token, I'll bet Egyptian cotton sheets are even better when they come from Egypt. (They are — I've bought from an Egyptian seller!)

FIGURE 5-5:
The International
Search Location
selector.

The Location Search option is pretty much an international version of Search, and it's best done by clicking the Advanced Search link at the top of the page. You have the choice of narrowing your search to countries that offer an item, and to which countries they ship to. (Most eBay sellers will ship to the United States, which is the default.)

Finding a specific seller

In eBay's Advanced Search, locate the By Seller link in the links on the left, shown in Figure 5-6; the By Seller pages show you a list of all the items a seller is selling, and it's a great way for you to keep tabs on people you have successfully done business with. The By Seller search, shown in Figure 5-6, is also a strategy that eBay users use to assess the reputation of a seller. You can find out more about selling strategies in Chapter 9.

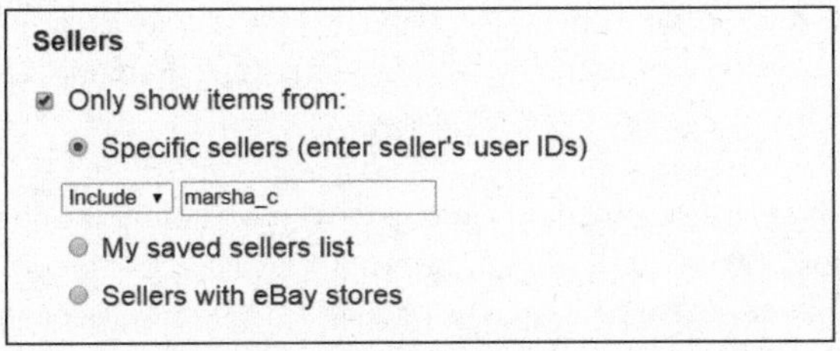

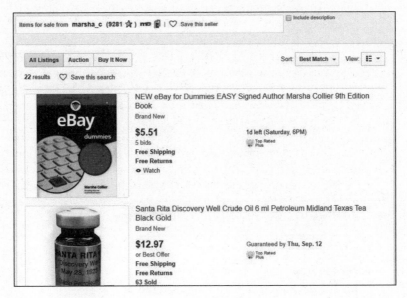

FIGURE 5-6: You can search for all items by an individual, or search for one item from many sellers.

Once you find a listing of the seller of your choice, you can also click the *See other items* link in the Seller Information box on an item page. Figure 5-7 shows you the results.

FIGURE 5-7: The results of a By Seller search.

MARSHA SAYS

FREE HANGING CHADS . . .

eBay gives you the opportunity to have the same fine museum-quality items as the Smithsonian Institution. In November 2001, the Palm Beach County Board of County Commissioners found themselves in a bit of a pickle. Due to the infamous presidential election of November 7, 2000 — fraught with hanging, pregnant, and dimpled chads — the announcement of the election winner was delayed for an unprecedented 37 days. As a result of this election, the Florida legislature outlawed the future use of punch-card voting systems — all Florida counties had to move to more stable, state-approved voting machines.

Palm Beach County chose to move to a touchscreen type of voting device, which cost its residents over $14 million. What to do with the old historic punch-card voting machines? Yep, donate one to the Smithsonian — and auction the rest on eBay. Palm Beach County donated machine #1 to the Auction for America; it netted $4,550.01 for the Twin Towers fund.

The rest? Well, the Palm Beach County folks should have read this book. They ran a Dutch auction for 3,055 of the basic voting packages, with a starting bid of $300. Included with the voting machine was the iniquitous "butterfly ballot" with official stylus; a brass plaque certifying that it was used in the November 7 election; a Certificate of Authenticity signed by Theresa LePore, Palm Beach County Supervisor of Elections; 25 demonstrator punch cards for playing polling place at home; a signed photograph of the folks in charge of recounting the ballots: Palm Beach County Supervisor of Elections Theresa LePore, Palm Beach County Commissioner Carol Roberts, and Judge Charles Burton; and "any chads which are in the machine from previous elections." What a package! There also were 569 Premier packages, which included an Official Ballot box, starting at $600.

In the 10-day auctions (run at the same time!), Palm Beach County sold 78 of the Premier packages and 389 of the Basic voting-machine packages. I called the County Commissioner's office to find out why my voting machine hadn't arrived and asked when the rest would be auctioned. I was assured they would be put back up on eBay auction, but at a higher starting bid.

Palm Beach County should have followed the strategies in this book, the way some smart eBay sellers did. Soon after, one of the basic packages sold after a 7-day auction for $670. Other entrepreneurial sellers have been selling voting machines from counties other than Palm Beach on eBay. Unfortunately for those who purchase them, only the Palm Beach County machines had the infamous butterfly ballot.

Finding items by keywords for multiple sellers

If you're looking for a specific item from a group of sellers, you can enter the sellers' IDs in the bottom half of the Advanced Search Find Items page. You can also search only within your Saved Sellers list. You may need to perform this type of search after you settle into shopping on eBay and have several sellers you like doing business with (or alternatively, you can exclude sellers you prefer not to do business with). With this method, you can limit the search for a particular item to just the sellers you want, rather than tens of thousands of sellers.

TIP

When you find a seller who you want to continue doing business with, you can add his or her link to your My eBay: Saved Sellers area. Just click the Save This Seller link on the item page. It then appears on your My eBay page, in the Sellers You Follow area. You can then search that seller's sales with a click of your mouse!

Shortcuts for a quick eBay search

After you become familiar with each of eBay's search options, you need a crash course in what words to type into those nice little boxes. Too little information and you may not find your item; too much and you're overwhelmed with information. If you're really into bean-bag toys, for example, you may be looking for Ty's Tabasco the Bull. But if you just search for *Tabasco*, you'll get swamped with results ranging from hot sauce to advertisements.

Some simple tricks can help narrow your eBay Search Results when you're searching from pages other than the main Search page (where you don't find all the searching bells and whistles). Table 5-2 has the details.

TABLE 5-2   **Symbols and Keywords for Conducting Searches with the eBay Search Engine**

Symbol	Effect on Search	Example
No symbol, multiple words	Returns auctions with all included words in the title.	**reagan letter** might return an auction for a mailed message from the former U.S. president, or it might return an auction for a mailed message from Boris Yeltsin to Ronald Reagan.
Separating comma without spaces (a,b)	Finds items related to either the item before or after the comma.	**(gi joe,g.i. joe)** returns all G.I. Joe items, no matter which way the seller listed them.

(continued)

TABLE 5-2 *(continued)*

Symbol	Effect on Search	Example
Minus sign (–)	Excludes results with the word after the –.	Type **box –lunch**, and you'd better not be hungry because you may find the box, but lunch won't be included.
Minus sign and parentheses	Searches for auctions with words before the parentheses but excludes words inside the parentheses.	**midge –(skipper,barbie)** means that auctions with the Midge doll won't have to compete for Ken's attention.
Parentheses	Searches for both versions of the word in parentheses.	**political (pin,pins)** searches for *political pin* and *political pins*.

Here are additional tips to help you narrow any eBay search:

>> **Don't worry about capitalization:** You can capitalize proper names or leave them lowercase; the search engine doesn't care.

>> **Don't use *and, a, an, or,* or *the*:** Called *noise words* in search lingo, these words are interpreted as part of your search. So if you want to find something from *The Sound of Music* and you type **the sound of music**, you may not get any results. Most sellers drop noise words from the beginning of an item title when they list it, just as libraries drop noise words when they alphabetize books. So make your search for **sound music**. An even more precise search would be **"sound of music"** (in quotes).

>> **Search within specific categories:** This type of search narrows your results because you search only one niche of eBay — just the specific area you want. For example, if you want to find Tabasco the Bull, start at the home page and, under the Categories heading, click Toys and Bean Bag. The only problem with searching in a specific category is that sometimes an item can be in more than one place. For example, if you're searching for a Mickey Mouse infant snuggly in the Disney category, you may miss it because the item might be listed in infant wear. It's best not to limit yourself to a category because some of the best deals are miscategorized by sellers. What makes them such good deals is that not everyone can find them. But you know better.

MARSHA SAYS

Often sellers misspell words in titles, so when searching, use the parentheses to list common misspellings of your search term. You can also visit a site, www.fatfingers.com, which offers misspellings that even you never thought of. One of my favorite dress designers is Diane Von Furstenberg, and using fatfingers, I have found many auctions for her items without any bids.

Chapter **6**

Get a Deal: The Art of Shopping eBay

Everyone who first buys one of my books says, "I know how to shop on eBay, that's not my problem!" But do you? I bet this chapter will give you a few tips that might help you find some better deals.

Browsing different categories of eBay, looking for nothing in particular, you spot that must-have item lurking among the others. You find that insanely expensive Dyson hair dryer being sold for way less than retail. Sure, it's refurbished, but it's refurbished by Dyson and sold in their eBay Outlet store. Did you know there were brand name outlet stores on eBay? Just stop by www.ebay.com/b/Brand-Outlet/bn_7115532402 and, according to eBay, "Here you'll find our best direct brands, authorized resellers, and trusted sellers."

Then again, lots of us are suckers for vintage clothing and accessories. eBay's fashion area is loaded with quality vintage items. I've found some incredible deals on quality '50s and '60s items. Of course, there's gobs of *Star Trek* paraphernalia in the Collectibles category. Sure, you *could* live without that faux-gold communicator pin, but life would be so much sweeter *with* it. And even if it isn't in mint condition, at least you can still accessorize your outfit on casual Fridays.

Once you find a store that you like, you can "Save" to your saved sellers and receive emails when they list new items for sale!

When you bid for items on eBay, you can get that same thrill that you would get at Sotheby's or Christie's for a lot less money, and the items you win are likely to be *slightly* more practical than a signed Banksy that you're afraid to leave at the framer's.

In this chapter, I give you info about ways to shop on eBay, as well as a rundown of the nuts and bolts of auction bidding strategies. I also share some tried-and-true tips that'll give you a leg up on the competition. (Hey, I buy lots of stuff on eBay.)

The Item Listing Page

At any given point, you have more than a million pages of items that you can look at on eBay, making item pages the heart (better yet, the skeleton) of eBay listings. All item pages on eBay — whether auctions, fixed-price items, or Buy It Now items — look about the same. For example, Figure 6-1 shows a conventional auction page with a Buy It Now option; Figure 6-2 shows a fixed-price sale; and Figure 6-3 shows a fixed-price sale with a twist — the Make Offer option, which you will often see on an auction as well. This gives the buyer an opportunity to make an offer on the item before any bids are placed. Once bids are placed on an auction with Best Offer, the option to make the offer disappears.

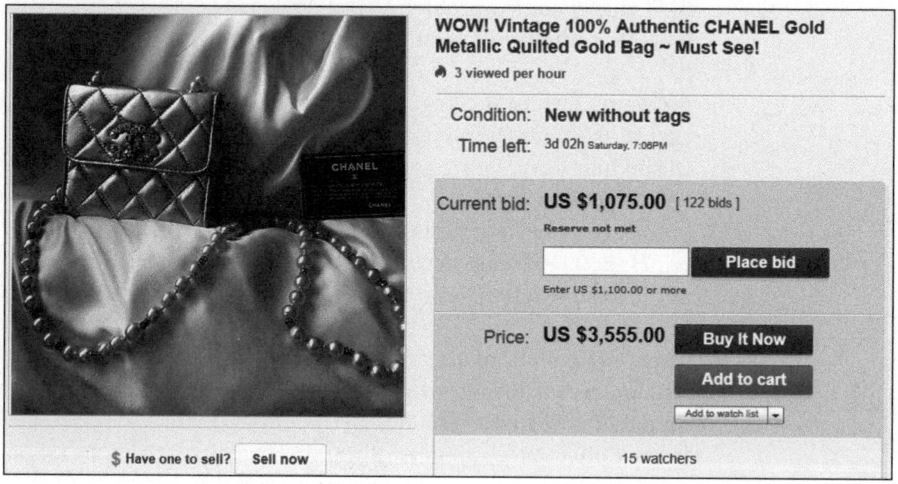

FIGURE 6-1:
Here's a typical auction, featuring the Buy It Now button and the Place Bid button.

	WOW! Vintage 100% Authentic CHANEL Gold Metallic Quilted Gold Bag ~ Must See!
	🔥 3 viewed per hour
	Condition: **New without tags**
	Time left: 3d 02h Saturday, 7:06PM
	Current bid: **US $1,075.00** [122 bids]
	Reserve not met
	[ ] Place bid
	Enter US $1,100.00 or more
	Price: **US $3,555.00** Buy It Now
	Add to cart
	Add to watch list ▾
$ Have one to sell? Sell now	15 watchers

FIGURE 6-2:
In a fixed-price sale, you see the Buy It Now button and the opportunity to place the item in your shopping cart, but no Place Bid button.

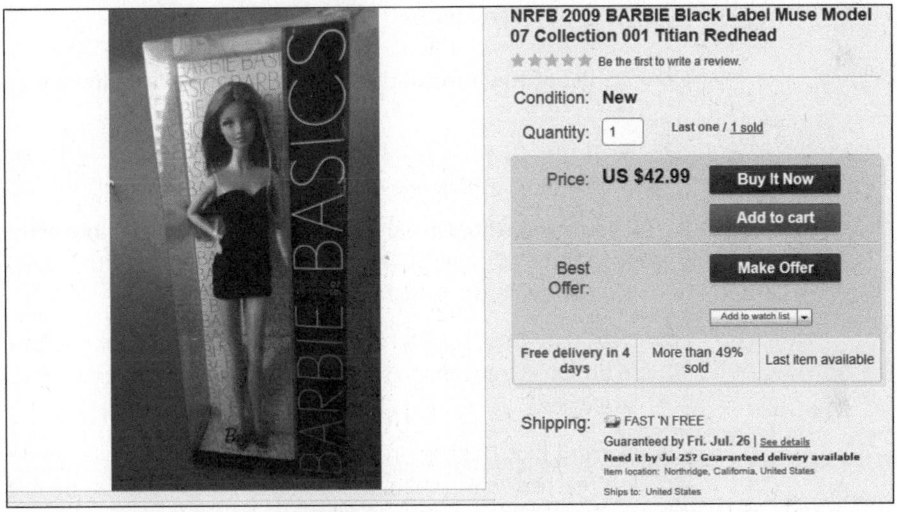

FIGURE 6-3:
Some sellers provide a Make Offer option on their fixed-price sales.

All item pages show the listing title at the top of the selling area, bidding or buying info in the middle, and seller info below that. The options appear similarly on eBay mobile (more on how to shop with the mobile app in Chapter 18). Below all this is a tabbed area that displays the complete description of the item, along with a tab for shipping and payment information.

The listing types have some subtle differences. Some listings feature multiple pictures at the left of the page, others only a single picture, depending on how the seller sets up the sale page. (Some sellers insert pictures within the item description.) Most listings have set item specifics in the description (as shown in Figure 6-4). This area is set up by eBay or filled in by the seller to give you a snapshot description of the item for sale. If you search for an item and end up finding it available in a fixed-price sale, you won't see the Place Bid button (refer to Figure 6-1). But overall, the look and feel of these pages will be the same.

FIGURE 6-4:
Item specifics are filled in by eBay or the seller according to the parameters eBay sets up for them.

Item specifics			
Condition:	Brand New: A new, unread, unused book in perfect condition with no missing or damaged pages. See the seller's ... Read more	Publication Year:	2011
Country/Region of Manufacture:	United States	Language:	English
Topic:	Online Customer Service	Format:	Hardcover
Subject:	Business & Economics	Special Attributes:	1st Edition, Signed
Brand:	Wiley	Edition Description:	Autographed
ISBN:	9780470637708		

When you come to a fixed-price listing with the Make Offer option, you can make an offer with a price that you'd like to pay for the item. (I talk about the best ways to make your offer later in this chapter.)

Here's a list of the information you see as you scroll down on a typical item page:

TIP

>> **Item Title:** The title describes the merchandise for sale. It's generally made up of key words (rarely a complete sentence) that identify the item.

If you're interested in a particular type of item, take note of the key words used in the title (you're likely to see them again in future titles). Doing so helps you narrow future searches.

>> **Item Category:** Located above the item, there's a link you can click if you want to do some comparison shopping. (Chapter 5 gives you more searching strategies.)

>> **Current Bid:** This field in an auction indicates the dollar amount the bidding has reached, which changes throughout the auction as people place bids. If no bids have been placed on the item, this field is called Starting Bid.

REMEMBER

Sometimes, next to the current dollar amount in an auction, you see the words *Reserve not met* in tasteful parentheses. This statement means that the seller has set a *reserve price* for the item — a secret price that must be reached before the seller will sell the item. If you don't see this note on a listing item page, don't be alarmed. Most auctions don't have reserve prices. Also, the moment a reserve is met, the indicator disappears.

>> **Buy It Now:** If you want the item immediately and the price quoted in this area is okay with you, click the Buy It Now link, which takes you to a page where you can complete your purchase. This is also an option in an auction listing (refer to Figure 6-1). In this case, you can still place a bid for the lower bid price and the listing will convert to an auction format.

>> **Add to cart:** If you're on a mini shopping spree and planning to buy a few items, click this box. The item will be added to your eBay shopping cart, and you can pay for everything simultaneously.

REMEMBER

Items placed in your shopping cart are not yours until you check out. If the seller has only one of an item in stock, another buyer can swoop in and buy it while you're browsing the site.

>> **Quantity:** This field appears only in multiple-item, fixed-price sales. This is where you indicate how many of an item you want to purchase. Next to the quantity, you see how many are currently available and how many of the item have been sold. You can be sure that it's a fixed-price sale because you have no opportunity to bid; you can just use the Buy It Now option (or Add to cart) for whatever quantity of the item you want. If a seller is selling two items for the price of one, the item quantity still shows up as 1 (as in 1 set of 2 bookends).

>> **Time Left:** The official clock keeps ticking down as time passes. When the item gets down to the last hour of an auction, eBay automatically starts an interactive clock that counts the minutes and seconds. This field tells you the time remaining in this particular auction.

REMEMBER

Timing is the key in eBay auction bidding strategies (covered in Chapter 7). eBay's headquarters is in California, so eBay uses Pacific standard time or Pacific daylight time as the standard, depending on the season. Not a major deal if you live on the West Coast as I do, but it can be an issue if you live anywhere else. Not to worry: My website, www.coolebaytools.com, has time charts that translate eBay time to time zones all over the U.S. and the world.

>> **Condition:** All sellers must clearly state the condition of the item (or items) for sale. eBay varies the guidelines a seller may use in this area, depending on the category in which the item is listed. But rest assured that if an item is listed as *new*, it will be a brand-new, unused, unopened, and undamaged item. If you'd like a peek at the category-specific parameters, go to www.ebay.com/help/selling/listings/creating-managing-listings/item-conditions-category?id=4765.

>> **Bids:** This field (next to the Current or Starting bid) tells you how many bids have been placed on an auction. To use the number of bids to your advantage, you have to read between the lines. You can determine just how much attention this item has received by comparing the number of bids the item has received over time. Based on how many bids an item has received, you can create a time strategy (which I talk about later in this chapter).

If you want to see the starting bid, you have to click the number of bids (as shown in Figure 6-5) to show the bid history. With that same click, you can also find out the number of individuals bidding and what dates and times the bids were placed. The dollar amount of each bid is shown in the bidding history, but all bidders' maximum bids are kept secret.

Click here to see the bid history.

Vintage Tonka Smokey the Bear " Smokey and His Forest Friends " Jeep & Truck Set

Condition: **Used**
"Very Nice condition"

Time left: 1 day 2 hours Monday, 5:48PM

Current bid: **US $228.00** [22 bids]

Enter US $230.50 or more

Place bid

Add to watch list

38 watchers   Ships from United States

Bucks You'll earn $2.28 in eBay Bucks. See conditions

FIGURE 6-5:
Clicking the "number of bids" link before or after an auction will give you an idea of how much competition you may have for an item.

REMEMBER

Bidding is more an art than a science. Sometimes an item gets no bids because everyone's waiting until the last second to bid. You see a flurry of activity as bidders all try to outbid each other (called *sniping,* which Chapter 7 explains). But that's all part of the fun of eBay.

>> **Shipping:** This area lets you know whether the seller offers free shipping or gives you the shipping price to your location. The Item Location field tells you (at the very least) the country where the seller is located, and you may also see more specific info, such as the city and geographic area where the seller is. (What you see depends on how detailed the seller wants to be.) Also listed are the countries to which the seller is willing to ship the item.

Factor in the geographic location of a seller when you consider bidding on an item. If you buy from someone in your own state, you may also have to pay sales tax on your purchase. If the item is in Australia, for example, and you're in Vermont, you may decide that you don't really *need* that wrought-iron doorstop. (Remember, *you* may have to pay the shipping charges.)

>> **Add to Watch list:** Click this link to magically add the item to the Watch section of your My eBay page. From there, you can keep an eye on the progress of the auction — without bidding. If you haven't signed in, you have to type your User ID and password before you can save a listing to your My eBay page.

MARSHA SAYS

Be sure to use the Watch feature as you shop on eBay. I often use it for fixed price comparison shopping. Organization is the name of the game, especially if you plan to bid on multiple auctions (or find the best deal on a fixed price item) while you're running auctions of your own. I figure you're in the game to win and save money, so start keeping track of items now.

>> **Social Sharing:** You can tip off a friend on a good find via email, get some advice from an antiques or collecting expert, or run the auction by a friend who's been around the eBay block a few times and ask for strategy advice. (You find this at the top of the listing with a small envelope icon.) There are also links to share the page on Facebook, Twitter, or Pinterest — but I say that if you're bidding on an auction, why invite the competition?

>> **Seller Information:** This area gives you links to the seller's profile (by clicking the seller's name) and to their feedback ratings (by clicking the number next to the seller's ID). By clicking these links, you can get a better idea of your trading partner. The number next to the seller's ID allows you to view his or her entire feedback history to make sure that you feel comfortable doing business with this person (as shown in Figure 6-6).

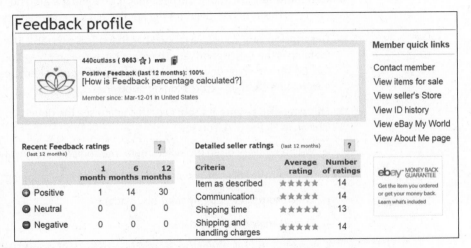

FIGURE 6-6: A quick glance will give you a good idea of who you're dealing with.

TIP

Keep in mind that no matter what the seller's rating is, your purchase is covered under the eBay Money Back Guarantee to be exactly as described.

On the item page you have the opportunity to follow the seller by clicking the heart (♡) next to Save this Seller. (From there you can decide whether you want your list to be public or private.) Another link takes you to a list of the other items the seller has up for sale.

If you see an icon of a golden seal that says Top Rated Plus or a blue ribbon with a white outlined star next to Top Rated Plus on the item page, you are on the page of one of eBay's sellers who have earned this title by giving the best customer service, according to their history and feedback.

Clicking through to the Feedback profile page, you get more options; some of the most-used are

- *Positive Feedback percentage:* The eBay computers cipher this figure. It's derived from all the positive and negative feedback that a user has received in the last 12 months.

- *Contact member:* Clicking this link connects you to eBay's message system. You can ask the seller a question regarding the item here.

- *View items for sale:* This link takes you to a page that lists all the seller's current auctions and fixed-price sales.

  If the seller has an eBay Store, a link to it appears next. I give you a step-by-step guide on how these links work later in this chapter.

>> **Item number:** Just above the description, you find the item number on the far right. This number identifies the item within the eBay servers.

>> **Description tab:** You see a tabbed bar that offers two tabs. The opening (default) is the Description tab. The other tab is the Shipping and Payments tab. Be sure to scroll down the page and read the entire item description information carefully *before* bidding or buying.

>> **Shipping and payments tab:** Click this tab to see the details on shipping (shown in Figure 6-7). You see

- Who pays (very often the seller offers free shipping, but you never know).

- Whether the seller offers alternatives like expedited shipping.

- Which states have to pay sales tax (if any).

- The estimated delivery date.

- Whether the seller is willing to ship to your area. (If the sellers won't ship internationally, they'll let you know here.)

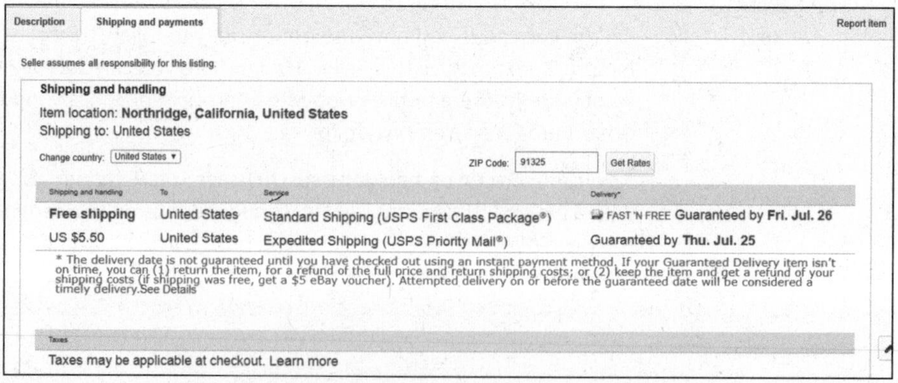

FIGURE 6-7:
Check the Shipping and payments tab next to the Description tab to find out about additional costs, shipping, and taxes that may apply when you buy.

TIP

Also, be sure to check the item description for other shipping information and terms.

If the item doesn't have free or flat-rate shipping, the seller may have conveniently included eBay's shipping calculator on the page to calculate your costs. eBay knows your ZIP code, so you're presented with the shipping cost to your location.

The seller's return policy will be listed here, too, so if you want to have the option to return an item (if it doesn't fit?), you'd better check here first.

The Payment details area tells you the payment methods that the seller accepts such as PayPal or the seller's own merchant credit card service. Some sellers allow you to pick up the item at their location. Often you're directed to read the item description for more details. (I explain how to decipher item descriptions later in this chapter.)

Beating the Devil in the Details

As with any sale — whether you find it at Joe's Hardware, Bloomingdale's, or Target — carefully check out what you're buying. The item page gives you links to help you know what you're buying — and who you're potentially buying from. If you take advantage of these features, you won't have many problems. But if you ignore these essential tips, you may end up unhappy with what you buy, who you buy it from, and how much you spend.

MARSHA SAYS

If you're teetering on a purchase and have a question, do yourself a favor and click Contact seller. If the seller replies quickly with a satisfactory reply, you have the information you need to make a decision. If the seller blows off your query, I'd think twice before continuing with the transaction. Yes, you have a Money Back Guarantee — but is it worth the hassle?

Read the item description carefully

The *item description* is the most critical item on the listing page. This is where the seller gives the details about the item being sold. Read this page carefully and pay very close attention to what is, and *isn't*, written.

Don't judge a book by its cover — but do judge a seller by his or her item description. If the sentences are succinct, detailed, and well structured, you're most likely dealing with an individual who planned and executed the listing with care. It takes time and effort to post a good listing. If you see huge lapses in grammar, convoluted sentences, and misspellings, you might want to ask the seller further questions (if you really want the item from this seller, that is — there may be others available on eBay). Make sure that you feel comfortable dealing with this person or business; decide for yourself whether he or she seems to be out to sell junk for a quick buck or to sell on eBay for the long term.

If additional pictures are available, take a good look. The majority of eBay sellers spruce up their listings with multiple photos of their items. The seller may answer a few general questions publicly in the item description. If these questions aren't answered, that doesn't necessarily mean that the seller's disreputable — only that if you're really interested, you should contact the seller (through eBay messages) and get those answers before you bid. In particular, ask questions like these:

>> Is the item a first edition or a reprint? An original or a reissue? (See Chapter 5 for tips on how to assess what you're buying.)

>> Is the item in its original packaging? Does it still have the original tags?

>> Is the item under warranty?

TIP

eBay requires that sellers spell out exactly how the item will be shipped. Check the Shipping and payments tab, which is next to the Description tab, to see whether an actual shipping charge applies — and if so, how much it'll cost you. Some sellers use eBay's incredibly convenient shipping calculator. Here are a few other things to consider regarding your item:

>> If you're in a hurry to get the item, is the seller shipping within a day?

>> If there are shipping charges, does the amount seem reasonable?

TIP

Most experienced eBay buyers know that, depending on the item, a tiny scratch on a vintage item here or there may be worth the risk of making a bid. But a scratch or two may affect the value *and* your bidding price. (Look at Chapter 5 for more expert advice for buying collectibles.)

>> Is this item the genuine article or a reproduction — and if it's the real deal, does the seller have papers or labels certifying its authenticity?

>> What size is the item, and how much does it weigh? (That life-size fiberglass whale may not *fit* in your garage. That baby grand piano might cost a lot to ship from Anchorage, so you need to factor in the cost of shipping when you consider how much you're willing to pay.)

Get the scoop on the seller

I can't tell you often enough that the single most important way you can make a transaction go well is to *know who you're dealing with.* Apparently, the eBay folks agree; they enable you to get info on the seller right from the feedback page. I recommend that you take advantage of the links offered there.

TIP

eBay, like life, is full of shades of gray. Some sellers are unfairly hit with negative comments for something that wasn't their fault. If you suspect that a seller has received a bum rap (after you've read all his or her positive feedback), be sure to look for the seller's response. (Look at Chapters 4 and 8 for more on reading and leaving feedback.)

View the seller's other items

To find out what other sales the seller has going on eBay, all you have to do is click the corresponding link on the item page; you're taken to a list of the other items the seller has up for sale. If the seller has no other items up for sale and has no current feedback, you may want to do a more thorough investigation and conduct a By Seller search that will show you all of that person's completed listings in the last 15 days. (See Chapter 5 for details.)

Contact seller

If anything about the transaction is unclear to you, remember this one word: *ask.* Find out all the details about that item before you bid. If you wait until you've won the item before you ask questions, you may get stuck with something you don't want. Double-checking may save you woe and hassle later.

You can find out more about payment options, shipping charges, insurance, and other fun stuff in Chapters 8 and 12.

SPELL CHECK PAYS OFF

A savvy eBay user I know benefited from a major seller error. The seller titled his auction "Swede Star Trek Cast Jacket." My friend checked out the item description and found that it was written with bad spelling and incoherent grammar, so she emailed the seller for more information. The seller explained that the jacket was a suede cast jacket given as a "wrap" gift to the cast and crew of the movie *Star Trek: Generations.* He had won it in a local radio contest, and it was brand new. Because of the seller's spelling mistake, only one bidder bid on this lovely green suede (silk-lined!) jacket, which my friend picked up for $150. Because of its *Star Trek* connection, the jacket is worth upwards of $400 to collectors. So study the item page carefully. You may get lucky and find that errors can work to your benefit. (And a word to the wise: Check your own spelling and grammar carefully when you put an item up for sale.)

MARSHA SAYS

If you're bidding on a reserve-price auction, don't be afraid to message the seller and ask what the reserve is. Yeah, reserves are mostly kept secret, but there's no harm in asking — and many sellers will gladly tell you.

Factoring In the Extras

Before you think about placing a bid on an item, you should consider the financial obligation you take on when you bid. In every case, the maximum bid you place won't be all you spend on an item. I recommend that you look closely at the payment methods that the seller is willing to accept — and also factor in shipping (if any). If you live in the same state as the seller, you may have to pay sales tax if the seller is running an official business.

Payment methods

Several payment options are available, but eBay only allows sellers to show electronic payment methods. Closer to 2021, eBay will be moving to a new Managed Payments program, which will offer more ways for a buyer to pay. Currently, most sellers are not required to accept any other form of payment but PayPal, and they may have a merchant account. These are the forms of payment available to you:

>> **Credit card:** Paying with a credit card is a favorite payment option for many buyers, offered mainly by businesses and dealers. I like paying with credit cards because they're fast and efficient. In addition, using a credit card offers you another ally — your credit card company — if you're not completely satisfied with the transaction. Credit cards can also be used for payment through the other electronic payment options a seller may offer. I still prefer PayPal.

>> **PayPal:** I pay for all my eBay purchases through PayPal. PayPal is the largest Internet-wide payment network. All sellers on eBay should accept PayPal and accept MasterCard, Visa, American Express, and Discover as well as electronic checks and debits. The checkout is integrated directly into eBay transactions, so paying for your item is a mouse click (or a tap on mobile) away.

After you register with PayPal to pay for an item, PayPal debits your credit card or your bank checking account (or your PayPal account — if you have earned some money from sales) and sends the payment to the seller's account. PayPal does not charge buyers to use the service. Buyers can use PayPal to pay any seller within the United States (and around the world in over 190 countries, in more than 20 currencies). Some international bidders can pay for their eBay items from sellers in the United States. To see a current list of PayPal's accepted currencies, go to www.paypal.com/selfhelp/article/FAQ2390.

PayPal deposits the money directly into the seller's PayPal account, from which the seller can withdraw to their own bank account. The service charges the seller a small transaction fee, so the seller absorbs the cost.

TIP

Your credit card information is known only to the PayPal platform; the seller never sees your credit card info. Another major advantage is that you have protection behind you when you use PayPal on the Internet. And you have the right to dispute charges if the item arrives damaged or doesn't show up at all.

For more details, check out the PayPal website at www.paypal.com.

» **PayPal Credit:** If you find that your credit card limit is about to hit, and you really want an item, this could be your answer. PayPal Credit is like using an online credit card; just select PayPal Credit as your payment choice when you check out on eBay. Keep in mind you're opening a credit account, so PayPal will need some personal information to approve your using their service.

Approval takes only seconds, and after your account is set up, you'll see PayPal Credit as a payment option when you check out through PayPal. Clicking PayPal Credit opens a window asking for your birth date and the last four digits of your Social Security number. After you accept the terms and are approved, credit is then added to your PayPal account.

» **Pay on pickup:** Sometimes you may buy an item from someone in your neighborhood and may be able to arrange a direct pickup, instead of waiting for an item to be shipped. You're on your own with this type of transaction — but at least you get to meet the person with whom you are transacting business.

TIP

Most business on eBay is conducted in U.S. dollars, and eBay converts foreign currency into U.S. dollars on the item page. If you want to make an exact conversion yourself, eBay has a currency converter, located at the following URL: pages.ebay.com/services/buyandsell/currencyconverter.html.

Just select your choice of currency, type the amount, and click Perform Currency Conversion.

Using an escrow service

Even though most sales on eBay are for items that cost $100 or less, using an escrow service comes in handy when you're buying a vehicle in the Motors category. *Escrow* is a service that allows a buyer and seller to protect a transaction by placing the money in the hands of a neutral third party until a specified set of conditions are met. Sellers note in their item descriptions whether they're willing to accept escrow. If you're nervous about sending a lot of money to someone you don't really know, consider using an escrow company.

WARNING

eBay has a partnership with `Escrow.com` to handle eBay escrow sales. After a transaction closes, the buyer sends the payment to the escrow company. After the escrow company receives the money, it emails the seller to ship the vehicle. After the buyer receives the item, he or she has an agreed-on period of time to look it over. If everything's okay, the escrow service sends the payment to the seller. If the buyer is unhappy with the item, he or she must ship it back to the seller. When the escrow service receives word from the seller that the item has been returned, the service returns the payment to the buyer (minus the escrow company's handling fee, of course).

Before you start an escrow transaction, make sure that you and the seller agree on these terms. Here are three questions about escrow that you should know the answers to before you bid:

» Who pays the escrow fee? (Normally the buyer does, although sometimes the buyer and seller split the cost.)

» How long is the inspection period? (Routinely, it's two business days after receipt of the merchandise.)

» Who pays for return shipping if the item is rejected? (The buyer usually pays.)

Shipping costs

Most eBay sellers don't charge for standard shipping. There may be an additional charge for expedited shipping, however, so read the options. Don't let the sale go down with the shipping. If the item is not an odd shape, excessively large, or fragile, experienced sellers calculate the shipping based on Priority Mail at the U.S. Postal Service, which is the unofficial eBay standard. Expect to pay a minimum of $6 for the first pound.

Some sellers smartly use First Class Mail for items that weigh less than a pound when packed, and sellers of media will often use the slower-delivery Media Mail for their items. These forms of shipping can save you big bucks!

It has also become somewhat routine for the seller to include a dollar or so for packing materials such as paper, bubble wrap, tape, and such. This is a fair and reasonable handling charge because the cost of these items can add up over time.

WARNING

You may come across sellers trying to nickel-and-dime their way to a fortune by jacking up the prices on shipping to ridiculous proportions. If you have a question about shipping costs, ask before you purchase the item.

Placing Your Bid on an Auction

Okay, so you've found the perfect item to track (say, a really classy Taylor Swift guitar for that budding pop star), and it's in your price range. You're more than interested — you're ready to bid. If this were a live auction, some stodgy-looking guy in a gray suit would see you nod your head and start the bidding at, say, $200. Then some woman with a fierce hairdo would yank on her ear, and the price on the guitar would jump to $300.

eBay reality is more like this: You're sitting at home in your fuzzy slippers, sipping coffee in front of the computer; all the other bidders are cruising cyber-space in their pajamas too. You just can't see 'em. (Be really thankful for the small things.)

When you're ready to jump into the eBay fray, you can find the bidding box at the top of the auction item page. If the item includes a Buy It Now option, you see that in the bidding box.

To fill out the bidding form and place a bid, first make sure that you're registered (see Chapter 2 for details), and then follow these steps. After you make your first bid on an item, you can instantly see the auctions you're bidding on from your My eBay page. (If you need some tips on how to set up My eBay, see Chapter 4.)

1. **Enter your maximum bid in the appropriate box.**

The bid needs to be an increment or more higher than the current minimum bid. The lowest amount you can bid is displayed just below the Place Bid box. (See the later section, "Bidding to the Max: Automatic Bidding," for more information about bidding increments.)

TIP

You don't need to put in the dollar sign, but *do* use a decimal point — unless you really *want* to pay $1,049.00 rather than $10.49. If you make a mistake with an incorrect decimal point, you can retract your bid (see "Retracting your bid," later in this chapter).

2. **Click Place Bid.**

The Review Bid page appears on your screen, filled with a wealth of legalese. This is your last chance to change your mind: Do you really want the item, and can you really buy it? The bottom line is this: If you bid on it and you win, you buy it. eBay really means it.

3. **At this point, you have to sign in if you haven't already; if you're signed in, skip to Step 4.**

4. **If you agree to the terms, click Confirm Bid.**

After you agree, the Bid Confirmation screen appears.

TIP

When you first start out on eBay, I suggest that you start with a *token bid* — a small bid that won't win you the auction but can help you keep tabs on the auction's progress. Personally, I keep an eye on the listing by adding it to my Watch list and letting my eBay Mobile app keep me apprised of the bidding action. (Learn more about the Mobile App in Chapter 18.)

After you bid on an item, the item number and title appear on your My eBay page, listed under the Bidding heading, as shown in Figure 6-8. (See Chapter 4 for more information on My eBay.) The Bid/Offers list makes tracking your auction (or auctions, if you're bidding on multiple items) easy.

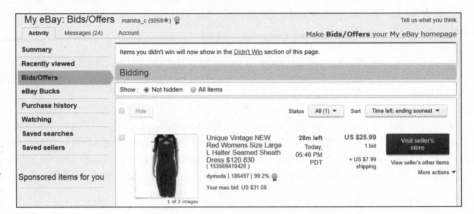

FIGURE 6-8:
Keep track of your bids on your My eBay page.

REMEMBER

eBay considers a bid on an item to be a binding contract. You can save yourself a lot of heartache if you make a promise to *never bid on an item you don't intend to buy.* Don't make practice bids, assuming that because you're new to eBay, you can't win; if you do that, you'll probably win simply because you've left yourself open to Murphy's Law. Therefore, before you go to the bidding form, be sure that you're in this auction for the long haul — and make yourself another promise: *Figure out the maximum you're willing to spend.* (Read the section "The Agony (?) of Buyer's Remorse," later in this chapter, for doleful accounts of what can happen if you bid idly or get buyer's remorse.)

Bidding to the Max: Automatic Bidding

When you make a maximum bid on the bidding form, you actually make several small bids — again and again — until the bidding reaches where you told it to stop. For example, if the current bid is up to $19.99 and you put in a maximum of $45.02, your bid automatically increases incrementally so that you're ahead of the competition — at least until someone else's maximum bid exceeds yours. Basically, you bid by *proxy*, which means that your bid rises incrementally in response to other bidders' bids.

No one else knows for sure whether you're bidding by proxy, and no one knows your maximum bid. And the best part is that you can be out having a life of your own while the proxy bid happens automatically. Buyers and sellers have no control over the increments (appropriately called *bid increments*) that eBay sets. The bid increment is the amount of money by which a bid is raised, and eBay's system can work in mysterious ways.

The current maximum bid can jump up a nickel or a quarter or even a Washington, but there is a method to the madness, even though you may not think so. eBay uses a *bid-increment formula* (see Table 6-1) that uses the current high bid to determine how much to increase the bid increment. As you can see, the higher you bid, the larger the proxy (automatic) bidding amounts become. Here are a pair of examples:

» A quart size bottle of body lotion has a current high bid of $14.95. The bid increment is $0.50 — meaning that if you bid by proxy, your proxy will bid $15.45.

» A 5-ounce can of top-notch caviar has a high bid of $200. The bid increment is $2.50. If you choose to bid by proxy, your proxy will bid $202.50.

TABLE 6-1

eBay's Proxy Bid Increments

Current Bid	Your Bid Increment
$0.01–$0.99	$0.05
$1.00–$4.99	$0.25
$5.00–$24.99	$0.50
$25.00–$99.99	$1.00
$100.00–$249.99	$2.50
$250.00–$499.99	$5.00
$500.00–$999.99	$10.00
$1000.00–$2499.99	$25.00
$2500.00–$4999.99	$50.00
$5000.00 and up	$100.00

Table 6-2 shows you what kind of magic happens when you put the proxy system and a bid-increment formula together in the same cyber-room.

TABLE 6-2   ## Proxy Bidding and Bid Increments

Current Bid	Bid Increment	Minimum Bid	eBay Auctioneer	Bidders
$2.50	$0.25	$2.75	"Do I hear $2.75?"	Joe Bidder tells his proxy that his maximum bid is $8.00. He's the current high bidder at $2.75.
$2.75	$0.25	$3.00	"Do I hear $3?"	You tell your proxy your maximum bid is $25.00 and take a nice, relaxing bath while your proxy calls out your $3.00 bid, making you the current high bidder.
$3.00	$0.25	$3.25	"I hear $3.00 from proxy. Do I hear $3.25?"	Joe Bidder's proxy bids $3.25, and while Joe Bidder is out walking his dog, he becomes the high bidder.
A heated bidding war ensues between Joe Bidder's proxy and your proxy while the two of you go on with your lives. The bid increment inches from $0.25 to $0.50 as the current high bid increases.				
$7.50	$0.50	$8.00	"Do I hear $8.00?"	Joe Bidder's proxy calls out $8.00, his final offer.
$8.00	$0.50	$8.50	"The bid is at $8.00. Do I hear $8.50?"	Your proxy calls out $8.50 on your behalf, and having outbid your opponent, you win the auction!

Specialized Categories

After you get the hang of bidding on eBay, you may venture to the specialized auction areas. You can purchase a car or car parts and accessories from eBay Motors, or your own piece of land or a new home in the Real Estate category. eBay is always adding new specialty areas, so be sure to check the announcements as well as the home page.

Should you reach the big-time bidding, be aware that if you bid over $15,000 in an auction, you *must* register a credit card with eBay. All items in the special categories are searchable in eBay's search, so don't worry about missing your dream Corvette when you use the Search page.

Speaking of Corvettes, visiting the automotive area of eBay is an auto enthusiast's dream. You can also find some great deals in used cars, and eBay offers creative ways to make buying vehicles of all shapes and sizes (as well as the largest array of parts you'll find anywhere on the planet) easy. Visit eBay Motors by clicking the Motors category link on the home page or by going to www.ebay.com/motors. When shopping for a vehicle on eBay, you'll find all sorts of ways to shop for a car with confidence.

>> **Specialized search:** If you want to search for cars without coming up with hundreds of die-cast vehicles, eBay Motors has its own search available from the eBay Motors home page. Here you can input makes, models, and your ZIP code to see if there are any vehicles available in your area. There is a separate search where you can find parts or accessories for your existing car.

>> **Vehicle shipping:** If you don't want to drive across the country to pick up your new vehicle, you can have it shipped through several eBay-recommended auto shippers. You can find shipping quotes on the listing pages.

>> **AutoCheck Reports:** With the vehicle's VIN (Vehicle Identification Number), a seller can provide a free history report.

>> **Financing:** Clicking the Get Low Monthly payments link, below the bidding area, takes you to the RoadLoans.com page to get an estimate. You can also apply for financing here for your purchase.

The Agony (?) of Buyer's Remorse

Maybe you're used to going into a shopping mall and purchasing something that you're not sure you like. What's the worst that could happen? You end up back at the mall, receipt in hand, returning the item. Not necessarily so on eBay.

(Top-rated sellers offer a 30-day return policy.) Even if you realize you already have a purple feather boa in your closet that's just like the one you bought yesterday on eBay, deciding that you don't want to go through with a transaction that's already underway *is* a big deal. Not only can it earn you some nasty feedback, but it can also give you the reputation of a deadbeat.

It would be a shame to float around eBay with the equivalent of a scarlet *D* (for *deadbeat*) above your User ID. Okay, eBay sellers use a kinder term — *non-paying bidder* — but for many members, it boils down to the same thing. If you win an auction or buy an item and have to back out of your obligation — even through no fault of your own — you need some info that can keep you in good (well, okay, *better*) standing. Look no further; you've found it.

Retracting your bid

Remember, many states consider your bid a binding contract, just like any other contract. You can't retract your bid unless one of these three outstandingly unusual circumstances applies:

>> If your bid is clearly a typographical error (you submitted a bid for $4,567 when you really meant $45.67), you may retract your bid. If this occurs, you should re-enter the correct bid amount immediately. You won't get any sympathy if you try to retract an $18.25 bid by saying you meant to bid $15.25, so review your bid before you send it.

>> You have tried to contact the seller to answer questions on the item, and he or she doesn't reply in a timely fashion.

>> If the seller substantially changes the description of an item after you place a bid (the description of the item changes from "can of tennis balls" to "a tennis ball," for example), you may retract your bid.

BUYER'S REMORSE CAN PAY OFF

Sometimes buyer's remorse does pay off. I know one eBay buyer who got a serious case of remorse after winning an auction. She decided to do the right thing and pay for the item even though she didn't want it. After receiving the item, she turned around and *sold* it on eBay for triple what she paid. If you really don't want the item, think like a seller — see whether you can turn a horrible mistake into a profitable venture. For more information on the benefits of selling, take a look at Chapter 9.

TIP

If you simply must retract a bid, try to do so long before the auction ends — and have a good reason for your retraction. eBay users are understanding, up to a point. If you have a good explanation, you should come out of the situation all right. So admit that you've made a mistake.

AFTER THE AUCTION: SIDE DEALS OR SECOND CHANCES?

WARNING

If a bidder is outbid on an item that he or she really wants — or if the auction's reserve price isn't met — the bidder may message the seller and see whether the seller is willing to make another deal. Maybe the seller has another similar item — or is willing to sell the item directly rather than run a whole new auction. You need to know that this could happen — but know also that eBay doesn't sanction this outside activity.

If the seller has more than one of the item, or the original auction winner doesn't go through with the deal, the seller can make a Second Chance offer. This is a legal, eBay-sanctioned second chance for *underbidders* (unsuccessful bidders) who participated in the auction. Second Chance offers can also be made in reserve auctions if the reserve price wasn't met.

Any side deals other than Second Chance offers are unprotected. Here's an example: My friend Jack collects autographed final scripts from hit television sitcoms. So when the curtain fell on *Seinfeld,* he had to have a script. Not surprisingly, he found one on eBay with a final price tag that was way out of his league. He placed a bid anyway; in those days, eBay showed bidders' User IDs in the bid history (which they no longer do). He figured another seller might contact him.

After the auction closed, he received a message from a guy who worked on the final show and had a script signed by all the actors. He offered it to Jack for $1,000 less than the final auction price on eBay. Tempted as he was to take the offer, Jack understood that eBay's rules and regulations wouldn't help him out if the deal turned sour. He was also aware that he wouldn't receive the benefit of feedback or any eBay Money Back Guarantee for the transaction.

If you even *think about* making a side deal, remember that not only does eBay *strictly* prohibit this activity, but eBay can also suspend you if you are reported for making a side deal. And if you're the victim of a side-deal scam, eBay's rules and regulations don't offer you any protection. My advice? Watch out!

If you've made an error, you must retract your bid prior to the last 12 hours of the auction. At this point, a retraction removes all bids you have placed in the auction. Mistakes or not, when you retract a bid that was placed within the last 12 hours of the listing, only the most recent bid you made is retracted — your bids placed prior to the last 12 hours are still active.

Here's how to retract a bid while the auction's still going on:

1. Go to http://offer.ebay.com/ws/eBayISAPI.dll?RetractBidShow.

2. Read the legalese, scroll down the page, and enter the item number of the auction you're retracting your bid from; then open the drop-down menu and select one of the three legitimate reasons for retracting your bid.

3. Click the Retract Bid button.

    You receive a confirmation of your bid retraction via email. Keep a copy of it until the auction is completed.

If you made a mistake when making a Best Offer, go to the following website: http://offer.ebay.com/ws/eBayISAPI.dll?RetractBestOfferShow.

WARNING

The seller may send you a message to ask for a more lengthy explanation of your retraction, especially if the item was a hot seller that received a lot of bids. Keep your replies courteous. After you retract one bid on an item, all your lower bids on that item are also retracted (unless the retraction is done within the last 12 hours), and your retraction goes into the bidding history — another good reason to have a really good reason for the retraction. The number of bids you've retracted also goes on your feedback-rating scorecard.

Avoiding deadbeat (unpaid item) status

Some bidders are more like kidders — they bid even though they have no intention of buying a thing. When honest eBay members spot these ne'er-do-wells, they often post the deadbeats' User IDs on Internet message boards. Some eBay members have created entire websites to warn others about dealing with the deadbeats . . . ahem . . . *non-paying bidders.* (Civilized but chilly, isn't it?)

Once a seller opens an unpaid-item case (say, if you do not pay within two days), and you don't want to pay, you can be excused by appealing the case. You may also contact the seller explaining why. The following human mishaps are generally accepted by most sellers:

>> A death in the family

>> Computer failure

>> A huge misunderstanding

REMEMBER

If you have a good reason to call off your purchase, make sure that the seller knows about it. The seller is the only one who can excuse you from the sale.

REMEMBER

There's no guarantee that your appeal will be accepted. eBay will contact you after an investigation and let you know whether your appeal was successful.

eBay has a message for non-paying bidders. The policy is pretty strict: After the first complaint about a non-paying (deadbeat) bidder, eBay gives the buyer a warning. After the third offense, the violator may be suspended from eBay for good and becomes *NARU* (Not a Registered User). Nobody's tarred and feathered, but you probably won't see hide nor hair of that user again on eBay.

Chapter **7**

Winning eBay Shopping Strategies

When people think about eBay, they initially think all sales on the site are auctions. This is not close to being true, of course, since many major brands have hung up their shingles on the site. Fixed-price sales have become the majority of eBay transactions — but the team at eBay (thank goodness) still lets us enjoy the fun of auctions. Bidders love them and so do sellers, even more — especially when the item up for sale is worth more than the seller ever expects to get.

On social media, I am often asked about eBay. I speak to so many people who find an auction on eBay, bid on it, and at the last minute — the last hour, or the last day — are outbid. Sad and dejected, they find losing an auction often cuts to the core and makes them feel like losers.

You're *not* a loser when you lose an auction on eBay. You just may not know the fine art of sneaky bidding (my way of saying *educated* bidding).

When the stakes are high and you really, really want the item, you have to resort to the highest forms of strategy. Sports teams study their rivals, and political candidates scout out what the opposition is doing. Bidding in competition against other bidders can be just as serious an enterprise. Follow the tips in this chapter and see if you can come up with a strong bidding strategy of your own. (Feel free to email me with any brilliant bidding plans; I'm always open to new theories.)

Make an Offer!

If you come across a fixed-price listing and you're in the mood to negotiate, why not make an offer? Sellers on eBay can apply the Best Offer option any time they list a fixed-price item — and many do. When the seller selects this option, it means he or she is willing to deal on the price — and you'll see the Make Offer button on a listing, which should indicate to you that you're dealing with a seller who's motivated to sell. This is a great way to get bargains. You make an offer on the item and the seller will either accept your offer, send you a counteroffer, or decline it.

The best way to find listings that accept offers is to search for your item. As you can see in Figure 7-1, you can refine an eBay search to see only those listings that "Accepts Offers."

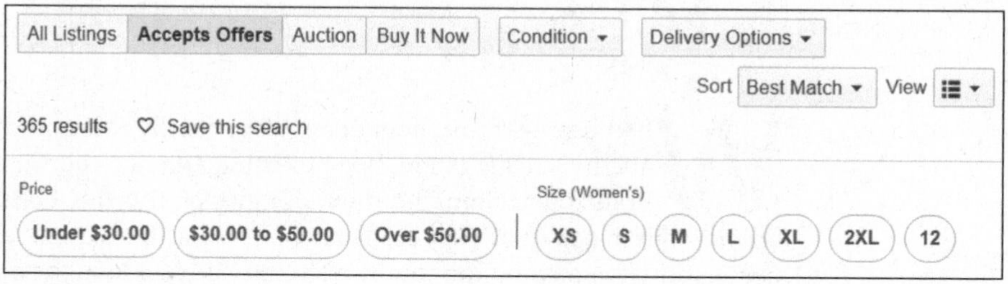

FIGURE 7-1:
Click the selection for Accepts Offers to find the negotiable bargains.

Making an offer to buy an item has a drawback: The seller has up to 48 hours to respond to you, and you may find the same item from another seller at a better price before then. By making an offer, you are duty-bound to buy the item, at the price your offer specifies, if the seller agrees to it. If that doesn't happen, you're off the hook and can find another of the item elsewhere.

To make an offer, click the Make Offer button (rather than the Buy It Now button); see Figure 7-2.

When making an offer, you might think you want to put in a really, really low offer. But be sensible; if the item is new, the seller may have only a small margin on the price. Also, putting in a ridiculously low offer (say $10 on a $25 item) may just annoy the seller; he or she may turn you down without giving you an opportunity to negotiate.

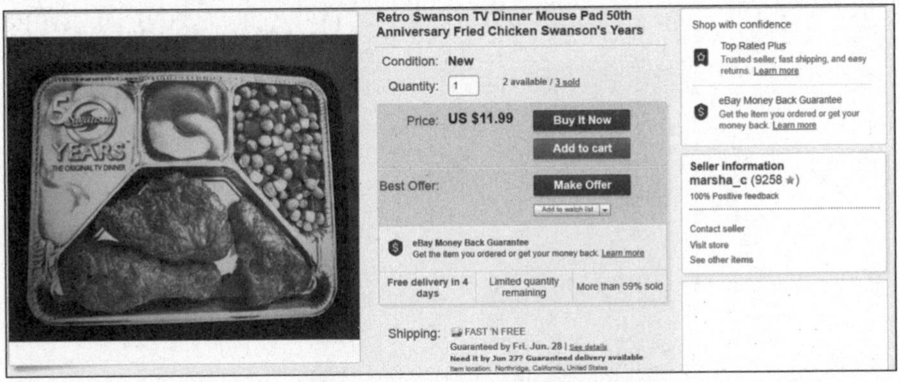

Retro Swanson TV Dinner Mouse Pad 50th
Anniversary Fried Chicken Swanson's Years

Condition: **New**

Quantity: 1   2 available / 3 sold

Price: **US $11.99**   Buy It Now

Add to cart

Best Offer: Make Offer

Add to watch list

eBay Money Back Guarantee
Get the item you ordered or get your money back. Learn more

Free delivery in 4 days | Limited quantity remaining | More than 59% sold

Shipping: FAST 'N FREE
Guaranteed by Fri, Jun 28 | See details
Need it by Jun 27? Guaranteed delivery available
Item location: Northridge, California, United States

Shop with confidence

Top Rated Plus
Trusted seller, fast shipping, and easy returns. Learn more

eBay Money Back Guarantee
Get the item you ordered or get your money back. Learn more

Seller information
marsha_c (9258 ★)
100% Positive feedback

Contact seller
Visit store
See other items

FIGURE 7-2:
Use the Make
Offer option any
time you're not in
a rush and want
to haggle a deal.

MARSHA
SAYS

To make your offer more attractive to the seller, don't lowball their asking price, just deduct a reasonable percentage (especially if they offer free shipping). After all, they need to make a profit on the sale. A super-low offer can feel insulting.

TIP

When placing an offer on an item, you officially have two further follow-up offers you can make should the seller turn down your first proposal.

Find Out an Item's Bidding History

You can access an active auction's bidding history by clicking the number of bids link, as shown in Figure 7-3, which appears to the right of the current bid on the item page. The bidding history lists everyone who is bidding on the item. You can see how often and at what time bids are placed, and unless you are the seller of the item, you can't see the bidders' real eBay usernames. To protect the innocent, eBay changes User IDs to a gibberish of asterisks and numbers. Each bidder is assigned a faux bidder ID in the history.

TIP

Pay attention to the times of day at which bidders are placing their bids; you may find that the people bidding in this auction seem to be creatures of habit — making their bids about once a day and at a particular time of day. They may be logging on before work, during lunch, or after work. Whatever their schedules, you have this data at your disposal in the event that a bidding war breaks out: Just bid after your competition traditionally logs out, and you increase your odds of winning the auction.

You'll also notice that you can reveal proxy bids by clicking the words *Show automatic bids*. This view shows when someone has placed a higher proxy bid — as when a single bidder continually ups the bid and still doesn't have the highest, winning bid. Look at Figure 7-4 to see the bidding history on an auction where someone busted the winning bidder's proxy.

The current number of bids.

CHANEL Crystal Baguette Wide Cuff Clear Silver
Cuff Bracelet New !

Condition: **New with tags**

Time left: **36m 48s** Today 4:48PM

Current US $440.00 [56 bids]
bid:

[   ] **Place bid**

Enter US $445.00 or more

Add to watch list ▼

🛡 eBay Money Back Guarantee
Get the item you ordered or get your money back. Learn more

| Limited time remaining | 29 watchers | Longtime member |

Bucks You'll earn $4.40 in eBay Bucks. See conditions

FIGURE 7-3:
Look for the number of bids in the tiny link next to the latest bid amount and click.

Bid history

Tell us what you think

Bidders: **12**   Bids: **56**   Time left: **34 mins 59 secs**   Duration: **7 days**

Only actual bids (not automatic bids generated up to a bidder's maximum) are shown. Automatic bids may be placed days or hours before a listing ends. Learn more about bidding.

Show automatic bids

Bidder ⓘ	Bid Amount	Bid Time
x***b (163 ★)	$440.00	24 Jun 2019 at 4:09:35PM PDT
x***b (163 ★)	$440.00	24 Jun 2019 at 4:09:26PM PDT
x***b (163 ★)	$440.00	24 Jun 2019 at 4:09:17PM PDT
x***b (163 ★)	$440.00	24 Jun 2019 at 4:09:08PM PDT
o***i (178 ★)	$435.00	24 Jun 2019 at 7:39:28AM PDT
x***b (163 ★)	$430.00	23 Jun 2019 at 8:24:31PM PDT
o***i (178 ★)	$430.00	24 Jun 2019 at 7:39:25AM PDT
o***i (178 ★)	$420.00	24 Jun 2019 at 7:39:23AM PDT

FIGURE 7-4:
The bidding history tells you the date and time of day at which the bidders placed their bids, as well as the amount.

Early in an auction, there may not be much of a bidding history for an item, but that doesn't mean you can't still check out the dates and times a bidder places bids. You can also tell that a bidder practices *sniping* (discussed later in this chapter) if his or her bid zips in during the last few minutes (or even seconds!) of the auction. You may have a fight on your hands if the bidder does practice sniping.

Get to Know the Other Bidders

It used to be an easy task to study up on your competition, but the brains at eBay got smart and made it all but impossible. That is, all *but* impossible to us! In this section, I show you how I figured out the now-circuitous route you can use to research your competition.

The anonymized ID of the person the item would belong to if the auction ended right now is listed on the auction item page. After clicking through to the bid history during the auction, you can see the personal bid history of an individual bidder.

By clicking an ID in the bid history, you are presented with a page like the one shown in Figure 7-5, which shows just what that bidder has been up to — bidding-wise.

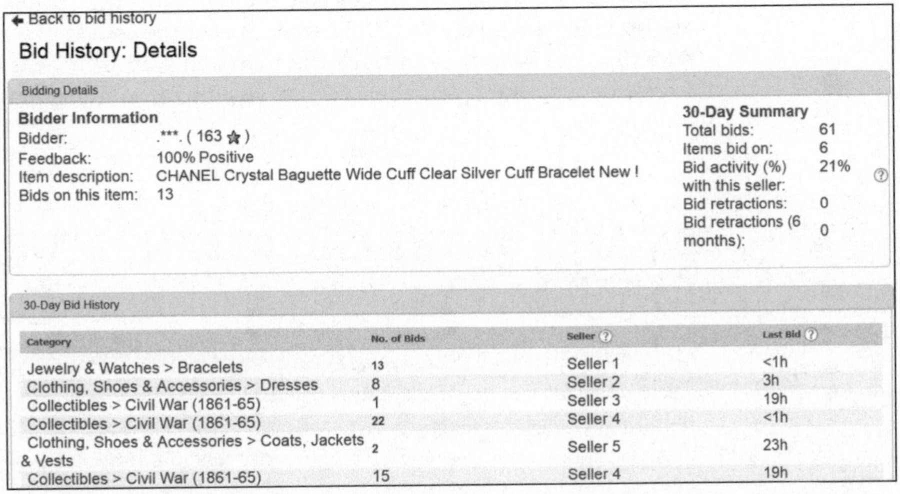

FIGURE 7-5: Clicking an ID in the bid history reveals a lot about the competition. Here someone is clearly highly interested in high-ticket collectibles. (A dealer, perhaps?)

← Back to bid history

Bid History: Details

Bidding Details

Bidder Information
Bidder: .***. (163 ★)
Feedback: 100% Positive
Item description: CHANEL Crystal Baguette Wide Cuff Clear Silver Cuff Bracelet New !
Bids on this item: 13

30-Day Summary
Total bids: 61
Items bid on: 6
Bid activity (%) with this seller: 21%
Bid retractions: 0
Bid retractions (6 months): 0

30-Day Bid History

Category	No. of Bids	Seller ?	Last Bid ?
Jewelry & Watches > Bracelets	13	Seller 1	<1h
Clothing, Shoes & Accessories > Dresses	8	Seller 2	3h
Collectibles > Civil War (1861-65)	1	Seller 3	19h
Collectibles > Civil War (1861-65)	22	Seller 4	<1h
Clothing, Shoes & Accessories > Coats, Jackets & Vests	2	Seller 5	23h
Collectibles > Civil War (1861-65)	15	Seller 4	19h

THE TALE OF THE 3-PLUS-NEGATIVE SELLER

A friend of mine took a risk and bid on an old Winchester rifle (now a banned item — see Chapter 9 for a rundown of what you're allowed and not allowed to sell on eBay) without reading the seller's feedback. The seller had a (3) next to his User ID, which at a glance might say that the user is new to eBay. Good thing my friend lost the auction. It turned out that the seller had a whopping 20 negative feedback messages. He had 23 positives, mostly posted by suspicious-looking names. These days, a seller like this might be suspended by eBay . . . eventually. Repeat after me: *Always check the feedback comments!*

Strategies to Help You Outsmart the Competition

MARSHA SAYS

Your two cents *do* matter — at least on eBay. Here's why: Many eBay members tend to round off their bids to the nearest dollar figure. Some choose nice, familiar coin increments such as 25, 50, or 75 cents. But the most successful eBay bidders have found that adding 2 or 3 cents to a routine bid can mean the difference between winning and losing. So I recommend that you make your bids in oddish figures (such as $15.12 or $45.57) as an inexpensive way to edge out your competition. If you have a proxy bid in, say for $22.57, and a sniper jumps in at the last second and places a bid for $22.50 — you still win! The highest bid placed always wins. For the first time ever, your 2 cents (or in this case 7 cents) may actually pay off!

That's just one of the many strategies to get you ahead of the rest of the bidding pack without paying more than you should. *Note:* The strategies in this section are for bidders who are watching an item over the course of a week or so — so be sure that you have time to track the item and plan your next moves. Also, get a few auctions under your belt before you throw yourself into the middle of a bidding war.

PIRATES OF THE CARIBBEAN . . . OR CARRIBEAN?

Just before the original *Pirates of the Caribbean* movie premiered, Disneyland gave out exclusive movie posters to its visitors. My then-college-student daughter, savvy eBayer that she is, snagged several copies to sell on the site. She listed them (one at a time) when the movie opened and couldn't get more than the starting bid of $9.99 for each of them.

When we searched eBay for *pirates poster,* we found that the very same posters listed with a misspelled title, "Pirates of the Carribean," were selling for as high as $30 each. After selling out her initial stock, my daughter found another seller who had ten for sale — in one auction — with the proper spelling. She bought those as well (for $5 each) and sold them with misspelled titles on the site for between $15 and $27!

The moral of this story is always to search alternate spellings of your item; you might possibly eke out a gem without any competition.

Here's a list of do's and don'ts that can help you win your item. Of course, some of these tips *are* eBay-endorsed, but I had to get you to notice what I have to say somehow:

>> **Don't bid early and high.** Bidding early *and* high shows that you have a clear interest in the item. It also shows that you're a rookie, apt to make mistakes. If you bid early and high, you may give away just how much you want the item.

Of course, a higher bid does mean more bucks for the seller and a healthy cut for the middleman. So it's no big mystery that many sellers recommend it. In fact, when you sell an item, you may want to encourage it too.

If you must bid early and can't follow the auction action (you mean you have a life?), use software or an online sniping service like BidRobot. Then feel free to place your highest possible bid! You can find out more about that website in Chapter 20.

>> **Do wait and watch your auction.** If you're interested in an item and you have the time to watch it from beginning to end, I say that the best strategy is to wait. Click the Watch This Item link to move it to your My eBay page — and remember to check it. But if you don't have the time, go ahead — put in your maximum bid early and cross your fingers.

>> **Don't freak out if you find yourself in a bidding war.** Don't keel over if, at the split-second you're convinced that you're the high bidder with your $45.02, someone beats you out at $45.50.

TIP

You can increase your maximum bid to $46.02, but if your bidding foe also has a maximum of $46.02, the tie goes to the person who put in the highest bid *first*. Bid as high as you're willing to go, but bid at the very end of the auction.

>> **Do check the item's bidding history.** If you find yourself in a bidding war and want an item badly enough, check the bidding history and identify your fiercest competitor; then refer to the previous section, "Get to Know the Other Bidders," for a pre-auction briefing.

TIP

To get a pretty exact picture of your opponent's bidding habits, make special note of the times of day when he or she has bid on other auctions. You can adjust your bidding times accordingly.

>> **Do consider sniping.** Further in this chapter I discuss *sniping* — a term I coined in the early days of eBay to describe a technique for bidding at the last possible second of an auction.

>> **Do remember that most deals go through without a problem.** The overwhelming majority of deals on eBay are closed with no trouble, which means that if the auction you're bidding in is typical and you come in second place, you've lost. Or maybe not . . .

If the winning bidder backs out of the auction or the seller has more than one of the item, the seller *could* (but isn't obligated to) come to another bidder and offer to sell the item at the second bidder's price through eBay's Second Chance option. (See Chapter 13 for more details on this feature.)

Time Is Money: Auction Strategy by the Clock

You can use different bidding strategies depending on how much time is left in an auction. By paying attention to the clock, you can find out about your competition, beat them out, and end up paying less for your item.

Most auctions on eBay run for a week; the auction item page always lists how much time is left. However, sellers can run auctions for as short as one day or as long as ten days. So synchronize your computer (or mobile) clock with eBay's master time and become the most precise eBay bidder around. eBay's official time page (Figure 7-6) is hard to find. Go directly to or `http://ofr.ebay.com/ws/eBayISAPI.dll?EbayTime` to check it out.

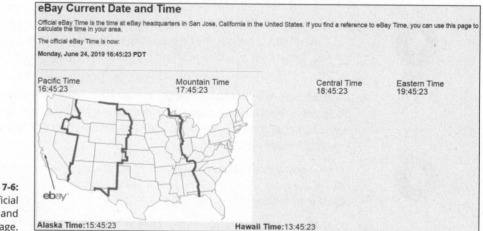

FIGURE 7-6: eBay's official date and time page.

To synchronize your clock, make sure that you're logged on to the Internet and can easily access the eBay website. Then follow these steps:

1. **Go into your computer's Control Panel and double-click your system's Date and Time functions.**

2. **Go to the link supplied in the previous paragraph.**

3. **Check your computer's time against eBay's current time.**

4. **Click the Change Date and Time Settings on your computer, and then click the Reload button on your browser.**

   Clicking to Reload ensures that you see the latest, correct time from eBay.

5. **Type the minutes displayed on the eBay official time page as soon as the newly reloaded page appears.**

6. **Repeat Steps 4 and 5 to synchronize your computer's seconds display with eBay's.**

This process takes a little practice, but it can mean the difference between winning and losing an auction.

You don't need to worry about the hour display unless you don't mind your system clock displaying Pacific time.

Most bidding on eBay goes on during East Coast work time and early evening hours, which gives you a leg up if you live out West. Night-owl bidders will find that after 10:00 p.m. Pacific time (about 1:00 a.m. eastern time), lots of bargains are to be had. And believe it or not, lots of auctions end in the wee hours of the morning. Monday holidays are also great for bargains, as are Thanksgiving and the day after. While everyone is in the living room digesting and arguing about what to stream on Netflix (or getting up at 5:00 a.m. to buy the big discount deal at Walmart), fire up eBay and be thankful for the great bargains you can buy.

For simplicity's sake, go over to my website and print my quick and easy eBay time-conversion chart. It's located at `www.coolebaytools.com/tools/usa-time-zones`.

Using a laid-back strategy

Sometimes the best strategy at the beginning of an auction is to do nothing at all. That's right; relax, take off your shoes, and loaf. Go ahead. You may want to make a *token bid* (the very lowest you are allowed) or mark the page to watch in your My eBay area. I generally take this attitude through the first six days of a week-long auction I want to bid on, and it works pretty well. Of course, I check in on the mobile app every day just to keep tabs on the items I'm watching, and revise my strategy as time goes by.

TIP

The seller has the right to up his minimum bid — if his auction has received no bids — up to 12 hours before the auction ends. If the seller has set a ridiculously low minimum bid and then sees that the auction is getting no action, the seller may choose to up the minimum bid to protect his investment in the item that's up for sale. By placing the minimum token bid when you first see the auction, you can foil a Buy It Now sale from another bidder (because the Buy It Now feature is disabled after a bid has been placed unless there is a reserve on the listing) or prevent the seller from upping the minimum.

REMEMBER

If you see an item that you *absolutely must* have, mark it to watch on your My eBay page (or make that token bid) and plan to revise your maximum bid as the auction goes on. I can't stress enough how important this is.

As you check back each day, take a look at the other bids and the high bidder. Is someone starting a bidding war? Look at the time that the competition is bidding and note patterns. Maybe at noon eastern time? During lunch? If you know what time your major competition is bidding, then — when the time is right — you can safely bid after he or she does (preferably when your foe is stuck in the dentist's chair while trying to use the eBay app, without a signal, to bid).

If you play the waiting game, you can decide if you really want to increase your bid or wait around for the item to show up again sometime. You may decide you really don't want this particular item after all. Or you may feel no rush because other sellers have posted the same item.

Using the beat-the-clock strategy

You should rev up your bidding strategy during the final 24 hours of an auction and decide, once and for all, whether you really *have* to have the item you've been eyeing. Maybe you put in a maximum bid of $45.02 earlier in the week. Now's the time to decide whether you're willing to go as high as $50.02. Maybe $56.03?

No one wants to spend the day in front of the computer (ask almost anyone who does). Set a notification on your smartphone, reminding you of the exact time the auction ends. If you're not going to be near a computer when the auction closes, bid on the eBay app on your phone or use an automatic bidding site to bid for you; see Chapter 20 for details.

In the last half-hour

With a half-hour left before the auction becomes ancient history, head for the computer and dig in for the last battle of the bidding war. I recommend that you log on to eBay about five to ten minutes before the auction ends. The last thing you want to have happen is to get caught in Internet gridlock and not get access to the website. Go to the item you're watching and click the auction title.

With an hour to go, if your auction has a lot of action, eBay reloads the bidding action every second so you can get the most current info on what people are bidding.

Sniping to the finish: The final minutes

The rapid-fire, final flurry of bidding happens because bidders are *sniping* — practicing the fine art of waiting until the very last seconds of an eBay auction and then outbidding the current high bidder just in time. Of course, you have to expect that the current high bidder is sniping back.

With a hot item, open a second window on your browser (you do that by pressing the Ctrl key and the N key together); keep one open for bidding and the other open to watch eBay's constant reloading during the final few minutes. With the count-down at 60 seconds or less, make your final bid at the absolute highest amount you will pay for the item. The longer you can hold off — I'm talking down to around 15 seconds — the better. It all depends on the speed of your Internet connection (and how strong your stomach is), so practice on some small auctions so you know how much time to allow when you're bidding on your prize item. Keep watching the time tick to the end of the auction, as in Figure 7-7.

Watch the bids go up in a popular auction. That stamp auction closed at $21.50 within the minute (see Figure 7-8).

THE STORY OF THE SNIPE SISTERS

Cory and Bonnie are sisters and avid eBay buyers. Bonnie collects vases. She had her eye on a Fenton Dragonfly Ruby Verdena vase, but the auction closed while she was at work and didn't have access to a computer. (This was before mobile bidding). Knowing that, her sister Cory decided to snipe for it. With 37 seconds to go, she inserted the high bid on behalf of her sister. Bang, she was high bidder at $63. But, with 17 seconds left, another bidder sniped back and raised the price to $73. It was, of course, Bonnie, who had found a way to get access to a computer from where she was. Bonnie got the vase, and they both had a good laugh.

FIGURE 7-7:
With 51 seconds left to go this stamp auction is at $16.50.

NobleSpirit NO RESERVE } Excellent US Nos. 219-229 Used Set =$268 CV!

Condition: --
Time left: **51s** Today 5:01PM

Current bid: **US $16.50** [9 bids]

Enter US $17.00 or more

Place bid

Add to watch list

eBay Money Back Guarantee
Get the item you ordered or get your money back. Learn more

SEE DESCRIPTION FOR ALL PHOTOS

FIGURE 7-8:
See how fast a price can go up?

NobleSpirit NO RESERVE } Excellent US Nos. 219-229 Used Set =$268 CV!

Condition: --
Ended: Jun 24, 2019, 5:01PM

Winning bid: **US $21.50** [11 bids]

Add to list

eBay Money Back Guarantee
Get the item you ordered or get your money back. Learn more

Shipping: $3.00 Standard Shipping | See details
Item location: Pittsfield, NH, United States
Ships to: Worldwide. See exclusions

SEE DESCRIPTION FOR ALL PHOTOS

If you want to be truly fancy, you can open a third window for bidding and have a back-up high bid in case you catch another sniper swooping in on your item immediately after your first snipe. (I recently received an email from one of my readers who used my somewhat paranoid method — which she learned from a previous edition of this book — and by using the second snipe, she won her item!) You can avoid the third-window routine if you've bid your highest bid with the first snipe. Then, if you're outbid, you know that the item went for more than you were willing to pay. (I know; it's some consolation, but not much.)

Some eBay members consider the practice of sniping unseemly and uncivilized — it's like when dozens of parents used to mob the department store clerks to get to the handful of limited-edition collectibles that were just delivered. Of course, sometimes a little uncivilized behavior can be a hoot.

TIP

I say that sniping is an addictive, fun part of life on eBay auctions. And it's a blast. So my recommendation is that you try sniping. You're likely to benefit from the results and enjoy your eBay experience even more — especially if you're an adrenaline junkie.

Here's a list of things to keep in mind when you get ready to place your last bid:

» Know how high you're willing to go. If you know you're facing a lot of competition, figure out your highest bid to the penny. You should have researched the item already, and you should know its value at this point. Raise your bid only to the level where you're sure that you're getting a good return on your investment; don't go overboard. Certainly, if the item has some emotional value to you and you just have to have it, bid as high as you want (and can afford — but you knew that). But remember, you'll have to pay the piper later. You win it, you own it!

» Know the speed of your Internet connection.

» Remember, this is a game, and sometimes it's a game of chance, so don't lose heart if you lose the auction.

Although sellers love sniping because it drives up prices, and bidders love it because it's fun, a sniper can ruin a week's careful work on an auction strategy. The most skillful snipers sneak in a bid so close to the end of the auction that you have no chance to counterbid, which means you lose. Losing too often, especially to the same sniper, can be a drag.

If you can make the highest bid with less than 10 seconds left, you most likely will win. With so many bids coming in the final seconds, your bid might be the last one that eBay records.

This stuff is supposed to be fun, so don't lose perspective. If you can't afford an item, don't get caught up in a bidding war. Otherwise, the only person who wins is the seller. If you're losing sleep, barking at your cat, or biting your nails over an item, it's time to rethink what you're doing. Shopping on eBay is like being in a long line in a busy department store. If it's taking up too much of your life or an item costs too much, be willing to walk away — or log off — and live to bid (or shop) another day.

Chapter **8**

Winner! Winner! Chicken Dinner?

Perhaps there's no chicken dinner, but the thrill of the chase is over, and you've bought (or won) your eBay item. Congratulations — now what do you do? You have to follow up on your victory and keep an eye on what you're doing. In this chapter, you can get a handle on what's in store for you after you buy your item. I clue you in on what the seller is supposed to do to make the transaction go smoothly and show you how to grab hold of your responsibilities as a buyer. I give you info here about following proper post-sale etiquette, including the best way to stay organized, communicate with the seller professionally, and send your payment without hazards. I also brief you on how to handle an imperfect transaction.

eBay Calling: You're a Winner

The Buy section of your desktop My eBay Summary highlights the titles of items you've won or purchased and indicates the amount of your purchase price. eBay will contact you via email or smartphone notification if you win, and you can check out the Purchase history section for yourself. Figure 8-1 shows my latest purchase. If you install eBay's mobile app on your smartphone, you can also pay for the item on the run. In Chapter 18, I help you with the plusses and minuses of the mobile app.

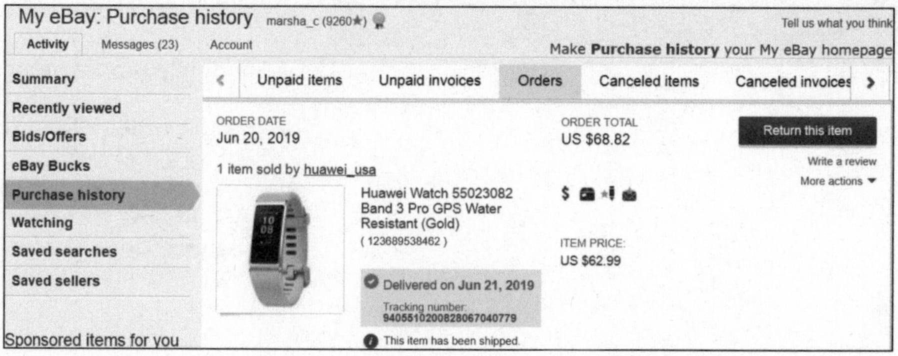

FIGURE 8-1:
Your My eBay:
Purchase history
page is the hub
for your buying
activities.

Throughout an auction's bidding process, dollar amounts of items that you're winning appear in green on your My eBay Bids/Offers tab. If you've been outbid, the bid amounts appear in red. After an auction ends, there's no marching band, no visit from a celebrity with a camera crew, no armful of roses, and no oversized check to duck behind. In fact, you're more likely to find out that you've won the auction from either a mobile notification or by visiting the Purchase history section of your My eBay page. Fortunately, eBay gets its Order Confirmation emails out pronto. For a look at the information in the winner's email, see Figure 8-2.

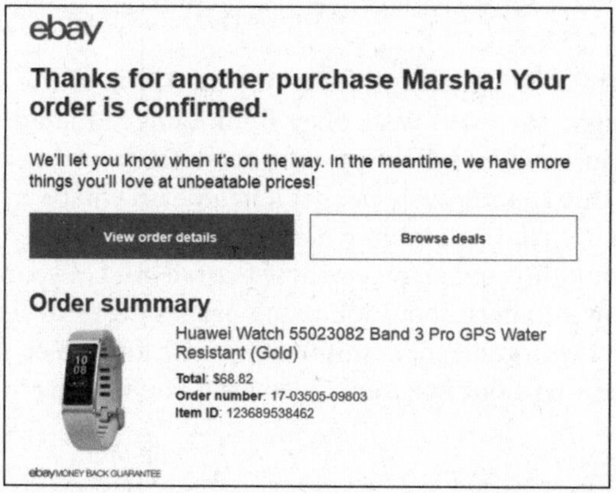

FIGURE 8-2:
Everything you
need to know
about your
transaction is
included in
eBay's email.

Getting Your Paperwork Together

Yeah, I know that PCs were supposed to create a paperless society, but cars were supposed to fly by the year 2000, too. Maybe it's just as well that some predictions don't come true (think of the way some people steer shopping carts). Paper still has its uses, and when you're just starting out on eBay, you *might* want to print copies of your purchase records to help you keep your records straight. If you're the techie type, like me, you might just want to highlight your email (which has a link to the item's description). Know that you can always go back and reference the details of the sale by clicking the item in your email or Purchase history.

**MARSHA
SAYS**

AN ORDER OF FRIES WITH
A MENU ON THE SIDE

In 1999, one seller auctioned an old menu from Howard Johnson's, estimating its era as the 1950s based on the cars pictured on the cover — and the prices (fried clams were $1.25). Also included was a separate menu card that listed fresh seafood and had a liquor menu (with Pieman logo) on the back — plus a list of locations in the New York City area. Except for a couple of staple holes at the top of the front cover (maybe evidence of daily specials past), the menu was in very good condition. The starting bid was $5; the item sold for $64. These menus are even harder to come by now, and rare editions are selling as high as $90. (I wonder how much they want for fried clams in New York City these days. . . .)

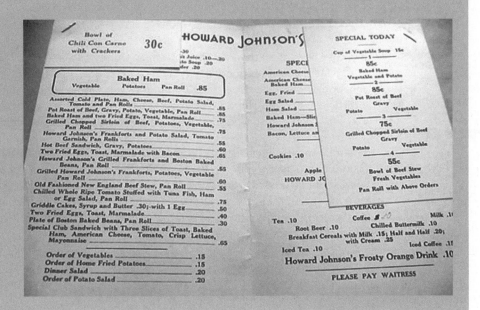

Many sellers have multiple listings going at the same time (and you may be buying many items at a time), so the more organized you are, the more likely you will receive the correct item (and quick feedback) from each seller. Here's a list of the virtual documents you should keep at the ready until your item is delivered and all is well:

>> Save your confirmation email from eBay. *Don't* delete the email! You may need to refer to the email later, and there's no way to get another copy — so if you want to print it out just in case, go ahead. Right-click on the item name to get the direct link to the Order details page on eBay.

>> Save copies of any messages between you and the seller that detail specific information about the item or circumstances of shipping arrangements.

>> Print, if you must, a copy of the final listing page.

WARNING

Sellers can update their listings while they're in progress, so keep your eyes peeled for changes in the listing as you monitor it. If the seller makes major changes, you are within your rights to retract your bid. (Check out Chapter 6 for more on the bidding process.)

Getting in Contact

If you've bought an item and intend to pay through PayPal, it's *de rigueur* for you to pay for the item as soon as you've purchased it. If the item is an auction that you won while away from your computer, you can pay from your smartphone. Whichever way you choose, you'll see a Pay Now link on the item page. Clicking that link takes you to a page where you can review your order and make payment.

To find out the seller's email address for your records, you'll find it in the eBay transaction page in your PayPal account after you pay. It's a good thing to tuck away should the need arise. Know that any contact you have with the seller should be done through eBay's monitored messages; they become part of the transaction's record. Should a problem arise, the folks at eBay will be able to see the communications between you and the seller.

Sending the Payment Promptly and Securely

So how many times have you heard the saying "The payment is in the mail?" Yeah, I've heard it about a thousand times, too. If you're on the selling end of an auction, hearing this line from the buyer but not getting the money is frustrating.

If you're on the buying end, it's very bad form and may also lead to bad feedback for you.

Being the good buyer that you are (you're here finding out how to do the right thing, right?), you'll get your payment out pronto via PayPal. Do it immediately — why wait? (The sooner you pay, the sooner you get that stunning vintage Chanel jacket you won!)

TIP

Most sellers expect to get paid within a day after the close of an auction. (Buy It Now items are paid immediately.) Although this timeline isn't mandatory, it makes good sense to let the seller know if there will be any delay in payment.

REMEMBER

Send your payment promptly. If you have to delay payment for any reason (you have to go out of town or you are over your credit card limit), let the seller know as soon as possible. If you know there may be a problem ahead of time, contact the seller to ask permission — maybe it just isn't okay. Most sellers do understand if you send them a kind and honest email. Let the seller know what's up, give him or her a date by which the money can be expected, and then meet that deadline. If the wait is unreasonably long, or the seller wants their money now, they may cancel the transaction.

The bottom line is that just about every eBay seller accepts PayPal as the main payment option, and you do not have to set up an account to use it. After a listing has ended with you purchasing the item, a checkout appears. You can generally make your payment in several ways:

>> **Credit or Debit Card:** You can use your American Express, Discover, Visa, or MasterCard to make your payment. The cost of the item is charged to your card, and your statement will reflect a PayPal (or eBay) payment with the seller's ID.

>> **eCheck:** Sending money with an eCheck is easy. It debits your checking account just like a paper check. It does not clear immediately, and the seller probably won't ship until PayPal tells him or her that the eCheck has cleared your bank.

>> **PayPal's Credit:** If you'd like to open up a credit line with PayPal, you can (as long as you qualify). By selecting the PayPal Credit option, you can open up a credit account in a minute or so. This option may not be available in the future — read belore clicking anything.

>> **Instant Transfer:** An instant transfer is just like an eCheck, except that it clears immediately and the money is directly posted to the seller's account. It is available only to users in the United States who have linked a U.S. bank account and a debit or credit card to their PayPal (or eBay) account. When you send an instant transfer, your credit or debit card will be a backup (should the payment from your bank be denied).

PayPal is my favorite payment service when shopping at other websites as well. PayPal also has a purchase-protection program, which covers your purchases in the case of possible fraud (if your item arrives not as described). *But eBay is ending the relationship with PayPal as their primary payment provider, and soon, you will make payments directly to eBay.*

FIXED-PRICE SALES: BUY IT NOW OR ADD TO CART?

When you are shopping and buying eBay Fixed Price listings, you'll notice a Buy It Now button — as well as an Add to cart button (both shown in the figure).

They represent two different procedures:

- **Buy It Now:** This button takes you to a checkout page, where you confirm that your item is the one you want and your mailing address is correct. Then you just click Pay Now and the item is yours.

- **Add to cart:** Clicking this button allows you to hold that particular item in your cart, so you can continue shopping around the site and find other items to buy. As you find them, just click Add to cart. When you've accumulated your full bounty, you can pay for all the items with just a click.

Keep in mind that any items in your cart are not yours until you pay for them. So if a seller only has one of the item left in stock, another buyer can swoop in and purchase it while you're dillydallying.

If you're new to PayPal, they take you step by step through the process of filling out a payment form to identify the item you're paying for, as well as your shipping information. Then you're all done. Your credit card information is held safely with PayPal, and the payment is deposited into the seller's PayPal account. The seller receives notice of your payment and notifies you about how quickly he or she will ship your item.

By paying with PayPal, you can instantly pay for an eBay item without hassle. Your credit card information is kept private, and your payment is deposited into the seller's PayPal account.

You can always view your Checkout status or track the package by going to your My eBay: Purchase history page. Click the drop-down menu in the Action column for the item in question.

Checking Out

When you buy something in a store, you need to check out to pay. eBay isn't much different. eBay's Checkout is a safe and convenient way to pay for your completed auctions and Buy It Now sales.

Checkout is integrated directly onto the item page so that you can win and pay for an item in less than a minute. You may also be forwarded to a link to the seller's Checkout page if the seller uses a third-party Checkout system.

If you find out about your win from an eBay email, you can click the Complete purchase link in the email to go to the Checkout page.

When you click the Pay Now button, you're taken through the Checkout process. You pay for the item, and the seller is notified. You also get an email confirming your payment, along with the seller's email address.

TIP

If you don't have a balance in your PayPal account (from selling items), PayPal defaults to taking the payment from your registered bank account. If you prefer to pay with a credit card, you must find the link (as I did in Figure 8-3) to change your payment method.

If you're dealing with a Buy It Now or fixed-price listing, the page won't change much after you've purchased the item. After you commit to buy and confirm to eBay that you want to make a purchase, you're taken immediately to a checkout page with a Confirm and Pay button.

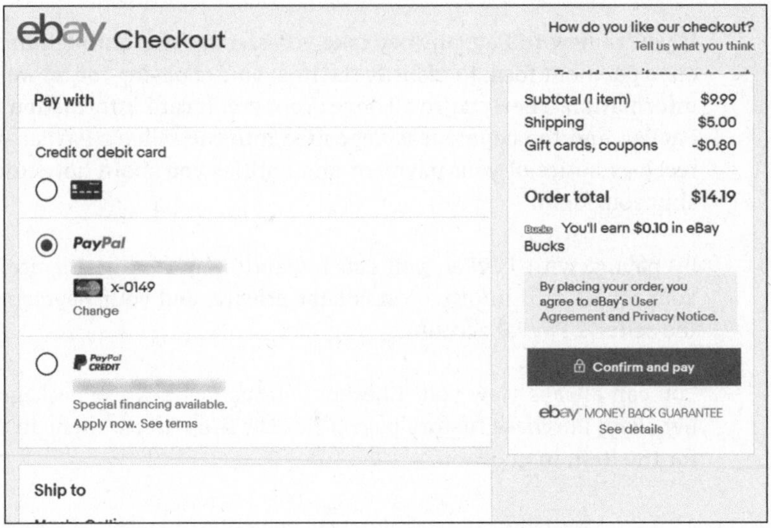

FIGURE 8-3:
Use the elusive drop-down menu to select your preferred payment method.

Communicating with the Seller

Top-notch sellers know that communication is the absolute key to a successful transaction, and they do everything they can to set a positive tone for the entire process with speedy and courteous responses to eBay messages.

After the transaction is over and it's time to leave feedback, communication is one of the points on which you're asked to rate the seller. Top Rated Sellers on eBay depend on high (5-star) ratings to maintain their reputation on the site. Things to consider when judging a seller's communication include (a) how accurate the seller's description was of the item and (b) how quickly you received confirmation of your purchase.

Contact you may receive from eBay might include the following information:

>> The link for paying with PayPal or a secure website for credit card processing

>> A review of the shipping options, if applicable

>> Contact information

>> The date the item will be shipped and when you should expect delivery

>> The tracking number so you can follow your item's progress through the mail

You should pay immediately upon receipt of the invoice. If you have a question before paying, contact the seller immediately — he or she will be expecting your payment.

If you see significant differences between the email you receive from the seller after the sale and what's on the item page, address those differences immediately with the seller before you proceed with the transaction. For more on clarifying payment options during the buying process, see Chapter 6.

Keeping in Touch: Dealing with an AWOL Seller

The eBay community, like local towns and cities, is not without its problems. With the millions of transactions that go on every week, transactional difficulties do pop up now and then.

You may be faced with an AWOL seller. Just as you're expected to hustle and get your payment off to the seller, the seller has an obligation to post tracking information after receiving your payment to let you know that the item has been shipped. If you sent the payment but you haven't heard a peep in a while, *don't* jump the gun and assume the person is trying to cheat you, but *do* follow up.

Follow this step-by-step approach if you've already paid for the item but haven't heard from the seller:

>> **The gentle-nudge approach:** In your My eBay Purchase history area, click the arrow next to More Actions on your transaction (see Figure 8-4). Click Contact Seller and send a message; ask whether your item has been shipped, and would they be so kind as to send you the tracking number. You'll find that the old saying, "You can attract a lot more bees with honey than with vinegar," works great on eBay.

FIGURE 8-4:
Use the drop-down menu to contact the seller, and more.

Orders		
● Not hidden ○ Show hidden items	See orders from: The last 60 days ▼ Filter by: All ▼	
ORDER DATE Jul 10, 2019	ORDER TOTAL US $14.99	Leave feedback
1 item sold by ▓▓▓▓▓		View order details
		More actions ▼
4 Marvelous Mrs. Maisel REVLON Lipsticks 616 001 720 Matte Creme (113804230964)	$ ▦ ✴▮ ▧	Contact seller
		View PayPal transaction
	ITEM PRICE: US $9.99	Ask to cancel order
		View seller's other items
		View similar items
		Sell this item
		Save this seller
ORDER DATE Jun 20, 2019	ORDER TOTAL US $68.82	Hide order

>> **Civil-but-firm approach:** Send a message through eBay again. Be civil but firm, and request the information.

>> **Take-action time:** If you still haven't heard from the seller within a week, go to your My eBay Purchase history area, and in the drop-down menu next to the item in question, choose Contact Seller again, but this time, click the radio button next to your complaint as shown in Figure 8-5. You can then open a case for an item not received (or for one stating that the item is not as described). Know that eBay will investigate the case — and if everything pans out, you will receive a refund.

FIGURE 8-5: This time, report that you haven't received your item or it's not as described.

You Get the Item . . . Uh-Oh, What's This?

The vast majority of eBay transactions go without a hitch. You buy, you send your payment, you get the item, you check it out, you're happy. If that's the case — a happy result for your transaction — skip this section and go leave some positive feedback for the seller!

On the other hand, if you're not happy with the item you receive, the seller may have some 'splaining to do. Message (through contact seller) and politely ask for an explanation if the item isn't as described. Some indications of a foul-up are pretty obvious:

>> The item's color, shape, or size doesn't match the description.

>> The item is scratched, broken, or dented in ways that don't match the description (the description said the doll was new, but the box is tattered and the doll has seen more than its share of action).

>> You purchased a set of candlesticks and received a vase instead.

TIP

A snag in the transaction is annoying, but don't go nuclear immediately. Contact the seller and see whether you can work things out. Keep the conversation civilized. The majority of sellers want a clean track record and good feedback, so they'll respond to your concerns and make things right. Assume the best about the seller's honesty, unless you have a real reason to suspect foul play. Remember, you take some risks whenever you buy something that you can't touch. If the item has a slight problem that you can live with and you paid a small price, leave it alone and don't go to the trouble of leaving negative feedback about an otherwise pleasant, honest eBay seller.

Of course, while I can give you advice on what you *deserve* from a seller, you're the one who has to live with the item. If you and the seller can't reach a compromise, and you really think you deserve a refund, ask for one.

If the item arrives at your home pretty well pulverized, contact the seller to alert him or her about the problem. Give the seller all the details needed to make an insurance claim (if the insurance was purchased by the seller).

With any luck, you and the seller can work things out. If not, file a claim with eBay's Money Back Guarantee to get your money back. Check out Chapter 12 for more tips on how to deal with shipping catastrophes. And jump over to Chapter 16 to find out how to file your claim.

Don't Forget to Leave Feedback

Good sellers should be rewarded, and potential buyers should be informed of good transactions. That's why no eBay transaction is complete until the buyer fills out the feedback form. Before leaving any feedback, though, always remember that sometimes no one's really at fault if some transactions get fouled up; communication meltdowns can happen to anyone. (For more info on leaving feedback, see

Chapter 4.) Here are some scenarios that give you an idea on what kind of feedback to leave for a seller:

>> **Positive:** If the transaction could have been a nightmare, but the seller really tried to make it right and meet you halfway, that's an easy call — give the seller the benefit of the doubt and leave positive feedback.

>> **Positive:** Whenever possible, reward someone who seems honest or tried to fix a bad situation. For example, if the seller worked at a snail's pace but you eventually got your item and you're thrilled with it, you may want to leave positive feedback with a caveat. Something like "Item as described, good seller, but slow to deliver" sends the right feedback message.

>> **Neutral:** If the seller worked at a snail's pace and did adequate packaging and the item was kinda-sorta what you thought, you may want to leave neutral feedback; the transaction wasn't bad enough for negative feedback but doesn't deserve praise, either. Here's an example of what you might say: "Really slow to deliver, didn't say item condition was good not excellent, but did deliver." Wishy-washy is okay as a response to so-so; at least the next buyer will know to ask very specific questions.

>> **Negative:** If the seller never shipped your item or the item seriously didn't match the description when it arrived, *and* you had to file a claim, you need to leave negative feedback. Make sure that both conditions apply. Never write negative feedback in the heat of the moment — and never make it personal. Keep it mellow and just state the facts. Do expect a response but don't get into a name-calling war. Life's interesting enough without taking on extra hassles.

The Accidental Deadbeat might be an intriguing title for a movie someday, but being a deadbeat isn't much fun in real life. See Chapter 6 for details on buyer's remorse and retracting a bid *before* the end of an auction.

Properly Giving the Detailed Seller Ratings (DSRs)

In addition to a feedback comment and rating (positive, negative, or neutral), buyers should leave detailed seller ratings, too. The DSR part of the feedback system asks you to rate sellers by filling in 1 to 5 stars. A 5-star rating doesn't cost you anything as the buyer, and if the sellers you buy from are Top Rated Sellers, feedback can affect a discount they receive on their eBay fees. Table 8-1 outlines what the stars mean to me when I leave a rating.

TABLE 8-1   **What the DSR Stars Mean**

Rating Question	# of Stars = Meaning	In the Real World
How accurate was the item's description?	1 = Very inaccurate 2 = Inaccurate 3 = Neither inaccurate nor accurate 4 = Accurate 5 = Very accurate	In my world, the item was either described right or wrong — to me, there is no in-between. So when I rate a seller, either the item is as advertised (5) or it isn't (1).
How satisfied were you with the seller's communication?	1 = Very unsatisfied 2 = Unsatisfied 3 = Neither unsatisfied nor satisfied 4 = Satisfied 5 = Very satisfied	As a buyer, I lean more with being very satisfied that I got enough communication from the seller, or not. If I get one email, or the item description is thorough, I'm usually satisfied and give a 5. But if I haven't heard from a seller until the item reaches my door and there's a problem, I'm definitely rating in the 2-star range.
How quickly did the seller ship the item?	1 = Very slowly 2 = Slowly 3 = Neither slowly nor quickly 4 = Quickly 5 = Very quickly	When you're a buyer, it's only fair to check the postmark on the package you receive. If the seller ships the next day or the next day after — you really should click 5 (Very quickly), no matter how long the postal service took to get it there. eBay keeps track of delivery dates, too.
How reasonable were the shipping and handling charges?	1 = Very unreasonable 2 = Unreasonable 3 = Neither unreasonable nor reasonable 4 = Reasonable 5 = Very reasonable	When I purchase an item, I know what the shipping cost will be. The only surprise here is when you get an item in a small envelope and you paid $9 for shipping — or if you paid for Priority Mail and it comes in another class of service. This is, to me, pretty black-and-white. The shipping and handling charges are either reasonable or unreasonable.

Here are some other items to keep in mind when you're deciding on what Detailed Star Rating to leave for a seller:

>> **Shipping takes time:** You have to realize that Ground shipping can take up to ten days. This isn't the seller's fault. So before leaving this rating, make sure to check the tracking details or the date on the shipping label.

>> **Shipping costs money:** Sellers have to add a little to cover the costs of tape, boxes, and packing materials. As a buyer, you have to keep that in mind. If you're unfamiliar with postage rates, you should also know that a package costs a lot more to ship across the country than to ship to the next state. So do a little homework and evaluate shipping costs *before* you buy. If the shipping is too high, go to another seller.

TIP

You may notice when leaving feedback that some star categories are grayed out (you can't click them). This is because the seller fulfilled requirements such as posting a tracking number quickly, or the package was delivered within the stated time.

If your seller is a Top Rated Seller, you should also know that your star ratings affect the fees he or she pays to eBay. Being a good seller (with high DSRs) can save as much as 20 percent on final value fees, so your rating is a very serious matter.

3

Making Money the eBay Way

Chapter 9

Selling Online for Fun and Profit

Selling on eBay is fun and profitable. I've been doing it for almost twenty years. My eBay selling is not my exclusive job; I sell on eBay part time. In the past, when I've needed cash, I'm all over my eBay, selling anything that isn't tied down, and it's been a blessing. My eBay sales paid for my daughter's college tuition, and more. You can make a living on eBay without turning your enterprise into a complicated monster. It's also one of the best side gigs ever.

Finding items to sell can be as easy as opening your closet (garage? kitchen drawer?) or as challenging as acquiring antiques overseas. (I've even taken the leap and imported items from China to sell on eBay.) Either way, establishing yourself as a successful eBay seller isn't as difficult as it seems when you know the ropes. In this chapter, you find out how to look for items under your own roof, figure out what they're worth, and turn them into ready cash. But before you pick your house clean (I know eBay can be habit-forming, but please keep a *few* things for yourself!), read up on the eBay rules of the road — such as how to sell, when to sell, and what *not* to sell. If you're interested in finding out how to set up your auction page, get acquainted with Chapter 10; if you want to read up on advanced selling strategies, the appendix is where to find them.

Why Should You Sell Stuff on eBay?

Whether you need to simply downsize or clear out 35 years of odd and wacky knickknacks cluttering your closets or you seriously want to earn much-needed money, the benefits of selling on eBay are as diverse as the people doing the selling. The biggest plus to selling on eBay is wheeling and dealing from your home in pajamas and slippers (every day is Casual Friday in my office). But no matter where you conduct your business or how you dress, many more important big-time rewards exist for selling on eBay.

Most people starting a business have to worry about rounding up investment capital (startup money they may lose), building inventory (buying stuff to sell), setting up a website, learning SEO, and acquiring customers. Today, even a garage-based startup can require a major investment. eBay helped to level the playing field a bit; everybody can get an equal chance to start a small business with very little money. Anyone who wants to take a stab at doing business can get started with just enough money to purchase initial items. eBay brings the customers to you.

TIP

Get a few transactions under your belt. I suggest you buy a few inexpensive items from other sellers. See how they handle their transactions. Does their way of business satisfy you as a customer? Ask yourself what you might do differently and apply that to your future sales. (A plus to this is that you build positive feedback with every transaction.)

Sell your old collection of postcards, ashtrays, concert souvenirs (you really never wear that Cher "farewell tour" hoodie — do you?), or your aunt's souvenir spoon collection. See how you like the responsibilities of listing, collecting money, shipping, and customer service. Grow a bit more, and you'll find yourself spotting trends, acquiring inventory, and marketing your items for maximum profit.

TIP

If you think you're ready to make eBay a full- or part-time business, take a look at Chapter 11 for some advanced sourcing strategies. If you still want to go long on eBay, please take a look at my book, *eBay Business All-in-One For Dummies* (Wiley Publishing, Inc.) — a complete reference for your online business (including your website). It will give you just what you need to ramp up from hobbyist to big-time e-commerce tycoon making several thousand dollars a month!

LIFE LESSONS LEARNED ON EBAY

MARSHA SAYS

If you have children, they will benefit if you get them involved with your eBay transactions. They'll get real-life lessons they can't learn in school. Give them a feel for meeting deadlines and fulfilling promises. Get them writing emails (if they aren't already), and when you sell, get them to help pack the items. eBay is a great place to learn basic economics and how to handle money. When I first started on eBay, I taught my preteen daughter about geography by using eBay. Every time I completed a transaction, she used a search engine to look up the city in which the buyer (or seller) lived — and then marked the city by placing a pin on a huge map of the United States. While helping me with shipping, she graduated from college, having majored in business and marketing, and has a good job today. (Thank you, eBay!)

Get creative and make eBay a profitable learning experience, too. Remember, however, that eBay doesn't let anyone under the age of 18 register, buy, or sell — so make sure that you're in charge of handling all transactions. Your kids can help out, but they need to be under your supervision at all times.

Again, a fun way to get your feet wet on eBay is to buy some small items. When I say small, I mean it. Some of the least expensive items you can buy on eBay are recipes. Type **recipe** in the search box and click the Home & Garden category. You'll find recipes that range from a penny up. You don't have to pay a shipping charge, either. The sellers are required to send you a copy in the mail, but they often also email the recipe direct to you after you pay. You can also begin selling your very own secret recipes. This is a great way to become familiar with how eBay works, and you'll be gaining experience with feedback — as well as building yours!

Finding Stuff to Sell

Finding merchandise to sell on eBay is as easy as checking your garage and as tough as climbing up to the attic. Just about anything you bought and stashed away (because you didn't want it, forgot about it, or it didn't fit) is fair game. Think about all those unwanted birthday and holiday presents (hey, it was the thought that counted — and the givers may have forgotten about them, too). Now you have a place you can try to unload them for cash. They could even make someone else happy. In Chapter 11, I give you more advanced tips for sourcing items. This is just for starters.

In your closet, find what's just hanging around:

REMEMBER

>> **Clothing that no longer fits or is out of fashion:** (Do you really want to keep it if you wouldn't be caught dead in it or you know it will never fit?) Don't forget the pair of shoes you wore once and put away.

You may not get top dollar for used items, but selling them will give you experience, build your feedback, and fill your pocket with a few well-earned dollars that you didn't have before.

>> **Any item with a brand-name label:** Especially if it's in new or almost-new condition.

>> **Gifts:** Have you received many well-meaning gifts that you've never used? You stashed them in the closet, right? One man's trash (mathoms for the LOTR fans) is another man's (or woman's) treasure.

>> **Kids' clothes:** (They outgrow things fast — sometimes before they wear them. Use profits from the old items to buy new clothes they can grow into. Now, that's going green.)

TIP

Have the articles of clothing in the best condition possible before you put them up for sale. For example, shoes can be cleaned and buffed till they're like new. According to eBay's policies, clothing *must* be cleaned before shipping.

And consider what's parked in your basement, garage, or attic:

>> **Old radios, stereo and video equipment, and 8-track systems:** Watch these items fly out of your house — especially the 8-track players (believe it or not, people love 'em).

>> **Books you finished reading long ago and don't want to read again:** Some books with early copyright dates or first editions by famous authors earn big money on eBay.

- » **Leftovers from an abandoned hobby:** Who knew that building miniature dollhouses was so much work?

- » **Unwanted gifts:** Have a decade's worth of birthday, graduation, or holiday gifts collecting dust? Put them up on eBay and hope Grandma or Grandpa doesn't bid on them because they think *somebody* needs another mustache comb!

Saleable stuff may even be lounging around in your living room or bedroom:

- » **Home décor you want to change:** Lamps, chairs, and rugs (especially if they're antiques) sell quickly. If you think an item is very valuable but you're not sure, get it appraised first.

- » **Exercise equipment:** If you're like most people, you bought this stuff with every intention of getting in shape, but now all that's building up is dust. Get some exercise boxing up all that equipment after you've sold it on eBay. *Remember:* The USPS will pick up for free.

- » **Vinyl records:** Have a few boxes of vintage vinyl? If you're not buying a turntable any time soon, put them up for sale! (Think records are dead? You may be very surprised.)

- » **Autographs:** All types of autographs — from sports figures, celebrities, and world leaders — are popular on eBay. A word of caution, though: A lot of fakes are on the market, so make sure that what you're selling (or buying) is the real thing. If you're planning on selling autographs on eBay, be sure to review the special rules that apply to these items. Here's where to find them:

    `http://pages.ebay.com/help/policies/autographs.html`

Know When to Sell

MARSHA SAYS

Warning . . . warning . . . I'm about to hit you with some of my time-honored clichés (these truths never change):

- » *Timing is everything.*
- » *Sell what you know and know when to sell.*
- » *Buy low and sell high.*
- » *Fast quarters are better than slow dollars.*

Okay, granted, my clichés may be painful to hear over and over, but they do contain nuggets of good information. (Perhaps they're repeated for a reason?)

Experienced eBay sellers know that when planning a sale, timing is almost everything. Fur coats don't sell well in July, and as a seller of collectibles you don't want to be caught with 200 Nintendo WiiU games during a run on Xbox. (Hold on to them; vintage games do sell well.) *Star Wars* action figures are traditionally good sellers unless a new sci-fi title is all the rage.

MARSHA SAYS

Some items — such as good antiques, rugs, comic books, and sports cars — are timeless. But timing still counts. Don't put your rare, antique paper cutter up for auction if someone else is selling one at the same time. I guarantee that will cut into your profits.

SNAPPING UP PROFITS

Way back in 1980, when Pac-Man ruled, my friend Ric decided to try his hand at photography. Hoping to be the next Ansel Adams — or to at least snap something in focus — he bought a Kowa 66, one of those cameras you hold in front of your belt buckle while you look down into the viewfinder. Soon after he bought the camera, Ric's focus shifted. The camera sat in its box, instructions and all, for over 15 years until he threw a garage sale.

Ric and his wife didn't know much about his Kowa, but they knew that it was worth something. When he got an offer of $80 for it at the garage sale, his wife whispered "eBay!" in his ear, and he turned down the offer.

Ric and his wife posted the camera on eBay with the little information they had about its size and color, and the couple was flooded with questions and information about the camera from knowledgeable bidders. One bidder said that the silver-toned lens made it more valuable. Another gave them the camera's history.

Ric and his wife added each new bit of information to their listing description and watched as the bids increased with their every addition — until that unused camera went for more than $400 in a flurry of last-minute sniping in 1999. These days, when Ric posts an item for sale, he always asks for additional information and adds it to the listing page.

What difference does a year make? You'll find that the values of all items on eBay trend up and down. In 2000, this camera sold on eBay for over $600; in late 2001, it sold for $455. In the winter of 2003, interest in it was waning; it sold in the $375 to $400 range. In 2009, one sold for $390, in 2011, $440. Believe it or not, in these days of digital cameras, one *just* closed on eBay for $425. Not bad, considering "everyone" is saying film cameras are dead merchandise.

TIP

Timing is hardly an exact science. Rather, timing is a little bit of common sense, a dash of marketing, and a fair amount of information gathering. Do a little research among your friends. What are they interested in? Would they buy your item? Use eBay itself as a research tool. Search Sold listings to see whether anyone's making money on the same type of item. If people are crazed for some fad item and you have a bunch of those, *yesterday* was the time to sell. (In other words, if you want your money out of 'em, get crackin' and get packin'.)

REMEMBER

If the eBay market is already flooded with dozens of an item and no one is making money on them, you can afford to wait before you start your listing.

Know Thy Stuff

At least that's what Socrates would have said if he'd been an eBay seller. Haven't had to do a homework assignment in a while? Time to dust off those time-trusted skills. Before selling your merchandise, do some digging to find out as much as you can about it.

Getting the goods on your goods

You may know a little about your item, but writing a detailed description of your collectible or rare item can increase your selling price immensely. Here are some ideas to help you flesh out your knowledge of what you have to sell:

>> **Hit the books.** Study historic guides and collector magazines; perhaps even check your local library (yes, they still exist) for books about the item. Especially out-of-print books will give you valuable information. To find some online, go to

   https://books.google.com/advanced_book_search

   and search your topic. I just went there, searched "Barbie collector," and found thousands of results!

WARNING

   Even though some collectors use published price guides when they put a value on an item, so much fast-moving e-commerce is on the Internet that printed (or even digital) price guides often lag behind the markets they cover. Take their prices with a grain of salt.

>> **Go surfin'.** Conduct a web search and look for info on the item on other e-commerce sites. If you find a print magazine that has some good information, check to see whether the magazine is available on the web by typing the title of the magazine into your browser's search window.

(For detailed information on using search engines to conduct a more thorough online search, check out Chapter 5.)

>> **When the shopping gets tough, go mobile.** If you're out and about searching tag sales or resale shops, use eBay's handy smartphone app and see whether (and for how much) the item is selling on eBay. (Find more about eBay's handy mobile app in Chapter 18.)

REMEMBER

When you understand the demand for your product (whether it's a collectible or a commodity) and how much you can realistically ask for it, you're on the right track to running a successful sale.

>> **Call in the pros.** Need a quick way to find the value of an item you want to sell? Call a dealer or a collector and say you have one to sell. A merchant who smells a good deal will make an offer; at that point, ask them what it would sell for in their store.

>> **Bing to the rescue.** Run a search of your keywords on Bing.com. You can run a search on Google, but Bing provides another view of Internet-wide results.

For information on how items are graded and valued by professional collectors, jump to Chapter 5, where I discuss grading your items.

WARNING

Be certain that you know what you have — not only what it is and what it's for, but also *whether it's genuine.* Make sure that it's the real McCoy. You are responsible for your item's authenticity; counterfeits and knock-offs are not welcome on eBay. In addition, manufacturers' legal beagles are on the hunt for counterfeit and stolen goods circulating on eBay — and they *will* tip off law enforcement.

Spy versus spy: Comparison selling

Back in the old days, successful retailers like Gimbel and Macy spied on each other to figure out ways to get a leg up on the competition. Today, in the bustling world of e-commerce, the spying continues, and dipping into the intrigue of surveilling the competition is as easy as clicking your mouse. Collectible items are often the most difficult to price.

Often what makes something valuable is the fact that it is controversial, although it didn't start out that way. Also, discontinued products gain in popularity. Scarcity is the name of the game. Take the beloved 1980s TV show, *The Dukes of Hazzard.* Its fans were legion and loyal to the innocent theme of the show, yet today it's looked at through a different lens.

Dukes of Hazzard stuff, such as DVDs of the show, movie memorabilia, General Lee models, and lunch boxes, are still huge sellers with millennials and Gen X-ers looking for memories of their childhood. That piece of tin that once held their lunchtime PB&J may very well fetch a nice sum. To find out for sure, you can do some research on eBay. To find out the current market price for a *Dukes of Hazzard* lunch box, you can conduct a Sold listings search (as described in Chapter 5) and find out exactly how many *Dukes of Hazzard* lunch boxes have been sold in the past few weeks. You can also find out their high selling prices and how many bids the lunch boxes received by the time the auctions were over. And repeating a completed search in a week or two is not a bad idea — you can get at least a month's worth of data to price your item. Figure 9-1 shows the results of a Sold listings search sorted by the highest prices first.

FIGURE 9-1:
Use the Sold listings search to find out the current selling price. Time to sell a rare lunch box!

TIP

You can easily save your searches for pricing research on eBay. Just click the heart emoji next to the *Save this search* link at the top of the results to add a search to your saved searches list. Then it's on your My eBay Saved Searches page, and you can repeat the search with a click of your mouse.

TIP

Look at the pictures on item pages for each item that your Sold listings search turns up. That way, you can confirm that the items (lunch boxes, for example) are identical to the one you want to sell. And when you do your research, factor in your item's condition. Read the individual item descriptions. If your item is in better condition, expect (and ask for) more money for it; if your item is in worse condition, expect (and ask for) less. You can always add a Make Offer option to your listing and decide on the fly whether you will accept a specific price suggested by a buyer. Note which categories the items are listed under; they may give you a clue about where eBay members are looking for items just like yours.

If you want to be extremely thorough in your price estimates, check out Worthpoint or Terapeak to see whether the results of your eBay search mesh with historical sales. (Chapter 20 explains these services). If you find that no items like yours are for sale anywhere else online, and are pretty sure that people are looking for what you have, you may just find yourself in a very profitable position.

REMEMBER

Don't forget to factor in the history of an item when you assess its value. Getting an idea of what people are watching, listening to, and collecting can help you assess trends and figure out what's hot.

Know What You Can (And Can't) Sell

The majority of items sold on eBay are aboveboard. But sometimes eBay finds out about listings that are either illegal (in the eyes of the state or federal government, or even those of international authorities) or prohibited by eBay's rules and regulations. In either case, eBay steps in, calls a foul, and makes the item invalid.

eBay doesn't have rules and regulations just for the fun of it. eBay wants to keep you educated so you won't unwittingly bid on, buy, or sell an item that has been misrepresented. eBay also wants you to know what's okay and what's prohibited so that if you run across an item that looks fishy, you'll help out your fellow eBay members by reporting it. And eBay wants you to know that if you do sell legally iffy items, getting your listing shut down is the least of your worries: You can be suspended if you knowingly list prohibited items. And I won't even talk about criminal prosecution.

You need to know about these three categories:

>> **Prohibited** lists the items that may *not* be sold on eBay under any circumstances.

>> **Restricted** lists the items that may be sold under certain conditions.

>> **Potentially Infringing** lists the types of items that may be in violation of copyrights, trademarks, or other rights.

WARNING

You may not even offer to *give away for free* a prohibited or an infringing item, nor can you give away a questionable item that eBay disallows; giving it away doesn't relieve you of potential liability.

TIP

The items that you absolutely *cannot* sell on eBay can fit into *all three* categories. Those items can be legally ambiguous at best — not to mention potentially risky and all kinds of sticky. To find a detailed description of which items are prohibited on the eBay website, follow these steps:

1. **Click the Policies link, located on the bottom of all eBay pages.**

    You arrive at the friendly eBay Rules & Policies page.

2. **Scroll to the Prohibited and restricted items link and click.**

    You are presented with the lists and links that help you decipher whether selling your item falls within eBay's policy boundaries.

    Or, if you're reading this in an e-book or you don't mind typing, you can go directly to www.ebay.com/help/policies/prohibited-restricted-items/ prohibited-restricted-items?id=4207.

Sometimes an item is okay to own but not to sell. Other times the item is prohibited from being *sold and possessed.* To complicate matters even more, some items may be legal in one part of the United States but not in others. Or an item may be illegal in the United States but legal in other countries.

WARNING

Because eBay's base of operations is in California, United States law is enforced — even if both the buyer and seller are from other countries. Cuban cigars are legal to buy and sell in Canada, but even if the buyer *and* the seller are from Canada, eBay says "*No permiso*" and shuts down sales of Havanas fast. Figure 9-2 shows an auction that was shut down soon after I found it. To see a current list of countries where trade is embargoed, visit http://pages.ebay.com/help/policies/ embargo.html.

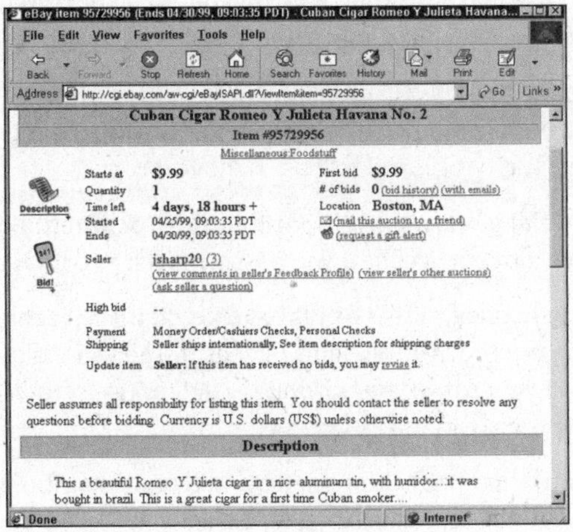

FIGURE 9-2:
In 1999, this auction for a Cuban cigar appeared and eBay swiftly removed it.

Prohibited items

The lists that follow are not fully comprehensive of everything that's prohibited on eBay. Please be sure to visit the Prohibited link just mentioned if you have further questions.

Even though possessing (and selling) many of the items in the following list is legal in the United States and elsewhere, you are absolutely, positively *prohibited* from buying and selling the following on eBay:

>> **Firearms of all types:** This also means firearm accessories — including antique, collectible, sport, or hunting guns; silencers; converters; kits for creating guns; gunpowder; high-capacity ammunition magazines (receptacles designed to feed ten rounds or more into a gun, not the publications about ammo); and armor-piercing bullets. You can't even sell a gun that *doesn't* work.

TIP

You *can* buy and sell single bullets, shells, and even antique bombs and musket balls — as long as they have nothing explosive in them.

>> **Firearms and weapons:** No way can you sell any type of firearm designed to propel a metal (or similar) projectile, regardless of whether it works. (If we're talking paintball, archery, or spud pistols — that's another story.) Military weapons? Items included in that category — and all *verboten* — are bazookas, grenades, and mortars.

>> **Police-related items:** Stop in the name of the law if you're thinking about buying or selling any of these items, including actual United States federal (or state or local) or reproduction badges. In fact, selling just about any U.S. government badge (even the Forest Service) can get you in hot water.

REMEMBER

You also can't own or sell those agencies' identification cards or credential cases or those really cool jackets they use in raids. Selling a copy or reproduction of any of these items is prohibited, too, because these items are copyrighted (see the section on infringing items in this chapter).

If you find a badge that's legal to sell and own, you need to provide a letter of authorization from the agency. The same letter of authorization is required for fake badges, such as reproductions or movie props.

>> **Replicas of official government identification documents or licenses:** Birth certificates, drivers' licenses, and passports fall into this category.

>> **Current vehicle license plates or plates that claim to resemble current ones:** Note that expired license plates (at least three years old) are considered collectible — as long as they are no longer valid for use on a vehicle and you mention the plate's age in the listing.

>> **Lock-picking devices:** These items can be sold only to authorized recipients. Federal law prohibits the mailing of such devices.

>> **Human parts and remains:** Hey, we all have two kidneys, but if you get the urge to sell one to pay your bills, eBay is not the place to sell it. You can't sell your sperm, eggs, blood, or anything else you manage to extricate from your body. What's more, you can't even *give* away any of these items as a free bonus with one of your auctions.

>> **Drugs or drug paraphernalia:** Narcotics, steroids, or other controlled substances may not be listed. Drug paraphernalia includes a swath of items that are primarily intended or designed for using a controlled substance, including vaporizers, bongs, and water pipes.

>> **Anything that requires a prescription from a doctor, a dentist, or an optometrist to dispense:** Listen, just because it's legal to use doesn't mean that it doesn't require special permission to get. For example, even though penicillin is legal to buy in the United States, only a doctor can prescribe it — which is why, when you get sick, you have to stand in that *loooong* line at the pharmacy sneezing on all the other sick people. And if you're looking for Viagra auctions on eBay, don't even *go* there.

>> **Stocks, bonds, or negotiable securities:** Nope, you can't sell stock in your new pie-baking company or an investment in property you may own. And if you're thinking of offering credit to someone, you can't do that either. (Note that collectible items are permitted.)

>> **Bulk email lists:** No bulk email or mailing lists that contain personal identifying information. You may not even sell tools or software designed to send unsolicited commercial email or promote social-media "likes" or recruit "followers."

>> **Animals and wildlife, including animal parts from endangered species:** If you've had it with Buster, your pet ferret, don't look to eBay for help in finding him a new home. And you can't sell your stuffed spotted owls or rhino-horn love potions, either. If you're in the animal business — *any* animal business — eBay is not the place for you.

>> **Child pornography:** Note that this material is strictly prohibited on eBay, but you can sell other forms of erotica.

>> **Forged items:** Autographs from celebrities and sports figures are big business — and a big opportunity for forgers. Selling a forgery is a criminal act. The state of New York is taking the lead on this issue, investigating at least two dozen suspected forgery cases linked with online auctions.

TIP

If you're in the market for an autograph, don't even consider bidding on one unless it comes with a *Certificate of Authenticity* (COA) or a letter of authenticity (LOA). eBay requires that sellers give buyers the right to a full refund if any doubt about authenticity crops ups. Figure 9-3 shows an item that comes with a personal COA from an auction on eBay.

The FBI investigates and takes down those who sell forgeries on the Internet. For some interesting reading, check out the FBI's `Operation Bullpen` at

`www.fbi.gov/sandiego/about-us/history/operation-bullpen`.

You can find out more about professional authentication services in Chapter 16.

>> **Items that infringe on someone else's copyright or trademark:** Take a look at the very next section for details on infringing items.

>> **Stolen items:** Need I say more? (Seems obvious, but you'd be surprised.) If what you're thinking about selling came to you by way of a five-finger discount or fell off a truck, don't sell it on eBay.

FIGURE 9-3:
When bidding on an item with a personal COA, be sure that the seller is reputable (check the feedback).

The item you are bidding on is a 3x5 Card, Autographed by the late James Stewart ....

The card is white and in mint condition... Signed bold and clear, in black felt tip pen ...

This Autograph is 100% Genuine, and I will provide my COA that Guarantees it for life...

REMEMBER

Ignorance is no excuse. If you list an item that's in any way prohibited on eBay, eBay will end your listing. If you have any questions, always check eBay's Trust & Safety department at

www.ebay.com/help/policies/prohibited-restricted-items/prohibited-restricted-items?id=4207.

Infringing items

In school, if you copied someone's work, you were busted for plagiarism. Profiting from a copy of someone else's legally owned *intellectual property* is an *infringement* violation. Infringement, also known as *piracy*, is the encroachment on another person's legal ownership rights on an item, a trademark, or a copyright. eBay prohibits the selling of infringing items at its site.

Here's a checklist of no-no items commonly found at the center of infringement violations:

>> Music that's been recorded from an original compact disc, cassette tape, or record.

HOT PROPERTY BUSTED

In 1961, a young jockey named John Sellers won his first Kentucky Derby on a horse named Carry Back. He was so emotional about the victory that he was crying as he crossed the finish line. Seventeen years later, someone broke into his California home and stole his priceless trophy. But today, more than two decades after it was stolen, it's back in his possession — thanks to an observant eBay member. The prized trophy was put up for auction in 1999, by a seller who had bought it legitimately. An eBay member who knew the history of the trophy saw that it was for sale and alerted the seller. The seller stopped the auction immediately, contacted the former jockey, and personally returned the trophy to him. Now that's a great finish!

>> Movies that have been recorded from an original DVD, laser disc, or commercial VHS tape.

>> E-books you purchased for your own use and do not have the rights to resell or distribute.

>> Television shows that have been recorded off the air, off cable, or from a satellite service.

TIP

Selling a used *original* CD, tape, commercial VHS movie cassette, DVD, or CD-ROM is perfectly legal. Some television shows have sold recorded episodes; you can sell those originals as well. But if you're tempted to sell a personal copy that you made of an original, you are committing an infringing violation.

>> Software and computer games that have been copied from CD-ROMs or disks (and that includes hard drives — anybody's).

>> Counterfeit items (also called *knock-offs*), such as clothes and jewelry, that have been produced, copied, or imitated without the permission of the manufacturer. (Bart Simpson knock-off T-shirts abounded in the early '90s.)

WARNING

If you pick up a brand-name item dirt cheap from a discount store, you can check to see whether it's counterfeit by taking a look at the label or comparing it with like items on a Google image search. If something isn't quite right, the item may be a knock-off.

REMEMBER

Trademark and copyright protection don't just cover software, music, and movies. Clothing, toys, sunglasses, and books are among the items covered by law.

Intellectual-property owners actively defend their rights and, along with help from average eBay users, continually tip off eBay to fraudulent and infringing auctions. Rights owners can use eBay's Verified Rights Owner (VeRO) Program, as well as law-enforcement agencies. (See "Intellectual Property Violations," later in this chapter, for info about the VeRO program.)

Restricted items: Know the laws

Because some items are prohibited in one place and not another, eBay lists a few items that you can trade but that are restricted and regulated. As a member of eBay, you're responsible for knowing the restrictions in your area — as well as those on the eBay website.

Certain items are illegal in one geographic area and not another. This list mentions a few of the major questionable items:

>> **Event tickets:** Laws regarding the resale of event tickets vary from state to state, even city to city. Some laws prohibit reselling the ticket for a price higher than the amount printed on the face of the ticket. Some states limit the amount you can add to the ticket's face value. Be sure to double-check your state website for laws covering ticket sales. An event search engine website, SeatGeek, keeps a pretty up-to-date listing of the laws. You can find the information in an article on SeatGeek at

   `http://seatgeek.com/blog/ticket-industry/ticket-resale-laws#lawsbystate.`

   Be certain that you're following the appropriate laws for your area.

>> **Wine and alcohol:** Selling wine and alcohol on eBay — and anywhere else, for that matter — is tricky business. For starters, you have no business in this business unless you're at least 21 years old and licensed to sell. eBay does not permit sales of any alcohol products unless they are sold without their contents for their "collectible" containers. You may sell wine for consumption if you have a license to sell and ship wine and are pre-approved by eBay.

Forbidden tactics

The folks on eBay didn't just fall off the turnip truck. eBay staffers have seen just about every scam to get around paying fees or following policy guidelines. Chances are good that if you try one of these scams, you'll get caught. Then eBay cancels the listing. Do it once, and shame on you (don't count on getting the listing fee credited back to you). Do it a lot, and you're no longer welcome on eBay.

The following items are definitely forbidden:

- >> **Raffles and prizes:** You need to *sell something* in your auction; you can't offer a chance to win a prize either by chance or a giveaway. You can offer to give away a bonus product with a sold item.

- >> **Advertisements:** An eBay listing is not the place to make a sales pitch (other than attractive copy describing your item, that is) for an item for sale elsewhere. Some eBay bad guys list an item name and then use the post to send bidders to some other auction or website. The Real Estate category and eBay Motors are exceptions. You can run a classified ad there to sell property.

- >> **Bait-and-switch tactics:** These are a variation on the ugly old sales technique of pretending to sell what you're not really selling. Some eBay users who are selling an unfamiliar brand of an item try to snag bidders by putting a more familiar brand in the title. For example, writing *Designer Chanel purse — not really, but a lot like it!* is a fake-out. eBay calls it *keyword spamming.* I call it lousy.

- >> **Mixing apples with oranges:** This gambit tries to attract more bidders to view an item by putting it in a high-traffic category where it doesn't belong. Forget it. eBay may move it for you if necessary, but keeping that rutabaga recipe book *away* from the list of automotive repair manuals is more considerate.

- >> **Go emoji-less:** Although it may seem that using emoji might be a way to get eyes on your title, don't. The folks at eBay saw this potential headache coming, and quickly banned the use of special characters, superscript, and subscript in titles and subtitles.

- >> **Duplicate listings:** You may not list more than one fixed-price listing of an identical item at the same time. If you are running an auction, you may have more than one listing for identical items. Auctions for identical items listed by the same seller will be filtered by eBay, and only one duplicate listing without bids will appear at a time.

Reporting a Problem Listing

You probably think that eBay can't possibly monitor millions of items for sale on a daily basis. You're right; it can't. eBay relies on eBay members like you to let it know when you suspect a shady listing is afoot. If you ever smell something fishy, for goodness' sake, report it to eBay. Sometimes eBay takes a few days to cancel a listing, but rest assured that eBay invests time to protect its users from fraudulent listings and violations of policy.

If you see something that just doesn't look right, you should report the listing using an online form by clicking the Report Item link, which is on the right, on the same line as the Description tab on every eBay item page.

Intellectual Property Violations

If you own intellectual property that you think is being infringed upon by an item for sale on the eBay site, you should take advantage of the eBay *Verified Rights Owner* (VeRO) Program. Owners of trademarked or copyrighted items and logos, as well as other forms of intellectual property, can become members of this program for free.

You can find out more about the VeRO Program by going to

www.ebay.com/help/policies/listing-policies/selling-policies/intellectual-property-vero-program?id=4349.

Read the information there; if you qualify, click to download the form, fill it out, and email or fax it to eBay. Then you're on your way to protecting your intellectual property from being sold to the highest bidder. Remember, only *you* can stop the infringement madness. If eBay agrees with you that your intellectual property is being infringed upon, it invalidates the sale and informs the seller by email that the item "is not authorized." The high bidders in an auction are also notified and warned that there was an issue with the listing.

I participate in the VeRO Program. Should someone think it's a good idea to digitize and sell counterfeit copies of my books, I file my VeRO notice, and the listing is removed within hours.

WARNING

eBay understands that sometimes people don't know that they're selling infringing items, but it draws a hard line on repeat offenders. eBay not only shuts down the offenders' listings but can also suspend repeat offenders. Also, eBay cooperates with the proper authorities on behalf of its VeRO Program members.

If eBay deems your listing or transaction to be invalid because the item doesn't meet eBay's policies and guidelines, you can find out why by checking the page at

www.ebay.com/help/selling/listings/creating-managing-listings/removed-listings?id=4656.

If you still feel that you're in the right, find the Contact Us link. Click there to plead your case.

eBay Fees? What eBay Fees? Oops . . .

The "Cliché Police" are going to raid me sooner or later, but here's one I'm poking a few holes in this time around: *You gotta spend it to make it.* This old-time business chestnut means that you need to invest a fair amount of money before you can turn a profit. Although the principle still holds true in the real world (at least most of the time), on eBay you don't have to spend much to start your business. This is one reason why eBay has become one of the most successful e-commerce companies on the Internet. eBay keeps fees low and volume high.

MARSHA SAYS

In this chapter I'm giving you a simple overview of fees, based on my assumption that you are just beginning to sell on eBay. When you move into the higher levels of selling, the fee structure can get more complex. Since I personally sell on eBay only part-time, these are the fees I pay attention to.

For the beginning seller (without an eBay Store), eBay charges the following types of fees for listing on the site:

>> **Auction and Fixed-price insertion fees:** Up to 50 listings are free per month. After that, $0.35 per additional listing. (Canada $.30)

>> **Real estate listing fees:** These vary because you have the choice of listing your property as an ad rather than an auction. Because eBay real estate auctions are *nonbinding* (due to legalities), you may be better off running an ad. (eBay Canada charges the same fees for auctions or fixed-price real estate listings). eBay charges different prices for different types of real estate:

- *Timeshares, manufactured homes, and land*

  Auction-style/fixed-price: 1-, 3-, 5-, 7-, or 10-day listing ($35); 30-day listing ($50)

  Classified Ad format: 30-day listing ($150); 90-day listing ($300)

- *Residential, commercial, and other real estate*

  Auction-style/fixed-price: 1-, 3-, 5-, 7-, or 10-day listing ($100); 30-day listing ($150)

  Classified Ad format: 30-day listing ($150), 90-day listing ($300)

>> **Motors (Automotive) fees:** For low-volume sellers (who post six or fewer vehicle listings per calendar year), both eBay U.S. and eBay Canada allow the first six listings free, with subsequent listings $50; motorcycles are only $20.

>> **Additional reserve-price auction fees:** $5; auctions with reserves over $150 are charged 7.5 percent of the reserve, with a maximum of $250.

>> **Final value fees:** A percentage of the sales price (read further on).

>> **Optional fees:** Vary.

TIP

Here's a snapshot of how a reserve price affects your auction insertion fee. If you set a starting bid of $0.99 for a gold Rolex watch (say what?), but your reserve price is $5,000 (that's more like it), you're charged a 7.5 percent reserve fee based on the $5,000 reserve price (but no more than $5. (See Table 9-1, for more fees.)

TABLE 9-1 **eBay Optional-Upgrade Fees**

Option	Fee (Auction)		Fee (Good 'Til Cancelled)	
	Starting at up to $150	Starting price over $150	Fixed price up to $150	Fixed price over $150
1- or 3-day duration	$1.00	$1.00	n/a	n/a
Boldface title	$2.00	$3.00	$4.00	$6.00
Gallery Plus (free in the Collectibles, Art, Pottery & Glass, and Antiques categories)	$0.35	$0.70	$1.00	$2.00
List in two categories	Double-listing and upgrade fees		Double-listing and upgrade fees per month	
Listing Designer	$0.10	$0.20	$0.30	$0.60
Subtitle	$1.00	$3.00	$1.50	$6.00
International site visibility	Auctions on a tiered scale based on starting price from $0.10 to $0.40		All fixed-price listings $0.50	
Auction BIN (Buy It Now)	Free			

So what does the insertion fee buy you on eBay?

>> A really snazzy-looking display page for your item that millions of eBay members can see, admire, and breathlessly respond to. (Well, we can only hope.)

>> The use of eBay services, such as the Trust & Safety program, which protects your selling experience. (Chapter 16 tells you how to use the Security Center (when necessary) during and after your sale.)

Final value fees

If you follow the movie business, you hear about some big A-list stars who take a relatively small fee for making a film but negotiate a big percentage of the gross profits. This is known as a *back-end deal* — in effect, a commission based on how much the movie brings in. eBay does the same thing, taking a small *insertion fee* when you list your item and then a commission on the back end when you sell your item. This commission is called the *final value fee* (FVF) and is based on the total amount of the sale (the selling price of the item, shipping, and any other fees a seller may charge, excluding any sales tax).

TIP

eBay doesn't charge a final value fee on a listing in the Real Estate/Timeshares category as they do in other categories; instead, they charge a flat *notice fee* of $35 rather than an FVF for Timeshares, Land, and Manufactured Homes. There's no fee for Residential, Commercial, and Other. But in the Motors category, you pay a "Successful listing" fee of $60 for passenger vehicles if your listing ends with a final amount under $2,000. If your item's final bid is over $2,000, you'll pay a $125 fee.

In real life, when you pay sales commissions on a big purchase such as a house, you usually pay a fixed percentage. It is the same on eBay. A listing's final value fee (whether auction or fixed price) is 10 percent (with a maximum of $750) in most categories. Books, DVDs & Movies, Music are 12 percent. This is taken from the total amount of the sale, including the final price of the item, shipping charges, and any other amounts you may charge the buyer. Sales tax is not included.

REMEMBER

Final value fees are different (and lower) for eBay Store owners. Chapter 11 explains that, and more.

Here's a sample final value fee calculation for a successful listing:

>> You sell an item for $95 with a shipping cost of $5.

>> Your final value fee on the total amount is 10 percent of $100 ($10.00).

Managed Payments and PayPal fees

Currently, sellers on eBay have options on how they want to collect their money in payment for sales on the site. I've used PayPal since eBay began because it's a safe way to transact online. I recommend it for you when you start out on the site. PayPal currently charges 2.9 percent of the total collected and $0.30 per transaction. Discounts are available as you move more money through the service, but if you bank on that, it's always a safe estimate. Further on, I recommend an eBay fee calculator. It's an excellent way to estimate your costs *before* you list an item.

But by 2021, all sellers will have to receive payments through eBay's new payment system, Managed Payments, and eBay will send the money to the seller's bank. eBay will be sending out information to sellers via email as this service progresses.

Keep calculating your profits

When you've finished all the legwork needed to make some money, do some brain work to keep track of your results. The best place to keep watch on your eBay sales is on your My eBay page, a great place to stay organized while you're conducting all your eBay business. (I describe all the functions of the page in Chapter 4.) When it comes to calculating your bottom line, it's best to get used to using a program like QuickBooks.

Before you list, calculate your fees; calculate every last penny! There's a free, eBay calculator Salecalc at `https://salecalc.com/ebay` shown in Figure 9-4.

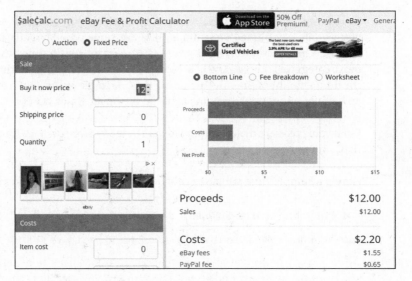

FIGURE 9-4:
As you type in your costs on Salecalc, graph bars move to show where your costs and profits rise and fall.

I personally use Salecalc because it includes all possible fees (even PayPal) and store discounts. They also update the site when eBay fees change. On Salecalc, you can work your math backward. If (say) you'd like to make 20 percent on an item, the calculator tells you how much profit you'll make — after calculating all the fees and costs for you. Salecalc also offers an app for Apple mobile devices: `https://appsto.re/us/2L0_3.i`.

TIP

Here's a checklist of what to watch out for after the sale ends:

>> **Keep an eye on how much you're spending to place items up for sale on eBay.** You don't want any nasty surprises, and you don't want to find out that you spent more money to set up your listing than you received selling your item.

>> **Keep track of your expenses for your taxes.** I explain Uncle Sam's tax position on eBay next. Stay tuned.

>> **Make sure that you get refunds and credits when they're due.**

>> **Double-check your figures to make certain eBay hasn't made mistakes.** If you have any questions about the accounting, let eBay know.

Uncle Sam Wants You — to Pay Your Taxes

What would a chapter about money be without a discussion of taxes? As Ben Franklin knew (and we've all found out since), you can't escape death and taxes. (Hey, it's not a cliché; it's accepted wisdom.) Whether in cyberspace or face-to-face life, never forget that Uncle Sam is always your business partner.

From 2011 on, the IRS receives a 1099-K form from PayPal that reflects the total transaction amounts for sellers who have completed over 200 transactions or who have had over $20,000 in transactions paid through their site. You will have to include this income on your annual income tax filing, so filing your taxes may become a bit more complex. To get more information on this IRS form from payment processors, visit this page: http://PayPal.com/IRS.

You will have to file a Schedule 1040-C, "Profit or Loss From Business." Here you will have to post your income (and expenses) for your eBay business.

REMEMBER

Be sure to keep track of all your eBay business expenses to offset your profits. If you live outside the United States, check the tax laws in that country so you don't end up with a headache down the road.

REMEMBER

As with offline transactions, knowledge is power. The more you know about buying and selling on eBay before you actually start doing it, the more savvy the impression you make — and the more satisfying your experience.

For in-depth details on taxes and bookkeeping, check out my book, *eBay Business All-in-One For Dummies.*

Two wild rumors about federal taxes

I've heard some rumors about not having to pay taxes on eBay profits. If you hear any variation on this theme, smile politely and don't believe a word of it. In this section, I discuss two of the more popular (and seriously mistaken) tax notions running around the eBay community these days.

The U.S. government uses two laws on the books to go after eBay outlaws. One is the Federal Trade Commission (FTC) Act, which prohibits deceptive or misleading transactions in commerce. The other is the Mail or Telephone Order Merchandise Rule, which requires sellers to ship merchandise in a timely manner or offer to refund a consumer's money. The FTC is in charge of pursuing these violations. If you have a question about federal laws, you can find a lot of information online. For example, I found these two websites keep current lists of U.S. law and federal codes that affect e-commerce sellers:

`www.ftc.gov/tips-advice/business-center/guidance/business-guide-ftcs-mail-internet-or-telephone-order`

`www.fourmilab.ch/ustax/ustax.html` (Click the Contents link for easy-to-locate links.)

Rumor #1: e-commerce isn't taxed

One story claims that "there will be no taxes on e-commerce sales (sales conducted online) for three years." No one ever seems to know when those three years start or end.

Well, presently it *is* three years down the pike from the Marketplace Fairness Act of 2013, and Internet sales tax has become a reality. The good news is most states have a threshold of $100,000 in sales before you have to collect sales tax from sales within their state. A good, updated reference is this chart from the Sales Tax Institute: `www.salestaxinstitute.com/resources/economic-nexus-state-guide`.

If your state charges sales tax, odds are you have to charge sales tax for orders within your own state. To get an idea of which states these are, visit this page: `www.salestaxinstitute.com/resources/rates`. On this page, click the name of your state for even more information on how sales tax is handled in your state.

Since I am not a tax professional, please check with your tax advisor or your state small-business portal as to how taxes will affect your sales.

Rumor #2: Profits from garage sales are tax exempt

"eBay is like a garage sale, and you don't have to pay taxes on garage sales." (Uh-huh. And the calories in ice cream don't count if you eat it out of the carton. Who comes up with this stuff anyway?)

This notion is just an urban (or shall I say *suburban*) legend — somebody's wishful thinking that's become folklore. If you make money on a garage sale, you have to declare it as income — just like anything else you make money on. Most people never make any money on garage sales because they usually sell things for far less than they bought them for. However, the opposite is often true of an eBay transaction.

WARNING

Even if you lose money, you may have to prove it to the government, especially if you're running a small business. You most definitely should have a heart-to-heart talk with your accountant or tax professional as to how to file your taxes. If something might look bad in an audit if you *don't* declare it, consider that a big hint.

To get the reliable word, I checked with the IRS's e-commerce office. The good folks there told me that even if you make as little as a buck on any eBay sale after all your expenses (the cost of the item, eBay fees, shipping charges), you still have to declare it as income on your federal tax return.

If you have questions about eBay sales and your federal taxes, check with your personal advisor, call the IRS Help Line at 800-829-1040, or visit the IRS website at www.irs.gov. And be friendly. (Just in case.)

State sales tax

If your state has sales tax, a *sales tax number* is required before you *officially* sell something. If sales tax applies, you may have to collect the appropriate sales tax for every sale that falls within the state that your business is in. A 1992 U.S. Supreme Court decision said that states can only require sellers that have a physical presence in the same state as the consumer to collect so-called use taxes, but all that may have changed.

In addition to the sales tax links listed in this section, to find the regulations for your state, visit the following site, which provides links to every state's tax board. The tax board should have the answers to your questions:

www.taxsites.com/State-Links.html.

State income taxes

Yes, it's true. Not only is Uncle Sam in Washington, D.C., looking for his slice of your eBay profits, but your state government may also be hankering to join the feast.

TIP

If you have a good accountant, give that esteemed individual a call. If you don't have one, find a tax professional in your area. Tax professionals actually do more than just process your income tax returns once a year; they can help you avoid major pitfalls even before April 15.

Here's how to find out what your responsibilities are in your home state:

>> You may need to collect and pay state sales taxes, but only if you sell to someone in your state.

>> You can get tax information online at this website:

www.taxadmin.org/state-tax-forms.

The site has links to tax information for all 50 states.

>> You can also call your state tax office and let the good folks there explain the requirements. The state tax office should be listed in the government section of your state government website.

IN THIS CHAPTER

» **Preparing to set up your listing**

» **Writing your item description**

» **Deciding on your options**

» **Making changes after your item is listed**

Chapter **10**

Time to Sell: Making Irresistible Listings

t's time to make some money. Are you ready? Yes? (Call it an inspired guess.) You're on the threshold of adding your items to all those that go up for sale on eBay every day (and perhaps also shedding from your home some of the valuable things you haven't touched in years). Some listings are so hot that sellers quadruple their investments. Other items, unfortunately, are so stone cold that they may not even sell. Although, when you pay attention to your listing and tweak as you go, I've found nearly everything sells eventually.

In this chapter, I explain the facets of setting up your listings and take the mystery out of the page you fill out to get your auction going (or item selling) on eBay. You get some advice that can increase your odds of making money and standing out from the over 1.2 billion active listings on the site worldwide. I also show you how to modify, relist, or end your listing when you need to.

MARSHA SAYS

A caveat here: To keep the marketplace up to date, eBay is constantly working to improve the site, and improvement means change. The form you use to list an item for sale (as I describe in this chapter) my change from time to time, but the basic decisions you need to make will not. The selling philosophy laid out in this chapter will help you ride the waves of change on eBay — whatever they may be.

Getting Ready to List Your Item

After you decide what you want to sell, find out as much as you can about it and conduct a little market research. Then you should have a good idea of the item's popularity and market value. To get this info, check out Chapter 9. You can start on a smartphone or tablet by uploading your photos to start a draft, or begin directly on a PC and import the photos from there. In Chapter 14, I show you how I start my listings on my phone and complete them on my laptop. The instructions that follow are for your computer. It's a much more robust listing tool.

Before you list your item, make sure that you have these bases covered:

>> **The specific category under which you want the item listed:** Ask yourself where you'd look for such an item — and also remember the categories you saw most frequently when you conducted your market research with the eBay search function. (Further on, I show you how eBay will help you here as well.)

TIP

Not everyone does, but you *may* see that eBay has two item-listing forms. There's a Quick Listing form and one with Advanced options. If you've landed on the Quick form, I recommend you select the Switch to Advanced Tool link at the top of the form. When you list items, not everything is intuitive (or perhaps your memory can fade), and I prefer to see all the options each time so that I can decide which ones I want to use for each individual listing.

>> **What you want to say in your item description:** Jot down ideas. Take a good look at your item; especially if it's in its original box, go over every inch of both the item and its box, and make a list of keywords that describe it. *Keywords* are single descriptive words that can include the following (this is hardly a complete list):

- Brand name

- Complete model name (research helps here)

- Size of the item (citing measurements if appropriate)

- Age, date, or country of manufacture

- Bar code to find the UPC (Universal Product Code) or GTIN (Global Trade Identification Number)

- Manufacturer's part number (MPN)

- Condition (new or used)

- Rarity

- Color

- Size

- Material

I know all about writer's block. If you're daunted by the listing page, struggle through it anyway. This way you've finished the hard work before you even begin.

>> **Whether you want to attach a picture (or pictures) to your description via a Uniform Resource Locator (URL):** Pictures sell items, and it's important to have multiples. You can upload photos to eBay easily from your computer, or store them on a website and use the URL to bring them into your item's description for extra punch. (This information won't be on the test, but if you want to know more about uploading pictures from your smartphone to a draft listing, see Chapter 14.) Figure 10-1 shows photos that were uploaded from my phone and are being edited on my computer in a listing draft.

>> **The price at which you think you can sell the item:** Be as realistic as you can. (That's where your market research comes in.)

FIGURE 10-1:
eBay's cropping and editing tools make picture-perfect a snap.

Examining the Create Listing Page

Begin by clicking the word *Sell* in the navigation bar at the top of the eBay page. After you've clicked, you land at your Seller Hub. On the top right is a link to Create Listing. Click there and you'll have a choice to list a single item or multiple listings, which helps you set up a template that will appear the same if you have many listings. You can fill in the individual details separately for each listing.

If you're not a product specialist, you may want to have different information for each of your items. I sell many different types of products, so I create each listing individually. That way I'm sure not to leave out any details. Once your business ramps up to dozens of items a week, you might automate more.

When you dive into the listing process, be sure to read what appears on the forms. Filling out this virtual paperwork requires a few minutes of clicking, typing, and answering numerous questions. The good news is that when you're finished, your listing is up and running and (I hope) starting to earn you money.

Before you begin, you have to be registered on eBay as a seller. If you still need to register, go to Chapter 2 and fill out the preliminary online paperwork. If you've registered but haven't provided eBay with your financial information (credit card or checking account), you'll be asked for this information to set up your seller account before you proceed. Fill in the data on the secure form, then you're ready to roll.

eBay can be like the dizzying menu in a Chinese restaurant: You have lots of choices for selling an item on eBay — three, in fact. Three ways may not seem to be very dizzying, unless you're trying to decide psychically which format is the best for you. Here's what you need to know about each type:

MARSHA SAYS

One of the most important parts of the listing (aside from the description) are the Item Specifics. These vary from category to category and include drop-down menus or fill-in items like ISBN numbers, materials, brand names, and so on. The more you can fill out in this area, the better. Your placement in searches may depend on as fully a filled-out form as you can provide. Later in this chapter, there's more information on how to use these.

>> **Auction:** This is the tried-and-true format that made eBay famous. People enjoy auctions for desirable items, and you can combine the format with a Buy It Now option for those who want to buy the item immediately. Often, if you're selling a collectible item, letting it go to auction may net you a much higher profit — just remember to do your research *before* listing.

>> **Fixed-price:** As with shopping at the corner store or any e-commerce shopping site, a fixed-price sale is easy for the buyer to comprehend and complete. This includes items you sell in your eBay Store.

TIP

A variation on a fixed-price listing is to add the Make an Offer option. This enables buyers to hope they can get a deep discount — but you have the opportunity to accept their offer, deny it, or make a counteroffer. Cultural leanings toward bargaining may lead some buyers to prefer this method. You may not. It can be fun, however, and is just another way to spur sales for a slow-selling product.

>> **Classified ad:** If you don't want to put your property, services, or other valuable items up for auction, and you'd like to correspond with the prospective buyer, this is the option for you. Although this option originated with eBay real estate sales, the Classified ad is available in specific categories; if it's available, you'll find it on the listing page under Format (on the advanced listing form). The cost of your ad is $9.95 for a 30-day listing ($150 in the Real Estate category).

When listing your item for sale or auction, here's *some* of the info you're asked to fill out (each of these items is discussed in detail later in this chapter):

>> **Category:** The category where you've decided to list your item (required).

>> **Title:** The name of your item (required).

>> **Description:** What you want to tell eBay buyers about your item (required).

>> **Photos:** Upload your images that you want to appear at the top of your listing. You are allowed 12 for free (the first picture becomes your Gallery photo, which appears in searches). You can add more to your description (there's no extra charge for this), if necessary. (Chapter 14 has more information on using images in your listings.)

>> **Item location:** The region, city, and country from which the item will be shipped (required).

>> **Quantity:** The number of items you're putting up for sale in this listing. In an auction it is always one (required).

>> **Starting price:** The starting price (sometimes called a *minimum bid*) you set (required in an auction).

>> **Selling price:** If this is a fixed-price listing, you have to post the selling price of the item.

>> **Best Offer**: Whether you want to allow potential buyers to make an offer for your item.

MARSHA SAYS

A sweet eBay feature is the option to send special deals to customers who have marked your item to "Watch." More on how to use this to build profits in Chapter 13.

>> **Duration:** The number of days you want the auction or fixed-price listing to run (required). The option *Good 'till cancelled* will repeat your listing every month until it sells.

>> **Reserve price:** The hidden target price you set for an auction. This is the price that must be met before this item can be sold (optional).

eBay charges a fee for the reserve-price feature. See Chapter 9 for the pricing of eBay's features.

>> **Private:** You can keep the identity of all bidders or buyers secret with this option (optional). This type of auction is used only in special circumstances.

>> **Buy It Now:** You can sell your item directly to the first buyer who is willing to pay this price. This is optional in auctions but required in fixed-price listings.

>> **List item in two categories:** If you want to double your exposure, you can list your item in two categories. Note that double exposure equals double listing fees (optional).

>> **Shipping details:** Here's where you can indicate where you're willing to ship an item. If you don't want the hassle of shipping out of the United States, check the option that restricts shipment to USA only. You can individually select different countries as well (optional).

You may want to consider whether you *really* want to be in the international shipping business early in your eBay career. Buyers pick up the tab, but you have to deal with customs forms and post-office paperwork. (You can make that easier by printing your customs forms along with your postage from your computer — see Chapter 12.) Keep in mind that if you don't ship internationally, you're blocking a bunch of possible high bidders. Depending on what you're selling, shipping internationally may or may not be worth the investment in extra time.

>> **Shipping and handling charges:** eBay requires you to show your shipping charge in the listing. Buyers are more likely to bid or buy right then and there if they feel your shipping costs are reasonable or free. Consider that when you list a flat shipping charge (or even free shipping) on your listing, eBay will take that into account when deciding how your item shows up in search results. For larger items, see information on eBay's handy shipping calculator, later in this chapter, in the section "Setting shipping terms."

>> **Payment instructions:** Here's the place you put any after-sale information. Until eBay changes to Managed Payments for all sellers, you are required to accept PayPal or at least one electronic payment or Internet merchant credit card option for your items. (These are the safest options anyway.) This information appears at the top of your listing when the sale is completed, under the Shipping and payments tab of the listing while it's active, and in the End of Listing email (optional).

When eBay Managed Payments takes over on the site, buyers will be able to pay for their items in a multitude of ways – but you will get *your* payments directly from eBay.

>> **PayPal and immediate payment:** Fill in this area if you want to require the high bidder to pay through PayPal immediately when using Buy It Now. Add the Immediate Payment option if you want the winner to pay with a click of the mouse (optional).

>> **Return policy:** You are required to state whether you are willing to accept returns. You can give the customer as few as three days to return the item (that cuts down on spurious returns). It's okay if you don't accept returns, but you must post that information in your listing.

Filling In the Required Blanks

Yes, the selling form looks daunting, but filling out its many sections doesn't take as long as you may think. Some of the questions you're asked aren't things you even have to think about; just click an answer and off you go. Other questions ask you to type information. Don't sweat a thing; all the answers you need are right here. In this section I describe all the required info; later in this chapter, I talk about optional stuff. After you click your category, you land on the official Sell page.

eBay has two different types of Selling pages. One is "advanced" and the other is the "quick listing tool." If you do not see all the options mentioned in the chapter, eBay may make some (unintended) decisions for you about how to list your item for sale. To be able to fully customize your listing and take control of all the options, click the Switch to Advanced Tool link in the upper right corner of the page to get the full-featured Sell Your Item form.

Selecting a category

Many eBay sellers will tell you that selecting the exact category isn't crucial to achieving the highest price for your item — and they're right. The bulk of buyers (who know what they're looking for) just input search keywords into eBay's search box and look for their items. Others may select a category and peruse the items for sale to see whether a particular one strikes their fancy (just like going to the mall but without the parking hassles).

On the first page of the Sell form, you select the main category for your item. Type the UPC or the ISBN number from the code of a new product. If there is no visible barcode, type at least three keywords that best describe your item into the box provided, and then click Search. Figure 10-2 shows you how the results came up after I typed words for a title into my smartphone, making it easier to identify my item and select a category. You can always change this before you launch the listing.

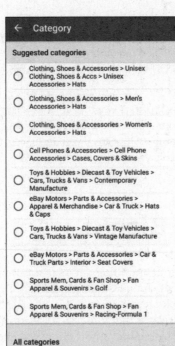

FIGURE 10-2:
Select the category where you feel your item belongs.

TIP

Here's where your creativity can come into play. Who says that a box of Blue Dog (the famous dog icon painted by Cajun artist George Rodrigue) note cards belongs in Everything Else (where most greeting cards are listed)? If you look around, you may find a better category, such as Art. The Find Categories tool appears the second you open the selling page. Just click the associated link to browse for categories. Check to see whether anyone else is selling the item (and in which category) — or just let this tool help you pick a good category.

You can also browse the categories by clicking (surprise!) the Browse Categories link on this page. This will help you select your main category, and the thousands of subcategories. eBay offers you this wealth of choices in a handy point-and-click way. If you're unfamiliar with the types of items you can actually *find* in those categories, you may want to pore over Chapter 3 before you choose a category to describe *your* item.

Most bidders scan for specific items in subcategories. For example, if you're selling a Bakelite fruit pin, don't just list it under Jewelry; keep narrowing your choices. In this case, you can put it in a costume-jewelry category that is especially for Bakelite. (I guarantee that the real Bakelite jewelry collectors out there know where to look to find the jewelry they love.) To narrow the category of your item, just keep clicking until you hit the end of the line.

SOME CATEGORIES AREN'T FOR EVERYONE

If you've chosen to list an item, bid on an item, or even just browse in the Everything Else: Adult Only subcategory, you need to follow separate, specific guidelines because that category contains graphic nudity or sexual content that may offend some community members. You must

- Be at least 18 years of age (but you already know that all eBay customers must be 18 or older in the first place).

- Have a valid credit card.

- Complete a waiver stating that you're voluntarily choosing to access adults-only materials. For more on how to do this (and a handy primer on privacy issues), see Chapter 15.

If you have adult or erotic items that you'd like to sell in a private auction, check out the later section, "I want to be alone: The private listing."

Creating the perfect item title

After you figure out what category you want to list in, eBay wants to get down to brass tacks — what the heck to call that thing you're trying to sell.

Think of your item title as a catchy Internet story title. The most valuable real estate on eBay is the 80-character title of your item. *The majority of buyers do title searches, and that's where your item must come up to be sold!* Give the most essential information right away in the form of keywords to grab the eye of the reader who's just browsing. Be clear and informative enough to get noticed by eBay's search engine.

Here are some ideas to help you write your item title:

>> Use the most common name for the item.

>> If the item is rare, vintage, or hard to find, mention that.

>> State the item's condition and whether it's new or old.

>> Include the item's special qualities, such as its style, model, or edition number.

>> Avoid fancy punctuation or unusual characters, such as $, multiple hyphens, and L@@K, because they just clutter up the title — and buyers don't search for them.

When you get into advanced selling mode, you should take a look at one of my other books, coauthored by Patti Louise Ruby, *eBay Listings That Sell For Dummies*. It covers eBay photography and HTML for your descriptions, in depth.

Ordinarily, I don't throw out French phrases just for the fun of it. But where making a profit is an issue, I definitely have to agree with the French that choosing or not choosing *le mot juste* can mean the difference between having potential bidders merely see your auction and having an all-out bidding war on your hands. Read on for tips about picking *the best words* to let your listing shine.

Look for a phrase that pays

Here's a crash course in eBay lingo that can help bring you up to speed on attracting buyers to your item. The following words are used frequently in eBay listings, and they can do wonders to jump-start your title:

>> Mint

>> One of a kind (or OOAK — see the abbreviation list in Table 10-1)

>> Vintage

>> Collectible

>> Rare

>> Unique

>> Primitive

>> Well-loved

MARSHA SAYS

In Table 10-1, you find collector-specific abbreviations. If you're looking to sell to a general audience, I recommend *not* using them. Consider these acronyms to be professional-grade terms that might just confuse a casual buyer.

There's a whole science (called *grading*) to figuring out the value of a collectible. You're ahead of the game if you have a pretty good idea of what most eBay members mean. Do your homework before you assign a grade to your item. If you need more information on what these grades actually mean, Chapter 5 provides a translation.

eBay lingo at a glance

Grading terms and the phrases in the preceding section aren't the only marketing standards you have at your eBay disposal. As eBay has grown, so has the lingo that members use as shortcuts to describe their merchandise.

TABLE 10-1
A Quick List of eBay Abbreviations

eBay Code	What It Abbreviates	What It Means
MIB	Mint in Box	The item is in the original box, in great shape, and just the way you'd expect to find it in a store.
MOC	Mint on Card	The item is mounted on its original display card, attached with the original fastenings, in store-new condition.
NRFB	Never Removed from Box	Just what it says, as in "bought but never opened."
COA	Certificate of Authenticity	Documentation that vouches for the genuineness of an item, such as an autograph or painting.
OEM	Original Equipment Manufacture	You're selling the item and all the equipment that originally came with it, but you don't have the original box, owner's manual, or instructions.
OOAK	One of a Kind	You are selling the only one in existence!
NOS	New Old Stock	A brand-new item from a bygone era that's been tucked away safely and never opened.
NR	No Reserve Price	A reserve price is the price you can set when you begin your auction. If bids don't meet the reserve, you don't have to sell. Many buyers don't like reserve prices because they don't think that they can get a bargain. (For tips on how to allay these fears and get those bids in reserve-price auctions, see "Writing your description," later in this chapter.) If you're not listing a reserve for your item, let bidders know.
HTF, OOP	Hard to Find, Out of Print	Out of print, only a few ever made, or people grabbed up all there were. (HTF doesn't mean you spent a week looking for it in the attic.)

Table 10-1 gives you a handy list of common abbreviations and phrases used to describe items. (*Hint:* Mint means "may as well be brand new," not "cool chocolate treat attached.")

Often, you can rely on eBay slang to get your point across, but make sure that you mean it and that you're using it accurately. Don't label something MIB (Mint in Box) when it looks like it's been Mashed in Box by a meat grinder. You can find more useful online abbreviations on my website, `www.coolebaytools.com/ tools/online-acronyms-and-ebay-abbreviations`.

Don't let your title ruin your salability

Imagine going to a supermarket and asking someone to show you where the "stringy stuff that you boil" is, rather than asking where the spaghetti is. You might end up with zoodles — delicious to some but hardly what you had in mind.

That's why you should check and recheck your spelling. Savvy buyers use eBay search to find merchandise; if the name of your item is spelled wrong, the search engine may (or may not) be able to find it. Poor spelling and incomprehensible grammar also reflect badly on you. If you're in competition with another seller, the buyer is likelier to trust the seller *hoo nose gud speling.*

WARNING

If you've finished writing your item title and you have spaces left over, ***please*** fight the urge to dress it up with lots of asterisks and exclamation points!!!!!!!!!!!! (See how annoying that is?) No matter how gung-ho you are about your item, the eBay search engine may overlook your item if the title is encrusted with meaningless **** and !!!! symbols. If bidders do see your title, they may become annoyed by the virtual shrillness and ignore it anyway!!!!!!!! (It's even more annoying the second time around.)

Another distracting habit is overdoing capital letters. To buyers, seeing everything in caps is LIKE SEEING A CRAZED SALESMAN SCREAMING AT THEM TO BUY NOW! Using all caps is considered *shouting,* which is rude and tough on the eyes. Use capitalization SPARINGLY, and only to finesse a particular point to attract the buyer's eye.

Giving the title punch with a subtitle

Subtitles are a handy feature on eBay. You can buy an additional 55 characters, which will appear under your item title on a search results page. The fee for this extra promotion for an auction is $1.00 for an item with a selling price of up to $150 and $3.00 for an item that sells for more. Fixed-price and Good 'till cancelled listings cost $1.50 and $6.00, respectively; in many circumstances, it's definitely worth your while. Any text that you input will really make your item stand out when many sellers have the same item up for sale. But (you knew there would be a *but* didn't you?) these additional 55 characters won't come up as part of a title search.

Adding item specifics

Item specifics can be a bit confusing until you understand what they accomplish in your eBay listing. Whereas many people find your item through eBay search, others may find it through a search on Google or Bing. Because each seller may list the same item with different keywords, there needs to be some universally identifiable information for most products.

TIP

Filling out the item specifics as thoroughly as possible advantages your item in eBay's search algorithm. Translation? It could show up near the top of the list of items for sale.

Each category on eBay has varying options for which items specifics are requested. Do yourself a favor, add as much identifiable information on your item in this area. It can make a huge difference in how many people find your item.

Here's how to fill out this area. Under the *Add item-specific* head, be sure to fill out as many of the requested specifics. Below each entry is a box with a drop-down menu; you may find the specific you are looking for there. If you don't see what you're looking for, select the *Enter your own* option and type in the appropriate identifier. If you have a specific that is not listed, click the plus sign next to *Add custom item-specific* and write it in yourself.

Most importantly, if available, add the following:

>> **GTIN** (Global Trade Identifier), which is also known as a **UPC** (Universal Product Code) number, that appears on almost every retail product. It can be found below the bar code on the package.

>> **ISBN** number for books. The ISBN number appears below the bar code on the back, or on the inside of the book on the publisher's information page.

>> **MPN:** If possible, find the manufacturer's part number on the item and type it in an existing or custom box.

>> **Brand:** Type in the manufacturer's name.

>> **Size, color, and edition** if applicable.

Writing your description

After you hook potential bidders with your title, reel 'em in with a fabulous description. Don't think Hemingway here; think QVC. You can write a description that sells as well — all you have to do is click in the box and start typing.

Here's a list of suggestions for writing an item description:

>> **Include a clear list of the item's features.** If you're not trying to sell an especially coveted collectible or used item, be brief and stick to the facts. Give every possible bit of information that your buyer might want to know about the item for sale, and stop there. There's no emotion in these descriptions; people just want the facts.

>> **Accentuate the positive.** Give the buyer a reason to buy your item, and be enthusiastic when you list all the reasons everyone should buy it. Unlike the title, here you can use as much space as you want. If there are any "industry specific" descriptors for your item, be sure to include them here, so fans of the item will know you understand the products you sell.

>> **Include the negative.** When it comes to used merchandise, don't hide the truth of your item's condition. Trying to conceal flaws costs you in the long run; you get tagged with bad feedback and a refund. If the item has a scratch, a nick, a dent, a crack, a ding, a tear, a rip, missing pieces, replacement parts, faded color, dirty smudges, or a bad smell (especially if cleaning might damage the item), mention it in the description. If your item has been overhauled, rebuilt, repainted, or hot-rodded, say so. You don't want the buyer to send back your merchandise because you weren't truthful about imperfections or modifications and report you to eBay because it arrived "not as described."

>> **While you're at it, promote yourself too.** This helps when you're selling an item against very competitive sellers. As you accumulate positive feedback, tell potential customers that quality customer service is the byword of your business. You can even take it a step further by inviting prospective bidders to your eBay profile page. Chapter 17 gives you some tips on how to get your listing seen by a wider audience.

>> **Wish your potential bidders well.** Communication is the key to a good transaction, and you can set the tone for your listing and post-sale exchanges by including some simple phrases that show your friendly side. When it comes to a one-of-a-kind item, offer that you will provide additional photos on request.

When you type your description, you have the option of jazzing things up with a bit of HTML coding, or you can use eBay's HTML text editor (see Figure 10-3). If you know how to use a word processor, you'll have no trouble touching up your text with this tool. Table 10-2 shows you a few additional codes if you'd like to manually insert the code in the HTML view.

TIP

You can go back and forth from the HTML text editor to regular input and add additional codes here and there by clicking from the Standard form to the HTML entry form tabs. I often prepare my listings ahead of time and save them in my eBay folder as plain HTML files — that way they're always retrievable for use (I just copy and paste) — no matter what program or form I'm using to list. See Chapter 20 for more on software to help you with your auctions.

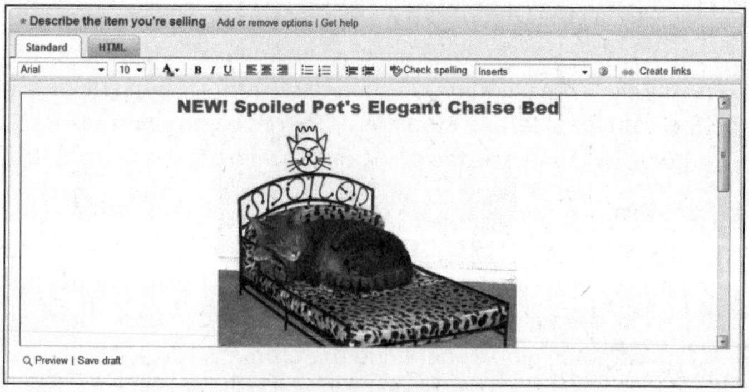

FIGURE 10-3:
The HTML text editor in Advanced Editing shows you the description area with HTML-coded text and additional free photo inserted.

TABLE 10-2   ## A Short List of HTML Codes

HTML Code	How to Use It	What It Does
`<b></b>`	`<b>cool collectible</b>`	**cool collectible** (bold type)
`<i></i>`	`<i>cool collectible</i>`	*cool collectible* (italic type)
`<b><i></i></b>`	`<b><i>cool collectible</b></i>`	***cool collectible*** (bold and italic type)
`<font color=red></font>`	`<font color=red>cool collectible</font>`	Selected text appears in red. (This book is in black and white so you can't see it.)
`<font size=+1></font>`	`<font size=+3>cool</font> collectible`	cool collectible (font size normal +1 through 4, increases size *x* times)
` `	`cool collectible`	cool collectible (inserts line break)
`<p>`	`cool<p>collectible`	cool collectible (inserts paragraph space)
`<hr>`	`cool collectible<hr>cheap`	cool collectible_____cheap (inserts horizontal rule)
`<h1></h1>`	`<h1>cool collectible</h1>`	cool collectible (converts text to headline size)

TIP

To insert additional photos in your description, use the following code. (Just insert the URL of your hosted picture, along with the photo's file name.) My example in Figure 10-3 used the following code:

```
<img scr=http://www.collierad.com/catbed.jpg>
```

TIP

Occasionally, sellers offer an item as a *presale,* or an item that the seller doesn't yet have in stock but expects to. If you're offering this kind of item, make sure that you spell out all the details in the description. eBay policy states that you must ship a presale item within 30 days of the auction's end, so be sure that you will have the item within that time span and include the actual shipping date. Putting an item up for sale without having it in hand is a practice fraught with risk. The item you're expecting may not arrive in time or may arrive damaged. I've heard of one too many sellers who have had to go out and purchase an item at retail for a buyer to preserve their feedback when caught in this situation.

Listing the number of items for sale

Unless you're planning on holding a Multiple Item listing, the number of items is always 1 — which means that you're holding a traditional auction, or listing a single item up for sale, or just selling a single unit of an item. If you need to change the quantity number from 1, just type the number in the box.

TIP

A matching set of cuff links is considered one item, as is the complete 37-volume set of *The Smith Family Ancestry and Genealogical History since 1270*. If you have more than one of the same item (two sets of cuff links), I suggest that you sell them one at a time. You are much more likely to get a higher final price for your items when you sell them individually. Never try to sell items that belong in a set as separate items.

TIP

Sellers can't have more than one identical fixed-price listing up at a time. You may have duplicate auctions, but only one of the duplicate auctions without bids will appear on eBay at a time.

Setting a starting price — how low can you go?

What do a baseball autographed by JFK, a used walkie-talkie, and a Jaguar sports car all have in common? They all started with a $0.99 starting price. eBay requires you to set a *starting price,* also called a minimum bid — the lowest bid allowed in an auction. You may be surprised to see stuff worth tens of thousands of dollars starting at just a buck. These sellers haven't lost their minds. Neither are they worried that someone could be tooling down the highway in a $100,000 sports car they bought for the price of a burger.

TIP

Setting an incredibly low minimum (just type it in the box *without* the dollar sign but *with* the decimal point) is a subtle strategy that gives you more bang for your buck. You can use a low starting price to attract more bidders who will, in turn, drive up the price to the item's real value — especially if, after doing your research, you know that the item is a hot seller.

If you're worried about the outcome of the final bid, you can protect your item by using a *reserve price* (the price the bidding needs to reach before the item can be sold). Then you won't have to sell your item for a bargain-basement price; your reserve price protects your investment. The best advice is to set a reserve price that is the lowest amount you'll take for your item and *then* set a minimum bid that is ridiculously low. Use a reserve only when absolutely necessary because some bidders just pass up reserve auctions. (For more info about setting a reserve price, see the section "Your secret safety net — reserve price," later in this chapter.)

TIP

When entering a starting price, type only the numbers and a decimal point. Don't use dollar signs ($) or cent signs (¢).

Buy It Now for auctions

eBay's Buy It Now (*BIN* in eBay-speak) is available for auctions. This feature allows buyers who want to purchase an item *now* to do so. Have you ever wanted an item really badly and didn't want to wait until the end of an auction? If the seller offers Buy It Now, you can purchase that item immediately. If you're the seller, you can entice your bidders to pay just a tad more to have the satisfaction of walking away with the item free and clear. Just specify the amount the item can sell for in the Buy It Now price area — the amount can be whatever you want. If you choose to take advantage of selling a hot item during the holiday rush, for example, you can make the BIN price as high as you think it can go. If you just want the item to move, make your BIN price the average price you see the item go for on eBay.

When your item receives a bid, the BIN option disappears, and the item goes through the normal auction process. If you have a reserve price on your item, the BIN feature doesn't disappear until a bidder meets your reserve price through the normal bidding process. To list an item with Buy It Now, the Buy It Now price needs to be·at least 30 percent higher than the auction's opening bid, and you need to list the item for at least $0.99.

Setting your auction time

How long do you want to run your auction? eBay gives you a choice — 1, 3, 5, 7, or 10 days. Just click the number you want in the box.

TIP

My auction-length strategy depends on the time of year and the item I'm selling, and I generally have great success. If you have an item that you think will sell pretty well, run a 7-day auction (be sure that it will cover a full weekend) so bidders have time to check it out before they decide to bid. However, if you know that you have a red-hot item that's going to fly off the shelves — such as a rare toy or a hard-to-get pair of Nikes — choose a 3-day auction. Eager bidders tend to bid higher and more often to beat out their competition if the item is hot and going fast. Three days is long enough to give trendy items exposure and ring up bids.

REMEMBER

No matter how many days you choose to run your auction, it ends at exactly the same time of day as it starts. A 7-day auction that starts on Thursday at 9:03:02 a.m. ends the following Thursday at 9:03:02 a.m.

Although I know the gang at eBay is a pretty laid-back group, they do run on military time. That means they use a 24-hour clock set to Pacific time. So 3:30 in the afternoon is 15:30, and one minute after midnight is 00:01. Questions about time conversions? Look at the table on my website in the Tools area, which has a printable conversion chart of eBay times (www.coolebaytools.com/tools/usa-time-zones). There's also one with international time conversions.

With items selling 24 hours a day, 7 days a week, you should know when the most bidders and buyers are around to take a gander at your wares. Here are some times to think about when running an auction or item for sale:

>> **Saturday/Sunday:** Always run your listing over a weekend. People log on and off eBay all day.

WARNING

Don't start or end your listing on a Saturday or Sunday — *unless* your completed auction research indicates that you should. Certain types of bidders love sitting at their computers waiting for auctions to end on the weekends, but many bidders are busy having lives, and their schedules are unpredictable. Although a few eager bidders may log on and place a maximum bid on your auction, you can bet that they won't be sitting at a computer making a last-minute flurry of competitive bids if they have something better to do on a Saturday or Sunday.

>> **Holiday weekends:** If a holiday weekend is coming up around the time you're setting up your auction, run your auction through the weekend and end it a day after the "holiday" Monday. This gives prospective bidders a chance to catch up with the items they perused over the weekend and to plan their bidding strategies.

WARNING

Don't end an auction on the last day of a three-day holiday; try the day after. People in the mood to shop are generally at department stores collecting bargains. If eBay members aren't shopping, they're out enjoying an extra day off.

>> **Time of day:** The best times of day to start and end your auction are during eBay's peak hours of operation, which are 5:00 p.m. to 9:00 p.m. Pacific time, right after work on the West Coast. Perform your sold item research, however, to be sure that this strategy applies to your item. Your timing depends on the item you're listing and whether 5:00 p.m. to 9:00 p.m. Pacific time is the middle of the night where you live.

TIP

Unless you're an insomniac or a vampire and want to sell to werewolves, don't let your items close in the middle of the night. Not enough bidders are around to cause any last-minute bidding that would bump up the price.

Your secret safety net — reserve price

Here's a little secret: The reason sellers list big-ticket items like Ferraris, grand pianos, and high-tech computer equipment with a starting bid of $1 is because they're protected from losing money with a *reserve price*. The reserve price is the lowest price that must be met before the item can be sold. It's not required by eBay but can protect you. eBay charges an additional fee for this feature that varies, depending on how high your reserve is.

For example, say you list a hardback book — a 1939 first edition of John Steinbeck's *The Grapes of Wrath*. You set the starting price at $1, and you set a reserve price at $500. That means that people can start bidding at $1, and if at the end of the auction the bidding hasn't reached the $500 reserve, you don't have to sell the book.

As with everything in life, using a reserve price for your auctions has an upside and a downside. Many choosy bidders and bargain hunters blast past reserve-price auctions because they see a reserve price as a sign that proclaims "No bargains here!" Many bidders figure that they can get a better deal on the same item with an auction that proudly declares *NR* (for *no reserve*) in its description. As an enticement to those bidders, you see lots of NR mentions in auction titles.

TIP

If you need to set a reserve on your item, help the bidder out. Many bidders shy away from an auction that has a reserve, but if they're really interested, they will read the item description. To dispel their fears that the item is way too expensive or out of their price range, add a line in your description that states the amount of your reserve price. "I have put a reserve of $75 on this item to protect my investment; the highest bid over $75 will win the item." A phrase such as this takes away the vagueness of the reserve auction and allows you to place a reserve with a low opening bid. (You want to reel 'em in, remember?)

TIP

On lower-priced items, I suggest that you set a higher starting price and set no reserve. Otherwise, if you're not sure about the market, set a low minimum bid but set a high reserve to protect yourself.

If bids don't reach a set reserve price, some sellers send a Second Chance offer through the eBay system. Two caveats if you try to circumvent eBay fees and contact the bidders:

>> *Side deals that circumvent eBay fees are strictly prohibited.* eBay can suspend the seller *and* the buyer if a side deal is reported.

>> eBay won't protect buyers or sellers if a side deal goes bad.

I want to be alone: The private listing

In a private listing, bidders' or buyers' User IDs are kept under wraps. Sellers typically use this option to protect the identities of bidders or buyers for high-priced, big-ticket items (say, that restored World War II fighter). Wealthy eBay users may not want the world to know that they have the resources to buy expensive items. Private auctions are also held for items from the Adult/Erotica category. (Gee, what a shock.)

MARSHA SAYS

A PRIVATE AUCTION MIGHT HAVE HELPED JOHN STAMOS

The famous sign that was pictured in almost every Disneyland promotion (for the first 40 or so years of Disneyland's existence) was put up for sale on eBay in 2000. Legend has it that the sign was purchased by actor John Stamos for a high bid of $30,700. Unfortunately for John, the Disney auction did not use the private auction feature (and in those days eBay did not mask bidder IDs). After news of the winner's name hit the tabloids, the entire world knew John's eBay User ID! He had to change his ID in a hurry to end the throngs of love-smitten emails headed to his computer!

TIP

If you can't find some of the options listed here (such as the Private Auction), click the Customize link within the sections on the Sell page. In the window that appears, select the option you want to use, and then click Save.

Filling out the item location

eBay wants to list the area and country where you live. The idea behind telling the bidder where you live is to give him or her a heads-up on what kind of shipping charges to expect. They'll fill in your location from your registration. If you live in a big area — say, suburban Los Angeles (who, me?), which sprawls for miles — you may want to think about narrowing your region a little. You may find a buyer who lives close to you, and that convenient fact could swing a sale. If you do a face-to-face transaction, doing it in a public place is a good idea. (I picked up an eBay purchase at Starbucks recently.)

Setting shipping terms

Ahoy, matey! Hoist the bid! Okay, not quite yet. Before you run it up the mast, select your shipping options. Here are your choices:

>> **Ship to the United States only:** This option is selected by default; it means that you ship only domestically.

>> **Will ship worldwide:** The world is your oyster. But make sure that you can afford the time for the extra processing of customs forms or use eBay's Global Shipping Program.

>> **Will ship to United States and the following:** If you're comfortable shipping to certain countries but not to others, make your selections here; they show up on your item page.

TIP

When you indicate that you will ship internationally, your item shows up on the eBay International sites, which is a fantastic way to attract new buyers! (Although, you will pay extra for U.S. seller's listings to appear on the International sites.) eBay has lots of good international users, so you may want to consider selling your items around the world. If you do, be sure to clearly state in the description all extra shipping costs — and that the buyer is responsible for any customs charges. (See Chapter 12 for more information on how to ship to customers abroad.)

The buyer pays for shipping (unless you choose to offer free shipping), and this is the point at which you must decide how much to charge. You also have to calculate how much this item will cost you to ship. If it's a small item (weighing under a pound or so), you may decide to charge a flat rate to all buyers. To charge a flat rate, click the Flat Shipping Rates tab and fill in the shipping amount. Before you fill in the amount, be sure to include your expenses for packing (see Chapter 12 for more info on how much to add for this task) and how much insurance charges will be (if any).

TIP

Although I recommend offering flat-rate or free shipping to attract customers, you may want to use eBay's versatile shipping calculator. Because UPS and the U.S. Postal Service now charge variable rates for packages of the same weight, based on distance, using the calculator simplifies things for your customers (and you). Be sure that you weigh the item and know how much your handling charge will be. The calculator allows you to input a handling amount and adds it to the overall shipping total but does not break out the amount separately for the customer. The calculator also conveniently calculates the proper insurance amount for the item.

The calculator also appears automatically on the item page so that prospective buyers can type in their ZIP codes and immediately know how much the shipping will be to their locations. Check out Chapter 12 for more information on shipping options.

Checking Your Work and Starting the Listing

After you fill in all the blanks on the Sell form, you come to the Preview Your Listing page. Scroll down the page and confirm that all the information appears as you intended. If you think you're ready to join the world of e-commerce, follow these steps:

1. Next to the Submit listing box, click the Preview link.

A pop-up page opens, showing you exactly how your listing will appear on eBay. Here's where you can catch mistakes before your item is listed.

You also may find the preview page helpful as a last-minute chance to get your bearings. You can go back to any of the areas that need correcting by clicking the Edit Listing link back on the selling form. Make category changes or any other changes and additions, and then head for the Verification page again.

2. Check for mistakes and review your fees for listings and options (if any).

TIP

Nitpick for common, careless errors; you won't be sorry. I've seen eBay members make goofs such as the wrong category listing, misspelling and grammatical errors, and missing information about shipping, handling, insurance, and payment methods.

3. When you're sure that everything's accurate and you're happy with your item listing, click List it button.

A Confirmation page pops up. At that precise moment, your listing begins, even though a little time may pass before it appears in eBay's search and listings updates. If you want to see your listing right away and check for bids, your Confirmation page provides a link for that purpose. Click the link, and you're there. You can also keep track of your items by using the My eBay page. (To find out how, see Chapter 4.)

WARNING

All item pages come with this friendly warning: *Seller assumes all responsibility for this listing.* Some eBay veterans just gloss over this warning after they've been wheeling and dealing for a while, but it's an important rule to remember. See Chapter 9 for details on the rules sellers must follow and Chapter 12 for tips on your role in closing the deal and receiving good feedback.

Midcourse Corrections: Fixing Current Listings

Don't worry if you make a mistake filling out the Sell page but don't notice it until after the auction is up and running. Pencils have erasers, and eBay allows revisions. You can make changes at two stages of the game: before the first bid is placed and after the bidding war is underway. The following sections explain what you can and can't correct — and when you have to accept the little imperfections of your item page.

Making changes before bidding begins

Here's what you can change about your auction before bids have been placed (and when there are more than 12 hours to go):

>> The title or description of your auction

>> The item category

>> The item's starting price

>> The item's Buy It Now price

>> The reserve price (you can add, change, or remove it)

>> The duration of your listing

>> The URL of the picture you're including with your auction

>> A private listing designation (you can add or remove it)

>> Accepted payment methods, Checkout information, item location, and shipping terms

When you revise a listing, eBay puts a little notation on your auction page that reads: `Description(revised)`. (Think of it as automatic common courtesy.)

To revise a fixed-price listing or any auction before bids have been received, follow these steps:

1. **Go to the page of the item you want to revise, and click the Revise your item link at the top left of the item page (see Figure 10-4).**

    If an auction hasn't received any bids, a message appears on your screen to indicate that you may update the item.

Your item is for sale	Manage Offers		
• Revise your item		**Listing info**	
• Sell a similar item		Page views:	7
• Change offer settings		Duration:	Good 'till cancelled
• Create shipping discounts		Start time:	Jul 23, 2019 15:29:20 PDT

2. **You arrive at the Revise Item page, which looks like the Sell form.**

3. **Make changes to the item information and then click the Save and Continue button at the bottom of the page when you're finished.**

A summary of your newly revised page appears on your screen.

4. **If you're happy with your revisions, click Save Changes.**

You're taken to your newly revised item page, where you see a disclaimer from eBay that says you've revised the listing before the first bid. If you instead want to make further revisions, click the Back button of your browser and redo the Edit Your Listing page.

Making changes after bidding begins

If your listing is up and running and already receiving bids, you can still make some slight modifications to it. Newly added information is clearly separated from the original text and pictures. In addition, eBay puts a time stamp on the additional info in case questions from early bidders crop up later.

After your item receives bids, eBay allows you to add to your item's description. If you feel that you were at a loss for words in writing your item's description, if you discover new information (that vase you thought was a reproduction is actually the real thing!), or if a lot of potential bidders are asking the same questions, go ahead and make all the additions you want. But whatever you put there the first time around stays in the description as well.

REMEMBER

Don't let an oversight grow into a failure to communicate — and don't ignore iffy communication until the item is purchased. Correct any inaccuracies in your description now to avoid problems later.

Always check your messages to see whether prospective buyers have questions about your item. If someone wants to know about flaws, be truthful and courteous when responding. As you get more familiar with eBay (and with writing descriptions), the number of buyer questions will decrease. If you enjoy good customer service in your day-to-day shopping, here's your chance to give some back.

Chapter **11**

Find Merchandise to Sell and the eBay Store Decision

As I suggest throughout this book, go through your home. Hone your selling skills on the items you can find in your closets, garage, and those stashed-away boxes that have not been revisited since you last moved. You've no doubt got a surplus of collectibles, old craft projects, children's clothes (outgrown before they were even worn), ties, purses, and souvenirs from past vacations that you're not paying attention to.

Once you pick clean everything not nailed down in your house, you may want to broaden your horizons. The key to successfully selling items on eBay is to find things people actually want to buy at the right price. I know it seems obvious, but having *stuff to sell* isn't always the same as having *things people want to buy*. Using this concept, you can teach yourself all kinds of effective marketing strategies. Finding the item that may be "the next big thing" takes lots of work, timing, and sometimes a dose of good luck.

As one who spends time online, you'll see tons of amazing seminars and entrepreneurial coaches offering a guarantee that if you just take their program, you will find the hottest-selling items (perhaps drop-ship) and you'll be a success on eBay.

Think about this for a second. If you knew the hot ticket to riches, wouldn't you be selling that on eBay with a staff and making the fortune yourself? The one fact that successful sellers will rarely share is the source of the items that sell best on eBay. It's naïve to think that eBay businesses would even sell you the secrets that make them successful; after all, you *are* their competition. These people aren't big-hearted millionaires; it's just easier to make money by preying on those who think there's a magic way to make money on eBay. There isn't. It takes old-fashioned elbow grease and research.

Knowing the Market

Just as successful stockbrokers know about individual companies, they also need to know about the marketplace as a whole. Sure, I may know about the top designer purses, and so do many others. To get a leg up on your competition, you need to understand the big picture, taking marketing trends and economics into consideration. Here are some questions you should ask yourself as you contemplate making serious money (well, I hope) by selling items on eBay:

>> **What items are currently hot sellers?** If you see everyone around you rushing to the store to buy a particular item, chances are good that the item will become more valuable as stocks of it diminish. (Smartphone accessories, anyone?) The simple rule of supply and demand says that whoever has something everyone else wants stands to gain major profits. Big-box warehouse stores like Costco usually have a full stock of popular items because their (very savvy) buyers purchase by the truckload months in advance — how about visiting a warehouse store to find items at discount?

MARSHA SAYS

Believe it or not, one day I was wheeling my cart around Costco and right in front of me was a huge display with women jumping around and grabbing at the merchandise. I glanced above to read the sign: Fendi Baugette Handbags $199.99. My daughter and I elbowed our way (in a not-too-ladylike fashion, I might add) through the crowd and saw the regularly $450.00 purses stacked like lunchmeat. In those days, the Baugette was new and sold on eBay for around $350.00. Needless to say, we bought all that our credit cards could handle for resale.

>> **Do I see a growing interest in a specific trend that might make it a big seller?** Are you starting to hear buzz about a particular item, or even an era? I just found some new-in-the-box copies of Windows 3.1 that were headed for the trash, but found I can still make money with them. What about '60s aluminum Christmas trees? Who knew they sell easily for over $100?

Listen carefully and think of what you already own (or can get your hands on) that can help you catch a piece of the trend's action.

» **Should I hold on to this item and wait for its value to increase, or should I sell now?** Knowing when to sell an item that you think people may want is a tricky business. Sometimes you can catch the trend too early and find out that you could have commanded a higher price if only you had waited. Other times, you may invest in a fad that's already passé and find that no one's interested anymore. It's best to test the market with a small quantity, dribbling items individually into the market until you've made back the money you spent to acquire them. When you have your investment back, the rest will be gravy.

» **Is a company discontinuing an item I should stockpile now and sell later?** Pay attention to items that are discontinued, especially toys and novelty items (and be sure you have a place to store them). If you find a collectible item that a manufacturer has a limited supply of, you could make a tidy profit. If the manufacturer ends up reissuing the item, don't forget that the original run is still the most coveted — and valuable. I once bought a case of last season's footless pantyhose at a huge discount — I sold them one at a time, at a 400-percent profit, over three years.

» **Was there a recall, an error, or a legal proceeding associated with my item?** If so, how it affects the value of the item takes a back seat to eBay policy: An error item, okay. But items that have been recalled for safety reasons can't be sold on eBay (for details, go to www.ebay.com/help/policies/prohibited-restricted-items/recalled-items-policy?id=4300). For example, a toy recalled for safety reasons may no longer be appropriate for the kids, but even if it's rare and collectible, you *still* can't sell it on eBay.

But here's another angle: Consider that paper stock shares of (and any paperwork to do with) the now-defunct 1998 Enron Corporation became highly prized collectibles after the scandal hit; they still sell for as high as $100 on eBay as collectibles.

MARSHA SAYS

Remember when Colin Kapernick threw shade on Nike's newest Betsy Ross sneakers? It was officially called the Nike Air Max 1 Quick Strike Fourth of July shoe (original price $140) and got the nickname "Betsy Ross sneakers" because they had an image of the original United States flag (designed by Betsy Ross) on the back. Nike recalled and discontinued the shoe because it did not align with their values. Those who already had these shoes put them up for sale on eBay. Many sold on eBay for several thousand dollars. Limited Nike shoes can sell on eBay for big money — a pair of Nike Air Max sold for $40,000. So, keep an eye out for these limited (or recalled) issues.

MARSHA SAYS

EVEN DUMPSTER DIVING PAYS OFF

I'm a huge fan of the artist George Rodrigue. When building my collection of his famous "Blue Dog" items years ago, I came across a seller who had "liberated" some early museum-exhibition catalogs from a dumpster. Although the old catalogs had been tossed in the trash, they were boxed and bundled — and in perfect condition. Being a true-blue Rodrigue fan, I thought perhaps these catalogs might make good future eBay items.

I asked the seller if he had 30 to sell; he said yes, and he sold them to me for $4 each. I have been selling them off and on for close to ten years for between $15 and $55 each. As a matter of fact, I still have a few to sell. Spotting something evergreen and seeing the future value in items is what it's all about.

Some people like to go with their gut feelings about when and what to buy for resale on eBay. By all means, if instinct has worked for you in the past, factor instinct in here, too. If you've done some research that looks optimistic but your gut says, "I'm not sure," listen to it; don't assume that you're just hearing that lunchtime burrito talking. Try testing the waters by purchasing *one* of the prospective items for resale on eBay. If that sale doesn't work out, you won't have invested a lot of money, and you can credit your gut with saving you some bucks.

Do You Have Talent, Provide a Service?

If you're talented in any way, you can sell your services on eBay. Home artisans, chefs, and even stay-at-home psychics are transacting business daily on the site. (In fact, psychics are doing a land-office business!) What a great way to make money on eBay — make your own product or service! Just make sure it's legal, okay? (But you knew that.)

Personalized and custom items do well on eBay (see Figure 11-1). There's a demand for personalized invitations, cards, and announcements — and even return address labels (and you thought you had all you needed). Calligraphic work or computer-designed items (customized with Fido's picture, awww) are in big demand today, but no one seems to have the time to make them. Savvy sellers with talent can fill this market niche.

FIGURE 11-1: One of the personalized gifts I found on eBay. This from eBay seller *440cutlass.*

People go to trendy places (when they have the time) like Soho, the Grove, or the Village to find unique custom jewelry. They may look on Etsy, but the smart ones also shop eBay.

The world is your oyster on eBay, and the sky is the limit. Use your imagination, and you might be surprised at what your new business will be!

Catching Trends in the Media

Catching trends is all about listening and looking. You can find all kinds of inside information from newspapers, magazines, television, and of course, the Internet. Believe it or not, you can even find out what people are interested in these days by bribing a kid. Keep your eyes and ears open. When people say, "That GEICO gecko is *everywhere*," instead of nodding your head vacantly, start getting ideas.

Trending on the web

Newspapers and websites are bombarded by press releases and inside information from companies the world over. Pay close attention to the various sections of the newspaper. Look for stories on celebrities and upcoming movies and see if any old fads are making a resurgence (you can sell items as "retro chic" — Lava Lamps, anyone?).

Trending sites on the web give you up-to-the-second information. Google, for example, has a couple. Take a look at `www.google.com/trends/hottrends` that lists Googles searches and updates by the hour.

Read the most recent stories about retail trade conventions, such as the New York Toy Fair or the Consumer Electronics show. New products are introduced and given the thumbs-up or -down by journalists. This way you can start to think about the direction your area of expertise is heading.

What's on television

No matter what you think of television, it has an enormous impact on which trends come and go and which ones stick. Why else would advertisers sink billions of dollars into TV commercials? And look at the impact Oprah's Favorite Things had. Just one Oprah appearance for a product could turn it into an overnight bestseller. More and more celebrities (even Homer Simpson, who's imaginary) are talking about eBay. The buzz brings people to the site.

Recently many classic TV shows are making a comeback. *Fuller House*? *The X-Files*? Collectibles from the past become even more profitable when the shows return to the public eye.

Tune in to news networks and popular talk shows. See what's being featured in the programs. The producers of these shows are on top of pop culture and move fast to be the first to bring you the next big thing. Take what they feature and think of a marketing angle. If you don't, you can be sure somebody else will.

Catch up with youth culture . . .

. . . or at least keep good tabs on it. There seems to be no catching up with it, just as there's no way to say this without sounding over-the-hill: If you remember cranking up The Beatles, New Kids on the Block, or The Partridge Family (say what?) until your parents screamed, "Shut that awful noise off," you may be at that awkward time of life when you hardly see the appeal of what young people are doing or listening to. But if you want tips for hot-selling items, tolerate the awful noise of today's music (how *did* that happen?) and listen to the kids around you. (Try to watch some popular YouTube videos, too.) Children, especially preteens and teens, may be the best trend-spotters on the planet. See what kind of marketing tips you get from your neighborhood Millennial when you ask questions like these:

>> **What's cool at the moment?** Or "rad" if you want to sound cool — whoops, that was '80s-speak, wasn't it?

>> **What's totally uncool that was cool two months ago?** Their world moves at warp speed!

>> **What music are you buying?** Kanye West, Kelly Clarkson, Coldplay, and Black-Eyed Peas — yup, all those hot bands with big hits — but maybe *ewww-that's-so-five-minutes-ago* by the time you read this.

>> **What could I buy you that would make you really happy?** *Hint:* If the kid says, "a classic red BMW Z-5," or "liposuction," look for a younger kid. (Sorry, iPads are not a useful answer — because almost everyone already has one.)

Check out pop-culture websites

Websites geared to the 18 to 34 age group (and sometimes to younger teens — they call them *tweens*) can help you stay on top of what's hot. See what the big companies are pitching to this target audience and whether they're succeeding. If a celebrity's suddenly visible in every other headline or site, be on the lookout for merchandise relating to that person. (Are we talking hysteria-plus-cash-flow here, or just hysteria?)

An interesting website to view is `http://trendsmap.com`. Visiting this site will show you a map of the country with trending topics from Twitter imposed over the map. The larger the words appear, the more people are talking about them.

Follow the trends on social media

Social media is the loudspeaker to the Millennials and the majority of forward-thinking cohorts — even Baby Boomers! According to the United States Census statistics, the demographic cohort known as the Millennials are the largest cohort (over 76 million) in history, eclipsing the Boomers (75.4 million). Their birth years range from about 1980 to the early 2000s.

I am on social media every day, and the first thing I check in the morning is Twitter trending topics. Topics on the Twitter web interface trend differently based on location. But on the mobile app (for smartphones and tablets), when I tap the magnifying glass, it opens a page of topics trending on the site. I like Twitter for finding news and trends because I don't always get dragged into conversations; I can observe and absorb.

Chapter 9 in this book gives you additional ideas on where to search for information about items you might want to sell.

COLLECTING MAGAZINE WEBSITES

Although not quite a plethora, the number of online magazines geared to collectors is definitely approaching a slew. Although these webzines won't help you catch a trend (by the time it gets into one of these magazines, somebody's already caught it), they can give you great information on pricing, availability, and general collecting information. And you can follow the course of a trend for a real-life example of how it works. Many are available on the web; here's a list of collectors' magazines that I like:

- *Antique Trader* has been the bible of the antique collecting industry for over 40 years. Visit its online home at www.antiquetrader.com for more articles and other information.

- *Dolls Magazine* has info on everything related to dolls of all types. Go to www.dollsmagazine.com.

- *Numismatic News* is an old standard that has been around for more than 50 years. The first issue each month includes a pullout guide to retail U.S. coin prices. Every three months, it also includes a U.S. paper-money price guide at www.numismaticnews.net.

The Hunt for eBay Inventory

If you're not sure what you want to sell for profit on eBay — but you're a shop-till-you-drop person by nature — you have an edge. Incorporate your advanced shopping techniques into your daily routine. If you find a bargain that interests you, chances are you have a knack for spotting stuff that other shoppers would love to get their hands on.

The goods are out there

When you shop to sell on eBay, don't rule out any shopping venue. From the trendiest boutique to the smallest second-hand store, from garage sales to the Nordstrom Rack online, keep your eye out for eBay inventory. The items people look for on eBay are out there; you just have to find them.

Check your favorite eBay category and see what the popular items are. Better yet, go to your favorite brick-and-mortar store and make friends with the manager. Store managers are often privy to this type of information a couple of months in advance of a product release. If you ask, they'll tell you what's going to be the hot new item next month. After you're armed with the information you need, seek out that item for the lowest price you can, and then you can give it a shot on eBay.

Keep these shopping locales in mind when you go on the eBay hunt:

>> Get on the email lists from bargain websites. I've purchased many items to resell from flash sales on the Internet. Here are some valuable sites to follow:

- **Brad's Deals** posts links to new sales online every day. `www.bradsdeals.com`

- **Slickdeals** is where I found one of the hottest, limited (and most profitable) items of my selling career. It is a crowdsourced site that updates deals by the minute, showing deep discounts from around the web. `http://slickdeals.net`

- **Woot** has been on the web since 2004 selling electronics. They became famous for their "one item a day" selling format, where they would feature one item with a slashed price on sale until they ran out. Woot was bought by Amazon in 2010, and is now a great place to find close-outs and refurbished items. `www.woot.com`

>> Upscale department stores, trendy boutiques, outlet stores, or flagship designer stores are good places to do some market research. Check out the newest items — and then head to the clearance area or online outlet store and scrutinize the bargain racks for brand-name items.

>> Tour some of the discount and dollar stores in your area. Many of the items these places carry are *overruns* (too many of something that didn't sell), *small runs* (too little of something that the big guys weren't interested in stocking), or out-of-date fad items that need a good home on eBay.

>> Thrift stores are packed with used but usually good-quality items. And you can feel good knowing that the money you spend in a nonprofit thrift shop is going to a good cause. (Look out for vintage Hawaiian shirts — and know which brands to search for.)

MARSHA SAYS

A sharp seller I know is always at his local Salvation Army when the trucks come in. One day, as workers unloaded the truck, he saw a plaque-mounted baseball bat. Withholding his excitement, he picked it up and found that it was a signed Ty Cobb bat with a presentation plaque. Although he didn't know exactly what it was, he took a gamble and brought it to the cash register, where he paid $33 minus the senior-citizen discount. He took the bat to his office and made a few phone calls, later discovering that the bat was indeed a rare Louisville Slugger bat that had been presented to *the* Georgia Peach, Ty Cobb. But he'll never sell it because it's his good luck bat, which now hangs above the desk in his warehouse.

>> Find going-out-of-business sales. You can pick up bargains by the case if a shopkeeper just wants to empty the shelves so the store can close.

» Take advantage of any flea markets or swap meets in your area.

» Gift shops at museums, monuments, national parks, and theme parks can provide eBay inventory — but think about where to sell the items. Part of your selling success on eBay is *access*. People who can't get to the Kennedy Space Center may pay handsomely for a baseball cap with the official NASA logo on the box. Consider sports venues and theme parks as well.

» Dollar Stores come in all shapes and sizes. They can be filled with junk or treasure, and it takes a practiced eye to separate the wheat from the chaff. Many an item can be found here that makes for great practice for beginning sellers — and often goes for ten times what they paid. Try going in with a Gen Z, and see whether he or she reacts to any of the items for sale. Sometimes only one in five visits works out, but you'll know when you see the item — and at these prices you can afford to go deep! Stock at these stores doesn't stay on the shelf for too long; if you pass on an item, it may not be there when you return for it the next day. (Maybe another savvy eBay seller picked up the values.)

» Another super selling chain is the **Big Lots** company, which encompasses the Pic N Save, Mac Frugal's, Big Lots, and Odd Lots stores. They may have items priced at more than a dollar, but they specialize in closeout merchandise. All their merchandise sells for well under what most discounters charge — and at deep discounts to retailers. This is a great place to find toys, household goods — almost anything. Troll their aisles at least once a month to find items that you can resell on eBay. The Big Lots company has stores in forty-six states; check its website at www.biglots.com for store locations near you.

» One of my editors is going to kill me for mentioning one of her favorite eBay merchandise sources — but here it is. **Tuesday Morning** has more than five hundred stores scattered over the United States. They sell first-quality designer and brand-name closeout merchandise at deep-deep discounts, 50 percent to 80 percent below retail. The key here is that the store sells recognizable brand names, the kind of items that eBay shoppers look for. I've seem items at their store from Samsonite, Thomas Kincade, Limoges, Wedgwood, Royal Doulton, Madame Alexander, and even Barbie! Find your local store at their website, www.tuesdaymorning.com. If you sign up for their eTreasures newsletter, you'll get advance notice of when the really good stuff arrives at the store. (Sometimes they have only a dozen of a particular item per store, so you have to be there when the doors open.)

» Hang on to conference swag you get. If you receive handouts (lapel pins, pencils, pamphlets, books, interesting napkins, flashlights, towels, stuffed toys) from a sporting event, premiere, or historic event — or even a collectible freebie from a fast-food restaurant — any of them could be your ticket to some eBay sales.

DON'T FORGET CLASSIC GARAGE AND ESTATE SALES

Garage sales, tag sales, estate sales, and moving sales offer some of the biggest bargains you'll ever come across. Check for vintage kitchen pieces, designer goods, and old toys, and make 'em an offer they can't refuse.

What can be better than getting up at 6:00 a.m. to troll the local garage sales? I say nothing — if you're motivated to find lots of good eBay merchandise and prepared for the garage sales. Buy the newspaper or check your local newspaper's classified ads online (just run a Google search for your local newspaper's name), and print maps of the sale locations from Google Maps. You know the neighborhoods, so you can make a route that makes sense from one sale to the next — and figure in bathroom stops and coffee breaks.

Neighbors often take advantage of an advertised sale and put out some stuff of their own. Bring a friend; you can cover more ground faster if two of you are attacking the sales.

A few tips on shopping garage sales:

- Fancier neighborhoods have better stuff than middle-class ones. I know that sounds unfair, but I know for sure that rich folks' trash is better than mine.

- Look for sales that say "Early Birds Welcome," and make them the first on your list so you can get them out of the way. It seems like a universal bell goes off somewhere and all garage sales start at 8:00 a.m. *sharp!*

- The stuff you find at estate sales is often of a higher quality. These sales feature things that have been collected over many, many years.

- Keep an eye out for "moving to a smaller house" sales. These are usually people who have raised children, accumulated a houseful of stuff (collectibles? old toys? designer vintage clothes?), and want to shed it all so that they can move to a condo in Palm Springs.

- I usually put sales that feature "kids' items and toys" on the end of my list, and I go only if I'm not too tired. These sellers are generally young couples (with young children) who are trying to raise money or are moving. More often than not, they're keeping the good stuff and are simply shedding the excess.

Salvage: Liquidation Items, Unclaimed Freight, and Returns

The easiest buys of all, *salvage merchandise* is retail merchandise that has been returned, exchanged, or shelf-pulled for some reason. Generally, this merchandise is sold as-is and where-is and may be in new condition. To buy this merchandise, you might have to have your resale permit (complete with sales-tax number) and be prepared to pay the shipping to your location — unless you're buying the merchandise on eBay.

Available all over the country, the liquidation business has been thriving as a well-kept secret for years — just search Google for *liquidation* and see what you find. (Even **Walmart** sells liquidation merchandise at `https://liquidations.walmart.com`). As long as you have space to store salvage merchandise and a way to sell it, you can acquire it for as low as 10 cents on the dollar. When I say you need storage space, I mean *lots* of space. To buy this type of merchandise at bottom-of-the-barrel prices, you must be willing to accept truckloads — think 40- to 53-foot eighteen-wheelers, loaded with approximately twenty-two to twenty-four 4-x-4-x-6-foot (or 7-foot) pallets — of merchandise at a time. Often these truckloads have manifests listing the retail and wholesale price of each item on the truck. If you have access to the more than 10,000 square feet of warehouse that you'll need to unpack and process this amount of merchandise, then you're in business.

Several types of salvage merchandise are available:

>> **Unclaimed freight:** When a trucking company delivers merchandise, a *manifest* (a document containing the contents of the shipment) accompanies the freight. If, for some reason, a portion of the shipment arrives incomplete, contains the wrong items, or is damaged, the entire shipment may be refused by the merchant. The trucking company is now stuck with as much as a truckload of freight. The original seller may not want to pay the freight charges to return the merchandise to his or her warehouse (or accept blame for an incorrect shipment), and so the freight becomes the trucker's problem. The trucking companies arrive at agreements with liquidators to buy this freight in the various areas that the liquidators serve. This way, truckers are never far from a location where they can dump, er, *drop off* merchandise.

>> **Returns:** Did you know that after you buy something, decide you don't want it, and return it to the store or mail-order house, it can never be sold as new again (in most states anyway)? Such merchandise is generally sent to a liquidator who agrees in advance to pay a flat percentage for goods. The liquidator must move the merchandise to someone else. All major retailers

liquidate returns, and much of this merchandise ends up on eBay or in closeout stores.

TIP

If you're handy at repairing electronics or computers, you'd probably do very well with a specialized lot. You may easily be able to revitalize damaged merchandise, often using parts from two unsalable items to come up with one that you can sell in like-new working condition.

>> **Liquidations:** Liquidators buy liquidation merchandise by truckloads and sell it in smaller lots. The merchandise comes from financially stressed or bankrupt companies that need to raise cash quickly.

>> **Seasonal overstocks:** Remember my motto? Here it is again: "Buy off-season, sell on-season." At the end of the season, a store may find its shelves overloaded with seasonal merchandise (such as swimsuits in August) that it must get rid of to make room for the fall and winter stock. These brand-new items become salvage merchandise because they're seasonal overstocks. If the brands are quality, they may sell well in the following year.

>> **Shelf-pulls:** Have you ever passed up one item in the store for the one behind it in the display because its box was in better condition? Sometimes the plastic bubble or the package is dented, and you'd rather have a pristine one. That box you just passed up may be destined to become a *shelf-pull.* The item inside may be in perfect condition, but it's cosmetically unsalable in the retail-store environment.

WARNING

A proportion of liquidation items, unclaimed freight, and returns may not be salable for the reasons that I discuss in the rest of this section. Although you'll acquire many gems that stand to bring you profit, you'll also be left with a varying percentage of useless items. Caveat emptor.

Items by the pallet

Some suppliers take the risk and purchase salvaged merchandise by the truckload. They then break up each truckload and sell the merchandise to you a pallet at a time. You'll probably find some local liquidators who offer this service, or you can go online to find one. Here's the rub: finding the right person to buy from.

WARNING

As in any business, you'll find both good-guy liquidators and bad actors. As you know, the world is full of scammers and multilevel marketers who are in business to take your money. No one trying to sell you merchandise can possibly *guarantee* that you'll make money, so beware of liquidators who offer this kind of promise. I don't care who they are or what they say. Carefully research whomever you choose to buy from. Use an Internet search engine and search for the words *salvage, liquidation,* and *pallet merchandise.*

Some liquidation sellers sell their merchandise in the same condition that it ships in to their location, so what you get is a crapshoot. You may lose money on some items while making back your money on others. Other sellers who charge a bit more will remove less-desirable merchandise from the pallets. Some may even make up deluxe pallets with better-quality merchandise. These loads cost more, but if they're filled with the type of merchandise that you're interested in selling, you'll probably write better descriptions and subsequently do a better job selling them.

Getting a pallet of merchandise shipped to you can cost a bundle, so finding a source for your liquidation merchandise that's close to your base of operations is a good idea. You'll notice that many liquidation sites have several warehouses, which translates to lower shipping costs for the buyer. (They can then also accept merchandise from places close to the various warehouses.) You might see FOB (freight on board) and a city name — which means that when you buy the merchandise, you own it in the city listed. You're responsible for whatever it costs to ship the merchandise to your door. Search around; you may have to go through many sources before you find the right one for you.

When you find a source from which you want to buy merchandise by the pallet, check out a few things before spending your hard-earned cash:

>> Does this vendor sell mostly to flea marketers (you might not want that kind of merchandise because you're looking for *quality* at a low price) or closeout stores (more retail-oriented)?

>> Did you get a reply within 24 hours after calling or emailing?

>> Does anyone you speak to appear to care about your doing business with them?

>> Are the available lots within your budget?

>> Are the lots general or have they been sorted to include only the type of merchandise that you want to sell?

>> How long has this liquidator been in business and where does its merchandise come from?

>> Does the source guarantee that you *will* make money or state that you *can* make money by buying the right merchandise? **Remember:** No one can guarantee that you'll make money.

>> Does the supplier offer on its website references that you can contact to find out some usable information on this seller's items and the percentage of unsalable goods in a box or pallet?

>> Is a hard sell involved? Or is it a matter-of-fact deal?

WARNING

Before you get dazzled by a low, low price on a huge lot and click the Buy It Now button, check the shipping cost. Many so-called wholesalers will lure you in with bargain-basement prices, only to charge you three times the normal shipping costs. Do your homework before you buy!

Job lots

Manufacturers often have to get rid of merchandise, too. Perhaps a particular manufacturer made five million bobble-head dolls and then sold only four million to retailers. It has to unload this merchandise (known as *job lots*) quickly so it'll have the cash to invest in next season's array of items. Job lots often consist of hundreds or thousands of a single item. You'd best enjoy what you're selling because you'll be looking at the stuff for a while.

REMEMBER

Remember supply and demand — don't ever flood the eBay market. Otherwise your item will become valueless.

Many websites specialize in job lots, but you have to visit them often because the deals are constantly changing. One worth checking out is Liquidation.com, shown in Figure 11-2. Visit them at `www.liquidation.com`.

FIGURE 11-2:
Liquidation.com
has desirable lots
of liquidation
merchandise.

Drop-shipping to your customers

Some middlemen, wholesalers, and liquidators specialize in selling to online auctioneers through drop-ship services or warehouses. Some crafty eBay sellers make lots of money selling lists of drop-shipping sources to eBay sellers — I hope not to you. Dealing with a drop-shipper means that you don't ever have to take possession of (or pay for) the merchandise. You pay a monthly fee for accessing the vendor's website to select items. You're given a photo of the item and, after you sell the item itself, you give the vendor the address of the buyer. The vendor charges your credit card for the item plus shipping, and ships the item to your customer for you.

This way of doing business can cost *you* more and lower your profits. If you're in business, your goal is to make as much money as you can. Because the drop-shippers are in business too, they'll mark up the merchandise they sell to you (and the shipping cost) so they can make their profit. Drop-shipping can work as a *supplement* to your basic eBay business.

Be careful when using a drop-shipper. Ask for references. Don't give them your credit-card number with carte blanche to keep charging your account month by month if you're not benefiting from their services. See whether a zillion sellers are selling the same merchandise on eBay — and not getting any bites. Check, too, that the price you will pay for the item leaves you room for profit based on prior eBay sales. I've researched some of these items on eBay and noted that many inexperienced sellers only mark up drop-ship goods by a fraction. They seem to be happy selling $5 over cost; they don't take into consideration how much the fees impact their profits. That's just not smart business on their part, hence they can ruin the market for such items for everyone else.

Also, what happens if the drop-shipper runs out of an item that you've just sold? You can't just say "oops" to your buyer without getting some nasty feedback. It's *your* online reputation at stake. If you find a solid source and believe in the product, order a quantity and have it shipped to your door. Don't pay for someone else's mark-up for the privilege of shipping to your customers.

Tips for the modest investor

If you're interested in making money in your eBay ventures but you're starting with limited cash, follow this list of eBay inventory do's and don'ts:

>> **Don't** spend more than you can afford to lose. If you shop at boutiques and expensive department stores, buy things that you like to wear yourself (or know you can give as gifts) in case they don't sell.

>> **Do** try to find something local that's unavailable in a wider area. For example, if you live in an out-of-the-way place that has a local specialty, try selling that on eBay.

>> **Don't** go overboard and buy something really cheap just because it's cheap. Figure out who would *want* the item first.

>> **Do** consider buying in bulk, especially if you know that the item sells well on eBay or if the item is inexpensive. Chances are good that if you buy one and it sells well on eBay, by the time you try to buy more, the item's sold out. If an item is inexpensive (say, 99 cents), I always buy at least five. If no one bids on the item when you hold your auction, you're only out $5. (Anyone out there need any Bicentennial Commemorative coffee mugs?)

Making the eBay Store Decision

Perhaps the second question I'm asked (after where to find merchandise) is "when should I open my eBay Store?" It isn't rocket science to run one and not really necessary when you're starting out.

The requirements for opening an eBay Store are basic. However, I highly recommend that you transact business (sell) on the site for quite a while before you open an eBay Store because — before you take that plunge — you need a solid understanding of how eBay works and how to handle all types of transactions. These are eBay's requirements:

>> You must be registered as an eBay seller, with a credit card on file.

>> Have an idea of how much you want to spend to run the store (*HINT: Not much at first*).

MARSHA SAYS

When I taught classes at eBay University, one of the first questions I'd hear from those new to eBay — I hear it a lot even now — was, "What *kind* of store should I get?" The answer is simple: You don't have to get one. You can continue to sell items on eBay and never open a store. I know many people who have been selling successfully on the site for over a decade without a store. Yes, there are benefits to having an eBay Store, but it all depends on how much you're selling on the site. Read on and make an educated decision that makes sense for you — and fits your commitment to selling.

Selling from Your Own Virtual Storefront

At an eBay Store, you are not constrained by the auction format of a 1-to-10-day maximum. You can list your fixed-price items in your eBay Store on a "good 'til cancelled" basis (and set an "on vacation" sign when you go out of town). Most of all, you can add custom pages to tell the world more about your business.

TIP

I don't like to pull punches with my readers, so let me give you a bit of advice. Opening an eBay Store without a large stock of items, or many items that you stock in multiples, makes no sense. Opening an eBay Store is really for experienced sellers — those who make a business on the eBay site selling merchandise they bought for the purpose of reselling. Retailers who come to the eBay site to expand their business can be successful with the stores, but certainly it helps to know the e-commerce ropes already. To catch up on all you need to know, you can always read my *eBay Business All-In-One For Dummies*, 4th Edition.

WARNING

Too many readers who are new to eBay email me after reading this book and tell me that they opened a store and have had no sales. Whoa, there; first things first. You must first list a bunch of items on eBay that attract eyes. Attracting eyes makes your listings more desirable (and affects your status in eBay's "Best Match" search). Also try to list some special items in the auction format to draw people to your store — simple as that.

Paying the landlord

When paid annually, the rent for a Starter eBay Store is as low as $7.95 per month (paid by the year $4.95 per month); Basic Stores are $27.95 ($21.95); Premium Stores pay $74.95 ($59.95); and Anchor Stores (just like your local department store) pay $349.95 a month ($299.95 paid by the year). The benefits of each level of store are based on your sales revenue: The more you sell, the better the deal you get on insertion fees. There are also other benefits to owning a store: cost-per-click advertising, sales management tools, vacation holds, Markdown Manager, and lots of promotional benefits for your merchandise.

The reasonable pricing behind eBay Stores is a remarkable bargain. For as little as $7.95 a month, you have the opportunity to sell your merchandise to over 500 million active users!

Stores get a prescribed number for free listings per month:

>> **Starter Store:** 100 of any listing

>> **Basic Store:** 250 fixed-price listings, 250 auctions

>> **Premium Store:** 1,000 fixed-price listings, 500 auctions

>> **Anchor Store:** 10,000 fixed-price listings, 1,000 auctions

After stores have exhausted their free listing insertions, they are charged a nominal fee. See Table 11-1 for the fees.

TABLE 11-1 **eBay Store Listing Fees after Using Free Quota**

Type of Store	Auctions	Fixed Price
Starter	30¢	30¢
Basic	25¢	25¢
Premium	15¢	10¢
Anchor	10¢	5¢

You can use your number of free insertion fee listings for your auction-style listings in the following categories:

>> Antiques

>> Art

>> Clothing, Shoes & Accessories

>> Coins & Paper Money

>> Collectibles

>> Dolls & Bears

>> Entertainment Memorabilia

>> Health & Beauty

>> Jewelry & Watches

>> Pottery & Glass

>> Sports Memorabilia, Fan Shop & Sports Cards

>> Stamps

>> Toys & Hobbies

Listing fees and monthly rent can be just the tip of the iceberg if you choose to get fancy by using all kinds of options. My recommendation? Don't spend too much on them until you're fully entrenched in an eBay business — by that time, you'll have the experience to know what to add and when. Stick with the basics.

A real benefit to having an eBay Store is that your *final value fees* are lower than the flat 10 percent charged to non-store owners. Final value fees for eBay Stores are charged differently by category based on the total amount paid by the customer, including shipping. Final value fees vary depending on your store size and what categories you sell in. They can run as low as 4 percent to as high as 12 percent when selling Books, DVDs, and Movies. Because these fees are often a moving target, I suggest you check eBay at www.ebay.com/help/selling/fees-credits-invoices/store-selling-fees?id=4122 to view the current pricing trends.

TIP

When pricing any of your items for sale — or even deciding whether to have an eBay Store, use a calculator like the one at www.salecalc.com to work out the numbers. (See Chapter 20 for more details.)

When you have an eBay Store, you'll have a bunch of fixed-price listings, but no doubt you'll want to run an auction from time to time. Your auctions are included in your free monthly listing quota; after you exceed that number, you have to pay an insertion fee. On the good side, your final value fees are lower than they'd be if you didn't have a store.

Opening your eBay Store

Because this book is your introduction to eBay, I just give you some ideas about opening an eBay Store. In my more advanced book, *eBay Business All-In-One For Dummies*, I take you step by step through the basics of opening your store.

Once open, your store will have its own personalized URL, which you can link to in your emails or from your Facebook business page (or other social media sites). The web address for my store is

http://stores.ebay.com/Marsha-Colliers-Fabulous-Finds

Naming your eBay Store is your first challenge. Choose a name that describes the types of items your store will carry or one that includes your User ID. Don't choose a name that is so esoteric or overly creative that it doesn't give possible shoppers a clue as to what you carry. A creative store name and logo are pictured in Figure 11-3.

As you can see on the ModelSupplies Store page, each store can have its own categories. You get to make them up yourself so your customers can find items within your store in an organized manner. You can define up to 300 custom categories up to three levels deep. Each category can have a maximum of 29 characters for each name in your store. (In Chapter 17, you can learn more about how Anita Nelson, owner of ModelSupplies, promotes her business on social media.)

FIGURE 11-3:
The eBay Store
page for
ModelSupplies.

Your eBay Store home page has links for your Store Information: Store Policies and About the Store page. The About the Store page is the same as your profile (which I discuss in Chapter 14).

Spend some serious time on eBay before you open an eBay Store. Study some of the successful stores. You need to have enough know-how to make your store a success!

Chapter 12

Take the Pain out of Closing the Deal and Shipping

The sale is made and you have a buyer, who has paid, and the money is in your account. Sounds perfect, doesn't it? It is if you watch your step, keep on top of things, and act like a professional.

In this chapter, I help you figure out how to stay organized by showing you what business information you need to keep and for how long. I also include tips and etiquette on communicating with the buyer so that you're most likely to come out with positive feedback. In addition, you find out how to pack your item, assess costs, and make sure that the item reaches the buyer when you said it would (oh, yeah . . . and in one piece).

eBay will be instituting Managed Delivery for sellers sometime in 2020. Although shipping can be the bane of your eBay business, after you learn the ropes, it can even be profitable.

MARSHA SAYS

Remember that whenever you farm out pieces of your business for others to do, you will be incurring expenses. For small and occasional sellers, this is not a good idea. Even though discounts are promised (they're mostly for large sellers), *please* do the math before participating in *any* program. You, as a small business, can learn the tricks of the shipping trade (outlined in this chapter) and keep the extra money for yourself, thereby raising your profits.

Remember, also, that if you plan to expand to a website (you should) or sell on other platforms, the services mentioned at the end of this chapter will serve you across the Internet — not just on eBay.

Bookkeeping and Staying Organized

Although I don't recommend lining your nest with every scrap from every sale you run, you can safely keep some documents without mutating into a giant pack rat. Even if you're not quite an eBay expert (yet), you may be comfortable storing this information electronically. I often use the Windows Snipping tool to take a screen shot of important data (if you are keeping important data, be sure to keep records with the following information). If you'd like, you can print and file these essentials:

>> **The listing page as it appeared when the item closed:** This page gives you a record of the item name and number and a lot of other useful information. The page also includes the item description (and any revisions you made to it), which is handy if the buyer argues that an item's disintegrating before his eyes and you honestly described it as just "well-loved."

If you're the buyer, you can look it up in your Purchase History on your My eBay page. Figure 12-1 shows how you can access your purchases as far back as three years. (If you're the seller, the information will be in your My eBay ⇨ Sell ⇨ Sold area.) However, if you use the custom link that appears in your End of Listing (or Order Confirmed in the case of a buyer) email (see the next bullet), you can access the listing online for up to 90 days. Print the page *before* you forget about it, file it where you know you can find it, and *then* forget about it.

>> **The Order Confirmed email you receive from eBay that notifies a buyer that the sale is over (sellers get an Item Sale Confirmed email):** If you lose this email, you can't get it back because eBay doesn't keep it. Sellers can find ended listings, whether sold or unsold, for the current month and the previous three months via their My eBay pages.

You can set up a separate folder in your email client for purchases and sold-item emails. When one comes in, just read it and then drag it over to its special folder. That way, you can always check this folder for the information you need.

MARSHA SAYS

>> **Messages between you and the buyer:** In the virtual world, email is as close to having a face-to-face conversation as most people get. Your email correspondence is a living record of all the things you discuss with the buyer to complete the transaction. When you use eBay messages, the record is archived online for you (or eBay) to inspect should there be an issue.

>> **Payment notices:** You get a notice from the payment provider when the buyer pays for the item. The notice has the listing information and the buyer's shipping information. (When that email arrives, the clock begins to tick on sending the item.)

>> **Refund requests you make or receive:** If you make a request to eBay for a refund from a sale that doesn't go through, keep revisiting it until you can view the credit on your statement.

>> **Tracking numbers:** eBay wants to have a tracking number for every item you ship. So as a sound business practice, sellers should upload tracking numbers as labels are printed. When you print your shipping labels on eBay, the numbers are automatically inserted into the transaction record. If a customer claims that an item never arrived, the tracking number can prove that it did. I explain more about tracking and electronic options later in this chapter.

>> **Receipts for items that you buy for the sole purpose of selling on eBay:** This documentation comes in handy at tax time.

FIGURE 12-1:
eBay Purchase
History holds
three years of
your purchases.

Purchase history	‹	Unpaid items	Unpaid invoices	Orders	Canceled items	Canceled invoices	Returns and canceled ord	›

Orders

essie nail polish, ballet
slippers, p...
$9.00
Buy It Now
Free shipping
Almost gone

○ Not hidden ○ Show hidden items

See orders from: The last 60 days ▾   Filter by: All ▾

2019
2018
2017

ORDER DATE
Aug 06, 2019

ORDER TOTAL
US $7.75

Return this item

Leave feedback
More actions ▾

1 item sold by

Essie Nail Polish Lacquer #162 Ballet Slippers Light Pink
Great Colors 0.42oz
(132696598885)

✓ Delivered on **Aug 08, 2019**
Tracking number: 9400109699937708402966
ⓘ This item has been shipped.

ITEM PRICE:
US $7.75

REMEMBER

Someday, the Internal Revenue Service (or government agency that collects taxes in your area) may knock on your door. Scary, but true. Like hurricanes and asteroid strikes, audits happen. Any accountant worth his or her salt will tell you that the best way to handle the possibility of an audit is to be prepared for the worst — even if every eBay transaction you conduct runs smooth as silk and you've kept your records sparkling clean. See Chapter 9 for more tax information.

TIP

When you accept online payments by PayPal (PayPal Premier or Business members only), you can download your transaction history for use in QuickBooks, Quicken, or Excel. Additionally, these programs are excellent sources for your documentation.

TIP

When it comes to printouts or electronic archives of emails and documents generated during transactions, you can dump them as soon as the item arrives at the destination and you get your positive feedback. If you get negative feedback, hang on to your documentation a little longer (say, at least for 30 days or until you're sure that the issues it raises are resolved and everyone's satisfied). If selling on eBay becomes a fairly regular source of income, save all receipts for items you purchased to sell; for tax purposes, that's inventory.

TIP

If you sell specialized items, you can keep track of trends — and who your frequent buyers are — by saving records and connecting with those buyers through social media. This prudent habit becomes an excellent marketing strategy when you discover that a segment of eBay users faithfully visits and purchases your items. A *community* of buyers. Imagine that.

Talking to Buyers: The ABCs of Good Communication

You've heard it countless times — talk is cheap. Compared to what? Granted, empty promises are a dime a dozen, but honest-to-goodness talk, comprehensive descriptions, and efficient messages are worth their weight in gold and good feedback — especially on eBay. Sometimes *not* talking is costly.

A smooth exchange of money and merchandise starts with you (the seller) and your attitude toward the transaction. Your listing description and then your first contact — soon after the sale is made — set the transaction in motion and the tone for that transaction. If all goes well, *no more than* a day should elapse between getting paid and sending the item.

If you haven't received your payment in two days, Chapter 13 gives you all the information you need to ramp up communication for your buyer.

If you haven't received a payment, I suggest you send an invoice. Here's how:

1. **Start at your My eBay Summary, All Selling.**

   Locate your newly sold item. *Hint:* It should be at the top of the listings.

2. **Select the Send Invoice item from the More Action menu on the left.**

   You are presented with a page that summarizes the transaction with a "working version" of the invoice.

3. **Examine the invoice displayed on this page and make any changes if necessary.**

   If the buyer has purchased more than one item from you and hasn't used the shopping cart, click the link to combine purchases.

4. **Double-check that the shipping amount is correct (be sure alternatives are offered if you have some) and when you're satisfied, click the Send Invoice button.**

   If you select the Copy Me check box on this invoice, you'll receive a copy of the invoice. The buyer's copy has a link in the invoice, enabling the buyer to pay directly to PayPal (if you accept PayPal for payment).

Another way to contact your buyers, should you have an additional message for them, is to go to your My eBay page, scroll down to the Items I've Sold area, find the transaction, and click the drop-down menu next to the View Order Details button. From there, click the Contact Buyer link.

Thank you — mean it

What do all the successful big-name e-commerce stores have in common? Yes, great prices, good merchandise, and nice-looking web pages. But with all things being equal, customer service always wins hands down. One department store in the United States, Nordstrom, has such a great reputation that the store happily took back a set of snow tires because a customer wasn't happy with them. No big deal, maybe — until you notice that Nordstrom doesn't even *sell* snow tires! (A word to the wise: They did that exactly once.)

A friend of mine who owns restaurants calls this level of customer satisfaction the Wow! factor. If customers (no matter what they're buying) say, "Wow!" during or after the transaction — admiringly or happily — you've satisfied the customer. A good rule to go by: *Give people the same level of service you expect when you're on the buying end.* The best eBay sellers are also regular eBay buyers.

TIP

A special way to add value to the transaction for your buyer is to send a personal "item shipped" email — the buyer's email can be found in the transaction record. I send them to buyers who purchase high-value items. Congratulate the person on buying the item — making him or her feel good about the purchase — by saying thanks. Send it when you ship the item. A comprehensive, friendly email provides these important details:

- » Item name.

- » Statement that you have shipped and what type of shipping you used.

- » Let the customer know the tracking number (you've already input that number into the selling record) and approximate delivery date.

- » Make it clear how much you care about their satisfaction with the transaction and ask that they contact you immediately if there is an issue with the item.

- » Offer a phone number and add your personal thanks for the transaction.

- » Suggest that if all goes well, you'll be looking forward to receiving their feedback. (See Chapter 4 for more on feedback.)

REMEMBER

Note that there is an email reference ID at the bottom of all eBay correspondence. (It looks something like *Email reference id: [#55619d4736a14099b3e741a4c-cb468b4#].*) This reference number, or one like it, appears on *all* official eBay emails. eBay uses them as a reference number to prove authenticity should you have to call them with an issue on your transaction.

Keep communication open

If you have a good transaction going (the majority of them *are* good), the buyer will reply to your email or pay the invoice within a business day. *Never* **let an email or eBay message go unanswered.**

Send a thank-you note in every package you ship. This note has a double purpose: It should promote you as a seller *and* thank the customer. The one I send in every shipment thanks the customer, mentions that I look forward to doing business with the buyer again, and provides a link to my website. I set up these notes to print four on an 8½-x-11-inch sheet of paper and print them on my color laser printer. (Don't forget to put in a plug for positive feedback.)

Shipping without Going Postal

Shipping can be the most time-consuming (and most dreaded) task for many eBay sellers. Even if the selling portion of your transaction goes flawlessly, the item has to get to the buyer in one piece. If it doesn't, the deal could be ruined — and so could your reputation.

This section briefs you on shipping etiquette, gives you details about the three most popular shipping options (the U.S. Postal Service, UPS, and FedEx Ground), and offers tips on how to make sure that your package is ready to ride.

The best way to avoid shipping problems is to do your homework beforehand, determine which method is likely to work best, and spell out in your item description exactly how you intend to ship the item that you're putting up for sale. It's beneficial to give buyers an option should they want overnight or Priority shipping. Here's how I handle the process:

1. Before listing an item, get a single package ready to ship.

You don't have to seal the package right away, but you should have it ready to seal because the two critical factors in shipping are weight and time. The more a package weighs and the faster it has to be delivered, the higher the costs. (I cover packing materials and tips later in this section.) The time to think about packing and shipping is *before* you put the item up for sale — that way, last-minute surprises are less likely to arise while your buyer waits for the item!

2. Know your carrier options.

In the United States, the three main shipping options for most eBay transactions are the U.S. Postal Service, UPS, and FedEx. See the section "Shopping for a shipper" (try saying *that* five times fast) for how you can get rate options from each service, painlessly and online. Compare costs and services.

MARSHA SAYS

In the over-twenty years I have been selling on eBay, I find the United States Postal Service to be the most flexible, reliable, and reasonably priced shipper for my small business. Plus, your letter carrier visits your house every day. He or she can be a helpful ally in your shipping because you can set up free carrier pickup on the USPS website for your outgoing packages. (No more trips to the post office.)

3. Before quoting the shipping fees in the listing, make sure that you gather all appropriate costs.

Offering Free Shipping is very common on eBay because it gives you an advantage in eBay searches. When you do, build the shipping cost into the price you ask for the item. When you budget your costs, you may want to add in a nominal handling fee (up to $1 isn't out of line) to cover your packing materials, labels, and time. These costs can add up quickly as you start making multiple transactions. You should also include any insurance costs and signature-confirmation costs, should they be necessary for the item. See the sidebar "Insuring your peace of mind (and your shipment)" for more information.

WARNING

Some shoddy eBay sellers inflate shipping and handling charges to make added profit. *Shame on them*. Purposely overcharging is tacky, ugly, and immature. (It will also penalize your listings in a Best Match search.) Often the buyer also figures it out after one look at the postage on the label — and that can easily net you a negative feedback.

If you don't offer Free Shipping, post a flat shipping amount (or use the eBay online shipping calculator — see Chapter 10 for more on how to use this tool). This way, buyers can calculate this cost when they consider their shopping strategies. Figure out what the packed item will weigh, and then give a good estimate; the online calculators can help.

If the item is heavy, you could indicate that the buyer should use the eBay shipping calculator. You give the weight of the package when you put together your listing; eBay calculates shipping costs for the buyer, based on your zip code and the buyer's.

4. **Send the package.**

When should you ship the package? Common courtesy says it should go out as soon as the buyer has paid for the item and shipping charges. If the buyer has followed through with his or her side of the bargain, you should do the same. Ship that package no more than a day after payment. If you can't, contact the buyer immediately.

Shopping for a shipper

If only you could transport your item the way they did on *Star Trek* — "Beam up that antique lamp, Scotty!" Alas, it's not so. First Class and Priority Mail via the U.S. Postal Service (USPS) are pretty much the eBay standard for domestic as well as international shipments.

WARNING

Know that if you don't insure an item, you are still responsible for making sure that the item arrives at the buyer's door. Federal mail–order laws state that when an item is paid for, it must be delivered to the buyer within 30 days unless there has been an agreement between the buyer and the seller for other arrangements. If it gets lost in the mail, you'll have to replace the item or refund the buyer's money.

INSURING YOUR PEACE OF MIND (AND YOUR SHIPMENT)

Sure, "damaged in the mail" is an excuse we've all heard hundreds of times, but despite everyone's best efforts, sometimes things do get damaged or misplaced during shipment. The universe can be a dangerous place; that's what insurance is for. I usually get insurance on expensive items, one-of-a-kind items, or very fragile items. On eBay, covering the expense for that insurance falls on the seller.

The major shippers all offer insurance that's fairly reasonably priced, so check out their rates on their websites. Remember also that all USPS Priority Mail packages include $50 insurance for free. But don't forget to read the details. For example, many collectibles and gift items on eBay are sold MIMB (Mint in Mint Box). True, the condition of the original box often has a bearing on the final value of the item inside, but the U.S. Postal Service insures only what is *in* the box. So, if you sold a Malibu Barbie MIMB, USPS insures only the doll and not the collectible value of the doll in the original box. Pack carefully so that your buyer gets what's been paid for. Be mindful that shippers won't make good on insurance claims if they suspect you of causing the damage by doing a lousy job of packing.

Alternatively, when you're selling on eBay in earnest, you can purchase your own parcel-protection policy from a private insurer such as U-PIC (http://u-pic.com), Stamps. com, or Endicia. When you use this type of insurance, combined with preprinted electronic postage, you no longer have to stand in line at the post office to have your insured package logged in by the clerk at the counter. If you're shipping a lot, you can have an ongoing policy with them, or you can insure a single package through the form on their site.

Some sellers have their own form of *self-insurance.* Realize that I use the term "self-insurance" as a descriptive phrase only. You may not charge your buyer for insurance on eBay. Here's what I offer my buyers at no cost to them:

- On lower-priced items, I am willing to refund the buyer's money if the item is lost or damaged, per eBay policy.

- On some items I sell, I have a *risk reserve.* That means I have more than one of the item I sold. If the item is lost or destroyed, I can send the backup item as a replacement.

TIP

Whether you're at the post office, UPS, FedEx, or your doctor's office, be ready, willing, and able to wait in line. There's definitely a "rush hour" at my neighborhood post office — everybody's in a rush, so everything moves at a glacial pace. Avoid both the noontime and post-work crunches (easier on the nerves). A good time to ship is around 10:30 a.m., when everyone is still in a good mood. If you have to go in the afternoon, go about 2:00 p.m., when the clerks are back from their lunch breaks and friendly faces (mine, too — I always smile!) can take the edge off those brusque lunchtime encounters. If you can ship from home, why not save yourself the time and stress by requesting a free carrier pickup? You can do this on the USPS Mobile app or from the post office website. Here's the link:

```
http://usps.com/pickup
```

U.S. Postal Service

The U.S. Postal Service (USPS) is the butt of many unfair jokes and cheap shots, but when it comes right down to it, I think USPS is still the most efficient and inexpensive way to ship items — eBay or otherwise. It also supplies free boxes and labels for Priority and Express Mail packages. Here are some ways eBay members get their items from here to there via USPS:

>> **Priority Mail:** As I mentioned earlier, this is the *de facto* standard method of shipping for eBay users. I love the free boxes, and I like the rates. The promised delivery time is two to three days, although I've experienced rare delays of up to four days during peak holiday periods. This class of service includes up to $50 of insurance for your item.

Cost? As of this writing (rates are always subject to change), Priority Mail costs as little as $6.95 for a 1-pound package within your local zone when you print your postage electronically. The fees go up from there, calculated according to weight and distance, unless you're using Flat-Rate boxes.

A $7.35 ($6.95 printed electronically) Flat-Rate Priority envelope is also available. You can ship as much stuff as you want — as long as you can fit it into the supplied 9½-x-12½-inch envelope. (You'll be surprised how much you can jam into those envelopes.) You can reinforce the envelope with clear packing tape.

Using Flat-Rate Priority Mail boxes (which come in a multitude of sizes), you can send heavy packages at reduced rates. Order the boxes directly from the USPS. Table 12-1 shows you some of the wide selection!

To order your free boxes, labels, forms, and just about anything else that you'll need to ship Priority Mail, go to the Postal Store (see Figure 12-2) at www.usps.com/shippingsupplies and click Free Shipping Supplies on the left. Orders can take up to a month to arrive, so be sure to order before you need more boxes.

>> To keep up on any changes in USPS service — like during the holiday season, the USPS delivered packages on Sunday — be sure to visit https://about.usps.com/newsroom every once in a while.

TIP

To save money, print your postage electronically. You can do this through a service such as Endicia.com, Stamps.com, eBay, or PirateShip.

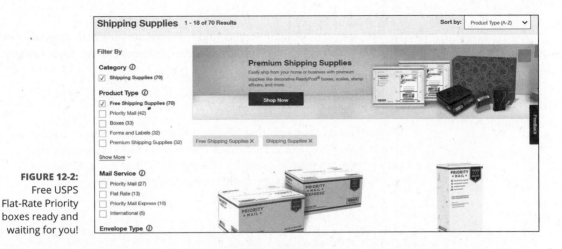

FIGURE 12-2:
Free USPS
Flat-Rate Priority
boxes ready and
waiting for you!

>> **Priority Mail Express 1-Day:** If the item needs to be delivered the next day, use Express Mail. The Postal Service promises delivery no later than 3:00 p.m. the following afternoon (even on weekends or holidays). It includes $100 worth of insurance and you can get free boxes and envelopes.

Cost? Priority Express Mail runs $31.30 for packages one pound and under. Express Mail also has a Flat-Rate envelope, which is the same size as the Priority Flat-Rate envelope and ships for $25.50. (When you print your postage electronically, you save about 5 percent — with the aforementioned items at $29.74 and Flat-Rate at $22.68.)

WARNING

Don't use Flat–Rate or Regional boxes unless your item weighs more than 20 pounds. Why? They're much more expensive to ship.

TIP

The Postal Service offers a free carrier pickup for Priority Mail and Express Mail, no matter how many separate packages are included. If you have several packages, carrier pickup is an excellent option.

Get to know your mail carrier and have your parcels ready and stacked up for him or her for the regular stop at your home. The mail carrier will be happy to take your packages back to the post office at no additional charge. (A bottle of icy-cold water for your letter carrier on hot days will go a long way to smooth your relationship!)

>> **First-Class Mail:** If your item weighs one pound or less (15.99 ounces to be exact), you can use First-Class Mail. First-Class Mail is considerably cheaper than Priority. I try to ship as much as I can via First-Class Mail so I can have the edge on other sellers by offering free shipping.

>> **Media Mail:** This is a popular option among those who sell books on eBay. It's the new name for two older products, Book Rate and Special Standard Mail. Media

Mail rates start at $2.75 for the first pound and increases for each additional pound. It's cheap and convenient, but your item can take up to ten days to arrive.

» **Other options:** For items over $750 in value, you need a signature confirmation — as well as shipping tracking information — to cover your shipment under eBay's Seller Protection.

You can check on whether the package was delivered (or whether an attempt was made to deliver it) by typing the number online at www.usps.com/shipping/ trackandconfirm.htm. You can also click the link to the tracking number in My eBay or PayPal after you've copied the number into the sales record.

ZONED BASE PRICING

In 2019, the USPS deemed that all packages (including First Class) will be charged not only by weight, but by zones. The USPS has eight zones within the contiguous United States and a ninth zone for outlying territories. Zones are based on what city you are shipping from. Below is a map showing the zones when shipping from Los Angeles. My website has more information at www.coolebaytools.com/tools/what-postal- zone-from-zip-code.

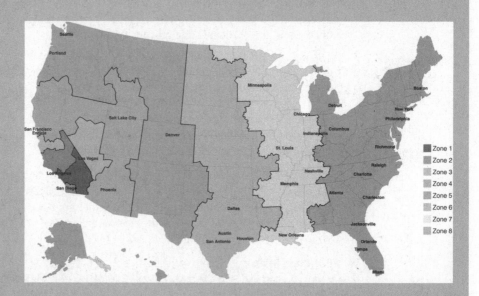

You'll also need to heed package size because larger boxes may incur higher postage costs when shipping via Priority Mail, Priority Mail Express, and Parcel Select. More on DIM (Dimensional Weight) pricing further on.

TABLE 12-1

Free Priority Mail Packaging

Size (in Inches)	Description
$7\frac{9}{16}$" x $5\frac{7}{16}$" x$\frac{5}{8}$"	Priority Mail DVD Box
$9\frac{1}{4}$" x $6\frac{1}{4}$" x 2"	Priority Mail Small (1096L)
$5\frac{3}{8}$" x $8\frac{5}{8}$" $1\frac{5}{8}$"	Small Flat Rate Box
$11\frac{1}{2}$" x $13\frac{1}{8}$" x $2\frac{3}{8}$"	Priority Mail Medium (1097)
$11\frac{7}{8}$" x $3\frac{3}{8}$" x $13\frac{5}{8}$"	Priority Mail Flat-Rate Medium 2
$12\frac{3}{8}$" x $15\frac{1}{4}$" x 3"	Priority Mail Large (#1095)
$12\frac{1}{8}$" x $13\frac{3}{8}$" x $2\frac{3}{4}$"	Priority Mail Medium (#1092)
10" x 7" x $4\frac{3}{4}$"	Priority Regional Rate A1
$10\frac{15}{16}$" x $2\frac{3}{8}$" x $12\frac{13}{16}$"	Priority Mail Regional Rate A2
12" x $10\frac{1}{4}$ x 5"	Priority Mail Regional Rate B2
$14\frac{3}{8}$" x $2\frac{7}{8}$" x $15\frac{7}{8}$"	Regional Rate B2
6" x 38"	Priority Large Triangle Tube 1098
6" x 25"	Priority Small Triangle Tube (1098S)
7" x 7" x 6"	Priority Mail Small Square 4
12" x 12" x 8"	Priority Mail Square 7
11" x $8\frac{1}{2}$" x $5\frac{1}{2}$"	Priority Medium Flat-Rate 1
$23\frac{11}{16}$" x $11\frac{3}{4}$" x 3"	Priority Large Board Game Flat-Rate (GBFRB)
12" x 12" x $5\frac{1}{2}$"	Priority Large Flat-Rate Box LARGEFRB
$7\frac{1}{2}$" x $5\frac{1}{8}$" x $14\frac{3}{8}$"	Priority Mail Shoe Box OSHOEBOX
$11\frac{5}{8}$" x $15\frac{1}{8}$"	Priority Mail Tyvek Envelope
$9\frac{1}{2}$" x $12\frac{1}{2}$"	Priority Mail Padded Flat-Rate Envelope
6" x 10"	Small Flat Rate Envelope
$12\frac{1}{2}$" x $9\frac{1}{2}$"	Priority Flat-Rate Envelope
5" x 10"	Priority Window Envelope

REMEMBER

Tracking numbers are important when you try to collect insurance for an item that was never delivered or if the buyer says the item was never delivered. It gives you proof from the Postal Service (or other shipper) that the item was sent. (I explain insuring shipments earlier in this chapter.) If your package gets lost in the mail for a few weeks, this number may not always reveal the location of your package until it's delivered.

The USPS website (www.usps.com) gives you an overview of the U.S. Postal Service rates so that you can see all your options. It sure beats standing in that endless line! For a complete explanation of domestic rates, check out www.usps.com/ship/mail-shipping-services.htm.

Even better, USPS has a page that can help you determine exactly what your item costs to mail (after you've packaged it and weighed it, of course). Start at the Rate Calculator page at http://postcalc.usps.gov and follow the instructions.

I know this may sound confusing, but you can find a DIM weight calculator at https://www.pirateship.com/usps/priority-mail-cubic to make your life simpler.

For example, (from Stamps.com), an 8-inch length x 6-inch height x 8-inch width (Tier 3) package weighing 8 pounds and being shipped to Zone 6 would cost $21.82 using Priority Mail Commercial Base rates. The same package would cost only $10.18 with USPS cubic pricing. That is a 53 percent savings!

UPS

The folks in the brown UPS trucks love eBay. The options they offer vary, with everything from Overnight service to Ground service. UPS also takes many of the odd-shaped large boxes, such as those for computer equipment that the U.S. Postal Service won't.

UPS makes pickups, but you have to know the exact weight of your package so that you can pay when the UPS driver shows up. UPS charges for this service unless you have a daily shipper account and ship a minimum number of packages with UPS per week.

WARNING

The rates for the same UPS shipment can vary based on whether you have a business account with UPS, whether the package goes to or is picked up at a residence, and whether you use the right kind of form. If you're going to use UPS regularly, be sure to set up an account directly with UPS. There are a lot of surcharges to small shippers.

SHIP SMALLER PACKAGES TO BENEFIT FROM USPS DIM AND CUBIC PRICING

Since June 2019, DIM weight pricing for packages over 1 cubic foot are applied to shipping Zones 1 to 9 for Priority Mail, Priority Mail Express, and Parcel Select. UPS and FedEx have been using DIM pricing since 2015. Calculate DIM rates by multiplying the width x height x length of your package in inches. If the result is more than 1 cubic foot (1,728 cubic inches), divide the result by 166 to determine the dimensional weight. If your box is larger than that, type in Large Package in your shipping software or on eBay's labels. Dimensional weight refers to how much space a package takes up during shipping and only applies to packages larger than 1 cubic foot.

Cubic pricing affords even more discounts on USPS shipping. Priority Mail packages weighing less than 20 pounds and measuring 0.5 cubic feet or less in volume, with no dimension longer than 18 inches, are eligible for Cubic pricing as long as you meet the minimum package requirements. For these packages, you pay shipping costs for the actual size of the package and the shipping distance *instead* of its weight.

Cubic pricing for your USPS package is measured by calculating length x width x height divided by 1728 = cubic feet. No dimension of your package can exceed 18 inches. Based on the size of the package, it will fall into five tiers of shipping costs. Note that eBay labels *do not support* cubic pricing at this time. You can only get cubic pricing from the electronic vendors I mention further on. Also, you cannot use USPS Priority boxes. If you can get away with a poly bag and bubble wrap, you're in the zone.

The table below shows you the savings:

2019 USPS Cubic Pricing by Zone (20 pounds and under)

Cubic Feet (Up to)	0.1	0.2	0.3	0.4	0.5
Zone 1 and 2	6.95	7.34	7.79	7.95	8.07
Zone 3	$7.28	7.68	7.99	8.27	8.56
Zone 4	$7.49	7.91	8.27	8.63	9.13
Zone 5	$7.65	8.12	8.92	9.50	10.34
Zone 6	$7.82	8.40	10.18	11.79	13.95
Zone 7	$7.99	8.61	10.73	12.94	15.75
Zone 8	$8.25	8.92	11.39	14.79	17.91
Zone 9	$9.91	10.92	15.90	20.09	24.96

**MARSHA
SAYS**

SÍ, OUI, JA, YES! SHIPPING INTERNATIONALLY

Money's good no matter what country it comes from. I don't know why, but lots of folks seem to be afraid to ship internationally. Of course, sending an item that far away may be a burden if you're selling a car or a street-sweeper (they don't fit in boxes too well), but I've found that sending a package across the Atlantic can be just as easy as shipping across state lines. I just sent a package to Sri Lanka and it arrived safely. The only down-side: My shipper of choice, the U.S. Postal Service, does not insure packages going to certain countries (check with your post office to find out which ones; they seem to change with the headlines), so I use private shipping insurance with U-PIC.

Here are a couple of other strategies for shipping internationally:

- You need to tell what's inside the package. Be truthful when declaring value on customs forms. Use descriptions that customs agents can figure out without knowing eBay shorthand terms. For example, instead of declaring the contents as "MIB Barbie," call it a "small child's doll." Some countries require buyers to pay special duties and taxes, depending on the item and the value. But that's the buyer's headache.

- Filling out customs forms is not a headache when you print your own labels via electronic postage. The vendors mentioned in this chapter generate these forms for you.

- Often foreign buyers request that you mark the package as a gift, or indicate a lower-than-actual valuation on the item. It's *not* a good practice to do this — because it's illegal, and eBay says you should report such buyers for asking you to commit customs fraud. If you do sell internationally, to protect your reputation from negative feedback, you must let your buyers know that this practice is illegal and your policy is not to do it. Here is sample text that I often use on my items that are popular with international buyers:

    NOTE to International Buyers: Import duties, taxes, and charges are not included in the item price or shipping cost. These charges are the buyer's responsibility. Please check with your country's customs office to determine what these additional costs will be prior to bidding or buying. Thank you for your business!

    If an international buyer leaves you negative or neutral feedback for not falsifying customs documents, and eBay sees text in your listing that clearly states your no-falsification policy, then eBay may expunge the feedback. I suggest you follow the rules listed here to be sure the customer gets the message:

- Text of your policy should be free-standing or set apart from other text in the item description.

- Use a font size no smaller than the majority of the other text in the item description.

- Prominently display your policy in the upper half of the item description.

To avoid all these issues, you can use eBay's Global Shipping Program to handle all the shipping information (including duty costs) with your buyer. With this program, you ship your package to a U.S. shipping facility and they handle all the details. This service is provided by Pitney Bowes, the nation's oldest provider of shipping solutions. This service is paid for by the buyer — and charges to the buyer will be higher than if you ship the item yourself.

The eBay Global Shipping Program is well worth the price when you choose to sell expensive or special items to remote locations. For the simple (under four pound) items that I sell to Canada and Europe, I ship via First Class International and print my customs forms through my Endicia electronic software.

For ongoing information on this program, go to `https://pages.ebay.com/seller-center/shipping/global-shipping-program.html`.

Although UPS offers "discounts" to eBay sellers (`https://pages.ebay.com/carriers/ups.html`), don't be fooled. If you ship mostly a few small packages a week and print electronic postage labels with tracking, you'd have to ship truckloads on a daily basis to compete with USPS rates.

You can find the UPS home page at `www.ups.com`. For rates, select your region, click the Quote tab, and then fill in your package information. (Note the ominous use of "estimate" rates.)

WARNING

The UPS.com Quick Cost Calculator prices are based on what UPS charges its regular and high-volume users. When you get to the counter, the price may be higher than what you find on the web.

My favorite link on the UPS site is the transit map that shows the United States and how long it takes to reach any place in the country (based on the originating zip code). If you're thinking of shipping that compact refrigerator to Maine, you can check out this fun and informative page at

`www.ups.com/maps`.

FedEx

I have used FedEx Express Air for rush business, but Express is rather expensive for my regular eBay shipping. However, if the buyer wants it fast and is willing to pay, I'll send it by FedEx overnight, you bet.

FedEx Ground service has competitive prices and carries all the best features of FedEx. I use FedEx Ground for items that are heavy (say, pro-style barbells) or extremely large (such as a 1920s steamer trunk), because FedEx ships anything up to 150 pounds in a single box — 80 more pounds than the U.S. Postal Service takes. FedEx also delivers on Saturdays — which UPS won't. It also charges to pick up items from shippers whose shipping incurs less than $60 in weekly package charges.

I also like the FedEx boxes. These boxes are small *and* tough. But if you're thinking of reusing these boxes to ship with another service, forget it: The FedEx logo is plastered all over every inch of the freebies, and the company may get seriously peeved about it. You can't use those fancy boxes for its Ground service.

TIP

The FedEx Ground Home Delivery service is a major competitor for UPS. The rates are competitive, and FedEx offers a money-back guarantee (if it misses the delivery window) for residential ground delivery. For residential delivery, FedEx charges an additional fee per package. A 2-pound package going from Los Angeles to a residence in New York City takes four days and costs $19.64 including the Home Delivery fee. To a business location, this package would cost $15.94. FedEx includes online package tracking and insurance up to $100 in this price. You have to be a business to avail yourself of home delivery — but plenty of home businesses exist.

Of course, eBay has a deal with FedEx; visit `https://pages.ebay.com/carriers/fedex.html` for more information. I recommend you double-check exactly how much of a discount you are actually getting by visiting the FedEx website.

You can find the FedEx home page at `www.fedex.com/us`. The link for rates is conveniently located in the center of the page.

Getting the right (packing) stuff

You can never think about packing materials too early. If you wait until the last minute, you won't find the right-size box, approved tape, or the labels you need. Start thinking about shipping even before you sell your first item.

Before you pack, give your item the once-over. Here's a checklist of what to consider about your item before you call it a wrap (gotta love Hollywood lingo):

>> **Is your item as you described it?** If the item has been dented or torn somehow in the time since you offered it for sale on eBay, email the winning bidder immediately and come clean. And if you sell an item with its original

box or container, don't just check the item; make sure that the box is in the same good condition as the item inside. Collectors place a high value on original boxes, so make sure that the box lives up to what you described in your listing. Pack to protect it as well.

>> **Is the item dirty or dusty, or does it smell of smoke?** Some buyers may complain if the item they receive is dirty or smelly, especially from cigarette smoke. Make sure that the item is fresh and clean, even if it's used or vintage. If something's dirty, check to make sure that you know how to clean it properly (you want to take the dirt off, not the paint), and then give it a spritz with an appropriate cleaner or just soap and water. If you can't get rid of the smell or the dirt, say so in your item description. Let the buyer decide whether the item is desirable, aromas and all.

TIP

If the item has a faint smell of smoke or is a bit musty, a product called Febreze may help. Just get a plastic bag, give your item a spritz, and keep it in the bag for a short while. **Note:** This is not recommended for cardboard; spray the unscented Febreze on a folded paper towel and put the towel in a big, open plastic bag so it doesn't come into physical contact with the item. And, as with any solvent or cleaning agent, read the label *before* you spray.

When the item's ready to go, you're ready to pack it. The following sections give you suggestions on what you should consider using and where to find the right stuff.

Packing materials: What to use

This may sound obvious, but you'd be surprised how many miss this: Any list of packing material should start with a box. But you don't want just any box — you want a quality cardboard type that's larger than the item. If the item is extremely fragile, you might use two boxes, with the outer box about 3 inches larger on each side than the inner box that holds the item, to allow for extra padding. And if you still have the original shipping container for such things as electronic equipment, consider using the original, especially if it still has the original foam inserts (they were designed for the purpose, and this way they stay out of a landfill a while longer).

As for padding, Table 12-2 compares the most popular types of box void-filler material.

TABLE 12-2   **Box Void-Filler Materials**

Type	Pros and Cons	Suggestions
Bubble wrap	**Pros:** Lightweight, clean, cushions well **Cons:** Cost	Don't go overboard taping the bubble wrap. If the buyer has to battle to get the tape off, the item may go flying and end up damaged. And for crying out loud, don't pop all the little bubbles, okay?
Newspaper	**Pros:** Cheap, cushions **Cons:** Can be messy, adds weight to the package	Seal fairly well. Put your item in a plastic bag to protect it from the ink. I like shredding the newspaper first. It's more manageable and doesn't seem to stain as much as wadded-up paper. I spent about $30 at an office-supply store for a shredder. (Or find one on eBay for much less.) Best use is in Flat-Rate boxes.
Cut-up cardboard	**Pros:** Handy, cheap **Cons:** Transmits some physical shock to item, hard to cut up, heavy	If you have some old boxes that aren't sturdy enough to pack in, this is a pretty good use for them. Again, this adds weight.
Foam packing peanuts	**Pros:** Lightweight, absorb shock well, clean **Cons:** Environmentally unfriendly, annoying	Your item may shift if you don't put enough peanuts in the box, so make sure to fill the box. Also, don't buy these; recycle them from stuff that was shipped to you (plastic trash bags are great for storing them). And never use plastic peanuts when packing electronic equipment because they can create static electricity. Even a little spark can trash a computer chip.
Air pillows	**Pros:** Extra lightweight **Cons:** Not quite enough protection for very delicate breakables	Air-filled packing pillows are perfect for filling in the area around smaller boxed items that you want to double-box. They are also handy if you have breakables that you've prewrapped in bubble wrap; just use the pillows to fill out the box. Most are crushproof and can support about 150 pounds without a blowout.
Air-popped popcorn	**Pros:** Lightweight, environmentally friendly, absorbs shock well, clean (don't use salt and butter, but you knew that), low in calories **Cons:** Cost, time to pop	You don't want to send it anywhere where there may be varmints willing to trash the box to get at it. The U.S. Postal Service suggests popcorn as a void-filler, however. (Hey, at least you can eat the leftovers!)

REMEMBER

Whatever materials you use, make sure that you pack the item well and that you secure the box. Many shippers will contest insurance claims if they feel you did a lousy job of packing. Do all the little things that you'd want done if you were the buyer — using double boxes for really fragile items, wrapping lids separately from containers, and filling hollow breakables with some kind of padding. Here are a few other items you need:

MARSHA SAYS

STORING BAGS OF RECYCLED PACKING MATERIALS

By now, you may have realized that I have commandeered a large chunk of my home for my eBay business, and you might think that I live in a giant swamp of packing materials. Not really. But I do have to store *loads* of packing peanuts, bubble wrap, and air pillows (that I collect from my online purchases). They're not heavy, but they sure are bulky!

If you have a house with a garage, you're set! Bear with me, now — my plan isn't as crazy as it seems. Go to your local store and purchase some large screw-in cup hooks. Then purchase the largest *drawstring* plastic bags you can find. (I'm partial to 39-gallon Lawn & Leaf bags.)

Screw the cup hooks into strategic locations on the ceiling rafters of your garage. Now fill the drawstring bags to capacity with packing peanuts or recycled bubble wrap, and hang. When you've finished, your garage will look like some bizarre art installation, but it gets the packing materials off the floor and out of your hair. I even set up a packing-peanuts barricade so I don't hit the end of my garage when I park!

>> **Plastic bags:** Plastic bags protect your item from moisture. I once sent a MIB doll to the Northeast, and the package got caught in a snowstorm. The buyer emailed me with words of thanks for the extra plastic bag, which saved the item from being soaked along with the outer box. (Speaking of boxes, if you send an item in its original box, be sure to bag it.)

   For any small items, such as mini stuffed animals, you should always protect them in a lunch baggie. For slightly larger items, go to the 1-quart or 1-gallon size. Be sure to wrap any paper or cloth products, such as clothing and linens, in plastic before you ship.

>> **Bubble-padded mailers:** The shipping cost for a package that weighs less than one pound (First-Class mail) is usually considerably cheaper than Priority. Many small items, clothing, books, and so on, will fit comfortably into the many available sizes of padded envelopes. You can find them made of kraft paper or extra-sturdy vinyl. A big plus is that they weigh considerably less than boxes — even when you use extra padding. See Table 12-3 for standard sizes.

>> **Address labels:** You'll need extras because it's always a good idea to toss a duplicate address label inside the box, with the destination address and a return address, in case the outside label falls off or becomes illegible.

>> **Shipping tape, 2 or 3 inches:** Make sure that you use a strong shipping tape for the outside of the box. Clear plastic will do just fine. There is also box-color tape that works very well for recycling boxes (taping over old shipping information). Remember not to plaster every inch of box with tape; leave space for those *Fragile* and *Insured* rubber stamps.

>> **Hand-held shipping tape dispensers:** It's quite a bit easier to zzzzzip! tape from a tape dispenser than to unwind it and bite it off with your teeth. Have one dispenser for your special shipping tape and one for your clear tape.

>> **Lightweight 2-inch clear tape:** Use this for taping the padding around the inside items. I also use a clear strip of tape over the address on the outside of the box so it won't disappear in the rain.

>> **Scissors:** A pair of large, sharp scissors. Having a hobby knife to trim boxes or shred newspaper is also a good idea.

>> **Handy liquids:** Three that I like are Goo Gone (which is available in the household supply section of most retail stores and is a wonder at removing unwanted stickers and price tags); WD-40 (the unstick-everything standby that works great on getting stickers off plastic); and Un-Du (the best liquid I've found to take labels off cardboard).

>> **Rubber stamps/stickers:** Using custom rubber stamps or stickers can save you a bunch of time when preparing your packages. I purchased some "thank you" self-inking rubber stamps to give my parcels some pizazz.

>> **Thermal label printer:** Once I thought this was a flagrant waste of money, but now I wouldn't be without one (I have two). When you begin shipping several packages a week, you'll find it far more convenient to use a separate label printer for addressing and delivery confirmations. Dymo has a good 4-x-6-inch label printer, the LabelWriter 4XL, for around $149 on eBay. If you want to go for an industrial-quality Wi-Fi model, try one of the Zebra thermal printers (I plan to try the ZD420, but it's pretty pricy). These printers can print labels for FedEx and UPS as well as USPS (you can also get deals on these on eBay).

>> **Black permanent marker:** These are handy for writing information ("Please leave on porch behind the planter") and the all-important "Fragile" all over the box or "Do Not Bend" on envelopes. I like the big, fat Sharpie markers.

If you plan to sell on eBay in earnest, consider adding a 10-pound weight scale (for weighing packages) to your shipping department. I'm using a super-small 13-pound-maximum scale, which I bought on eBay for only $29.95.

TABLE 12-3

Standard Bubble-Padded Mailer Sizes

Size	Measurements	Suggested Items
#000	4" x 8"	Collector trading cards, jewelry, computer disks, coins
#00	5" x 10"	Postcards, paper ephemera
#0	6" x 10"	CDs, DVDs, Xbox or PS2 games
#1	7¼" x 12"	Cardboard-sleeve VHS tapes, jewel-cased CDs and DVDs
#2	8½" x 12"	Clamshell VHS tapes
#3	8½" x 14½"	Toys, clothing, stuffed animals
#4	9½" x 14½"	Small books, trade paperbacks
#5	10½" x 16"	Hardcover books
#6	12½" x 19"	Clothing, soft boxed items
#7	14¼" x 20"	Much larger packaged items, framed items, plaques

Packing material: Where to find it

The place to start looking for packing material is the same place you should start looking for things to sell on eBay: your house. Between us, I've done thousands of eBay transactions and never once paid for void fill. I make most of my personal purchases from online vendors (I love e-commerce) and save all the bubble wrap, padding, and packing peanuts I get in the boxes with my orders. Just empty the boxes of void fill and place it into large plastic trash bags — that way, they don't take up much storage space. If you recently got a mail-order shipment box that was used only once — and it's a good, sturdy box with no dents or dings — there's nothing wrong with using it again. Just be sure to completely cover any old labels so the delivery company doesn't get confused.

Beyond the ol' homestead, here are a few other suggestions for places where you can rustle up some packing stuff for your beginning eBay sales:

>> **Your local supermarket, department store, or drugstore:** You won't be the first person pleading with a store manager for boxes. (Ah, fond memories of moving days past.) Stores like giving them away because it saves them the work of compacting the boxes and putting them in the trash or recycling bin. Places like Kmart, Walmart, Target, and office-supply stores often have good selections of packing supplies.

I have found that drugstores and beauty-supply stores have a better variety of smaller boxes. But make sure you don't take dirty boxes reeking of food smells.

TIP

>> **Shippers such as UPS, FedEx, and the U.S. Postal Service:** These shippers offer all kinds of free supplies as long as you use these supplies to ship things with their service.

TIP

The Postal Service also ships free boxes, labels, and shipping forms for Priority Express Mail, Priority Mail, and Global Priority Mail to your house. In the United States, you can order by phone (800-222-1811) or online (shop.usps.com). Here are a few rules for USPS orders:

- Specify the service (Priority Mail, Priority Mail Express, or Global Express Guaranteed) you're using because the boxes and the labels all come with the service name printed all over them, and you can use them only for that specific service.

- Order in bulk. For example, address labels come in rolls of 500 and boxes in packs of 25.

- The boxes come flat, so you have to assemble them. Hey, don't look a gift box in the mouth — they're free!

>> **eBay and online sellers:** Many terrific eBay sellers are out to offer you really good deals. (You can't beat eBay sellers for quality goods, low prices, and great service.) I recommend the following online stores:

- **BubbleFAST** — an eBay seller from the Chicago area — sells tons of reasonably priced bubble wrap, mailers, and lots of shipping accessories. Find them on eBay or on the website www.bubblefast.com.

- **Uline** is where I buy shipping boxes for items that do not fit into free Priority Mail boxes. They have shipping boxes for almost any size package, and because they ship from several locations in the United States, the cost (and time) of shipping is kept to a minimum. Find them at www.uline.com.

Take into account where these vendors are located. When you're ordering a large shipment, the distance it has to travel from the vendor's place to yours can tack on quite a bit of cash (and time) to your shipping costs!

Buying and Printing Postage Online

Isn't technology great? You no longer have to schlep to the post office every time you need stamps. What's even better, with the new print-it-yourself postage, you can give all your packages directly to your mail carrier. When you sign up for your Internet postage software, you apply for a USPS postal license that allows you to print your own *Information-Based Indicia* (IBI) for your postage. IBI is a barcode printed either on labels or directly on an envelope; it has both human- and machine-readable information about where it was printed, along with some security-related elements. IBI provides you, and the post office, with a much more secure way of getting your valuable packages through the mail.

You can print postage for First Class Packages, Priority, Priority Express, Media Mail, and International shipments as well as add insurance. If your printer mangles a sheet of labels or an envelope, you can send the printed piece to your Internet postage provider or apply online for a refund. Several vendors of Internet-based postage exist, but `Endicia.com`, `Stamps.com`, and `PirateShip.com` are the most popular.

TIP

Printing your postage electronically gives a real benefit: the Commercial Base price reduction, which is available for Priority Mail and Priority Mail Express. For Priority Mail packages weighing 10 pounds or less, Commercial Base prices are considerably lower than retail (at the post office) prices and are based on zone and weight. For Priority Mail Express, the commercial base prices are 3.5 percent lower than the retail prices.

For international shipping, you'll get 5- and 8-percent discounts on Priority Mail International and Global Express Guaranteed.

Preparing postage with Endicia

In the early '90s, a couple of guys came up with new software to enable people to design direct-mail pieces from the desktop. Wow! What an innovation. With the inexpensive software, you could also produce your own barcoding for the Postal Service. I used that software then, just as I use their DAZzle now.

DAZzle — combined with the patented Dial-A-Zip — became the basis for the software that comes free with the Endicia Internet Postage service. There isn't a more robust mailing program on the market. (You can also use their online portal to print your postage at `https://print.endicia.com/SignIn`.)

Endicia has all the basic features and more:

>> **Prints postage for all classes of mail, including international:** From Anniston, Alabama, to Bulawayo, Zimbabwe, the DAZzle software not only prints postage but also lists all your shipping options and applicable rates. For international mailing, Endicia advises you about any prohibitions (no prison-made goods can be mailed to Botswana), any restrictions, any necessary customs forms, and areas served within the country.

>> **Prints tracking numbers for Priority Mail, First Class, and Media Mail:** Tracking numbers are printed directly on the label.

>> **Packaging Advisor:** The Endicia software gives you options for your package. After pasting in the recipient's address, you can click to compare the costs of various USPS options based on the zip codes provided. I checked one of today's shipments in Figure 12-3.

>> **Fetches your eBay orders from eBay (and any other online sales platform you use):** After connecting your eBay account, the premium version of the service imports your sales and allows you to print in bulk — or one by one and automatically sends the tracking number back to eBay.

>> **Prints customs forms:** You no longer have to go to the post office with your international packages. Just print the customs form from the DAZzle software (some are integrated into the label) and give the package to your letter carrier.

>> **Enables you to design mail pieces:** The software enables you to design envelopes, postcards, and labels with color graphics, logos, and text messages. You can print your labels with postage tracking on anything from plain paper (tape it on with clear tape) to 4-x-6-inch labels in a label printer.

>> **Integrates with private insurance:** Private package insurance saves time and money. All your package insurance appears in one place no matter whether you sold from eBay or your own website.

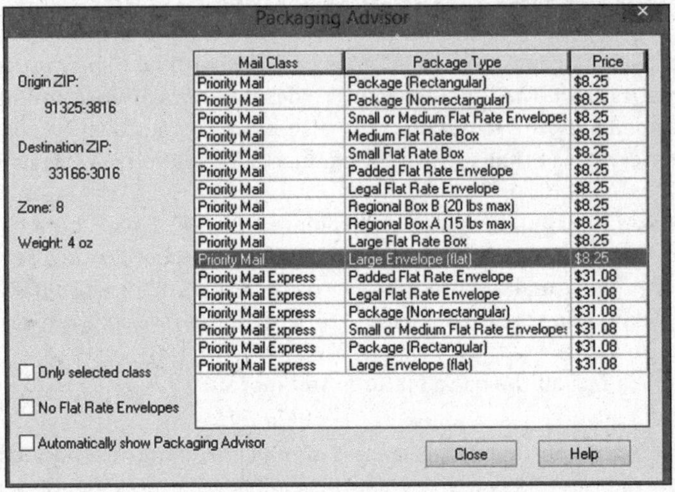

FIGURE 12-3: DAZzle software, showing my shipping options and costs.

Endicia offers three levels of service, one of which is for online sellers. The online seller plan adds special features, customizable email, enhanced online transaction reports and statistics, business reply mail, return shipping labels (prepaid so your customers won't have to pay for the returns), and stealth indicias for $17.99 a month.

TIP

You can get more information on their services at

www.endicia.com/online-seller.

Shipping with Stamps.com

I'd love to say that Stamps.com is way better than Endicia, but it's not really. It's really a matter of taste. Stamps.com purchased Endicia and they are basically one company — but still operate on different platforms. All your printing from Stamps.com is done online. Shipping with Stamps.com gives you all the benefits of Endicia:

» Domestic: Up to 40 percent off.

» International: Up to 5 percent off.

» Other Discounts Supported: Commercial Base, Commercial Plus, Cubic Pricing, and Negotiated Service Agreements.

» Insurance: Save up to 40 percent on insurance compared to USPS. Faster claims, too!

There's a free four-week trial, and after that you will be charged $17.99 a month. To see if Stamps.com is the right fit for you, go to www.stamps.com/shipping.

Ahoy matey! Print labels free from Pirate Ship

First off, one thing you can't argue with: Free is a good thing. But when free comes with lots of features, it's even better.

I learned about Pirate Ship (see Figure 12-4) when I was on vacation in Alaska. I often meet with eBay sellers when I travel because I like to know what the eBay experience is like from different perspectives. I learned that Pirate Ship automatically integrates cubic shipping into their free platform. If you read about Priority Mail cubic pricing earlier in this chapter, you can imagine how excited I was to learn about this provider.

I spoke to the CEO, Cap'n Bjorn Borstelmann, and learned that everything I'd heard was true. You can use Pirate Ship to ship for any e-commerce platform at the lowest USPS prices and at any time online. No ups or extras. According to their website, "Save up to 90% off retail USPS rates with the deepest commercial discounts and no markup, monthly fees, or hidden costs." Amazing, right?

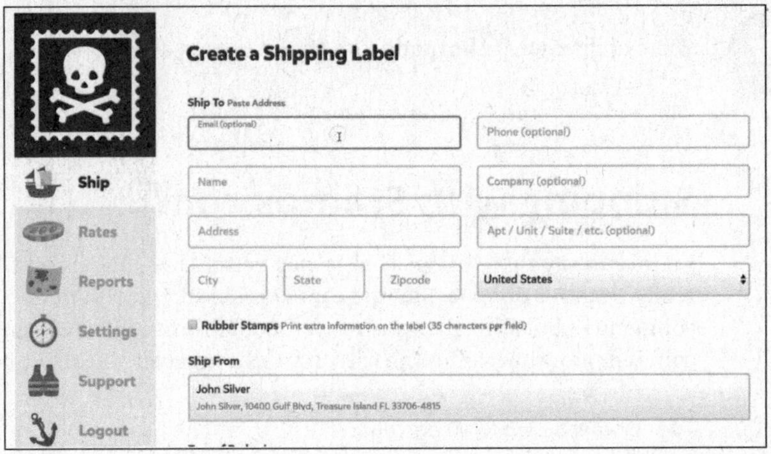

FIGURE 12-4:
Print labels and postage from Pirate Ship's online platform.

Check them out at www.pirateship.com and watch their videos. Give them a try and they might just be the perfect alternative to printing shipping labels and postage for all your online sales.

Shipping directly from eBay

I consider printing labels from eBay to be required for all beginning sellers. By using their service, a seller can streamline the buyer's shopping experience, making it simple to buy, click, and pay. Those out in the eBay world who haven't used it find the service to be a life-changing experience. Because you don't need to use additional software or sign up with an additional service, shipping with eBay is a convenient system for those who don't have to ship many packages each week.

TIP

eBay shipping services work great when you're just starting out in your business — but after you get rolling, you need a mailing service that includes recordkeeping, such as Endicia, Stamps.com, or PirateShip.

Chapter **13**

Saving and Troubleshooting Sales

There's no getting around it: You are doing business with strangers. There's no face-to-face handshake and a smile when you make a purchase (or sell to someone). You'll find that the more transactions you conduct on eBay, the more chances you have of facing some potential pitfalls.

In this chapter, I give you pointers on how to handle a difficult buyer as if he or she is your new best friend (for a little while anyway). In addition, I explain how to keep an honest misunderstanding from blowing up into a vitriolic war. You find out how to handle a sale that's (shall I say) on a road to nowhere, how to get some attention, and if it all goes sour, how to sell to someone else legally. There's no way that all of what I mention here will ever happen to you, but the more you know, the better prepared you'll be.

Dealing with a Buyer Who Doesn't Respond

Most of the time, the post-transaction between buyers and sellers goes smooth as glass. However, if you have difficulty receiving payment from the winner of your auction or fixed-price sale, you should know the best way to handle the situation.

You've come to the right place if you want help dealing with potential nonpaying buyers. Of course, you should start with an item description and listing that leaves no questions in the buyer's mind; see Chapter 10 for details. (For more information on how to deal with a difficult seller, see Chapter 16.)

Requesting immediate payment

One convenient way to avoid payment issues with a buyer is to request an immediate payment upon purchase. When you list an item for sale, you get the option on fixed-price sales (and auctions with a Buy It Now option) to require an immediate payment from the buyer. When buyers click the Buy It Now button, they are presented with a payment window requesting immediate payment. In this scenario, the item is not considered sold until the buyer completes the payment.

Setting buyer requirements

In your My eBay Summary Account area, under Site Preferences, there's an area where you can specify who can bid on or buy your items. Click Site Preferences and then scroll down the page until you see Buyer requirements. In this area, click Edit at the right to see the options afforded to sellers.

Here you can require that anyone who buys or bids on one of your items falls into some safe categories on eBay. If you decide you have to block some buyers, eBay suggests that you may "reduce your selling success." I say that limiting your buyer field to those who play by the rules is just smart business. You can require several things from your buyer, including

>> Not have five or less feedback (newbies) and attempt to purchase multiples of an item (usually by accident) or be bad actors who try to run the board and purchase multiple items without intending to pay

>> Have no Unpaid Item strikes in a set prior period

>> Have no negative feedback score

>> Have a shipping address only in the countries where you state you will ship

I recommend that you check out this area and select requirements that make you feel more confident that you'll get paid.

Going into nudge mode

Despite my best efforts, sometimes things fall through the cracks. Buyers should pay for their items without delay — or at least pay within the next 48 hours after the close of the sale. Most times, buyers check out directly from the item page and pay for the item immediately, which saves you hassle. However, if you don't hear from the buyer within three business days of your initial contact, my advice is *don't panic.*

People are busy; they travel, they get sick, their computers crash, or sometimes your item simply slips the winner's mind. After three days of no payment or communication (allow for weekends), you can go to your My eBay page and send a payment reminder message. You find the Contact member link on the item's transaction on the My eBay Sold page, or by clicking the Feedback number next to a buyer's ID. Clicking that number takes you to the buyer's feedback profile (Figure 13-1), where you'll find a link labeled Contact member on the right.

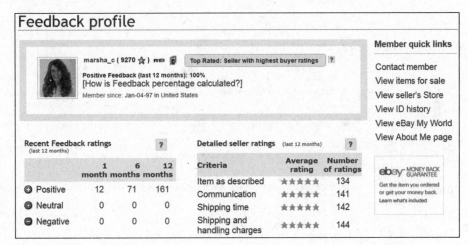

FIGURE 13-1: The Contact member link in the buyer's feedback profile.

Send a polite-but-firm message letting <random eBay user> know that when he/she won or bought your item, they became obligated to pay and complete the transaction. If the buyer doesn't intend to buy your item for any reason, he needs to let you know posthaste.

WARNING

Don't threaten your buyer. The last thing you want to do is add insult to injury in case the buyer is facing a real problem. Besides, if the buyer goes to sleep with the fishes, you'll *never* see your money.

Here's what to include in your nudge-nudge email:

» A gentle admonishment, such as, "Perhaps this slipped your mind" or "You may have missed the eBay notification of your purchase."

» A gentle reminder that eBay's policy is that every bid is a binding contract.

» A gentle inquiry as to whether there was a problem. Did the buyer order the item by mistake?

» A date by which you expect to see payment. Gently explain that if the deadline isn't met, you'll have no other choice but to consider the transaction invalid.

Do a little sleuthing

I'd like to say that history repeats itself, but that would be a cliché. (All right, you caught me, but clichés are memorable because they're so often true.) After you send your polite message, but before you decide that the transaction is a lost cause, take a look at the bidder's Feedback as a buyer on their Feedback profile page. Figure 13-2 shows you what that feedback looks like.

| Feedback as a seller | Search seller feedback | Feedback as a buyer | All Feedback | Feedback left for others |

1,309 Feedback received (viewing 1-25)   Bid retractions (last 12 months): 0

Period: All

Feedback	From Seller	When
You are truly 5 STARS! A+ Please leave us 5 stars too --	dymoda (187540 ★) --	During past month
Amazing Buyer Fast Payment!!! Thank you --	nosoup_4u (1075 ★) --	During past month
Great communication. A pleasure to do business with. --	huawei_usa (23 ☆) --	During past 6 months
Good buyer, prompt payment, valued customer, highly recommended. --	lovecustomers5 (1184 ★) --	During past year
Excellent Ebay Buyer and Transaction!	ditchdaisy (1418 ★)	During past year

FIGURE 13-2: You can get a good idea of whether a buyer will complete a sale by looking at his or her Feedback as a buyer.

To check a bidder's feedback (starting at your item page), do the following:

1. **Click the number in parentheses next to your winner's User ID.**

   This action takes you to the member's Feedback profile page.

2. **Click the Feedback as a buyer tab.**

3. **Scroll down the Feedback profile page and read the comments.**

Check to see whether the bidder has received recent negative feedback from prior sellers. Make a mental note of it in case you need some background information (should you be chastised at a later date for blocking an unwanted bid).

Blocking a customer

If you've had a bad experience with a particular customer and you don't want that person to be able to bid on or buy your items in the future, you can set up a bidder block for his or her User ID. If you block bidders, they can't bid; eBay tells them that they have to contact you before their bids will be accepted. You can add or delete bidders from your list at any time. eBay has managed to make the page difficult to find, so try going directly to the Buyer/Bidder Management area at

`pages.ebay.com/services/buyandsell/biddermanagement.html` or `http:// offer.ebay.com/ws/eBayISAPI.dll?BidderBlockLogin`.

If the buyer's feedback profile provides any indication that the buyer has gone AWOL in the past, start thinking about getting out of the transaction before too much time passes. If the buyer looks to be on the level, continue to give him or her the benefit of the doubt.

Other Possible Problems

I'm not quite sure why, but where money is involved, sometimes people act weird. Buyers may suddenly decide that they can't purchase an item after they've made a commitment, or there may be payment problems or shipping problems. Whatever the problem, look no further than this section to find out how to make things better.

Buyer backout? Try Second Chance Offer

Every time eBay members place a bid or click the Buy It Now button, they make a commitment to purchase the item in question — in theory, anyway. In the real world, people have second thoughts, despite the rules. But you also have every right to be upset that you're losing money and wasting your time. Unfortunately, if the buyer won't pay up, you can't do much except apply for a Final Value Fee credit and lick your wounds. Jump to Chapter 6 to find out more about buyer's remorse.

A SELLER'S NIGHTMARE

I was on Facebook, messaging with some other eBay sellers (feel free to find me on Facebook at www.facebook.com/MarshaCollierFanPage — all my readers are my friends!), and one was bemoaning a recent transaction. A seller always wants to sell a product, and a cooperative buyer makes the entire process pleasant. This particular seller was having a problem receiving payment from a buyer. Here's what she said:

"The buyer first said her boss opened a PayPal account for her under his email address and she couldn't access it and now her daughter used her credit card so she can't pay me. I tried to tell her she can add another email address to the PayPal account and make it the primary but . . ."

Is this fair? I recommended to the seller that she offer to mutually close the deal through eBay so she'd be free to resell the item to someone else. A buyer has a responsibility to carry out his or her part of the transaction as seamlessly as we expect service from the seller when we buy.

TIP

You can also sell additional merchandise by making a Second Chance Offer when you have multiples of the same item in stock and want to accept any of an auction's underbidders' final bids.

Keeping your cool

By all means, if the buyer of your item tells you that the transaction can't be completed, no matter what the reason, remain professional despite your anger. Hopefully, such a would-be buyer has the heart to break the news to you instead of ignoring your messages.

When Plan A fails, try Plan B, or even C — Auction Second Chance Offer

You have several options if the winner backs out:

>> **You can make a *Second Chance Offer:* Offer the item to another bidder from the auction.** eBay offers a little-known feature called Second Chance Offer, which invites underbidders just as if they were the winner of the auction. This is a great feature that turned the *previously* eBay-prohibited practice of side deals into fair and approved deals. You can make a Second Chance Offer to any underbidder from your auction (at the amount of that bidder's high bid) for up to 60 days after the auction's end. The steps that follow this list detail how to make a Second Chance Offer.

>> **You can request an unpaid item claim after 48 hours, and then relist the item and hope it sells again.** (I give you more information on requesting a Final Value Fee credit and relisting your item later in this chapter.) Who knows? This bidder may actually *earn* you money in the long run if you relist the item and get a higher winning bid.

You can make a Second Chance Offer in two ways. Just follow these steps:

1. **Go to the completed auction page.**

On the top of the page, you'll see some transaction-related links, as shown in Figure 13-3.

2. **Click the Make a Second Chance Offer link.**

You're taken to the Second Chance Offer page, which has the auction number already filled in.

3. **Click Continue.**

A page appears, showing all your underbidders and their high bids.

4. **Select an underbidder (or more than one underbidder if you have multiples of the item) to offer the item to; then click the Review Second Chance Offer link.**

When you make a Second Chance Offer, you can give the recipient one, three, five, or seven days to take you up on the offer. You are not charged a listing fee for the item, but you are responsible for Final Value Fees if the transaction is completed.

5. **Check over the offer and then click Submit to send it to the underbidder.**

Alternatively, you can go to your My eBay Summary Sold page, select the transaction and click the drop-down menu next to the item listing. Choose Second Chance Offer, and you'll arrive at the decision-making page from there, as shown in Figure 13-4.

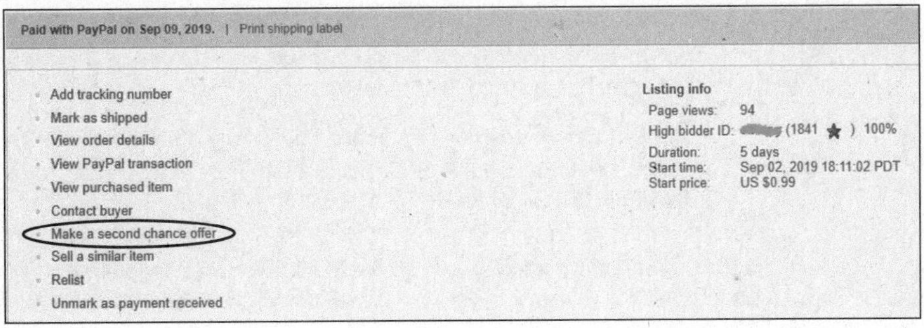

FIGURE 13-3:
After an auction is completed, you find a bunch of handy links on this page.

Order number 13-03849-61294

Ship by Sep 10 at 11:59pm PDT
Make sure you ship your order within the handling time you specified in the listing.
Estimated delivery date shown to buyer: **Sep 16, 2019**

Buyer's note: I am delighted to be the lucky winning bidder! :)

| Print shipping label | ▾ |

Add tracking number
Print shipping labels or invoices
Mark as shipped
Unmark as payment received
Cancel order
View PayPal transaction
Add/edit note
Relist
Second chance offer
Sell similar
Contact buyer
Report buyer
Archive

Purchase details

Buyer	~~Getxxxxxxxxxx Stanley~~ (1841)
E-mail	~~xtxxtxy@xx.bell.xxt~~
Phone	~~xxxxxxx-xxxx~~
Date sold	Sep 7, 2019
Date paid	Sep 9, 2019 via Paypal
Sales record number	9660

Shipping deta

Shipping method	
Tracking	
Ship to	
Street	
City	
State/province	
Zip code	
Country/region	

Copy full address to clipboard

FIGURE 13-4: Here's where you may get out of a difficult situation by offering your item to one of the underbidders in the unsuccessful auction.

TIP

You can also make a Second Chance Offer in the situation where a reserve price is not met in a reserve-price auction.

LEAVING FEEDBACK AFTER AN IMPERFECT EBAY EXPERIENCE

MARSHA SAYS

If a buyer never materializes, backs out, or moves slower than a glacier to send your payment (but wants the item sent overnight from Boston to Khartoum at your expense), you need to think about how you want to word your feedback. As a seller, you can no longer leave negative feedback, but you can still write in a "neutral" comment for other sellers to take heed. But if you do that, remember to stick to the facts and don't get personal. You can always also leave *no* feedback and block the buyer from your listings.

Here are a few feedback tips:

- If the transaction was shaky but everything turned out all right in the end, go ahead and leave positive feedback, but gauge it, depending on how tough things went.

- If a blizzard stopped planes out of Chicago for three days and that's why it took a long time to get online to pay, take a deep breath, blame the fates, and leave positive feedback with a fair comment.

- If the buyer was a living nightmare, take a long break before getting nasty — and have someone you love and trust read it before you send something into the virtual world that you can't take back.

For more information on leaving feedback, check out Chapters 4 and 6.

The item you send is busted — and so are you

Uh-oh! Could it be true? Could you have sent the wrong item? Or is it possible that the crystal vase you thought you packed so well is a sad pile of shards at the bottom of a torn box? If so, read Chapter 12 as soon as you take care of this catastrophe so that you can get some hints on packing and insurance.

It's time to do some serious problem-solving. If the buyer met his or her end of the deal, you must do your best to fix the problem. Your communication skills are your number-one asset in this situation, so get to work.

Picking up the pieces

No matter how carefully you pack an item, sometimes it arrives on the buyer's doorstep mangled, broken, or squashed. News of this unfortunate event travels back to you fast. Shortly after opening the package, the buyer will let you know — hopefully in a message, versus filing a complaint — how unhappy he or she is. (Sometimes such missives aren't very polite, but stay calm.)

TIP

When you send an item of value to a customer, it's best to insure the package. eBay holds you responsible for seeing that the item arrives as described when it reaches the customer, so it's best to insure irreplaceable or high-value items. (See Chapter 12 for more on shipping insurance.)

If a package is lost, you'll know it because the tracking number never shows delivery, and the buyer tells you the package is a no-show. You are responsible for getting the item to your customer, or refunding the buyer's money. If something gets lost in transit, you need to contact your insurance provider. If your item isn't located in 30 days, it's declared lost, and there's a round of paperwork and processing to do before you get your money.

TIP

If you have private package insurance of the sort available through U-PIC, Endicia, or Stamps.com, the process is much simpler than dealing with the USPS or UPS. You don't have to contact the shipper; you merely have to contact the insurance company and place a claim.

WARNING

Lots of online sellers seem to think that if a buyer doesn't pay for insurance and the package gets lost in transit, then it's not the seller's problem. They couldn't be more wrong. The Federal Trade Commission has a strict rule covering mail-order and Internet merchandise delivery. The short version is that if your item doesn't get to the buyer within 30 days, you must refund the payment. The long version can be found at the FTC website:

`www.ftc.gov/tips-advice/business-center/guidance/business-guide-ftcs-mail-internet-or-telephone-order`.

Boxed out of a claim

In my experience, neither UPS nor the U.S. Postal Service will pay on an insurance claim if they feel you did a lousy job of packing. Always use good packing products, wrap carefully, and be prepared to plead your case.

REMEMBER

Every shipping company has its own procedure for complaints. But here's the one thing they do have in common: No procedure is hassle-free. If you have insured through your shipper, contact those folks just as soon as a problem arises — and have your value documentation at the ready.

You have regrets — seller's remorse

You've undoubtedly heard about buyer's remorse. Here's a new one for you — *seller's remorse.* If you're selling your velvet Elvis footstool because your spouse said, "It's me or that footstool!" and then decide that your spouse should have known how much you revered the King when you went to Graceland on your honeymoon, you can end the listing. Read "Making changes or canceling bids" and "Ending your listing early," later in this chapter.

Going Badly? Cut Your Losses

So your auction is cruising along just fine for a couple of days when you notice that the same eBay user who didn't pay on a previous auction is your current high bidder (and you had neglected to block them). You don't want to get burned again, do you? Of course not; *cancel* this deadbeat's bid before it's too late (perhaps you should have put that person on your Blocked Bidder list?). Canceling bids — or, for that matter, entire auctions — isn't easy (you'll have a load of explaining to do, pardner), but eBay does allow it.

If you feel that you have to wash your hands of a listing that's given you nothing but grief, it doesn't mean that you have to lose money on the deal. Read on to find out the protocol for laying a bad transaction to rest and beginning anew.

TIP

Many of these functions are also available from the drop-down menus on the right side of the item's listing on the My eBay Sell ⇨ Active link.

Making changes or canceling bids

Face the facts: Oftimes things don't go as planned. You did your very best, and things didn't work out. Before you kill an auction completely, if there are no bids, see whether you can improve it by improving your description or reducing your opening bid. You may also cancel a bid, which removes a bidder from your auction, but the auction continues running.

When you cancel a bid, you need to provide an explanation, which goes on record for all to see. You may have a million reasons for thinking your auction is a bust, but eBay says your explanation had better be good. Here are some eBay-approved reasons for canceling a bid (or even an entire auction):

>> A bidder informs you that he or she is retracting a bid, or asks you whether it's okay to back out.

>> Despite your best efforts to determine who your high bidder is, you can't find out — and you get no response to your messages or phone calls.

>> You decide, mid-auction, that you can't sell your item because you've learned it was already sold in an outside venue — or the dog ate it. (You must cancel all bids and end the listing in this instance.)

WARNING

I can't drive this point home hard enough: *Explain why you're canceling a bid, and your explanation had better be good.* You can cancel any bid for any reason you want, but if you can't give a good explanation of why you did it, you'll be sorry. Citing past transaction problems with the current high bidder is okay, but canceling a bidder who lives in Japan because you don't feel like shipping overseas — after you said you'd ship internationally — could give your feedback history the aroma of week-old sushi.

To cancel a bid placed on one of your auctions, do the following (you can also reach the Bidder Cancellation Form by going to `http://offer.ebay.com/ws/ eBayISAPI.dll?CancelBidShow` and typing in the item number):

1. **Go to the listing page.**

2. **Click the Bid History link.**

   You're taken to the Bid History page.

3. **Scroll to the bottom of the bidding history and click the Cancel Bids link.**

   You'll be brought to a page outlining eBay's policies on bidding.

4. **Scroll down to the Canceling Bids area and click the Canceling Bids link.**

   You arrive at the Canceling Bids page, as shown in Figure 13-5.

5. **Type the item number, the User ID for the bid you're canceling, and the reason for canceling the bid.**

6. **Click the Cancel Bid button.**

WARNING

Be sure that you really want to cancel a bid before you click the Cancel Bid button. Canceled bids can never be reinstated.

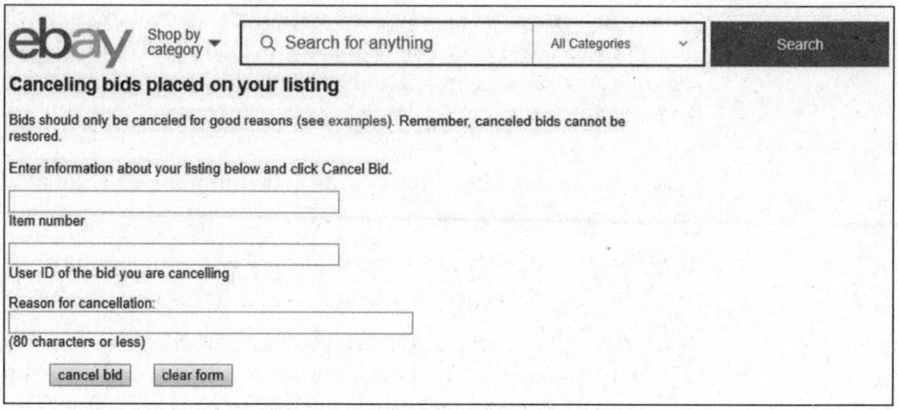

---

ebay Shop by category ▾ | 🔍 Search for anything | All Categories ▾ | Search

Canceling bids placed on your listing

Bids should only be canceled for good reasons (see examples). Remember, canceled bids cannot be restored.

Enter information about your listing below and click Cancel Bid.

[   ]
Item number

[   ]
User ID of the bid you are cancelling

Reason for cancellation:
[   ]
(80 characters or less)

[cancel bid]   [clear form]

FIGURE 13-5:
Use this form to remove a bidder from one of your auctions.

Canceling bids means that you removed an individual bidder (or several bidders) from your auction, but the auction itself continues running. If you want to end the auction completely, read on.

Editing your Fixed Price listing

You just listed an item for sale and click through to see your masterpiece. What's this? You misspelled the brand name? Made the price too high (or low)? You do have some options to revise your listing, even if (in case of selling multiple items) you've sold a few.

If no purchases have been made on your listing, eBay leaves things wide open. You can click to revise the item and change almost everything, with these exceptions:

>> A fixed-price listing cannot change formats. In other words, you cannot turn it into an auction. You must end the existing listing and relist it as an auction.

>> The duration of a fixed-price listing can't be changed two hours after the listing has been submitted.

For more information on what you can change, turn to Chapter 10.

Ending your listing early

If you put your auction up for a week and the next day your boss says you have to go to China for a month, or your landlord says you have to move out immediately so he can fumigate for a week, you can end your auction early. But ending an auction early isn't a decision to be taken lightly. You miss all the last-minute bidding action.

Also know that sellers are not allowed to cancel bids and end listings early merely to avoid selling an item that did not meet the desired sale price. That would be a violation of eBay's reserve-price policy. (*Hint:* You should have put a reserve price on the item.)

There are only two circumstances in which eBay will allow you to cancel a listing without violating policy:

>> The item is lost, broken, or otherwise no longer available for sale.

>> You made a mistake when creating the listing or entering the starting price or reserve price.

You also cannot end an auction listing if there are less than 12 hours to go before the item ends. If there is a bid on your item, you are bound by the rules to sell it to the high bidder for his or her bid price.

WARNING

eBay makes it clear that ending your auction early does not relieve you of the obligation to sell this item to the highest bidder. To relieve your obligation, you must first cancel all the bids, and then end the auction, and you'll be charged a Final Value Fee for the amount of the highest bid. Of course, if no one has bid yet, you have nothing to worry about.

When you cancel an auction, you have to write a short explanation that appears on the bidding history section of your auction page. Anyone who bid on the item may message you for a written explanation. If bidders think your explanation doesn't hold water, don't be surprised if your inbox becomes nasty.

WARNING

Bidding on your own item is against the rules. Once upon a time, you could cancel an auction by outbidding everyone on your own item and then ending the auction. But some eBay users abused this privilege by bidding on their own items merely to boost the sales price. Shame on them.

To end an auction early, go to your My eBay Active Selling page, and in the drop-down menu in the Actions column, choose End item. You'll be required to sign in again. You can also go directly to

```
http://offer.ebay.com/ws/eBayISAPI.dll?CancelBidShow
```

to cancel bids, and then to

```
http://offer.ebay.com/ws/eBayISAPI.dll?EndingMyAuction
```

to end an auction.

Then follow these steps:

1. **Click the appropriate link: either Cancel Bids and End Listing Early or Sell Item to High Bidder and End Listing Early.**

2. **On the next page, select a reason for ending your listing.**

3. **Click the End Your Listing button.**

   An Ended Listing page appears, and eBay sends an End of Listing Confirmation email to you and to the highest bidder.

Opening an Unpaid Item case

If closing a successful auction is the thrill of victory, finding out that your buyer is a nonpaying bidder is the agony of defeat. Adding insult to injury, eBay still charges you a Final Value Fee, even if the high bidder never sends you a cent. But you can do something about it. You may get a *Final Value Fee credit*.

To qualify for a Final Value Fee credit, you must prove to eBay that one of the following events occurred:

>> The winning buyer never responded to invoices or reminders.

>> The winning buyer backed out of the sale.

>> The winning buyer's payment did not clear or was never received.

>> The winning buyer returned the item to you, and you refunded the payment.

TIP

If both you and the buyer decide that it's okay not to go through with the transaction, that's okay with eBay, too. eBay will allow you to get back your Final Value Fee by going through the Resolution Center process. You'll find an option that will absolve the buyer of any wrongdoing with eBay's unpaid-item policy.

The instant you open a case, eBay shoots off an email to the buyer of your item (copying you on the email) and warns the eBay user of his or her nonpaying status.

There are two ways to handle this situation. You can open a case manually through the Resolution Center or use eBay's automated Unpaid Item Assistant.

The Unpaid Item Assistant will open and close cases for you. Once the assistant opens a case, the buyer has four days to make payment. If the buyer pays, the case is closed. If the buyer doesn't pay, the case is automatically closed and you get a Final Value Fee credit.

To use the Unpaid Item Assistant, you'll need to opt in from your My eBay page:

1. **Move your mouse pointer over the Account tab.**

2. **Click the Site Preferences link on the drop-down menu that appears.**

3. **Scroll down the page to the Unpaid Item Assistant heading.**

4. **Click the Show link (and then Edit if it appears) to the right of the heading, and then click Edit.**

   A page will open as shown in Figure 13-6.

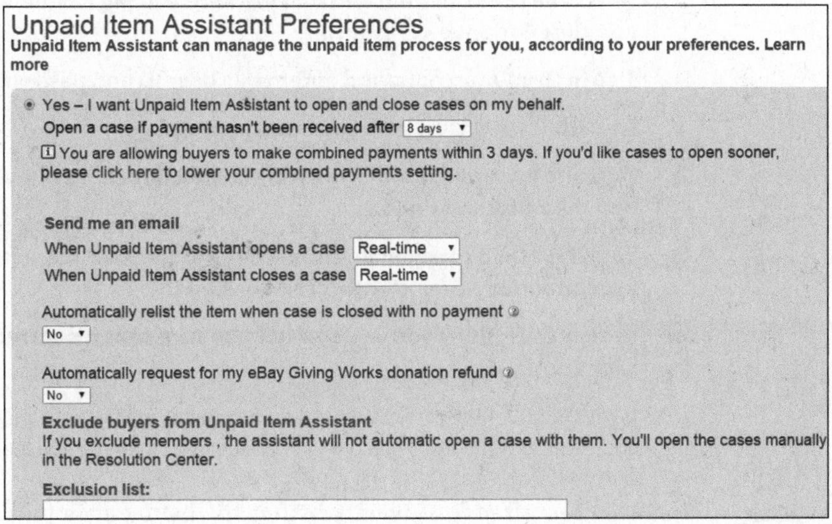

Unpaid Item Assistant Preferences
Unpaid Item Assistant can manage the unpaid item process for you, according to your preferences. Learn more

⦿ Yes – I want Unpaid Item Assistant to open and close cases on my behalf.
Open a case if payment hasn't been received after 8 days ▾
ⓘ You are allowing buyers to make combined payments within 3 days. If you'd like cases to open sooner, please click here to lower your combined payments setting.

Send me an email
When Unpaid Item Assistant opens a case Real-time ▾
When Unpaid Item Assistant closes a case Real-time ▾

Automatically relist the item when case is closed with no payment ⓘ
No ▾

Automatically request for my eBay Giving Works donation refund ⓘ
No ▾

Exclude buyers from Unpaid Item Assistant
If you exclude members , the assistant will not automatic open a case with them. You'll open the cases manually in the Resolution Center.

Exclusion list:

FIGURE 13-6: Setting up the automated Unpaid Item Assistant.

5. **Click the radio button next to *Yes I want Unpaid Item Assistant to open and close cases on my behalf* to indicate you want cases opened automatically.**

   A drop-down menu appears.

6. **Select a number of days that you want to allow your buyer to pay for the item before closing a case on the transaction.**

7. **Opt in to receive emails from eBay when a case opens or closes by the system.**

   At this point you can approve other options like instant relisting of the item and excluding certain buyers from this rule. Once you've read and approved the options, scroll down and follow the next step.

8. **Click Save.**

If you want to do this manually, and at least 48 hours — no more than 32 days — have elapsed since the end of the listing, you can apply for a Full Final Value Fee credit. First, however, you must file an Unpaid Item Alert:

1. **Go to your My eBay Sold view.**

   Find the transaction in question on the list of sold items.

2. **Click the drop-down menu in the Actions column of the listing and then choose Resolution Center.**

   You're taken to the Resolution Center.

3. **Select the I Sold an Item and Haven't Received My Payment Yet option and click Continue.**

4. **Sign in to your account and enter your User ID and password.**

   The Report an Unpaid Item Case form appears.

5. **Type the item number of the listing in question (if it's not already there), and then click Continue.**

6. **You'll be asked to select an issue from a drop-down menu that applies to your situation. After you do, click Continue.**

7. **Review everything you've entered to be sure that it's correct, and then click Continue.**

   If you and the buyer mutually agreed not to complete the transaction, when you click Continue, you see the Final Value Fee Credit Request page.

TIP

You need to wait *at least* two days after the listing ends to file a case and then another four days before you can apply for a Final Value Fee credit. I think it's jumping the gun to label someone a nonpaying bidder after only two days — try to contact the bidder again unless the bidder sends you a message about backing out (or you have good cause to believe that you have a deadbeat on your hands). To close the case and receive your Final Value Fee credit, do the following:

1. **On your My eBay page, hover your cursor over the Account tab and, on the Account page, choose Resolution Center.**

   You're taken to the Resolution Center.

2. **Under the Your Cases heading, find the transaction in question.**

3. **Click the View Dispute link under the status column.**

   You're now in the area where you may respond to any comments the buyer has left regarding why he or she hasn't yet paid for your item.

4. **Enter your response (if any) to the buyer in the messages area and click Submit Response, or to get your Final Value Fee refund, click Close Dispute.**

5. **Click the Close Dispute button on the bottom of the page.**

   You're taken to the Credit Request Process Completed page, which confirms that eBay is processing your refund.

WARNING

Anyone caught applying for a refund on a successful item transaction can be suspended or something worse — after all, such an action is a clear-cut case of fraud.

If you want to verify eBay's accounting, grab your calculator and use Table 9-1 in Chapter 9 to check the math. (Ah, calculators. Why couldn't I have had one of those in high school algebra class?)

TIP

In the case of an unsold or unpaid item, you may (only in this situation) qualify for an Insertion Fee credit by relisting the item within 90 days. If the item sells the second time, eBay will refund the Insertion Fee for relisting.

MARSHA SAYS

BUT IS SHE A NATURAL BLONDE?

Here's an example of an item that would have made the seller a bundle if he or she had done a little more strategizing up front:

1991 Platinum Mackie Barbie: Beautiful Platinum Bob Mackie Barbie. MIB (removed from box once, only to scan). The doll comes with shoes, stand, booklet, and Mackie drawing. The original plastic protects her hair and earrings. Buyer adds $10 for shipping and insurance. The starting price was $9.99, and even though the bidding went to $256, the seller's reserve price was not met, and the item didn't sell. And the Second Chance Offer didn't bite.

When relisting this item, the seller might do well to lower the reserve price and add much more to the description about the importance and rarity of the doll (unless, of course, $256 was far below what the seller wanted to make on the doll).

You *must* only use eBay's Relist feature to receive the credit. After the item is filed as unpaid, you can use the Relist link on the unpaid item page or do the following:

1. **Go to your My eBay page.**

2. **On the left side of the page in the Selling area, click the Unsold link.**

   You arrive at the Unsold listings page.

3. **Click the Relist link from the Actions drop-down menu next to the unpaid item.**

When you're listing using the Advanced Listing form (versus the Quick one), you can automatically relist an auction up to eight times if it doesn't sell.

TIP

The more specific your item title, the more you improve your odds of being profitable. If you're selling an old Monopoly game, don't just title it **Old Monopoly board game**; call it **Rare 1959 Monopoly Game Complete in Box**. For more information about listing items, see Chapter 10.

Here's a list of ideas that you can use to improve your auction's odds for success:

>> **Change the item category.** See if the item sold better in another category (see Chapter 3).

>> **Add a picture.** If two identical items are up for auction at the same time, the item with a photo gets more and higher bids. Zoom in on Chapter 14.

>> **Spruce up the title and description.** Make it enticing and grab those search engines. Breeze on over to Chapter 10 for pointers.

>> **Set a lower minimum bid.** The first bidders will think they're getting a bargain, and others will want a hot item. Mosey on over to Chapter 10.

>> **Set a lower reserve price or cancel the reserve.** A reserve price often scares away bidders who fear it's too high. See (yup) Chapter 10 for ways to make your reserve more palatable to prospective bidders.

>> **Change the duration of the auction.** Maybe you need some more time. Go to (you guessed it) Chapter 10.

TIP

Long-time eBay veterans say that reducing or canceling your reserve price makes an auction very attractive to buyers.

» Taking picture-perfect images with a smartphone

» Uploading your smartphone pictures to eBay

» Letting others meet you on your Profile

Chapter **14**

Increase Profits with Photography and Other Strategies

Y ou may be enjoying most of what eBay has to offer, and you're probably having some good buying adventures. If you're selling, you're experiencing the excitement of making money. But there's more.

Once you are on eBay for any length of time, you'll notice that listings with good pictures are more attractive. By saying "good pictures," I mean detailed photos taken by the seller of the actual item that's up for sale. People don't trust what they can't see, and often just using stock photography doesn't instill very much.

Although eBay requires you to have at least one photo of your item (at *least* 500 pixels on the longest side), the more images you add to your listing, the more it will be noticed.

In this chapter, you go to the head of the class by discovering some insider tips on how to enhance your listings with images and descriptive text. Successful eBay sellers know that pictures (also called *images*) really help sell items. This chapter gives you the basics on how to create great images. I also give you advice on linking pictures to your items so that buyers around the world can view them.

Using Images in Your Listings

Would you buy an item you couldn't see? Most people won't, especially if they're interested in purchasing items that they want to display or clothes they intend to wear. Without a picture, you can't tell whether a seller's idea of good quality is anything like yours — or if the item is really what you're looking for.

MARSHA SAYS

I coined this phrase ages ago when adding pictures to eBay listings was just an option. It is even truer today: "Take your pictures as if you have no description and write your description as if you had no pictures." As we know, some people are visual and others prefer to read the facts. By making this your mission, you will reach anyone who wants to know about what you have for sale. (There's more tips for writing a description in Chapter 3.)

Welcome to the cyberworld of *imaging,* where pictures are called not pictures but *images,* and your monitor or screen isn't a monitor but a *display.* (Certainly your smartphone isn't exactly just a "phone" either, but a tiny computer.) With a smartphone, digital camera, or scanner and software, you can manipulate your images — spin, crop, and color-correct — so that they grab viewers by the lapels. Even cooler: When you're happy with your creation, you can add it to your eBay listing for others to see.

TIP

Don't rule out using smartphone images on eBay. These days, pictures taken on many smartphones rival those taken on bigger digital cameras. Consider the top phones from manufacturers like Samsung, Apple, Huawei, and Google. Many tech news websites feature a page that offers updated reviews and compares smartphone cameras head to head. Be sure to check out the latest before you buy by searching Google for "top smartphone cameras."

Sellers, take heed and read these other reasons why you should use your *own* well-made digital images in your item pages, as well as eBay's stock photos (when available for new items only):

>> If you don't have your own picture, potential buyers or bidders may wonder whether you're deliberately hiding the item from view because you know something is wrong with it. Paranoid? Maybe. Practical? You bet.

>> Some fickle shoppers don't even bother reading an item description if they can't see multiple pictures of the item for sale. Maybe they were traumatized in English class.

>> Taking your own pictures shows that you actually have the item in your possession — and shows the item details. By contrast, some sellers take images from a manufacturer's website to illustrate their bogus sales. Why risk appearing suspect? Snap a quick picture!

>> Everyone's doing it. I hate to pressure you, but lots of digital images are *de rigueur* for items on eBay, so if you're not using more than one, you're not reaching the widest possible number of people who would buy your item. eBay requires that you use at least one. From that point of view, if you don't use multiple images, you're not doing the most you can to serve your potential customers' needs; it's just smart business to shoot the works (so to speak).

So which is better for capturing images: smartphones, digital cameras, or digital scanners? As with all gadgets, here's the classic answer: It depends. For convenience, it's hard to beat a good quality smartphone camera. But before you go snag one, decide what kind of investment (and how big) you plan to make in your eBay sales.

TIP

Whether you buy new or used digital equipment on eBay, consider buying a warranty from SquareTrade (squaretrade.com). If you *don't* get a warranty, Murphy's Law practically ensures that your digital equipment will break the second time you use it. There's more about SquareTrade in Chapter 20.

Choosing your camera

Having a dedicated home studio for your eBay photography is not just a luxury but a necessity once you start listing many items at a time. For your home studio, use the highest-quality digital camera you can afford, especially if you plan to use images for items that vary in size and shape. By *highest quality*, I don't necessarily mean a camera with vast amounts of megapixels; I mean a camera from a quality manufacturer that has a high-power optical zoom and a good (nonplastic) lens.

You can buy a used smartphone on eBay and use that with your home Wi-Fi exclusively for listing eBay items.

A great place to shop for these devices is (surprise!) eBay. Just do a search of some popular manufacturers, and you'll find pages of listings of both new and used digital cameras.

PRODUCT SHOOTING FOR EBAY, NOW WITH YOUR SMARTPHONE OR CAMERA

MARSHA SAYS

I've been on eBay since 1996, so I've taken lots of pictures to promote my online sales. I'm pretty happy with the quality of most of my own images. When I've sold paper ephemera, I usually just lay the item on a scanner — and scan away. It's still the best way to get a good image of that type of item (or vintage photographs). I started early on with an Olympus camera, but quickly changed to the Sony Mavica FD-73 (because it had a floppy drive as a storage device). The FD-73 was one of the first that had a 10X digital zoom, which helps with intricate close-ups. Then I upgraded to a used FD-92 with an 8X optical zoom (a newer model that added a memory stick). There was another Sony, a Canon, and a Nikon after that.

A smart camera was my next transition. A smart camera is just like a smartphone, only it turns a pocket camera into something special. I bought a fancy Android-powered Wi-Fi 14+-megapixel camera with an 18X zoom. To be honest, it's way too much camera for my eBay photoshoots, but it's reasonably priced and you can buy them now for around $130 (in used condition as low as $40).

One handy feature of a smart camera is the capability to send images over Wi-Fi from the camera to online storage or even to a smartphone — either approach makes for easy uploading to eBay. Newer cameras (and smartphone cameras) add not only Wi-Fi and fantastic zoom capabilities but also *image stabilization* — which holds the camera steady when zoomed in for ultra-macro close-ups. If you've ever taken a picture fully zoomed, you know that the slightest breath can jiggle the camera and blur the resulting image. If you're familiar with camera settings, the camera can also be set to Manual mode, if you don't want to use the auto features.

Prices are getting lower for cameras that are loaded with features. Consider buying a smart camera for eBay images; they are well worth the price!

When shopping for a smartphone or digital camera, look at the following features:

>> **Resolution:** Look for a camera that has a lower resolution setting (3MB is fairly common). This isn't hard to find because new cameras tout their strength in multiple *megabytes* (which translates to millions of pixels). You don't need that high a resolution for eBay because your pictures will not be printed; instead, they're shown ultimately on a monitor. A *pixel* is a tiny dot of information that, when grouped with other pixels, forms an image onscreen. The more pixels an image has, the clearer and sharper the image is.

When you upload images to eBay, the site compresses them for optimum viewing and loading as part of the item page.

The minimum requirement (eBay's rules) is that your image must be 500 pixels on the longest side; they recommend images to be at least 1600 pixels for best reproduction. 1600 pixels will generally be 1200 in the other direction (2MB). That's about perfect for any monitor or mobile device. You can always crop the picture if it's too large. eBay picture hosting will accept an image file of up to 7MB.

TIP

You want only high-pixel, high-resolution images for printing. The terms *ppi* and *dpi* (*pixels per inch* and *dots per inch,* respectively, found when you scan photos) only affect the printed size of the final picture. The human eye sees photo prints with printer-output resolutions over 240 ppi (pixels per inch) as continuous-tone images, even though the image is actually made up of slightly overlapping dots of ink.

>> **Optical zoom:** Here's where some camera manufacturers pull the wool over consumer's eyes. They sell cameras with an optical and a digital zoom. The *optical zoom* is a true zoom done by the camera, using its lens and its built-in CCD (computer chip in cameras that converts light into electronic data) — but a *digital zoom* is virtual; it's *interpolated* through software in the camera. That means it makes up data to fill in any holes it doesn't capture. You've seen this effect if you've ever tried to enlarge a picture from the web in a software program — it gets all blurry. A hybrid zoom works very well in the newest smartphone cameras.

TIP

If you ever plan on shooting close-ups in macro format, opt for a high-quality optical zoom.

>> **Storage type:** Smart card? SDHC? MicroSD card? CompactFlash card? Memory stick? (Whew.) The instructions that come with your camera explain how to transfer images from your media type to your computer. (No instructions? Check the manufacturer's website.) Many computers have card slots into which you can insert your camera's memory card; the computer reads the card like it's a teeny-tiny disk drive. I rarely take out my camera's card; I upload my images directly to eBay or to OneDrive via Wi-Fi, and then edit if necessary on my computer.

Using a light diffuser (versus using a flash) and a small tripod is an easy way to get the best images of items that require extreme close-ups (such as jewelry, stamps, currency, and coins). When photographing complex items, no matter how good your camera is, you may find it difficult to capture the item cleanly and exactly (especially the colors and brightness of gems and metals). Try using a diffuser like a photo tent or light box; your camera on a tripod points inside and takes pictures of the product inside the device. Figure 14-1 shows you my setup with a tent.

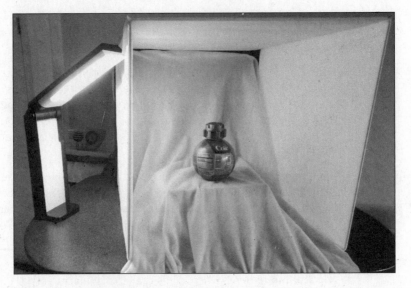

FIGURE 14-1:
Taking pictures
with a diffuser,
in this case,
a light box
(or photo tent).

Choosing a scanner

If you plan to sell flat items such as autographs, stamps, books, or documents — or if you need a good piece of business equipment that can double as a copier, printer, and fax machine — consider getting an all-in-one printer that has a digital scanner. I have a laser (versus inkjet) because I resent paying for ink refills continually, and it was quite reasonably priced. Whether you choose inkjet or laser, you can find used all-in-ones on eBay for around $100, or a brand new one for about $200.

Here's what you need to look for when you buy a scanner:

>> **Resolution:** As with printers and copiers, the resolution of digital scanning equipment is measured in *dots per inch* (dpi). The more dpi, the greater the resolution.

Some scanners can provide resolutions as high as 12800 dpi, which looks awesome when you print the image, but all the rez you need to dress up your eBay listings is (are you ready?) 72 or 96 dpi (dots or pixels per inch)! That's it. Your images will look great and won't take up much storage space on your computer's hard drive. Basic scanners can scan images at resolutions of up to 1200 dpi, so even they are far more powerful than you need for your eBay images.

>> **Flatbed:** If you're planning to use your scanner to scan pictures of documents (or even items in boxes), a flatbed scanner is your best bet. Flatbeds work just like old-school copiers: You simply lay your item or box on the glass and scan away.

Making Your Picture a Thing of Beauty

The idea behind using images in your listings is to attract tons of potential buyers. With that goal in mind, you should try to create the best-looking images possible, no matter what kind of technology you're using to capture them.

Get it on camera

Point-and-shoot may be okay for a group shot at some historical monument, but illustrating your sale is a whole different idea. Your digital camera or smartphone might be best used in manual mode (versus auto) so you can make adjustments to your images. Now that we have gone digital, experimenting takes a lot less time, especially because newer smartphone cameras integrate artificial intelligence to get the right snaps every time. However you use your camera, there are some basic photographic guidelines that can give you better results.

For more on using scanners, read ahead to the next section, "Yes, I scan." Then c'mon back to these picture do's and don'ts to ensure that your image is a genuine enhancement to your online sale:

» **Do** take the picture of your item in daylight whenever possible. That way the camera can catch all possible details and color.

» **Do** forget about fancy backgrounds; they distract viewers from your item. Put small items on a neutral-colored (preferably white), nonreflective towel or cloth; put larger items in front of a neutral-colored wall or curtain. You might even buy an *infinity board* on eBay to use as a background. You'll cut out almost all the background anyway when you crop your images. (This chapter explains how to prepare your picture.)

» **Do** turn off your flash and use extra lighting. You can do this with extra photo lighting on stands or even desk lamps. Consider using extra lighting even when you're taking the picture outside. The extra lighting acts as *fill light* — it adds more light to the item, filling in some of the shadowed spots.

» **Don't** get so close to the item that the additional light washes out (overexposes) the image. The easiest way to figure out the best distance is by trial and error. Start close and keep moving farther away until you get the results you want. You can see the picture seconds after you shoot it, keep it and modify it, erase it, and start again.

» **Do** take many acceptable versions of your image; you can choose the best ones later before you upload them.

>> **Don't** use incandescent light bulbs or fluorescent kitchen lighting to illuminate your photos. Incandescent lighting can make items look yellowish, and fluorescent lights lend a bluish tone to your photos. Some sellers use LED lighting; LEDs throw a good-quality light which, when combined with natural daylight, produces an even tone.

>> **Do** set the white balance setting on your camera or phone to *Auto*. You may see this as AWB, and this setting will often compensate for lighting differences.

>> **Do** take a wide shot of the entire item if your item relies on detail (for example, an engraved signature or detailed gold trim). Then take a tight close-up or two of the detailed areas that you want buyers to see, and include them in your description.

>> **Do** make sure that you focus the camera by tapping on the object on your smartphone screen; nothing is worse than a blurry picture. Most cameras today are auto-focus, so holding the camera still is (as ever) the biggest challenge for a shutterbug.

TIP

Taking pictures of your item from different angles gives the prospective buyer more information. When you have several images to upload to eBay, you can also use your photo–editing program to put them in a single composite image for your description, as shown in Figure 14-2.

TIP

Some eBay sellers, out of laziness, steal images from other eBay members. (They simply make a digital copy of the image and use it in their own listings. This is bad form because then the copied image doesn't represent the actual item being sold.) If you find yourself in a position where somebody has lifted one of your pictures, use the Ask a Question link below their description and ask them to remove your photo. If you don't get any cooperation, you can try using the Report Item link.

FIGURE 14-2:
Take several pictures from different angles to give the buyer a better idea of how your item looks.

Yes, I scan

If you use a scanner to create images for your eBay items, you've come to the right place. (Also check out the tips in the preceding section.) Here's how to get crisp scans of your items:

>> Select items to scan on glossy paper if you have an option; it scans best.

>> Scan the box that the item came in by laying it on the flatbed, or if there's a photo of the item on the box, scan that portion of the box.

>> If you're scanning a three-dimensional item (such as a doll, jewelry item, or box) and you can't close the scanner lid, drape a black or white T-shirt over the item after you place it on the scanner's glass plate; that way you get a clean background and good light reflection from the scanner.

>> If you want to scan an item that's too big to put on your scanner all at once, scan the item in sections and assemble the digital pieces with your image-editing software. The instructions that come with your software should explain how to do this.

Software that adds the artist's touch

After you take the picture (or scan it), you can upload it to eBay immediately or edit it in your smartphone with its native tools first. But if you're selling a high-ticket item (and you're a perfectionist), transfer it to your computer according to the manufacturer's instructions and edit the picture. You have to approach the image as a book or magazine editor would: Cut, fix, resize, and reshape your picture until you think it's good enough to be seen by the public. If you're a non-techie type, don't get nervous; many programs have one-button magical corrections that make your pictures look great.

A software program puts at your disposal an arsenal of editing tools that help you turn a basic image of your item into something special. Although each program has its own collection of features, a few basic tools and techniques are common to all:

>> **Image quality:** Enables you to enhance or correct colors, sharpen images, remove dust spots, and increase or reduce brightness or contrast.

>> **Size:** Reduces or increases the size or shape of the image.

>> **Orientation:** Rotates the image left or right; flips it horizontally or vertically.

>> **Crop:** Trims your picture to show the item, rather than extraneous background.

>> **Create an image format:** Gives your edited picture a specific format, such as JPG, GIF, or others when you save it. The best format for putting photos on the web (and thus the preferred format on eBay and the one I strongly recommend) is JPG (pronounced "JAY-peg").

QUICK AND EASY EDITING WITH PIXBY PHOTOPREP

Every image-editing software program has its own system requirements and capabilities. Study the software that comes with your camera or scanner. If you feel that the program is too complicated (or doesn't give you the editing tools you need), investigate some of the other popular programs. A simple-to-use program called Pixby PhotoPrep was developed by an eBay seller with us in mind. If you sell collectible, vintage, or one-of-a-kind items, you probably edit a lot of photos. The more you edit, the more you will appreciate the convenience of PhotoPrep's guidance for editing photos that conform to eBay photo requirements. It's incredibly simple to use, and the learning curve is small. I use it and love its simplicity and speed.

It has convenient one-click edit commands, a built-in image browser, an image uploader, unlimited undo and redo, and previewing of uploaded images in a web browser to check size and verify links. When it comes to editing, the PhotoPrep tools let you Resize, Rotate, JPEG Optimize, Sharpen, Add a Text Watermark, Add a Border, create a Gallery Thumbnail, Enhance, and Upload an image with one mouse click. It costs only $29.95, and you can get a free 30-day trial (as well as a 30-day money-back guarantee) to test it out at www.pixby.com/photoprep.

WARNING

Copying a manufacturer's text or images without permission can constitute copyright infringement, which may result in a very unfriendly "Cease and Desist" letter. If the copyright holder alerts eBay through the VeRO program, that action may end your listing.

Making Your Images Web-Friendly

Because digital images are made up of pixels — and every pixel has a set of instructions that has to be stored someplace — you have two difficulties facing you right after you take the picture:

>> Digital images contain computer instructions, so bigger pictures take up more memory.

>> Very large digital images take longer to *build* (appear) on the buyer's screen, and time can be precious on a web page.

TIP

Keep in mind that when you upload an image to eBay for your Gallery pictures (the ones that appear at the top of your listing and next to your item's title in search results), you really don't need to worry about size. eBay will standardize their size after you upload them, but they must be a minimum of 500 pixels on the longest side — with 1600 being optimal. That said, be sure your images aren't larger than 7MB.

There are some sellers who want to include more than the 12 pictures permitted by eBay. (Although I think 12 pictures is just fine). To get around this, when you add additional photos to your description, think small. Here's a checklist of tried-and-true techniques for preparing your fast-loading images to display on eBay:

>> **Set your scanner image resolution at 96 pixels per inch.** You can do this with the settings for your scanner. Although 96 ppi may seem like a low resolution, it only nibbles at bandwidth, shows up fast on a buyer's screen, and looks great on eBay.

>> **When using a digital camera, set the camera no lower than the 2MB setting.** At about 1600 x 1200, this gives you room to crop and edit the image to eBay's image size.

>> **If you add images to your description, be sure they are no larger than 480 pixels wide.** When you size your picture in your image software, it's best to keep it no larger than 300 x 300 pixels or 4 inches square, even if it's a snapshot of a classic 4 x 4 monster truck. These dimensions are big enough for people to see without squinting, and the details of your item show up nicely.

>> **Crop any unnecessary areas of the photo.** You need to show your item only; everything else is a waste. No props and no extraneous decoration. You can do this directly on the eBay listing page too.

>> **Use your software to brighten or change the photo's contrast.** When the image looks good on your computer screen, the image looks good on your eBay item page.

>> **Save your image as a JPG file.** When you finish editing your picture, save it as a JPG. (To do this, follow the instructions that come with your software.) JPG is the best format for eBay; it compresses information into a small file that builds fast and reproduces nicely on the Internet.

WARNING

>> **Reduce the size of an image used in your description if it's larger than 50K.** Small is fast, efficient, and beautiful. Big is slow, sluggish, and dangerous: Impatient eBay users will move on to the next listing if they have to wait to see your image. Software like Pixby, mentioned earlier in this chapter, can reduce images easily.

The Image Is Perfect — Now What?

Now that your masterpiece is complete, you want to emblazon it on your item page for all the world to see. You can upload your images to eBay, but they will only be kept on the site for a short period of time — then poof!

Although the best way to display your listing pictures is through the eBay uploader at the top of the listing, you may want to store your images as an archive. Stay tuned . . . .

TIP

Trade secret: Keep an archive of your pictures. Should you ever want to use them again (or to link to them from your description), you need to store the originals off eBay. This way you have your original images, no matter what; meanwhile, eBay makes optimized copies of your images to use in your listing — and stores them for the requisite 90 days.

If you have your image stored on the web, all you have to do is type its URL address in the picture uploader section of the "Sell" listing form. Just click the Import From web link in the picture uploader, and then type the address in the URL text field. Then, by clicking the Import button, you tell eBay to go ahead and copy your photos into your listing.

If you use eBay's picture uploader, your photo will reside on eBay's servers and will upload once, directly from your computer. I talk more about that in just a minute.

TIP

You can highlight your image's URL with your cursor, right-click your mouse, and copy the image to your computer's clipboard. Then go to the item page you're filling out on eBay, put your cursor in the Picture URL box, and paste the address into the box.

A typical address (for someone using a WordPress blog) looks something like this:

```
http://www.coolebaytools.com/wp-content/uploads/marsha.jpg
```

Because your image needs an address, you have to find it a good home online. You have several options:

>> **Your own website or blog:** If you have a website, why not set up a separate folder for eBay pictures? Web hosts give you so much space that there's generally plenty to spare. You're already paying for the space, so you can park pictures there at no extra charge.

>> **An image-hosting website:** Websites that specialize in hosting pictures are popping up all over the Internet. Some charge a small fee; others are free. The upside here is that they're easy to use.

>> **Your server:** If you have your own server (those of you who do, well, you know who you are), you can store those images right in your own home.

>> **eBay:** You can find out about using eBay's photo uploader later in this chapter. It's the simplest and easiest way to go.

Getting Pictures from Your Smartphone to eBay

These days I take all my photos with my smartphone camera. I have a great camera and rarely have to do any editing. Even if I need more editing than my camera's app provides, there are further tools I can use after I upload the pictures to eBay.

You have two options to get your images on eBay (note that these screenshots were taken on an Android phone; iOS looks a bit different):

1. **Take pictures using the camera that comes with the eBay app.**

To begin a listing and use the eBay mobile app

TIP

- Tap Selling on the opening page and tap List an Item (shown in Figure 14-3).

  Don't worry that you are listing an item for sale. It may seem that you are listing an item, but what we are doing is creating a draft listing that you can edit later.

- Type in a few keywords to describe your item for sale, then tap the magnifying glass on your keyboard.

- eBay shows you active listings that may be a duplicate of your item. If you find an exact duplicate, tap on it and eBay will begin a listing for that particular item. Once you do, you see a sample listing like the one in Figure 14-3.

- If you don't find a duplicate of your item, tap Create a New Listing at the bottom of the screen.

- Select the condition of your item.

- On the next page, select the condition of your item and you will be shown an upload (or take) photo option.

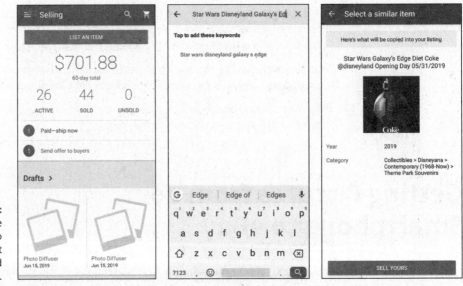

FIGURE 14-3:
A close duplicate of what I want to sell, but I will edit the title and description later.

Figure 14-4 illustrates the steps.

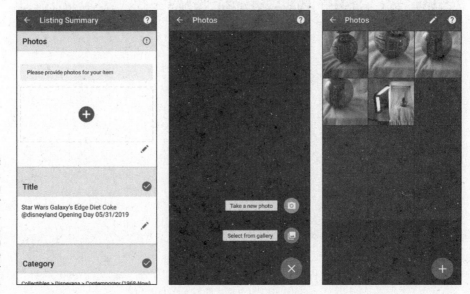

FIGURE 14-4:
Within the app, decide if you want to take or upload an image. To add photos, click the + sign and you'll be taken to your phone's gallery.

TIP

Don't worry if your photos are not centered or even need editing. Once you open up the draft listing on eBay with a computer, you can take care of that.

If your smartphone camera has a particularly good quality camera, I recommend using the native one. I'm using a Huawei P30 Pro that's known for the quality of the camera. It has AI (artificial intelligence) built in and takes incredible pictures of my products (see Figure 14-5).

2. **If you haven't taken the pictures in the eBay Mobile App, open it now, start the listing, then click the photo box to go to your photos.**

    Select which ones you want to use for your listing and tap to upload.

3. **Once you've selected and uploaded your images as in Figure 14-5, scroll to the bottom of the screen and tap Save for Later.**

    Do not tap List Your Item, or the listing will go live on the site.

4. **Open eBay in your computer's web browser and go to your drafts, which will be found either in your My eBay ⇨ Selling Overview or in the Seller's Hub ⇨ Drafts.**

    The My eBay page is shown in Figure 14-6.

5. **Find the draft you want to complete and click Complete Draft.**

6. **The Create your listing page appears; fill in all the information to complete the listing or just go to the photos you've uploaded.**

Photos
Uploading...
Pending...

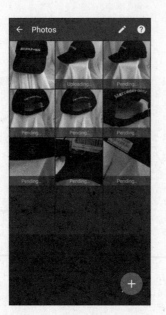

FIGURE 14-5: After you select your photo, it will be ready for uploading. You can upload as many as 12 at a time.

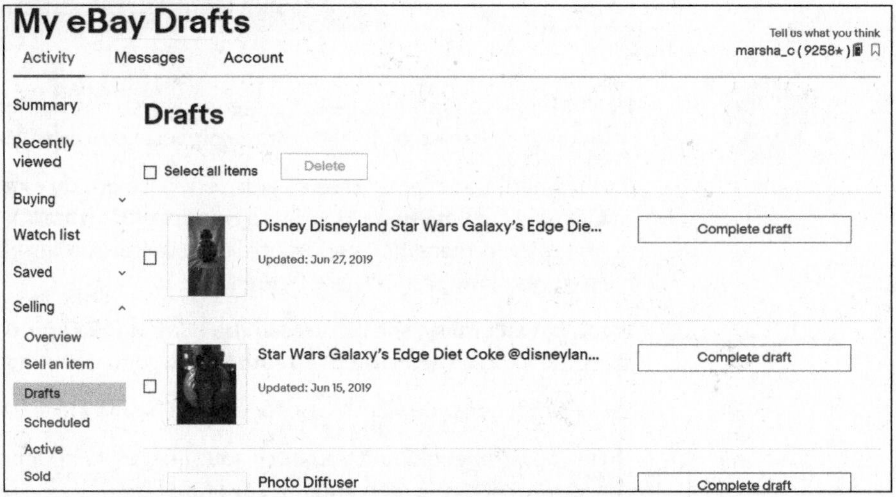

My eBay Drafts
Activity
Messages
Account
Tell us what you think
marsha_c (9258★)
Summary
Recently viewed
Buying
Watch list
Saved
Selling
Overview
Sell an item
Drafts
Scheduled
Active
Sold
Drafts
Select all items
Delete
Disney Disneyland Star Wars Galaxy's Edge Die...
Updated: Jun 27, 2019
Complete draft
Star Wars Galaxy's Edge Diet Coke @disneylan...
Updated: Jun 15, 2019
Complete draft
Photo Diffuser
Complete draft

FIGURE 14-6: Pending drafts are safely waiting for you.

7. **As you can see in Figure 14-7, your unedited photos are ready for editing.**

   To select and edit a photo

   - Click a photo to put it into the edit box.
   - Use the first symbol below the image to crop your photo to the appropriate size.
   - If you need to rotate the photo, use the circular arrow. Click it to turn the photo.

- Before you use the sun icon (for brightness and contrast) or the triangle (for sharpening), try tapping the magic wand icon. That usually corrects your image without guesswork. Click Save after your editing is done.

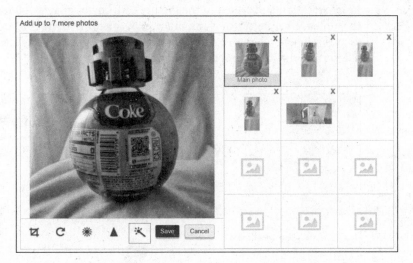

FIGURE 14-7:
One photo edited, four more to go.

8. **Click the other images to perform the edits as needed.**

9. **To change the order of the images, just click and drag them to a different spot.**

10. **Double check that all your details are correct for your listing, then go to the bottom of the page (shown in Figure 14-8) and tap List item.**

   If you'd still rather fill in the details later, tap Save as draft and revisit the draft when you want to list it.

FIGURE 14-8:
Tap List item to launch the listing now or Save as draft to finish later.

| List item | Preview | Save as draft | Cancel |

Using Your Website to Store Images

If you have a website, you can easily upload your images from there. A simple website where you can blog and post promotions to your eBay images can be as inexpensive as $3 to $4 a month. All you need to do is set up an eBay folder for your item's pictures and get FTP (file transfer protocol) login information from your webhost.

TIP

After you've uploaded your images to your website folder, get the address of your item's location and type it in the Picture URL box of eBay's Sell form. You can use the uploaded images for your main eBay pictures or within descriptions. The pictures appear whenever someone views your item pages. Figure 14-9 shows you a description with an embedded brand image.

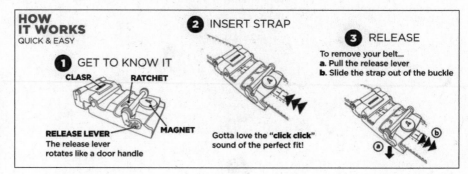

FIGURE 14-9: Mission Belt Company (of *Shark Tank* fame) embedded an instructional image in their description.

If your images are stored on a WordPress site, just upload them and use your own version of the URL as referenced earlier.

You can also use a service like Photobucket to host your images. More on image-hosting services in Chapter 20.

Using the Photo Uploader

eBay hosts up to 12 images per listing for free. The first photo (you can change the order after you have uploaded them) appears as your main Gallery photo in search results and as the featured photo on the listing page. Under the featured photo, a viewer appears where the buyer can scroll and click to enlarge your other images; the enlarged views automatically appear in the larger photo area.

When you upload photos to eBay, keep these tips (rules) in mind:

» Every item for sale on eBay is required to have at least one image to display the item.

» Photos *must* be a minimum of 500 pixels on the longest side. eBay recommends that they be at least 1600 pixels.

>> You can choose from several image types: JPG (JPEG), PNG, TIF (TIFF), BMP, or GIF. Most sellers use photos with the .jpg file extension.

>> Do not get fancy. Images with borders, text, or graphics embedded in them are a violation of policy (plus they're supposed to be pictures of your items, not ads).

>> When you export your JPG images for eBay, and your software gives you a choice, select an image quality of 90 or more. Then eBay will optimize it for viewing on the site.

When you prepare to list an item for sale, you will be asked whether to add photos. If you don't want to upload from your computer — but have product images on your website — eBay gives you the option of copying your website images. Just input the URL of your picture in the tab called Copy Your Photos from a Web Address in the enhanced photo uploader. Then follow the directions onscreen to upload your image from your computer to eBay.

To post your photo, you have options:

1. **Click Add/Edit Photos to use the photo uploader.**

2. **After clicking the Classic Uploader link, click the Browse box.**

   An Open File dialog box appears.

3. **Find your image on your computer and click Open.**

   The name of the image appears in the Pictures list (but not in your listing). Figure 14-10 shows the upload page.

FIGURE 14-10:
Click Add Photos and you're on your way.

4. **Add more pictures if you want, and click Add Photo.**

5. **At this point, follow the same process described previously in "Getting Pictures from Your Smartphone to eBay" for editing and arranging.**

Here are a couple things to keep in mind:

>> eBay keeps an image online for the duration of your listing and for up to 90 days (as long as you have the link available to access the page). After that, the image disappears (unless you relist the item).

>> You can always post the image again if you need it later; be sure to archive a copy of the image on your computer.

When you do your own photo hosting on eBay, you can use a different photo for your Gallery image.

MULTIPLE PICTURES IN YOUR DESCRIPTIONS

Here's the answer to *the most-asked* question when I teach a class on eBay. Many sellers have additional pictures within the listing description area. This isn't magic; you can easily do it too. Just add a tiny bit of HTML code in your description. Here is the HTML code to insert one picture in your description area:

```
<img src="http://www.yourserver.com/imagename.jpg">
```

Be sure to use the brackets to open and close your code (they're located above the comma and the period on your keyboard). This code reflects the URL of your picture, and the coding img src= tells eBay's server to insert a picture.

When you want to insert two pictures, just insert code for each picture, one after the other. If you want one picture to appear below the other, use the HTML code for line break, <BR>. Here's how to write that:

```
<img src="http://www.yourserver.com/imagenumber1.jpg"> <BR>
<img src="http://www.yourserver.com/imagenumber2.jpg">
```

Tell Your Story on Your Profile Page

If staying social is the key to the new web, your eBay profile is the hub of your eBay user interaction. Your profile page is there for customers and the eBay community. People like to know about other people, and your eBay pages let folks know with whom they are transacting.

Although my editors would love for me to give you a long, drawn-out, step-by-step list to show you how to get to your profile page, I won't. It's all too simple: To get to your profile page, click your User ID on your My eBay page — or on any eBay page, for that matter — even when you click your User ID after clicking "Hi" at the top left of any page.

When your profile page appears, it will be pre-populated with items you're selling, your reviews (if you've reviewed an item on eBay), your bio, and a profile picture (provided you previously uploaded the bio and photo to the now-defunct My World page). If you have no profile picture, read further on.

Remember: Whenever you click your name or User ID, you arrive at your own profile page. Your profile page contains basic information about you as a seller, your recent feedback, your eBay Store (if you have one), and some further handy details:

>> **Items for sale:** Images and links to your current listings.

>> **Following:** When you choose to follow an item search, or an eBay seller, they will show up here.

TIP

If you're following a search or seller for your own personal research, you can choose to make those selections private by clicking Settings on the right side of the page, then the word Private under the image on the profile page.

Take an opportunity to edit the page. Here's the lowdown on what you can do to personalize your page after clicking the Edit Profile button under your User ID. When you click that button, small pen icons appear, showing you where you can edit the page:

>> **Upload a profile photo:** Click the pen icon in the corner of the square next to your User ID. The page will prompt you to upload your profile image. Choose a profile photo that portrays you and your personality. There are no set requirements for size at this point, so I suggest using a close-to-square headshot. If you do not select a headshot, your face might be too small for folks to see.

>> **Upload a cover photo:** Just as on Facebook, you may upload a photo for the top of your page. Keep in mind that text covers a good deal of the cover photo, so don't select a picture where the most important spot is at the bottom. When you're selecting (or cropping) an image for use as a cover photo, also keep in mind eBay's recommended 1200 pixels x 270 pixels size for best viewing. Also, eBay requires cover-photo image files to be smaller than 4MB.

>> **Add content:** Here you have 250 characters to talk about yourself, your eBay life, or the items you enjoy selling or buying.

It is easy to share a link to your profile or find other buyers and sellers by typing an eBay ID into an eBay URL, like this: `http://www.ebay.com/usr/marsha_c` (pictured in Figure 14-11). I can't wait to see your creativity on *your* eBay profile page!

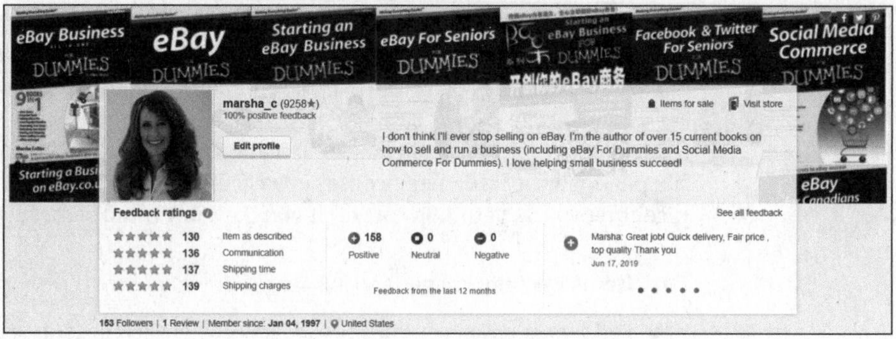

FIGURE 14-11:
Welcome to my
eBay profile page!

4

Even More of eBay's Special Features

IN THIS CHAPTER

about you

» **Determining how safe your information is online**

» **Setting up two-step authentication**

» **What to do when your account's been hacked**

» **Protecting your data**

Chapter **15**

Security: Protect Yourself Online and on eBay

On the Internet, as in real life, you should never take your personal privacy or security for granted. Sure, you're ecstatic that you can shop and sell on eBay from the privacy of your home, but remember: Just because your front door is locked doesn't mean that your security is protected. If you're new to the Internet, you may be surprised to find out what you reveal about yourself to the world, no matter how many precautions you take. (Yes, we all know about that avocado-green facial you wear when you're shopping online . . . just kidding . . . honest.)

All moves across the Internet have become part of the "big data" movement. You have most likely heard of *data mining,* which takes enormous amounts of data from every Internet citizen's posts, movements, and clicks. This data is also collected from your smartphone, tablet, and home Wi-Fi network. There is so much information available that data science specialists have to go in and pull sets and subsets to decipher the data. Once they have this information, they can spot business trends, plan cities, discover crime, and more.

Our government invested over $200 million in the White House's Big Data Research and Development Initiative to figure out what to do with this data. The Facebook/Cambridge Analytica scandal showed us that privacy is a thing of the past. We live in a data economy powered by surveillance capitalism. There's no escaping it.

You can imagine that the amount of information eBay gets from you is infinitesimal compared to the personal information collected by the various branches of the government. In this chapter, you find out how much eBay knows about you and with whom eBay shares this information. I explain what you can do to protect your privacy and tell you some simple steps you can take to increase not only your Internet privacy but also your personal safety.

What eBay Knows about You

The irony of the Internet is that although you think you're sitting at home working anonymously, third parties such as advertisers and marketing companies are surreptitiously getting to know you.

While you're busy collecting Winter Olympic memorabilia or buying that hot new Kate Spade purse, eBay is busy collecting nuggets of information about you. eBay gets some of this information from you and some of it from your computer. All the data eBay gets is stored in the mammoth eBay data bank.

What you tell eBay

eBay gets much of what it knows about you *from* you. When you sign up, you voluntarily tell eBay important and personal information about yourself. Right off the bat, you give eBay all or some of these basic tidbits:

>> Name

>> Email address

>> Snail-mail address

>> Phone number

>> Your date of birth

>> Password

"Okay, that's no big deal," you say, but if you're using your credit card to settle your eBay fees (and using PayPal), you're also giving the following personal financial information:

>> Credit card number

>> Expiration date

>> Bank account number

>> Credit card billing address

>> Credit card history

REMEMBER

Don't worry about giving this information to eBay or PayPal. The bottom line is that *every time* you pay by check or with a credit card in the real world, you give away personal info about yourself. The eBay companies carefully lock up this information (in a high-security area on their servers), but other companies or individuals may not be so protective. eBay has a vested interest in your safety.

What cookies gather

Websites collect information about you by using *cookies.* No, they don't bribe you with oatmeal-raisin goodies. Cookies are nothing more than tiny pieces of data that companies (such as eBay) put in your web browser to store data about your surfing and item-viewing habits. In a nutshell, they use this data to sell you more products and to improve the user experience.

Most web designers install cookies in the site code to help you navigate their sites. Sometimes the cookie becomes sort of an "admission ticket" so that you don't need to register or log in every time you land on the site.

TIP

Cookies can't steal information from other files on your computer. A cookie can access only the information that you provide to its website.

Aside from internal data scientists, eBay also has partnerships with third-party companies that provide page-view and data-tracking technology — and with advertisers who display the ads on eBay pages, whether you want to see them or not. If you click a banner, a cookie from that particular advertiser *may* go onto your computer, usually to prevent you from seeing it again.

TIP

The ads you see on eBay are served up by Ad Choice. If you do not want to participate in eBay's ad-customization programs, you can opt out at the Ad Choice program page (you will have to sign in first) shown in Figure 15-1:

www.ebay.com/adchoice

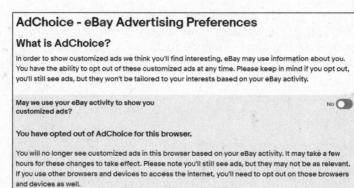

AdChoice - eBay Advertising Preferences

What is AdChoice?

In order to show customized ads we think you'll find interesting, eBay may use information about you. You have the ability to opt out of these customized ads at any time. Please keep in mind if you opt out, you'll still see ads, but they won't be tailored to your interests based on your eBay activity.

May we use your eBay activity to show you   No 〇
customized ads?

You have opted out of AdChoice for this browser.

You will no longer see customized ads in this browser based on your eBay activity. It may take a few hours for these changes to take effect. Please note you'll still see ads, but they may not be as relevant. If you use other browsers and devices to access the internet, you'll need to opt out on those browsers and devices as well.

FIGURE 15-1:
You must go to this page in every web browser you use for it to be fully effective.

Note that if you opt out, you will still see ads, but they will not be relevant to your online searches, since no data is collected.

Another example, DoubleClick, acquired by Google in 2018, is a major player in the cookie-tracking field. They say that it uses your information to limit the number of times that you see the same advertisement. DoubleClick also measures the kinds of ads that you respond to — and tracks which member websites you visit and how often. The bottom line is that DoubleClick is just trying to finesse how you buy stuff with ads based on your personal interests. The upside is that you get to see stuff that you may like.

These cookies, wherever they come from, target various criteria. Targeting is accomplished by using IP addresses or by referencing information about users stored within other cookies on your computer. Common information picked up by some cookies includes

>> What web browser you are using

>> Which operating system your computer uses

>> Who your Internet Service Provider is

>> Your bandwidth

>> Your IP address

>> The time of day you viewed the advertiser's cookie

TIP

If you want to keep your browsing information private, you can get more information on how to remove yourself from the cookie system or adjust your privacy settings by going to this website:

```
https://policies.google.com/technologies/ads
```

Your eBay sign-in cookie

There are several types of cookies; the most common ones you will encounter are as follows:

>> **Session:** This cookie type remains on your computer, tablet, or mobile phone as long as your browser is open or until you log out of the site. When you close your Internet browser (Microsoft Edge, Firefox, Safari, or Chrome), the cookie disappears as completely as if you snarfed it up with icy-cold milk.

>> **Persistent (tracking):** This flavor of cookie is perfect if you don't share your device with anyone else; it permits your computer, tablet, or mobile phone to always remain signed in to a particular website. Generally, these cookies have a timer that will expire within a pre-prescribed period of time (say, a year). Each time you visit a site with such a cookie, it pings the server's owners to let them know you are a repeat visitor. They may also record from where you came to the website. For this reason, persistent cookies are also called *tracking cookies.*

Some third-party service providers may also leave cookies when you visit eBay.

California, the state where eBay resides, has strong "Do Not Track" laws. As of this writing, eBay states: "Because there currently isn't an industry or legal standard for recognizing or honoring DNT signals, we don't respond to them at this time."

The quote comes from eBay's article on *Cookies, Web Beacons, and Similar Technologies,* which you can find here: https://www.ebay.com/help/policies/member-behaviour-policies/ebay-cookie-notice?id=4267.

I would suggest you check back there if this topic is of interest to you. I'm sure these policies will change over time.

REMEMBER

eBay's "keep me signed in" sign-in cookie is a good thing. It prevents the repetitive task of typing your User ID and password at every turn. This cookie simplifies your participation in bidding, watching items, viewing completed listings, and so on. Because you don't have to sign in every moment that you're doing business on eBay, it's a real timesaver.

Web beacons

Web beacons are transparent, single-pixel images placed in the HTML (or Internet page code) for individual pages. They are also commonly called *tracking bugs* or *pixel tags.* Web beacons, like cookies, are used mainly for collecting marketing information. They track the traffic patterns of users from one page to another.

Web beacons are also often used in emails. Ever wonder how someone knows you've received an email? Or why you may receive an email from a company whose website you've just visited? Blame the sneaky-but-harmless beacons.

Web beacons are as invisible as cookies and are incorporated into web pages without your knowing. Turning off cookies on your browser won't disable beacons, but this action does protect your anonymity. Web beacons are not as ominous as they may seem; the information collected is not personally identifiable; they just track your passage along the site.

What web servers collect

Every time that you log on to the Internet, you leave an electronic trail of information; it's just like when you're on a scavenger hunt. eBay, like millions of other websites, uses *servers*, which are immense pieces of hardware that do nothing but collect and transfer bits (and bytes) of information day and night. Your Internet connection has a special address (IP address) that identifies you to all servers when you surf the Net. This is called an *IP (Internet Protocol) address* and is often used by law enforcement to track those whose shenanigans wreak havoc on websites — or on other users.

TIP

If you're curious, you can find out your personal IP address by asking Google *What is my IP address* (just type it in the Google search box). The resulting page will show you your IP address without exposing your data to any spurious website.

Web servers all over the Internet track some or all of the following information:

>> What website you came in from

>> The ISP (Internet Service Provider) that you use

>> The items that you're selling or viewing on eBay

>> The websites you linked your listings to

>> Your favorite websites (if you link them to your profile page)

eBay collects the following information while you visit the eBay site or use the mobile app:

>> What you do while logged on to the site

>> Which categories you tend to browse

>> Which items you've viewed recently

>> What times you log on and log off

Like incredible Internet archivists, eBay's servers keep a record of everything you bid on, win, and sell — which is great news if you have a problem with a transaction and need eBay to investigate. Also, eBay couldn't display feedback about you and other users if its servers didn't store all the feedback you write and receive. Have you ever sent a message to eBay? eBay's servers record it and keep it in some murky recess of eBay's memory. Remember, we live in the age of digital commerce, and the people on eBay run a serious business that depends on e-commerce. They have to keep everything in case they need it later.

To keep up with changes to the policies, you must go to the *User Privacy Notice*, which has all the legalese, presented in an easy-to-read fashion. To get there, click the link you will find in the eBay copyright notice at the very bottom of almost every eBay page that says Privacy (Figure 15-2).

```
www.ebay.com/help/policies/member-behaviour-policies/user-
privacy-notice-privacy-policy?id=4260
```

FIGURE 15-2:
Find the Copyright notice at the bottom of eBay's home page (and others) and click Privacy.

eBay has a much more user-friendly page, called the Privacy Center. To Get there

1. **Go to the About eBay section of the site links at the bottom of the home page.**

2. **Under the About eBay header, click the link for Company Info.**

3. **On the resulting page, click Privacy Center and you'll land at the page in Figure 15-3.**

A direct link to the page is www.ebayinc.com/our-company/privacy-center.

TIP

You *can* also surf the Internet free of cookies and tracking if you use Google's Chrome browser, Firefox, Safari, or a recent version of Microsoft Edge. These browsers have an option that allows you to visit the web without giving off a trace of who you are. It's called *Incognito, InPrivate browsing,* or *invisible* mode. You can get into this mode easily, after you've installed the browser, by typing Ctrl+Shift+N.

FIGURE 15-3:
The Privacy
Center gives you
eBay's corporate
policies
worldwide.

If you're apprehensive about all the information that web servers can collect about you while you innocently roam the Internet, I understand. But before you start looking out for Big Brother watching over your shoulder, consider this: On the World Wide Web, *everybody's* collecting information — and very little is private anymore.

The odds are excellent that all the information that eBay knows about you is already in the hands of many other folks, too — your bank, your grocer, the staff of any magazines you subscribe to, clubs you belong to, any airlines you've flown, and any insurance agencies you use. That's life these days. And if you're thinking, "Just because everybody knows all this stuff about me, that doesn't make it right," all I can say is, "You're right." But maybe you'll sleep better knowing that eBay is a place where the privacy issue is taken seriously. See the next section for details.

To be sure the eBay site (itself) is safe, eBay subscribes to digicert (who acquired Symantec and Norton Security). You'll see the Norton Secured logo at the bottom of almost every page. If you click it, you see the current status of eBay's certification, shown in Figure 15-4.

There are even two links to report any SSL/TLS issues on the site. If you're interested in learning more about how all this works, click the link on this page to Learn More.

Unfortunately, no website — including the CIA's website — is completely secure, so you still have to be on your guard while you're online.

6/28/2019 16:35
www.ebay.com uses these DigiCert security services. DigiCert, Inc., with the acquisition of Symantec Website Security, is the leading global provider of digital certificates.

SITE NAME:	www.ebay.com
SSL/TLS CERTIFICATE STATUS:	Valid (Aug 9, 2018 to Sep 28, 2019)
COMPANY/ ORGANIZATION:	eBay, Inc. San Jose California, us

🔒	**Encrypted Data Transmission**	This website secures your private information using an SSL/TLS Certificate. Information exchanged with an address beginning with https is encrypted using SSL/TLS.
👤	**Identity Verified**	eBay, Inc. is verified as the owner or operator of the website on www.ebay.com. Official records confirm that eBay, Inc. is a valid business.
🐞	**Malware Scan**	www.ebay.com passed the malware scan on Jun 28, 2019 (UTC).

Security tip: When you visit a site, check that the internet address (URL) matches the address that you expect, so that your personal information doesn't end up in the wrong hands. If the address starts with "https", information you enter on the site will be encrypted and more secure than sites with just "http".

This site chose the Norton Secured Seal, the most trusted mark on the Internet, to promote trust online with consumers.

REPORT MISUSE

LEARN MORE

FIGURE 15-4: eBay's up-to-the-minute safety certified status.

MARSHA SAYS

GRATEFUL DEAD COOKIE JAR

In 1999, an auction description read: "This is one of the grooviest jars I have ever come across — a real find for the die-hard Grateful Dead fan or for the cookie jar collector who has it all. Made by Vandor, this Grateful Dead bus cookie jar looks like something the Dead *would* drive. Beautiful detailing on the peace signs; the roses are running lights. Painted windows. You have just got to see this piece. Only 10,000 made, and I have only seen one other. Comes with box that has Grateful Dead logos on it. Buyer pays all shipping and insurance."

The cookie jar started at $1 and sold on eBay for $102.50. When I updated this book in 2002, it sold on eBay for $125; when I updated again in 2004, it went for $150. Today, there's one for sale at $250. The Grateful Dead's bus cookie jar is riding the tracks these days; in 2009 an auction closed with the final bid at $125, and in 2016, $275. Perhaps the Baby Boomer Deadheads are feeling the economic crunch. I haven't seen a sold one, but there is one mint version asking $375 (or best offer). The price of the original has skyrocketed from the original issue price, so much so that Vandor just came out with a 40th anniversary replica. Buy it now for your Deadhead friends — and buy it quick. Only 1,200 were made, and the asking price is $499 (and it's not in mint condition).

What Does eBay Do with Information about Me, Anyway?

Although eBay knows a good chunk of information about you, it puts the information to good use. The fact that it knows so much about you actually helps you in the long run.

Here are some of the things that eBay uses personal information for:

>> **Upgrading eBay:** Like most e-commerce companies, eBay tracks members' use and habits to improve the website. For example, if a particular item generates a lot of activity, eBay may add a category or a subcategory.

>> **Clearing the way for transactions:** If eBay didn't collect personal information such as your email address, your snail-mail address, and your phone number, you couldn't complete the transaction you started after you made a purchase.

>> **Billing:** You think it's important to keep track of your merchandise and money, don't you? So does eBay. It uses your personal information to keep an eye on your account and your paying habits — and on everybody else's. (Call it a gentle encouragement of honest trading habits.)

>> **Policing the site:** Never forget that eBay tries to be tough on cybercrime; if you break the rules or regulations, eBay will hunt you down and boot you out. Personal information is used to find eBay delinquents, and eBay makes it clear that it cooperates with law enforcement and with third parties whose merchandise you may be selling illegally. For more about this topic, read up on the VeRO program in Chapter 9.

WARNING

Periodically, eBay runs surveys asking specific questions about your use of the site. It uses your answers to upgrade eBay. In addition, eBay asks whether it can forward your information to a marketing firm. eBay says that it does not forward any personally identifiable information, which means that any info you provide is given to third parties as raw data. However, if you're nervous about privacy, I suggest that you make it clear that you don't want your comments to leave eBay should you decide to participate in eBay surveys. But if you don't participate in the surveys, you won't have any hand in creating new eBay features — so you can't complain if you don't like how the site looks and works the next time it makes some changes.

What Do Other eBay Members Know about Me?

eBay functions under the premise that eBay's members are buying, selling, working, and playing in an honest and open way. That means that anyone who's surfing the site can immediately find out some limited information about you:

>> Your User ID and history

>> Your feedback history

>> All the auctions and fixed-price sales you run

>> Sellers you have purchased from in your feedback profile

eBay clearly states in its policies and guidelines that email addresses should be used only for eBay business. If you abuse this policy, you can be suspended and possibly be in violation of state or federal privacy laws.

REMEMBER

eBay provides limited eBay member registration information to its users. If another member involved in a transaction with you wants to know the following facts about you, they're available:

>> Your name (and business name if you have provided that information)

>> Your email address

>> The city, state, and country data that you provided to eBay

>> The telephone number that you provided to eBay

REMEMBER

Following the transaction, buyers and sellers exchange some real-world information. As I explain in Chapters 6 and 12, the exchange of merchandise, money, and information is all part of an eBay transaction. Make sure that you're comfortable giving out your home address. If you're not, I explain alternatives in this chapter.

Hack-proof Your Account with Two-Factor Authentication

MARSHA SAYS

Because data breaches have become a common occurrence, many websites allow (and encourage) two-factor authentication. eBay is one of the websites where you need to set this up. After you activate this, your account will be doubly safe.

It works by your adding your mobile phone number to your online account. If you request to reset your password (because you forgot it) or try to sign in from a new device, a code will be sent to your smartphone via text message. Type that code onto the platform and you've been authenticated.

Here's how to set it up it:

1. **Go to your My eBay Summary page by clicking the word Summary under the My eBay link on the home page.**

2. **On the My eBay Summary page, click the tab for your Account.**

3. **On the Account page, click the Personal Information link at the top of the left column.**

4. **On the Personal Information page, scroll down to Security Information.**

   You will see "2 step verification"; click Edit to the far right.

5. **You'll land on a page where you can set up two-step verification (shown in Figure 15-5).**

6. **Personally, I want to receive a text message and remove eBay from any hacker's equation, so I'll click Turn On next to Text Message.**

7. **On the next page (Figure 15-6), you'll be prompted for your mobile number; type it in, click Text Me, and eBay will text you a code.**

8. **eBay texts a six-digit code to your cell phone; type it in on the page that appears after eBay sends the code.**

   Voilà, you're one step closer to being hack proof. You will be sent a six-digit code anytime you newly log in to eBay to confirm that it's you.

Setting up 2FA is not only safe, it's the smart thing to do.

Spam — Not Just a Hawaiian Delicacy

Although you can find plenty of places to socialize and have fun on eBay, when it comes to business, eBay is . . . well, all business. eBay's policy says that requests for registration information can be made only for people with whom you're transacting business on eBay. The contact information request form requires that you type the item number of the transaction you're involved in, as well as the User ID of the person whose contact info you want. If you're not involved in a transaction, as a bidder or a seller in the specified item number, you can't access the user information.

When it comes to email addresses, your secret is safe. A PayPal transaction page (as well as other payment providers) contains your email address so that the person on the other end of the transaction can contact you. Using eBay messages is a far more efficient way to check on a transaction because the messages are archived by eBay. After the other user has your email address, eBay rules state that the user can use it only for eBay business.

Sending spam versus eating it

Sending email to other members is a great way to do business and make friends. But don't cross the line into spam. *Spam*, a Hormel canned meat product (I give Spam its own sidebar), now has an alternate meaning. When you spell it with a small *s*, *spam* is unsolicited email — most often, advertising — sent to multiple email addresses gleaned from marketing lists. Eventually, it fills up your inbox the way "Spam, Spam, Spam, and Spam" filled up the menu in an old *Monty Python* restaurant skit.

Think of spam as the electronic version of the junk mail that you get via the U.S. Postal Service. The original Spam may be okay for eating (if you're into that kind of thing), but sending the electronic variety can get you in a bunch of trouble.

REMEMBER

If you send an email that advertises a product or service to people who haven't agreed (opted in) that they wanted this sort of email, you're guilty of spamming.

WARNING

You are not allowed to add any eBay user, even a user who has purchased an item from you, to your mailing list (email or physical mail) without their express consent.

Trashing your junk mail

Sometimes spam can come in the form of mail from people you know and expect mail from. Your closest friend's computer may have been abducted by some weird

Internet virus that replicated the virus to everyone in his or her email address book. Obviously, this is not a good thing for those who receive and open the email.

As a matter of fact, my Skype account was hacked years ago and was sending out random links to my contacts. I quickly signed into my account — before the n'er-do-well who hacked my account could lock me out; I changed my password and locked them out first. If I'd set up two-factor authentication, this may not have been a problem.

WARNING

Don't open email from anyone you don't know, especially if a file is attached to it. Sometimes, if a spammer is really slick, it's hard to tell that you've received spam. If you receive an email with no subject line, however — or if the email has an addressee name that isn't yours, or is coming from someone you've never heard of — delete it. You never know; it could be just annoying spam — or worse, it could contain a computer virus as an attachment, just waiting for you to open and activate it.

Email spoofing

Email spoofing has become the bane of the online community and can wreak havoc. *Spoofing* is accomplished when crafty techno-geeks send an email and make it appear to come from someone other than themselves — someone you know and expect email from. Most often, this type of email is programmed to invade your privacy or, even worse, bilk you out of confidential information.

MY MESSAGES SAFEGUARD YOUR PRIVACY

Being the conscientious company it is, eBay has set up a private area, accessible only through one of the links on your My eBay page, called Messages. Messages enables you to communicate with other eBay members without revealing your email address. All your missives with other members, such as Contact the Seller communications, appear in this area. You can answer messages, send new messages, and delete communications from this area, just as if it was your own email software.

This service can protect you from most of the most dangerous forms of spam. For safety's sake, whenever you receive an email sent (in reality or purportedly) from eBay or an eBay member, don't click the email link to Respond Now. Open your browser (or mobile app) and go directly to your Messages area. If the email is legitimate, it will appear there. Merely click the email to open it, read it, and reply. Your privacy (in the form of your email address) isn't exposed to the receiving party.

WARNING

A spate of emails may appear, purportedly sent from eBay, PayPal, and other major e-commerce or finance sites, claiming that your membership has been suspended or that your records need updating. The opportunistic email then asks you to click a link to a page on the site, which then asks you to input your personal information. Don't do it!

REMEMBER

Most sites will *never* ask you to provide sensitive information through email, so don't respond to it. If you receive an email saying your "account has been suspended," close the email and go directly to the site in question — *without* using the supplied link in the email. You'll know soon enough if there is a problem with your account.

If you get this sort of email and want to confirm whether it is really from eBay, visit this eBay security page for legitimate things to look for:

```
www.ebay.com/help/account/protecting-account/recognising-
spoof-emails?id=4195
```

To help eBay in its investigation of these information thieves, send a copy of the email to spoof@ebay.com. When forwarding the email, do not alter it in any way.

I Vant to Be Alone — and Vat You Can Do to Stay That Vay

The Internet has a long reach. Don't be surprised if you furnish your personal information freely on one website, and it turns up somewhere else. If you don't mind people knowing things about you (your name, your hobbies, where you live, and your phone number, for example), by all means share. But I personally think you should give only as much information as you need to do business on the site.

REMEMBER

Privacy is not the same as security. Don't feel obligated to reveal anything about yourself that isn't absolutely necessary. (Some personal facts are in the same league as body weight — private, even if hardly a secret.)

FIGHTING BACK

Robbin was minding her own business, selling software on eBay, when she ran into one of the world's nastiest eBay outlaws. He was a one-stop-shopping outlet of rule-breaking behaviors. First, he ruined her auctions by bidding ridiculously high amounts and then retracting bids at the last legal minute. He emailed her bidders, offering the same item but cheaper. He contacted Robbin's winning bidders to say he was accepting her payments. Then he started leaving messages on her answering machine. (None of this could happen today, thankfully, because eBay changed their bidding and privacy policies.) When she finally had enough, she contacted eBay's Security Center, which suspended him.

But like a bad lunch, he came back up — with a new name. So Robbin fought back on her own. She got his registration information and sent him a letter. She also informed the support area at his ISP about what he was doing, and because he used his work email address, she also contacted his boss.

Her efforts must have done the trick. He finally slipped out of eBay and slithered out of her life. The lesson: Don't rely completely on eBay to pick up the pieces. If you're being abused, stand up for your rights and fight back through the proper channels!

In the virtual world, as in the real world, cyberstalking is scary and illegal. If you think someone is using information from eBay to harass you, contact eBay immediately — as well as your local police. Chapter 16 gives you the ins and outs of contacting eBay's security team.

Although you can't prevent privacy leaks entirely, you can take some precautions to protect yourself. Here are some tips to keep your online information as safe and secure as possible, starting with how to change your User ID and password:

>> **User ID:** When eBay first started, members used their email addresses to buy and sell. Today, users appear on the site with a *nom de plume* (okay, User ID, but *nom de plume* sounds oh, so chic). Your first line of defense against everyone who surfs the eBay site is to choose a User ID that doesn't reveal too much about you — unless you want to promote your personal brand or an existing business. Chapter 2 gives you some pointers on how to choose your User ID.

>> **Password:** Guard your password as if it were the key to your home. Don't give anyone your password. If a window requesting your password pops up in an auction or purchase, skip it — it's somebody who is up to no good. Use your password *only* on the official eBay sign-in screen. (See Chapter 2 for tips on choosing passwords.)

If you're concerned that someone may have your password, change it immediately:

1. **Go to your My eBay Summary and click the Account tab to go to Personal Information.**

2. **On your arrival in the Personal Information area, find the Password line and click the Edit link.**

3. **Follow the instructions to change your password.**

   Your password is immediately changed.

» **Credit card information:** Whenever you use your credit card on eBay, you can make sure that your private information is safe. Look for an SSL (SSL stands for *Secure Socket Layer*) lock icon in the URL line. SSL is an encryption program that scrambles the information so that hackers have almost no chance of getting your information. (I explain more about SSL in Chapter 2.)

   When buying from any website that accepts credit cards, carefully weigh the risks of giving your credit card number to someone you don't know, versus paying through PayPal. PayPal is the safest way to pay because your credit card number is not released.

IF YOUR ACCOUNT'S BEEN HACKED AND YOU CAN'T GET IN

If you haven't set up 2FA and a bad actor has changed your password and you can't sign in to your account, go to the eBay home page.

1. Click the Help & Contact link at the top of the page.

2. Scroll to the bottom of the page and click Call Us.

3. On the next page, click the Account topic.

4. Finally, on the Call Us page, click Get Help with a Hacked Account.

5. On the next page, you'll come to the sign-in page. (Don't cry yet.) Scroll to the bottom of the page and click the Continue box below "New to eBay, or need help signing in?"

6. You arrive at a page with a real phone number to call.

You'll be in touch with a live human being who can help you secure your account before damage can be done.

Never give anyone your Social Security number online. Guard yours as if it were the key to the Crown Jewels.

» **Registration information:** When you first register, eBay requests a phone number and address for billing and contact purposes. I've never had a problem with anyone requesting my registration information and then misusing it. However, many people want an added measure of anonymity. You can give eBay the information it wants in several ways without compromising your privacy:

- Rather than your home phone number, provide eBay with a mobile number, a work phone number, Google Voice, or a SkypeIn number. Screen your calls with voice mail.

- Use a mail box store rather than your home address.

- Start a bank account solely for eBay transactions. If you're a business and file a DBA (doing business as), start a business account so you can use an alternate name. Your bank can help you with this process.

Never say anything online that you wouldn't feel comfortable saying to the next person who passed you on the street. Basically, that's who you're talking to. You can find stories of romances blossoming in the eBay community and on social media — and I'm delighted for the happy couples, I swear — but come on, that doesn't mean that you should lose your head. Don't give out any personal information to strangers; too often that's asking for trouble. Have fun online but hang on to your common sense.

» **Check feedback:** Yep, I sound like a broken record (in case you don't remember, *records* were the large, black, prone-to-breaking vinyl disks used by people to play music on electric turntables before iPods and CDs were invented — and they're currently trendy again in some quarters), but here it is again: *Check feedback.* eBay works because its participants police it. The best way to find out about the folks with whom you're dealing is to see how others felt about them. If you take only one thing away from this book, it's to check feedback *before* you bid or buy!

Chapter **16**

Rules, Policies, and Etiquette (and How to Get Help)

Millions of people transact business every day online and on eBay. If you're new to this sort of commerce, you may need a reality check. With hundreds of millions of items for sale worldwide, and millions of new listings every day, the law of averages dictates that you may run into some rough roads eventually. E-commerce is anonymous; at least on eBay the playing field is covered by serious ground rules.

In this chapter, I take you through the hard-and-fast policies for users, plus the resources you might need for reporting abuses. This chapter explains how eBay enforces its rules and regulations — and points out how to go outside eBay for help if you run into some really big-time problems.

Keeping eBay Safe with eBay Security

The Security Center area of eBay focuses on protecting eBay buyers and sellers from those who aren't playing by the rules. Through this department, eBay issues warnings and policy changes — and in some cases, it gives bad guys the heave-ho by suspending their accounts.

TIP

You should know about two important safety areas on eBay:

>> **Security Center:** You reach the Security Center from a small link found at the bottom of many eBay pages (in the fine print). From here you can find and report safety violations. If eBay ever moves this link, just type `https://pages.ebay.com/securitycenter` into your browser, and you're there.

>> **Resolution Center:** Find this link at the bottom of many eBay pages. This is where you can report transactional issues: unpaid items, items received not as described, and more. Chapter 13 addresses the quickest ways you (as a seller) can resolve issues. If necessary, you can find this resource directly at `https://resolutioncenter.ebay.com`.

The Security Center (shown in Figure 16-1) is more than just a link to policies and information. You get the latest tips on staying safe on the Internet. It also connects you with a group of eBay staffers who handle complaints, field incoming tips about possible infractions, and dole out warnings and suspensions. eBay staffers look at complaints on a case-by-case basis, in the order they receive them. Some common complaints they receive are about these problems:

>> Shill bidders (see the section on "Selling abuses" in this chapter)

>> Feedback issues and abuses (see the section on "Feedback abuses" in this chapter)

TIP

Keep in mind that eBay is a widely varied community of people, most of whom have never met each other. No matter what you buy or sell on eBay, don't expect eBay transactions to be any easier than buying or selling from a complete stranger. Whatever the personality (or reputation) of the seller, however, know that your purchase is covered by eBay's Money Back Guarantee.

If you've read previous chapters in this book, you probably know about eBay's operating rules and regulations. For a closer online look at them, click the Policies link (located at the bottom of most eBay pages) or visit `www.ebay.com/help/policies/default/ebays-rules-policies?id=4205`, and then click the User Agreement link on that page or go direct to `www.ebay.com/help/policies/member-behaviour-policies/user-agreement?id=4259`. The agreement is revised regularly, so check it often.

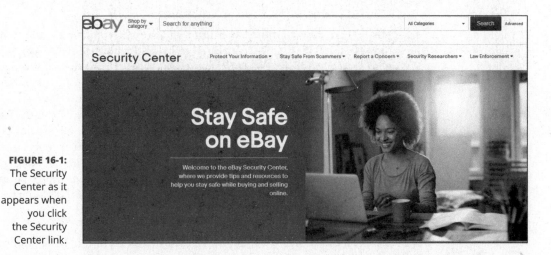

FIGURE 16-1:
The Security
Center as it
appears when
you click
the Security
Center link.

Buyers Are Safe When Shopping on eBay

One of the reasons people flock to the United States eBay marketplace is the eBay Money Back Guarantee. Under this policy, all purchases (with some exclusions listed below) are covered, and the buyer can get a full refund through their PayPal account if the item doesn't arrive or arrives not as described. Even shipping costs are refunded.

The way it works is that eBay hosts a *resolution* process (somewhat like mediation) when a buyer claims that their item was not received or that the item they received was different from what was described in the listing.

Items not eligible for the Money Back Guarantee are

>> Items covered for businesses under eBay's Business Equipment Purchase Protection

>> Items listed (or belong) in these categories:

- Vehicles (for which there is the eBay Vehicle Protection)

- Real estate

- Classified ads and services

- Digital content

- Items purchased from Sotheby's

- Websites and businesses for sale

- Items shipped to another location after being received at the buyer's address as specified in the PayPal transaction

There are defined steps that the buyer has to go through to make a claim. Buyers should always — and first — contact the seller through eBay Messages and attempt to resolve the issue. If the buyer doesn't hear from the seller or can't resolve the issue with the seller, he or she can then file a case with eBay. Buyers who don't hear back, or don't otherwise resolve the issue after contacting the seller, can file a claim within 30 days after the estimated delivery date at the Resolution Center. Sellers have three business days to respond to an official claim before eBay steps in. eBay reviews the case, checks to be sure that there is no fraud history on the part of the buyer, and contacts the seller. Before contacting the seller, eBay reviews the transaction information and any messages sent between the buyer and the seller through eBay Messages, as well as checking on package transit time.

TIP

As a seller, you can protect yourself by following the tips in this book. Additionally, when shipping an eBay item that sells for over $750, get proof of delivery in the form of a Signature Confirmation. (Personally, I request a Signature Confirmation for any item that sells for over $250.) PayPal also requires a signature to prove delivery for expensive items.

Abuses You Should Look Out For

Before you even consider blowing the whistle on someone by reporting him or her to eBay, make sure that what you're encountering is actually a misuse of eBay. Some behavior isn't nice (no argument there), but it *also* may not be a violation of eBay rules — in which case, eBay can't do much about it. Note that the reporting system is monitored, and abuse by an eBay member may result in a range of unpleasant actions. The following sections list the primary reasons you may start an investigation.

Selling abuses

If you're on eBay long enough, you're bound to find an abuse of the service. It may happen on an auction you're bidding on; or a seller whose listings compete with your items may do something really, really wrong. Be a good community member and be on the lookout for the following:

>> **Shill bidding:** A seller uses multiple User IDs to bid, or has accomplices place bids to boost the price of his or her auction items. eBay investigators look for six telltale signs, including a single bidder putting in a really high bid, a bidder with really low feedback but a really high number of bids on items, a bidder with low feedback who has been an eBay member for a while but who's never won an auction, or excessive bids between two users.

>> **Payment interception:** An unscrupulous user, pretending to be the actual seller, contacts the winner to set up terms of payment and shipping in an effort to get the buyer's payment. You can easily avoid this situation by paying with PayPal through the eBay site as soon as you've won or purchased an item.

>> **Fee avoidance:** There are many ways a seller can attempt to avoid fees; to keep up with the current scams, check www.ebay.com/help/policies/selling-policies/selling-practices-policy/avoiding-ebay-fees-policy?id=4354.

>> **Bidding manipulation:** A user, with the help of accomplices, enters phony bids to make an auction appear to have a lot of bidding action. Let the experts at eBay decide on this one; but you may wonder if you see loads of bids come in rapid succession, but the price moves very little.

Bidding abuses

If you want to know more about bidding in general, see Chapter 6. Here's a list of bidding abuses that eBay wants to know about:

>> **Bid shielding:** Two users working in tandem. User A, with the help of accomplices, intentionally bids an unreasonably high amount and then retracts the bid prior to the 12-hour cancellation deadline of the auction — leaving a lower bid (which the offender or an accomplice places) as the winning bid.

>> **Bid siphoning:** Users send emails to bidders of a current auction to offer the same merchandise for a lower price elsewhere.

>> **Transaction interference:** Users warn other bidders through email to stay clear of a seller or item, presumably to decrease the number of bids and keep the prices low.

>> **Bid manipulation (or invalid bid retraction):** A user bids a ridiculously high amount, raising the next highest bidder to a maximum bid. The manipulator then retracts the bid and rebids *slightly* over the previous high bidder's maximum.

>> **Nonpaying bidder:** People call them deadbeats; the bottom line is that these people win auctions but never pay up. Your bid on eBay is a legal contract to buy if you win — it is *not* a game.

>> **Unwelcome bidder:** A user bids on a specific seller's auction despite the seller's warning that he or she won't accept that user's bids (as in the case of not selling internationally and still receiving international bids). If you want to bar specific bidders from your auctions, you can exclude them. See Chapter 13 for the scoop on how to block bidders.

Feedback abuses

All you have on eBay is your reputation, and that reputation is made up of your feedback history. eBay takes any violation of its feedback system very seriously. Because eBay's feedback is transaction related, unscrupulous eBay members now have less opportunity to take advantage of this system. Here's a checklist of feedback abuses that will get you into trouble. These can all be reported through the Security Center:

>> **Feedback extortion:** A buyer threatens to post reputation-destroying feedback if the seller doesn't follow through on some unwarranted demand. Typical extortion attempts include demanding a refund or a generous discount after the bad buyer has won the item.

>> **Personal exposure:** A member leaves feedback for a user that exposes personal information that doesn't relate to transactions on eBay.

>> **Malicious feedback:** Writing malicious feedback is a sick game played by those who have very little to do with their time but upset upstanding eBay sellers. These sickies register on eBay with a new User ID and use the Buy It Now function to buy many items from a seller who has a high positive-feedback rating. A few hours later, they leave dastardly negative feedback. The only goal of this action is to ruin the seller's reputation.

REMEMBER

After you post feedback, your words are out there. They become part of cyberspace — effectively forever — and are there for all to see. Your words are a reflection of your online persona.

MARSHA SAYS

Know that eBay wields its power on a case-to-case basis. If the Customer Support representative doesn't see things your way, you might just be out of luck. Keep in mind that they have access to more data on the situation than you do, and in the end, their word is the final decision.

Identity abuses

On eBay, who you are is as important as what you sell (or buy). eBay monitors the identities of its members closely — and asks that you report any great pretenders in this area to Customer Support. Accurate information is critical so that eBay knows who — for real — is doing business on the site. Here's a checklist of identity abuses:

>> **Identity misrepresentation:** A user claims to be an eBay staff member or another eBay user, or he or she registers under the name of another user.

- » **False or missing contact information:** A user deliberately registers with fraudulent contact information or an invalid email address. If you come across someone on eBay who has false information registered on the eBay site, it's worth reporting them.

- » **Under age:** A user falsely claims to be 18 or older. (You must be *at least* 18 to enter into a legally binding contract.)

- » **Dead/invalid email addresses:** When emails bounce *repeatedly* (single bounces are almost a fact of life on the Internet) from a user's registered email address, chances are good that the address may be dead — and it's doing nobody any good.

- » **Doxxing:** One user publishes another user's contact information on the eBay site.

When there is any form of contact information violation, eBay can put a squeeze on the wrongdoing member(s). When such members attempt to log on to the eBay site, they are faced with a message that lets them know they can't proceed onto the site without correcting their information.

Operational abuses

If you see someone trying to interfere with eBay's operation, eBay staffers want you to tell them about it. Here are two roguish operational abuses:

- » **Hacking:** A user purposely interferes with eBay's computer operations (for example, by breaking into unauthorized files). If someone attempts to alter any of the eBay-generated information in a listing, such as a feedback rating or User ID, that person is violating important eBay rules.

- » **Spamming:** The user sends unsolicited email to eBay users. Just because you are in a transaction with someone doesn't give you the right to email the person after the auction is over to solicit future business. You're not allowed to send a newsletter or solicitations unless your recipients have expressly opted in to your list. No one has the right to send you email unrelated to your transaction without your permission.

Miscellaneous abuses

The following are additional problems that you should alert eBay about:

- » A user is threatening physical harm to another eBay member.

- » A person uses racist, obscene, or harassing language in a public area of eBay.

For a list of selling irregularities to report and how eBay runs each investigation, go to www.ebay.com/help/policies/selling-policies/selling-policies?id=4214.

Reporting Abuses to eBay Security

If you suspect a seller of abusing eBay's rules and regulations, you can report him or her directly on the item page. Look to the far right of the Description and Shipping tabs (above the description) on the page of the item in question and click the Report Item link.

When you click that link, you'll come to the only area on eBay where you can report listing violations. On the File a report page, select the reasons for your report and further information from the drop-down menus. It may be frustrating, but keep trying. After you make your selections, click Submit Report as shown in Figure 16-2.

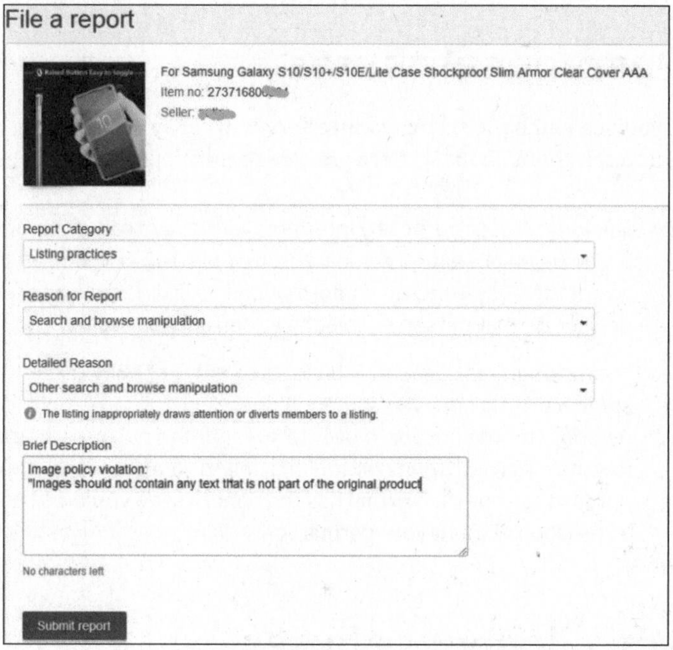

File a report

For Samsung Galaxy S10/S10+/S10E/Lite Case Shockproof Slim Armor Clear Cover AAA
Item no: 273716808
Seller:

Report Category
Listing practices

Reason for Report
Search and browse manipulation

Detailed Reason
Other search and browse manipulation
The listing inappropriately draws attention or diverts members to a listing.

Brief Description
Image policy violation:
"Images should not contain any text that is not part of the original product"

No characters left

Submit report

FIGURE 16-2:
Luckily I was able to quote the eBay policy. Most options leave you no chance to explain the violation.

If your issue is connected to a transaction that you're currently involved in with another eBay member, click the Resolve a Problem link on the Security Center page discussed earlier. You're presented with the Resolution Center, a page that suggests answers to the various questions you may have and allows you to open a case.

To actually reach eBay, click the link on the top of the home page to contact Customer Support. You can also go directly to www.ebay.com/help/home to file a report.

On this page you'll find the Customer Service portal, which presents you with some of the most popular questions about eBay, as well as clickable links to find answers. To *really* (this time I promise) contact eBay, scroll down the page to the *Need more help?* text and click the Call Us (or Have Us Call You) box.

If you encounter any of the abuses outlined in this chapter, be sure to report the problem. Community policing is what makes eBay work.

The Security Center offers a wealth of good general information that can help you prevent something from going wrong in a future transaction. Be sure to use these pages as a resource to help prevent problems.

eBay used to provide an option for filing a report via email, but presently offers only a "call us" option as an alternative to the Report Item link.

After eBay receives your report, you most likely will never hear back from eBay. Know that eBay investigates your allegations and uses internal data to take action (or not).

If your problem becomes a legal matter, eBay may not let you know what's going on. The only indication you may get that some action was taken is that the eBay member you reported is suspended or the listing in question ended.

Unfortunately, suspended members can show up again on the eBay site. Typically, nefarious sorts like these just use a different name and credit card to register back on the site. If you suspect that someone who broke the rules once is back under another User ID, alert Customer Support. If you're a seller, you can refuse to accept bids from that person (see Chapter 13).

Although receiving no response can get frustrating, avoid the temptation to initiate a reporting blitzkrieg by sending reports over and over until eBay "can't ignore" you. This practice is annoying at best and inconsiderate at worst; it just slows the process for everyone — and it won't endear the insistent reporter to the folks who could help. It's better to just grin and bear it and pray that action will be taken.

Stuff eBay Won't Do Anything About

People are imperfect everywhere, even online. (Ya think?) You probably won't agree with some of the behavior that you run into online or on eBay (ranging from slightly annoying to just plain rotten). Although much of that conduct is just plain nasty, it can (and does) go on as long as it doesn't break eBay rules.

In some cases, you may need to bite your tongue and chalk up someone's annoying behavior to ignorance of the unwritten rules of customer service. Just because people have computers and some things to sell or buy doesn't mean that they possess grown-up social skills. (But you knew that.)

Here's a gang of annoying issues that crop up pretty regularly in e-commerce but that *aren't* against eBay's rules and regulations:

>> **A seller sets astronomical shipping costs.** eBay policy says that shipping costs must be reasonable. Basically, eBay is wagging its finger and saying, "Don't gouge your buyers." There are shipping-rate caps in some categories to protect you. But when sellers gouge their buyers with uber-high shipping fees, eBay penalizes them in their Best Match search results.

Under the rules, eBay will stop someone from charging excessive amounts for shipping. For more information on policy, go to www.ebay.com/help/policies/selling-policies/selling-practices-policy?id=4346 and click the Guidelines link, then click Shipping and handling costs.

Prior to bidding or buying, you should always check shipping terms on the item page. You need to decide whether to agree to those terms *before* you bid or buy. The best way to protect yourself from being swindled is to buy only from a seller whose shipping costs feel fair to you (or are free).

>> **A seller or buyer refuses to meet the terms that you mutually set.** eBay has the power only to warn or suspend members. It can't make anyone do anything — even someone who's violating a policy. If you want to make someone fulfill a transaction, you're more or less on your own. I heard one story of a seller who refused to send a product after being paid. The seller said, "Come and get it." The buyer happened to be in town on business — and did just that!

But if your item never arrives, you can apply to eBay for a refund under the Money Back Guarantee. Information on how to file is further on in this chapter.

Often, reluctant eBay buyers just need a nudge from eBay in the form of a warning to comply. So go ahead and file a case report to get a Final Value Fee credit request (I explain how to do this in Chapter 13).

TIP

New eBay users are often the unwitting perpetrators of annoying behavior, but you're ahead of the pack now that you know what *not* to do. You can afford to cut the other newbies some slack and help them learn the ropes before you report them.

Knowing the Deeds That Can Get You Suspended

Playing by eBay's rules keeps you off the eBay Security radar screen. If you start violating eBay policy, the company is going to keep a close eye on you. Depending on your infractions, eBay may be all over you like jelly on peanut butter. Or you may safely lurk in the fringes until your feedback rating is lower than the temperature in Nome in November.

Here's a top-level list of eBay no-no's that can get a member's permanent record damaged — and the member possibly *suspended:*

>> Feedback rating of –4

>> Multiple instances of deadbeat bidding

>> Repeated warnings for the same infraction

>> Feedback extortion

>> Bid shielding

>> Unwelcome bidding after a warning from the seller

>> Shill bidding

>> Auction interception

>> Fee avoidance

>> Fraudulent selling

>> Identity misrepresentation

>> Bidding or selling when younger than age 18

>> Hacking

>> Physical threats

If you get a suspension but think you're innocent, respond directly to the eBay employee who suspended you to plead your case. Reversals do occur. Don't broadcast your suspicions online. If you're wrong, you may regret it. Even if you're right, it's bad form.

Be careful about accusing others of cheating. Unless you're involved in a transaction, you don't know all the facts. *Law & Order* moments are great on television, but they're fictional for a reason. In real life, drawing yourself into a possible confrontation is senseless. Start the complaint process, keep it businesslike, and let eBay's staff figure out what's going on.

eBay Motors Vehicle Purchase Protection

Another beneficial defense is eBay's Vehicle Purchase Protection, which offers a *free* limited warranty to anyone who purchases a vehicle and completes the transaction on eBay. Look for the Vehicle Purchase Protection Shield above the description area to see whether the vehicle you're interested in is covered.

Your vehicle purchase is protected for up to $100,000 or the vehicle purchase price, whichever is lower. You can find more information at eBay Motors:

http://pages.motors.ebay.com/buy/purchase-protection/index.html

PayPal Purchase Protection

In addition to offering a safe way to purchase, PayPal offers an even better reason to pay through its service. If you purchased your item on a website and pay via PayPal, you're covered for your original purchase price, plus shipping. This protection covers you only for nondelivery of tangible items and tangible items that are received significantly not as described — not if you are just disappointed with the item.

Know that PayPal is a payment processor, a middle man between you and your credit card company. If you pay for an eBay purchase with a credit card through PayPal, and need to make a claim, be sure to make a claim with eBay to get the ball rolling. If you pay with a credit card through PayPal for a web transaction, make your claim with PayPal. Do *not* make a claim with your credit card company. You can't open two claims at once. If you are not satisfied with the resolution from eBay or PayPal, you can then file a claim with your credit card company.

For the latest information on this program, go to

www.paypal.com/webapps/mpp/paypal-safety-and-security

Launching a Report or a Return

The moment that you complain about a seller who's taken money but hasn't delivered the goods (or has sent the wrong item), an investigation team gets in gear. The Resolution Center is where you can go to file a formal complaint when you run into trouble with a transaction.

The first thing you need to keep in mind is that buyers and sellers are all human beings. As human beings, we all make mistakes. Contacting the seller to solve the problem prior to opening a case on eBay may be a much more humane process. Get in touch with the seller and see if he or she will work things out with you. You can contact your seller through eBay's Message Center. If you don't get the treatment you feel you deserve, file your case and eBay will mediate for you.

MARSHA SAYS

Click Help and Contact at the top of eBay pages and hopefully you will manage to find a link to return your item. If, after clicking though, you're still not at the Resolution Center, go to the link mentioned further on.

The Resolution Center is the place to go if your item hasn't arrived or if you want to work out a solution to a problem (but don't want to return the item). The most common problems are Item Not Received and Significantly Not as Described. To get to the Resolution Center to resolve any problem that you can't work out with the seller during or after a transaction, you've got three ways to go:

>> Click the Resolution Center link at the bottom of the eBay home or your Account page.

>> Go to the original item page and click View order details. On the resulting page, click Return item.

>> Go to My eBay ⇨ Purchase History, scroll down to Orders, and click Return this item in that order's details.

If you can't find the Resolution Center through any of the links I've mentioned, you can go directly there via http://resolutioncenter.ebay.com as shown in Figure 16-3.

When a buyer hasn't paid for an item, a seller can open a case within two days after the item closes (and within 30 days thereafter).

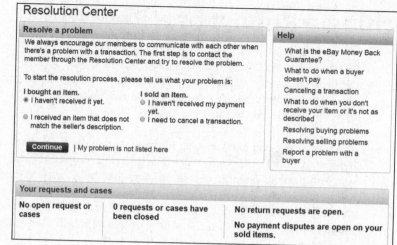

Resolution Center

Resolve a problem

We always encourage our members to communicate with each other when there's a problem with a transaction. The first step is to contact the member through the Resolution Center and try to resolve the problem.

To start the resolution process, please tell us what your problem is:

I bought an item.
○ I haven't received it yet.

○ I received an item that does not match the seller's description.

I sold an item.
○ I haven't received my payment yet.

○ I need to cancel a transaction.

[Continue] | My problem is not listed here

Help

What is the eBay Money Back Guarantee?

What to do when a buyer doesn't pay

Canceling a transaction

What to do when you don't receive your item or it's not as described

Resolving buying problems

Resolving selling problems

Report a problem with a buyer

Your requests and cases

| No open request or cases | 0 requests or cases have been closed | No return requests are open. |
| | | No payment disputes are open on your sold items. |

FIGURE 16-3:
Resolve problem transactions through eBay's Resolution Center.

MARSHA SAYS

Don't procrastinate, you have only up to 30 days after the eBay estimated delivery date to make the claim. But be careful not to jump the gun and register a complaint too soon. Be sure to check the tracking number on your item transaction page. Don't jump the gun! If the carrier hasn't confirmed that the package has been delivered, you may just have to wait. Be sure to click through on the tracking number to get the tracking history. In Figure 16-4, you'll see one. Be sure to use the scroll bar on the right to see every stop your package has made on its way. I have observed packages sent miles out of the way for them to still make their way to my home a few extra days later.

Your item was delivered.

Shipped
Thu, Jul 11 — In transit — Out for delivery — Delivered
Fri, Jul 12

Tracking details
USPS tracking #9400109699938587095911

Jul 12, 2019 2:11pm	DELIVERED IN/AT MAILBOX NORTHRIDGE, CA 91325
Jul 12, 2019 8:34am	OUT FOR DELIVERY NORTHRIDGE, CA 91325
Jul 12, 2019 8:24am	SORTING/PROCESSING COMPLETE NORTHRIDGE, CA 91325
Jul 12, 2019 6:06am	ARRIVAL AT UNIT NORTHRIDGE, CA 91324

FIGURE 16-4:
Clicking the tracking number in your Purchase History opens this information.

After you register a complaint, eBay informs the other party that you're making a claim. eBay says that it will try to contact both parties and help reach a resolution. *Registering* the complaint is not the same thing as *filing* for a refund. Registering starts the process; filing for a refund comes after a grace period if the situation isn't resolved.

Returning an item for a refund

Even if the seller doesn't accept returns, you are covered under eBay's Money Back Guarantee. There's a very simple way to return an item. To initiate a return, follow these steps:

1. **Go to your My eBay Summary page.**

2. **Click the Purchase History link on the left side to take you to the item you've purchased.**

3. **To confirm shipment information or details of your order, click the link to View order details.**

4. **On the resulting page, click the Show additional actions box (shown in Figure 16-5).**

5. **To return the item, click Return this item and select the appropriate reason from the list displayed:**

   - Doesn't fit
   - Changed my mind
   - Found a better price
   - Just didn't like it
   - Ordered by mistake
   - Doesn't work or defective
   - Doesn't match description or photos
   - Wrong item sent
   - Missing parts or pieces
   - Arrived damaged
   - Doesn't seem authentic

6. **Add any further needed information in the text box.**

7. **Upload any photos that will confirm your complaint.**

8. **Click Return item and the seller will be notified.**

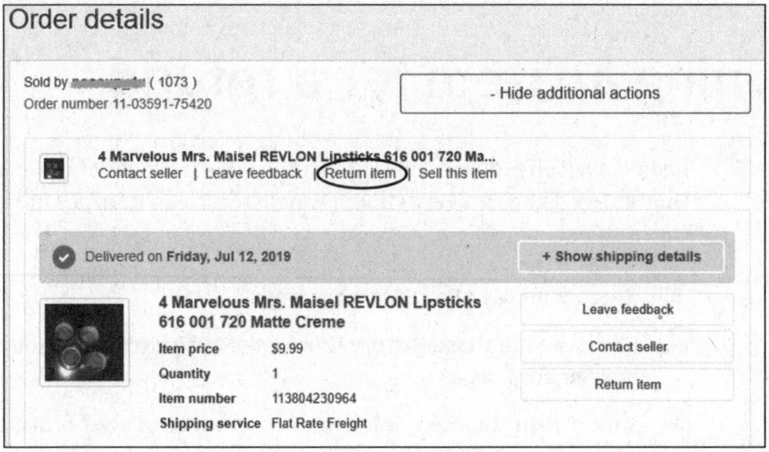

Order details

Sold by ~~nnnnmgxtn~~ (1073)
Order number 11-03591-75420

- Hide additional actions

4 Marvelous Mrs. Maisel REVLON Lipsticks 616 001 720 Ma...
Contact seller | Leave feedback | (Return item) | Sell this item

✓ Delivered on **Friday, Jul 12, 2019**

\+ Show shipping details

4 Marvelous Mrs. Maisel REVLON Lipsticks 616 001 720 Matte Creme

Item price	$9.99
Quantity	1
Item number	113804230964
Shipping service	Flat Rate Freight

Leave feedback

Contact seller

Return item

FIGURE 16-5:
Click Return item.

Once the seller receives the notification that a return has been initiated, they have three days to respond. The seller can respond through eBay to either accept the return or offer a partial refund, or the seller can message you directly to negotiate an alternative solution.

When a seller accepts a refund, the buyer has five days to repack and return the item. If the fault lies with the seller, he or she may send you a return label through eBay or negotiate a refund of your shipping costs.

Getting the Real Deal? Authentication and Appraising

Despite eBay's attempts to keep the buying and selling community honest, some people just refuse to play nice. After the New York City Department of Consumer Affairs launched an investigation into counterfeit sports memorabilia sold on the web, errant online outlaws experienced some anxious moments. I can always hope that they mend their ways, while at the same time advising you *don't bet on it.* Fortunately, eBay offers a proactive approach to preventing such occurrences from happening again.

Topmost among the countermeasures is easy member access to several services that can authenticate specific types of merchandise. The good news here is that you know what kind of item you're getting; the bad news is that, as does everything else in life, it costs you money.

MARSHA SAYS

Have a good working knowledge of what you're buying or selling. Before you bid, do some homework and get more information. I recommend you check out the website Worthpoint.com for unique items to see what the item has sold for in the past. (Chapter 20 gives you more information about their services.) And check the seller's or bidder's feedback. (Does this advice sound familiar?) See Chapters 5 and 9 for more information about conducting research.

TIP

Before you spend the money to have your item appraised and authenticated, ask yourself a few practical questions (regardless of whether you're buying or selling):

>> **Is this item quality merchandise?** Am I selling or buying merchandise whose condition is subjective but important to its value — as in, *Is it really "well-loved" or just busted?* Is this item graded by some professionally accepted standard that I need to know?

>> **Is this item the real thing?** Am I sure that I'm selling or buying a genuine item? Do I need an expert to tell me whether it's the real McCoy?

>> **Do I know the value of the merchandise?** Do I have a good understanding of what this item is worth in the marketplace at this time, considering its condition?

>> **Is the merchandise worth the price?** Is the risk of selling or buying a counterfeit, a fake, or an item I don't completely understand worth the cost of an appraisal?

If you answer "yes" to any of these questions, consider calling in a professional appraiser.

As for *selling* a counterfeit item — otherwise known as a knock-off, phony, or fake item — that's a no-brainer: No way. Don't do it.

If you need items appraised, consider using an appraisal agency. You can access several agencies by going to the overview page at http://pages.ebay.com/help/buy/authentication.html. eBay offers links to various appraising agencies that *may* offer their services at a discount to eBay members. These are my tried-and-true favorites:

TIP

>> The **PCGS** (Professional Coin Grading Service), **NGC** (Numismatic Guaranty Corporation), **ANACS** (American Numismatic Association Certification Service), and **IGC** (Independent Coin Graders) serve coin collectors by encapsulating and grading coins for sale (shown in Figure 16-6). Visit www.pcgs.com, www.icgcoin.com, www.anacs.com, and www.ngccoin.com.

When selling coins on eBay, you cannot put a grade within the title unless the coin has been graded by an authorized grading service.

>> **PSA/DNA** (a service of Professional Sports Authenticators), **James Spence Authentication**, and **Global Authentics** authenticate your sports autographs. These companies keep online databases of thousands of certified autographs for you to compare your purchases against. Their respective online addresses are www.psacard.com, www.spenceloa.com, and www.globalauthentics.com.

>> **APEX** (American Philatelic Expertizing Service) authenticates your postal stamps: http://stamps.org/stamp-authentication.

>> **CGC** (Comics Guaranty) grades and restores comic books. Visit www.cgccomics.com.

>> **IGI** (International Gemological Institute) grades, authenticates, and identifies loose gemstones and jewelry. Visit http://igionline.com.

>> **PSA** (Professional Sports Authenticators) and **SGC** (Sportscard Guaranty) help guard against counterfeiting and fraud with sports memorabilia and trading cards. You can connect with these services to grade and authenticate your trading cards. Visit the respective addresses of these agencies at www.psacard.com and www.sgccard.com.

FIGURE 16-6:
Graded and serial-numbered coins bring in much higher profits.

TIP

Even if you use an appraiser or an authentication service, do some legwork yourself. Often two experts can come up with opposing opinions on the same item. The more you know, the better the questions you can ask.

If a seller isn't sure whether the item he or she is selling is authentic, you may find an appropriate comment (such as *Cannot verify authenticity*) in the item description. Knowledgeable eBay sellers like to share what they know, and I have no doubt that someone on the Internet may be able to supply you with scads of helpful information. But be careful — some blarney artist (one of *those* is born every minute, too) may try to make a sucker out of you.

If It's Clearly Fraud

After filing either a fraud report or a Final Value Fee credit request, you can do more on your own. If the time is up with eBay to file a case, you still have some places to go. When the deal involves the post office in any way — if you mail a check or the seller sends you merchandise that's completely wrong and refuses to make good — file a mail-fraud complaint with the postal inspector.

TIP

In the United States, you can file a complaint online at www.uspis.gov/report. After you complete the form, the USPS sends the bad guy a notice that you've filed a fraud complaint. Perhaps that *will* get his or her attention.

In addition to the post office, you can turn to some other agencies for help:

>> **The National Consumer's League:** NCL has an online site devoted to combating fraud on the Internet. NCL works closely with legal authorities. File a claim at https://secure.nclforms.org/nficweb/Online ComplaintForm.aspx.

>> **Law enforcement agencies:** Contact the local district attorney (or state Attorney General's office) and the local and state Consumer Affairs Department in the other person's state and city. (Look online for contact information or try your local agencies for contact numbers.)

>> **Federal Trade Commission:** The FTC accepts complaints and investigates repeated cases of fraud. File a claim at www.ftccomplaintassistant.gov.

>> **Internet Service Provider:** Contact the member's ISP. You can get this bit of info from the person's email address, just after the @ symbol. (See? This easy access to information does have its advantages.) Let the ISP know whom you have filed a complaint against, the nature of the problem, and the agencies that you've contacted.

TIP

Any time you contact another agency for help, keep eBay up to date on your progress by writing to its representatives the old-fashioned way — yep, on paper, with a stamped envelope (you might want to keep some Forever stamps around for just such occasions). Address your letter to eBay, ATTN: Fraud Prevention, 2145 Hamilton Ave., San Jose, CA 95125.

WARNING

A very thin line separates alerting other members to a particular person's poor behavior and breaking an eBay cardinal rule by interfering with a sale. Don't make unfounded or vitriolic accusations — especially if you were counting on them never getting back to the person they were about (or, for that matter, if you hoped they *would*). Trample the poison out of the gripes of wrath *before* you have your say.

TIP

Communication and compromise are the keys to successful transactions. If you have a difference of opinion, write a polite email outlining your expectations and offer to settle any dispute by phone. See Chapters 12 and 13 for tips on communicating after the listing ends — and solving disputes *before* they turn wicked, aggressive, or unprintable.

Chapter **17**

Marketing Sales with Social Media and the Community

To be successful in selling it helps to include some marketing. Marketing is promoting your sales. In today's world, this relies on social media and advertising. This doesn't require you to spend money; you can promote your sales online through social media — the 21st century's answer for free marketing. You can build your own community online to increase sales with only a little bit of effort. In this chapter you'll get some beginner's tips; if you're interested in more advanced lessons, you might like my *Social Media Commerce For Dummies* book (also published by Wiley).

MARSHA SAYS

Note how I will always refer to a social media community, versus followers. From my experience having an inclusive community — where you follow back those who participate or comment — is the most effective (unless you're a Kardashian). Following back goes far to build a community that's invested in you as a human and your success. Too many approach social media as a place to "grow followers" and not follow back, versus to participate in a community. This isn't a broadcast medium. It's called "social" for a reason.

There is also a social community on eBay. On eBay, community is a long-standing tradition. Back in 1996 when eBay first began, the community was very strong, with thousands of eBay users; Customer Service representatives attended the boards (mostly to keep everyone in line), and they were a fun place to be. As in real-life communities, you participate as much as works for you. When it comes to the eBay community, you can get involved in all sorts of activities, or you can just sit back and concentrate on your sales. With the advent of social media, more eBay members participate in these open communities where they can also promote their businesses.

As you've probably heard by now, one of the main ways to participate in the eBay community is through transaction feedback (which I explain in detail in Chapters 4 and 6). In this chapter, I show you some other ways to build your community. You can socialize (making friends who live near you or who live across the planet). Also, whether on Facebook, Twitter, or eBay's boards, you can gain knowledge from others, post messages, or just read what everybody's talking about. I include tips here on how to use all these places to your benefit, and then give you a change of scenery by surfing through some off-site social media sites that can help you with your buying and selling.

I also wrote a book on online customer service; there's a preview of it on my site:

http://theultimateonlinecustomerserviceguide.blogspot.com

MARSHA SAYS

Although spending time on social media and community chats are fun, they take away from time spent on your business. It isn't "marketing" until you have a successful business to market. Those who are successful at eBay know that spending spare time listing and sourcing is the key. You need to work it, no way around that.

Joining the eBay Community

On the bottom of almost every eBay page is a group of links: Click Community to connect to other eBay members, or click the Announcements link to check proposed changes to the site on the Announcements page. Keep in mind, when you see the tips and suggestions on these pages, they may come right from corporate spokespersons in disguise. For example, I have seen catchy headlines about saving on shipping with free package pickup, electronic postage discounts, and free tracking — as if these offers were exclusive to eBay. You know, from reading this book, that these benefits are open to anyone. Take a little time to explore this area for yourself and separate the important messages from the PR spin.

News and chat, this and that

It's not quite *The New York Times*, but you can find announcements, groups, and discussion board links from the Community Overview page. Figure 17-1 shows you the important links on the page. (eBay is continually making changes to the community, so note that this page will change with regularity.) Although thousands of people used to discuss everything (including events of the day) on eBay's boards, the online buzz is now a shadow of its former self, as most people have moved to social media for discussions.

FIGURE 17-1: The main Community page features links to places to get information on eBay.

> **eBay** Shop by category ▾   Search for anything
>
> **The eBay Community**
>
> Home   Seller News ⌄   Knowledge Base ⌄   Discussions ⌄   Groups ⌄

MARSHA SAYS

The tech editor for this book is Patti Louise Ruby (eBay ID aunt*patti — although she has another secret buyer ID). She's been the tech editor for all my books on eBay. Why? Because she was one of two of the first eBay staff to man the original eBay chat rooms with Jim "Griff" Griffith. We also toured the country teaching eBay for "eBay University" in almost every state of the union. She knows eBay at its core. She goes over everything I write, and while I'm writing we text back and forth for reference. We both agree, the most important place for you to visit in the community are the Seller Updates. eBay sends out information on all the important changes for the site here. To save you time, just go directly to `https://pages.ebay.com/seller-center/seller-updates/index.html`.

Joining in the social media conversation

There are many places to connect with other eBay community members. Many are active on social media networks. You can find me on Twitter (@MarshaCollier), `http://twitter.com/MarshaCollier`, or through Facebook. If you have a quick question, ping me, and I will try to answer ASAP.

I also maintain a Twitter list of experienced eBay sellers who have a presence on Twitter. They are interested in helping others and are a valuable reference. More on them further on. Also further in this chapter, you'll find tips on how to connect and market your items on Twitter.

Filling in your eBay profile

Did you know that if you click your User ID on any eBay page, you arrive at your very own profile page? (You also have a link on your Feedback profile page.) Unlike the old About Me page, which you had to choose to set up yourself, every eBay member has an automatically generated profile page. Yours is ready and waiting for you to embellish. Figure 17-2 shows you mine.

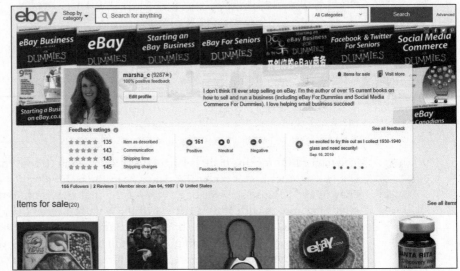

FIGURE 17-2:
At a glance, my page shows you my feedback and that I've been on eBay since January 1997.

In Chapter 14, I show you the basics of how to set up your own. You can also add custom features to this page to share your other community moments.

Your profile page can reflect your many varied interests. From here, eBay gives you other ways to express yourself:

» **Items for sale:** A few of your items you are selling will appear on the page.

» **Reviews:** Wondering what other eBay members think of a particular product, book, or movie? Selected items on eBay are reviewed by users, and you can contribute one of your own. Reviews you have posted show up when someone lands on an item for which eBay users have posted reviews. Figure 17-3 shows the review page for the previous edition of this book, written by eBay members. To add your own review, click the Write a review button.

» **Following:** A sample of which sellers and searches (Interests) you follow. Also, when you save a seller to follow, it shows up on that person's profile page.

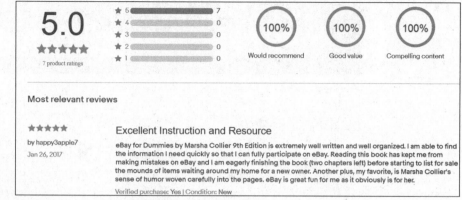

FIGURE 17-3:
eBay members review everything, including books. There are seven reviews for the book.

Hear ye, hear ye! eBay's Announcements Board

If you were living in the 1700s, you'd see a strangely dressed guy in a funny hat ringing a bell and yelling, "Hear ye, hear ye!" every time you opened eBay's Announcements Board. (Then again, if you were living in the 1700s, you'd have no electricity, Internet, fast food, or anything else you probably consider fun.) In any case, eBay's Announcements Board is an important place to find out what's going on (directly from the home office) on the website. And no one even needs to ring a bell.

The Announcements Board is where eBay lists any news that affects buyers and sellers, new features, and policy changes. Visiting this page is like reading a morning eBay newspaper because eBay adds comments to this page almost every week. You find out about upcoming changes in categories, new promotions, and eBay goings-on. eBay also uses it to help users become aware of critical changes in policies and procedures. Reach this page at http://announcements.ebay.com.

Figure 17-4 shows you eBay's Announcements Board with information that could affect your sales.

Help! I need somebody

If you ever have specific eBay questions to which you need answers, click the Knowledge Base link in the Community.

These boards work differently from eBay's old chat rooms. Chat rooms are full of people who are hanging out and talking to each other all at the same time, whereas users of discussion boards tend to go in, leave a message or ask a question, and pop out again. Also, in a discussion board, you need to start a thread by asking a question. Title your thread with your question, and you'll hopefully get a swift reply to your query.

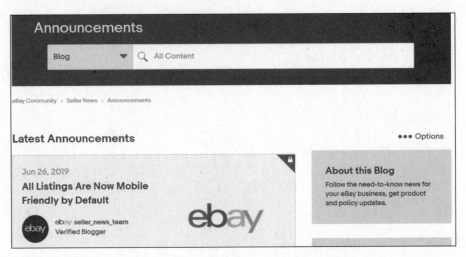

FIGURE 17-4:
Keep up to date on what's new at eBay by visiting the Announcements Board.

These boards cover almost any topic regarding selling and buying on eBay. Just post your question, and some kind eBay member will probably suggest an answer (but remember to double-check your answer, just as you would any advice from someone with unknown credentials). Keep in mind that the Knowledge Base is to answer questions; if someone tries to sell you something there, I'd say turn the other way.

One of the best solutions is to find one of the eBay Social Media sellers on Twitter (more about that later in this chapter); many are very active on the site, and you'll probably get an answer *tout suite*. (I'm on there and Facebook — daily — and answer whatever questions I can.)

User-to-user discussion boards

eBay has some other boards that take a different tack on things. They're *discussion* boards as opposed to *chat* boards, which basically means that the topics are deliberately open-ended — just as the topics of discussion in coffeehouses tend to vary depending on who happens to be in them at any given time. Check out these areas and read ongoing discussions about eBay's latest buzz. Post your opinions to the category that suits you. You can find quite a few discussion boards on various topics relating to doing business on eBay.

There's one cardinal rule for eBay boards: Conduct no business. No advertising items for sale! Not now. Not ever. eBay bans any repeat offenders who break this rule from participating on these boards.

Remember that you're visiting eBay and that you're a member. It's not Speakers' Corner — that spot in London's Hyde Park where protesters are free to stand on a soapbox and scream about the rats in government. If you feel the need to viciously complain about eBay, take it outside, as the bar bouncers say.

Category-specific groups

Want to talk about Elvis, Louis XV, Justin Turner, or Mickey Mouse? Currently a bunch of category-specific discussion boards enable you to tell eBay members what's on your mind about merchandise and auctions. You reach these boards going to the Community and then mousing over the word Groups. A drop-down menu appears where you can click Special Interest Groups.

Of course, you can buy and sell without ever going on a discussion board or group, but you can certainly benefit from one. Discussions mainly focus on merchandise and the nuts and bolts of transactions.

WARNING

On eBay, you get all kinds of responses from all kinds of people. Take a portion of the help you get with a grain of salt; some of the folks who help you may be buyers, competitors, or have something to sell you down the line.

TIP

Don't be shy. As your second-grade teacher said, "No questions are dumb." Most eBay members love to share their experiences.

Learning and Selling through Social Media

Social media is no longer in its infancy; it's long since made off with the car keys, so to speak. These days it has become the go-to destination for 69 percent of American adults. The burgeoning number of social media sites draws many eBay sellers and buyers because they are a tech-savvy group. All cultural changes began with words — as do many marketing campaigns — and the experts have decided that the dominant marketing tool today is social media. Social media is now the hub for "word of mouth" (WOM) recommendations and comments.

Social media sites have grown well beyond their initial role as tools of social contact. Following and friending like-minded people on social media networks (and connecting with them) not only builds a sense of community but also gives you a built-in support group.

When I say to *connect,* I mean to *converse.* You don't have to sit on the sites regularly; you do need to drop by and respond to people who have commented to you. You also need to reach out and comment to others. Marketing can be a natural next step — if you handle it right. But keep this distinction in mind . . .

REMEMBER

Social media discussion is *not* the same as advertising. You will see many online sellers promoting their goods, one after the other, as their sole "conversation." That's actually more broadcasting — like commercials on TV in the old days. Everyone skipped over commercials then — and they skip over them now. Ads-as-faux-conversation is old school and not very interesting to *anyone* who's following you online.

Best practices on social media commerce require engagement with other community members. If you want to share the items you have listed on eBay on your social pages, use this strategy sparingly. Be sure shared listings are not the only (or last five) posts in your stream.

TIP

Many small businesses on social media try to get hundreds of followers for their social media pages. A multitude of friends and followers does not equate to producing massive sales. The quality of your conversation and the people you connect with is what draws people to you.

Finding friends and customers on Facebook

You have a Facebook page, right? You share fun thoughts and ideas with your family and friends, right? Well, when you set up an eBay business, you can have a page for your small business. I'm not suggesting that you'll be directly selling from your Facebook page (although you can), but having a page is an efficient way to meet people online and interest them in what you're selling.

Your initial base for building a business page comes from your friends. When you get over 25 people to "like" your business page, you can get a custom URL from Facebook for the page. Mine is `www.facebook.com/MarshaCollierFanPage` (because it was established a long time ago — when they were called "fan" pages). The page is different from my personal page at `www.facebook.com/marsha.collier`. I try to treat each page differently, encouraging more intimate contact on my personal page, and posting business information and conversation on my business page. Even my pictures are selected for a different style.

WARNING

Unless your political and religious views reflect your core self and/or your business, it's best to stay away from making public statements on these topics. Whatever you put on the Internet is indexed and recorded somewhere — and your prospective customers may be put off if they do not hold the same views as you.

As a subtle touch on my business page, I use an application (see Figure 17-5) called *Auction Items* (despite the name, the app also posts your fixed-price listings). Applications such as this can only be used on business pages. The application will be listed in the links on the left side of your business page. I find this app gives my items punch, and yet isn't as "in-your-face" as other marketing programs. You can find it to put on your page (if Facebook qualifies your page) at www.facebook.com/AuctionItems.

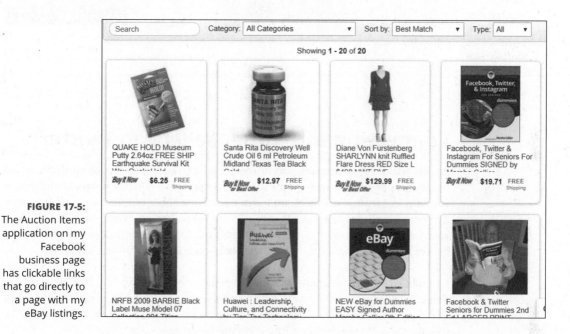

FIGURE 17-5:
The Auction Items application on my Facebook business page has clickable links that go directly to a page with my eBay listings.

The publishers of the app also offer other free tools. They enable eBay sellers to embed their listings into their websites by inserting a short HTML code into the website or via a WordPress plug-in. You can learn more about these by visiting http://esoftie.com and clicking Products.

Another example is my friend (and fellow eBay seller — *dnasupplies*) Anita Nelson. She has two Facebook pages as well: one personal and one for her business, ModelSupplies (see Figure 17-6). She is also @ModelSupplies on Twitter.

TIP

For a more detailed explanation of how to best use Twitter and Facebook, you might like my *Facebook, Twitter & Instagram For Seniors For Dummies* (even if you're not a senior)!

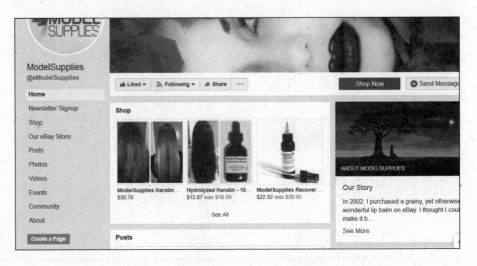

FIGURE 17-6:
The
ModelSupplies
Facebook page
builds her eBay
business on
Facebook.

Connecting with other sellers on Twitter

At this writing, Twitter has 500 million total users (more than 330 million active users) and serves up over 500 million tweets a day. What's a *tweet*? Not just a sound effect from a parakeet anymore. Now it's a short online comment from one Twitter user to another; tweets often flit back and forth between users who follow each other. Tweets are not only comments but also other quick notes that can be quotes, links to news stories, and the occasional self-promotion.

If you like to chat, comment, and read news stories, I'll bet you'll like Twitter. You don't have to be there all day, because when people "talk" to you there, you will see it in your "Notifications" column (you can see that on my Twitter page in Figure 17-7). To answer, you just click the Reply link.

FIGURE 17-7:
When I talk to
folks on Twitter,
they appear as
my "tweets &
replies."

You'll find that your conversations on Twitter will engage you — but only if you engage with your followers. Those who are constantly broadcasting are just trying to build follower numbers — but it's been proven that this practice will not increase sales.

So if you go to Twitter.com and sign up, you need to give your Twitter stream a name. I suggest that you use your real name — for several solid reasons:

>> Friends will find you easier.

>> If you change businesses down the line, you won't have to start over with a new name.

>> On the Internet, you are the face of your business — and everything you post is archived somewhere. Your tweets on Twitter are archived in the National Archive (no joke).

>> If it's good enough for @MichaelDell (founder of Dell), @SteveCase (founder of AOL), and @RichardBranson (founder of Virgin Group), I'd say it's a good idea for you too.

After you sign in, you need to put up a picture and fill out a short bio. The first thing you need to do is put up a picture — preferably yours. People like to see what you look like when they find you on Twitter. Do everyone a favor and describe yourself clearly, as best you can, in the allotted 160 characters. Take a look at Figure 17-8 for a good example from the Twitter mobile app on my phone. Although Anita maintains a separate Twitter account personally, the account represents her @ModelSupplies brand.

FIGURE 17-8: eBay seller dnashopper (Anita Nelson) shows an informative bio.

After you fill out all the cyber-paperwork, you'll see your very own Twitter page. It will be a very blank page. Don't be sad and lonely — you can begin by following me, @MarshaCollier. Say Hi, and I'll follow you back.

When you visit my Twitter page, you'll see a tab that, when clicked, reveals Lists that I've made of people on Twitter. I've made one full of eBay Social Sellers that lists eBay sellers who participate in social media and are fun to follow. Just click on the link or go to `http://twitter.com/MarshaCollier/ebay-social-sellers`. On the list page, just click the link and you will automatically be following everyone on the list.

When you see their tweets in your stream, click the Reply link to say hello — or share something interesting. No doubt they will follow you back.

To find other people to follow, I suggest that you go to the search box on Twitter. Here you can type keywords that reflect your interests or the items you sell, and you will be presented with a list of accounts who have mentioned this word in their tweets. I put in a search for antiques, clicked the *People* tab in Results, and found a long list of people with similar interests, shown in Figure 17-9.

FIGURE 17-9: A built-in list of people who have a passion for antiques on Twitter.

Type in your hobbies and your interests. You'll find a bunch of people to follow, and your Twitter home page will become far more interesting.

Chapter **18**

eBay Bucks Rewards, Charitable Buying and Selling, and Going Mobile

Although eBay is a site where we buy and sell, there are a few perks that make participating on the site a whole lot more fun. In this chapter, I familiarize you with my favorites.

Rewards Program for Shoppers: eBay Bucks

Personally, I'm a fan of loyalty programs; they keep my attention as a customer. For the uninitiated, a loyalty program is a cashback, discount, or bonus program designed by a brand to reward their loyal customers — to keep you coming back. Usually the more you spend, the better the bonuses.

That's how it works with *eBay Bucks*. Based on your purchases in a calendar quarter (three month period), you can earn 1%, up to $100 in a single transaction and (1%) up to $500 in a calendar quarter. To join the party you need to sign up (see Figure 18-1). Here are the steps for your Internet browser:

1. **Go to your My eBay ⇨ Summary page.**

2. **Click the Account tab.**

Once at your Account tab, scroll down to Communication Preferences and click.

3. **At the very bottom of the preferences is the option for Promotions and Surveys; click the word Show at the right end.**

4. **On the next page, click to put a check in the box next to General Email Promotions and click the Save button at the bottom.**

5. **While you're at it, why not select (or deselect) some of the other promotional communications.**

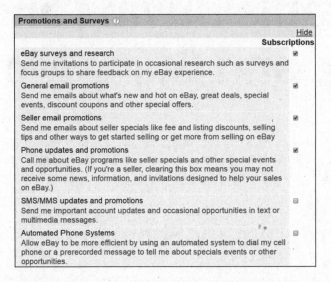

FIGURE 18-1:
Sign up for other eBay communications here as well.

Even if you're not a big shopper on the site, getting one percent back for qualified purchases is still not a bad deal (especially these days). To keep up with the current rules, type `http://pages.ebay.com/rewards/faq.html` in your browser and go to the eBay Bucks FAQ (Frequently Asked Questions) to discover all the ins and outs.

You may find some other restrictions, but purchases in these categories do not apply:

>> eBay Motors (but Parts & Accessories within the Motors category will qualify for eBay Bucks)

>> Classifieds

>> Real Estate

>> eBay Gift Cards, Gift Cards, and Digital Gifts within the Gift Cards & Coupons category

>> Coins & Paper Money, but only for Bullion within that category

>> Heavy Equipment within the Business & Industrial category

Your qualified purchases, after you sign up, are totaled by each calendar quarter. You can check your progress by clicking the eBay Bucks link in your My eBay: Buy section. Then eBay sends you an eBay Bucks Certificate to apply to purchases in the next calendar quarter.

TIP

You can't save up the certificates, and you must use them within 30 days of issuance.

Check the current status of your eBay Bucks by clicking the eBay Bucks link on your My eBay: Summary page left column.

Selling and Buying: Helping Nonprofits

Most of us have donated to charity in one form or another. But here on eBay, charities really rock. Do you need a *Jurassic Park* helmet signed by Steven Spielberg to round out your collection (and deflect the odd dino tooth)? Post a bid on one of the charity auctions. How about a signed original photograph of Jerry Seinfeld from *People* magazine? Yup, you can get that, too. All these and more have turned up in charity auctions. In short, having a big heart for charities has gotten a whole lot easier thanks to eBay.

eBay for Charity

November 2003 was a lucky time for this country's charities. That's the month that eBay launched the eBay Giving Works Charity auction platform. eBay originally teamed up with one of the first charity-giving sites on the Internet, MissionFish, which now runs the PayPal Giving Fund. After 9/11, as "9/11 Auction for America" (see sidebar further on), eBay's giving program originally raised over $10 million through online charity auctions for organizations supporting the victims of the tragedy and their families. More than 911 million dollars have been raised since 2003 on eBay for Charity, supporting more than 66,000 organizations.

If you're involved with a charity, and are certified as a 501(c)(3), you can register your charity to get on the list of beneficiaries. You can also run your own fundraising events on eBay! Just go to `http://charity.ebay.com`, and you'll arrive at the eBay for Charity hub (as shown in Figure 18-2).

FIGURE 18-2: Where eBay buyers and sellers work for good.

The best part is that *you* can run an auction or fixed-price listing to benefit your favorite charity. Sellers can list items for sale and designate those items to benefit a charity from the eBay for Charity directory at `http://charity.ebay.com/charity/search` (which lists tens of thousands of charities). The seller can also specify what percentage (from as little as 10 percent up to 100 percent) of the sale's proceeds go to the charity. You can browse to select the charity of your choice on the Giving Works page. When you list your item for sale, you can indicate — on the Sell form's Create Your Listing section — to which charity you'd like to donate proceeds, and what percentage of the final sale price to donate.

TIP

As you visit different areas of eBay, you can recognize the charity listings by the small blue-and-gold ribbon icon next to them in searches and the Category list.

9/11 AUCTION FOR AMERICA

In late 2001, eBay took on one of its most ambitious attempts at fundraising: the Auction for America. In response to requests by New York Governor George E. Pataki and Mayor Rudolph Giuliani, eBay called on the community to raise $100 million in 100 days. eBay and Billpoint (eBay's payment service at the time) waived all fees, and community members gave their all, donating and buying all kinds of items to benefit the New York State World Trade Center Relief Fund, the Twin Towers Fund, the American Red Cross, and the September 11 Fund.

In early November, Patti Ruby (this book's tech editor) and I worked with eBay to introduce non-eBay sellers to Auction for America at an event in Southern California. We brought hundreds of people to the site who participated in buying and selling to benefit the victims. There were many such events across the country.

Community member Jay Leno sold his celebrity-autographed Harley Davidson for over $360,260; Tim Allen sold his 1956 Chevrolet Nomad for $46,000; and countless corporate sponsors joined in with the person-to-person community to raise funds. Over 100,000 sellers participated, and over 230,000 items were listed.

The auction ended on December 25, after raising $10 million. This is an amazing tribute to the eBay members and their community spirit.

Creative charity auctions

New charities are popping up all the time on eBay. To see the sales that benefit nonprofits, go to the Giving Works page and click the Shop for Charity link. Here are some of the more creative charity auctions that have been held on eBay:

>> The highest-grossing charity auctions tend to be the annual event from billionaire Warren Buffett. He donates a private power lunch to benefit the Glide Foundation. The 2019 auction grossed $4,567,888; see more about Warren Buffett's Glide Foundation in Chapter 1.

>> Oprah Winfrey has jumped onto eBay with a bang! In 2003, to fund her charity, the Angel Network, Oprah auctioned two chairs from her set. These were not just any chairs. Aside from being luxurious leather chairs designed by Ralph Lauren, they had housed the behinds of famous names such as John F. Kennedy, Jr., Halle Berry, Tom Hanks, Jim Carrey, and Michael Jordan. The 7-day auction netted the charity an amazing $64,100. In 2010 through this year, the media mogul cleaned out her own closet for her Leadership Academy for Girls.

» To celebrate Chivas Regal's 200th year, the company chose eBay for CHIVAS 200, the largest online charity auction in the world. From September 6 to October 31, 2001, the Chivas folks auctioned more than 200 of the world's most-wanted items and experiences — such as an opportunity to become a Russian space-station cosmonaut — all for the benefit of charity partners around the world.

» Music producer and singer Pharrell Williams decided to put his famous Vivienne Westwood park ranger–style hat up for sale to benefit his non-profit organization, One Hand to AnOTHER. Pharrell wore the famous hat during his performance at the Grammy broadcast in 2014. Folks commented that the hat resembled the logo for the Arby's restaurant chain, so he tweeted through his Twitter account @Pharrell, "Hey @Arbys, you want my hat?" He started the listing on eBay for $200 (what he paid for it), and it did eventually sell to Arby's for $44,100. Arby's thanked Pharrell for the return of their hat on Twitter; the Tweet is shown in Figure 18-3.

» When I appeared on *The View* with Barbara Walters and Star Jones, all four stars of the show autographed a coffee cup that we auctioned off on eBay to benefit UNICEF. We raised over $1,000 on eBay for a single coffee cup! Now that a couple of the hosts have moved on, I wonder what that little cup's worth.

FIGURE 18-3: Arby's remarks to Pharrell on Twitter that they are happy to get their hat back.

Go Mobile — for Buying and Selling

Now you can take eBay along! I use the eBay mobile app when I'm out looking for items to resell on eBay. It's especially helpful at a garage sale to see how much I can sell an item for — and to find out how many people are selling an item. If you prefer a different view, you can also type `http://m.ebay.com` into your phone's browser to see a mobile enhanced version of the site.

The eBay mobile app is available for download on smartphones: iOS (for the iPhone and iPad) and Android. If you don't have one of those operating systems on your smartphone, you can always type the previous address into your mobile browser (or, if you're reading this as an e-book, tap the link in that sentence).

Several categories of auctions are featured at the top of the screen on mobile, just below the search box. Tapping the words show you different views (see Figure 18-4):

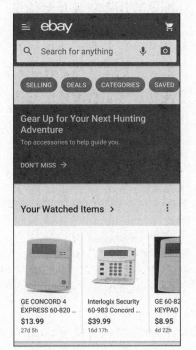

FIGURE 18-4:
Access your eBay pages and see views of Selling, Deals, Categories, Saved, and more.

>> **Categories:** This functions similarly to your My eBay ⇨ Buy pages. Here you can see your recently viewed items, and by scrolling your Watched Items list, you can see both your buying overview and your Selling overview. There's a link at the bottom of each section to "view all" in that category.

>> **Saved:** Here you'll find searches and sellers you've saved for future reference as well as an area to input products you're interested in.

>> **Deals:** Very much like the eBay home page, tapping Deals shows you special promotions and deals of the day — and points you to various items that (based on your search history) eBay suggests you might want to purchase.

   In the Deals view, you can swipe side-to-side to see different categories and featured specials within those interest areas.

>> **Selling:** In traditional eBay fashion, Sell is where you click to list an item for sale. You also see your selling history and listing drafts you started and haven't yet completed.

The experience is exactly the same on a tablet, but a tablet's screen gives you a lot more real estate to use. This is especially beneficial if you want to list an item for sale. When it comes to getting the most out of eBay on mobile, I personally prefer the tablet experience to using my smartphone.

If you're out and about and find an item you think might do well on eBay, you can easily search for the item by tapping the text box next to the magnifying glass on the app. Your mobile keyboard pops up, and you can type in the keywords for the item you're looking for.

TIP

Inside secret: Once you tap in the text field on the mobile app, you also see a tiny microphone. Tap there to input your text from speech. There is also an icon that looks like the lines of a barcode. This is a scan option. Just tap there to scan a barcode on an item to see whether that item is being sold on eBay (as shown in Figure 18-5).

The mobile barcode scanner is very fast and accurate; you get the results immediately. Then you can further refine your search to Sold Items Only to see at what price that item is currently selling.

When you're starting out on eBay, I recommend listing your eBay items for sale from your laptop or desktop computer. The text-formatting features available on the website's Sell an Item page (such as bulleted lists and boldface) are harder to use on the mobile app.

The app does have an HTML description writer, so if you learn a little bit of HTML code (as outlined in Chapter 10), you can give your descriptions a little extra character.

Because my tablet has a great camera, I do enjoy listing from mobile. My smartphone also has a great camera, but I prefer the bigger screen so I don't miss a detail when I'm getting a shot of the item.

I start some of my listings on my tablet by writing my title, adding some details, and uploading the photos; Chapter 14 gives you step-by-step instructions. I often complete a good portion of the listing on mobile, but I tend to click Save and then reopen the listing as a saved template on my computer. Once I am on my computer, I can search eBay more efficiently for top-selling keywords and pricing ideas.

When I do complete a full listing on the mobile app, I still go to the website on my computer and buff up the description and double-check the options for the listing. Never forget: The purpose of your listing is to sell the item. So, as with a lady's makeup, dolling up plain text (tastefully, please!) goes a long way toward making your item more desirable to a buyer.

5

The Parts of Tens

More tips for buying and selling items

Software and services that can lighten your selling workload

Chapter **19**

Ten (Or So) Golden Rules to Succeed on eBay

No matter how much experience pilots may have, they always keep numerous checklists to go over on a daily basis. The same is true on eBay (although the only crashing that you need to worry about is on your computer). No matter how many times you buy or sell, the advice in this chapter will help you survive and thrive on eBay.

Although conducting business on eBay is relatively smooth overall, any venture is bound to have a few bumps here and there. There's a certain etiquette that goes along with everything we do in life. If you follow these simple rules, your time on the site will be a whole lot more pleasant for everyone. That said, here are ten (or so) easy, important golden rules for eBay. I note which tips are geared toward buyers or sellers. Happy hunting and gathering!

MARSHA SAYS

After a while, posting listings and bidding can become rote. You can all too easily forget the basics, so *please* look at this book every now and again to jog your memory: As a successful eBay member, you're part of a very special person-to-person community.

Buyer: Research Your Treasure Before You Buy

In the excitement of finding just what we want, many of us may develop a tendency to leap before we look. I have often bought an item in a furious spurt of excitement, only to find that it wasn't *exactly* what I needed or wanted after it arrived.

Even if the item is closing soon, carefully read the item description. Does the item have any flaws? Can you live with them if it does? Is something missing from the description that should be there? Did you read the terms of payment and shipping? *(Do you really, really want it?)*

Don't be too shy or embarrassed. If you have any questions, ask the seller a question! You're better off covering your bases before you place a bid or buy an item than you are facing disappointment when the item arrives.

REMEMBER

Keep this in mind *before* you click the Bid or Buy button; you are *legally and morally obligated* to go through with the transaction if you win or purchase. Make sure that everything is as you want it and check for a warranty or return policy. Clarify everything up front. If the seller doesn't answer back, consider that non-response an early warning that dealing with this person may be a mistake — or at least a hassle!

Buyer: Check the Seller's Feedback

Never bid or buy without checking the seller's feedback. You need to be able to trust the person you're buying from. Look for the Top Rated Plus Seller icon, but even if you see one, you may not find enough information. When you are considering buying a very pricey item, dig a little deeper. Don't just evaluate the percentage of positive and negative feedback: Investigate the seller's feedback more deeply by clicking the number next to his or her User ID. Take the time to read the comments left by others who have transacted with this seller.

In my years on eBay, I have found that even the rarest of items show up sporadically on eBay. Don't just settle on a listing if you don't feel good about a seller. Save the search and the item will most likely come up for sale again. As badly as you may want something, sending a payment to someone with a high feedback rating *who recently got a bunch of negatives* could lead to a *big* disappointment.

Buyer: Check the Price Tag and Bid Wisely

Before you bid, make sure that you have some knowledge of how much you should pay for the item, even if you limit your search to completed listings to get an idea of how much the item went for in the past.

WARNING

Caveat emptor: If a deal sounds too good to be true, it may well be.

I love eBay — but not for every single thing that I buy (okay, almost). Make sure that you can't get the item cheaper at the store or from another online seller.

Beware of getting caught up in the frenzy of last-minute bidding: It's an easy thing to do. Whether you choose proxy bidding or sniping (see Chapter 7 for my discussion on sniping), decide how much you're willing to pay *before* you bid. If you set a limit, you won't be overcome with the urge to spend more than an item is worth — or, worse, more than you have in your bank account.

Although eBay is lots of fun, it's also serious business. Bidding is a legal and binding contract. Don't get a bad reputation by retracting bids or becoming a deadbeat.

Buyer: Leave Positive Feedback for a Good Seller

I have noticed that many buyers neglect to leave a feedback comment for the seller of an item they've purchased. Whoa, people, that's bad form (this isn't Amazon). Realize that eBay is a person-to-person marketplace, and that many of the businesses that sell on the platform are home-based businesses. College students, single moms, family businesses, they're all on eBay to earn some money. Your positive feedback means a lot to these sellers. Even neutral feedback can leave a tip to other prospective shoppers.

Sellers are judged on your Detailed Star Ratings. A low star rating can even cost them money (eBay discounts Final Value Fees to sellers who have top service ratings in their DSRs). Leaving feedback, and thereby helping other members, is your responsibility as a community member.

Always leave feedback after you receive an item and it's exactly as you expected and has arrived in a timely manner. eBay's feedback system judges sellers on several different points. Did you get your item as described? Did the seller send tracking numbers keeping you abreast of your shipment progress? Shipping times can be deceiving; mistakes happen. Be sure to check the tracking history on the package label to see when your seller sent the item. It's not fair to ding the seller's reputation because an item rerouted itself in the mail.

Keep in mind that the transaction isn't complete until the buyer receives the merchandise and is happy with the purchase. Not all sellers leave automatic positive feedback, so don't expect positive feedback just because you paid in a timely manner. Many feel that feedback is quid pro quo.

Buyer: Protect Your Privacy

Remember that just because you're conducting transactions from the privacy of your home doesn't mean that you're doing everything you can to protect your privacy. Legitimate buyers and sellers *never* need to know your password or Social Security number. *Do not respond to any email that asks for that information.* See Chapter 15 about how to handle such phishing scams.

Seller: Really Know Your Stuff

Do some homework. Know the value of your item. At the very least, get an idea of your item's value by searching completed listings for similar items. If it's a new item, check out other online sites and see what your item is selling for by running a Google product search for your item at www.google.com/shopping, like the one I ran in Figure 19-1. On searches I run for products I'm interested in, I often find the item at a price that was worth buying from a wholesaler. Keep your eyes open for opportunities like this! Knowing about your product also means that you can accurately describe what you have — and never, *ever* (even accidentally) pass off a fake as the real deal. Make sure that your item isn't prohibited, illegal, questionable, or infringing. It's your responsibility!

Before posting your listing, you should take the following actions:

>> Write an honest, thorough description.

>> Take a good, clear photo.

>> Work out your shipping costs and offer free shipping whenever possible.

Add each of the preceding pieces of info to your item's description to avoid any unnecessary disputes later.

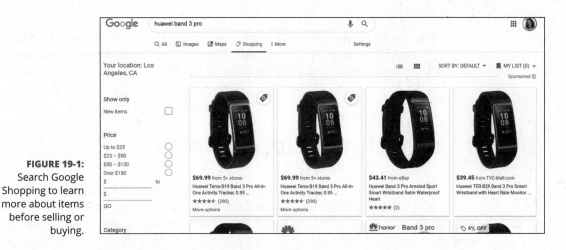

FIGURE 19-1:
Search Google
Shopping to learn
more about items
before selling or
buying.

Seller: Polish and Shine

Make sure that your title is descriptive enough to catch the eye of someone browsing a category and detailed enough for a buyer to identify. Don't just write *Old
Board Game.* Instead, give some details: *1952 Candy Land Vintage Retro Board Game
Complete.* Taking advantage of as many of the 80 characters that eBay allows for
your title gives you a fighting chance for your keywords to be found when prospective buyers search. The more search keywords you list, the easier it will be for
someone to find your item.

Play editor and scrutinize your text for grammar mistakes and misspellings.
Typos in either your title or description can cost you money. For example, a search
engine will keep skipping over your *Mikky Mouce Choklit Cookie Jare.* Spelling
counts — and pays. Always double-check your work!

Seller: Picture-Perfect Facts

Your photos can be a boon or a bust on eBay. Double-check the photo of your item
before you post it. Is the lighting okay? Does the photo paint a flattering image of
the item? Are the colors as accurate as possible? Use a white background with
nothing to distract the buyer's eye. Would *you* buy this item?

**MARSHA
SAYS**

Take your picture as if you didn't have a description; be sure that it totally illustrates the item. Also, write your description as if you didn't have a photo. Some
buyers are visual and some just want to read the facts; cover yourself so the buyer
will have an exact idea of what you're selling. For more about taking excellent
photos of your items, flash on over to Chapter 14.

Be factual and honest. On eBay, all you have is your reputation, so don't jeopardize it by lying about your item or terms. Tell potential buyers about any flaws. Give as complete a description as possible, with all the facts about the item that you can include.

Seller: Communication Is Key

Respond quickly and honestly to all questions sent via eBay Messages, and use the contact to establish a good relationship. Don't let more than 24 hours pass without sending a response. If a bidder makes a reasonable request about payment or shipping, going along with that request is usually worth it to make a sale. *Note:* The customer is always right. (Well, most of the time, anyway.)

Be up front and fair when charging for sending merchandise to your buyer. You can't make much by overcharging for shipping and handling. Besides, charging outrageous fees will penalize you in an eBay search and is a violation of eBay's policies; you could get yourself in trouble. Unreasonable charges inevitably lead to bad feelings, negative feedback, and low DSRs.

Seller: Be a Buyer's Dream

Just because you're transacting through the computer doesn't mean that you can forget your manners. Live by the Golden Rule: Do unto others as you would have others do unto you. Ship the item within a day of the buyer's payment — immediately is even better. (Better yet, why not always ship the item that quickly? I try to.) And keep all your correspondence polite.

Ship the goods as soon as you can (in accordance with the shipping terms you outline in the item description, of course). Be sure to input, as eBay requires, the tracking number into the transaction online, too. That way, buyers can eagerly anticipate the arrival of their goods.

REMEMBER

When shipping your items, use quality packing materials and sturdy boxes to prevent disaster. Broken or damaged items can lead to reputation-damaging negative feedback. Pack as if a gang of clumsy robots is out to destroy your package (or as if *you* had made this purchase). Your buyers are sure to appreciate the effort.

Seller: Listen to the Music

As I state in the golden rules for buyers, don't underestimate the power of positive feedback. Your reputation is at stake. Always generously dole out feedback when you complete a transaction. Your buyers will appreciate it and will hopefully return the favor.

What should you do if you get slammed unfairly with negative feedback? Don't freak out! If you feel it's unjustly posted, do, however, contact the buyer and find out how you can make things right. If that doesn't work, at least post a follow-up response for others to see. Those who read your feedback can often see past a single disgruntled message, especially if they can see you handled it well.

Keep in mind that, in most cases, negative feedback results from misunderstandings. Contact the buyer the moment you smell a problem arising and see if you can work things out to your satisfaction. Always work to keep your eBay reputation pristine.

Buyers and Sellers: Keep Current, Keep Cool

You'd be surprised at how many users get suspended even though they have automatic credit card payments. Maybe they move. Or their email addresses change because they change Internet Service Providers. Regardless, if you don't update your contact and credit card information, and that leaves eBay and other users unable to contact you, you can be suspended.

If you make any major moves (home address, billing address, ISP), let eBay know this new contact information. Click My eBay on the main navigation area at the top of eBay pages, click the Account tab, scroll down the links on the left side of the page to Personal Information, and update the appropriate data.

IN THIS CHAPTER

» Illustrating clothing sizes more competitively

» Sizing clothing for resale with Sizely

» Taking automatic aim with BidRobot

» Financing new merchandise with Kabbage

» Finding the value of your collectibles on Worthpoint

» Becoming a Top Rated Seller through good customer service

Chapter **20**

Ten (Or So) Services to Make Life Easy

R eady to take your sales to the next level? Are you looking for extra tools to help make your sales go off the charts and make your items say, "Buy me!"? Need to slip in a bid in the middle of the night without losing sleep? Perhaps you've found a great deal on some merchandise to sell and need to pony up the cash to buy it. If so, here's a list of ten (or so) platforms to help put your sales ahead of the pack and make your bidding life easier. In this chapter, I recommend some reliable companies, and many of them offer free solutions!

As online sales grow in popularity, software developers are continually upgrading and developing new auction and selling software to support eBay's evolution. Many of these programs update automatically as changes are made on the site.

TIP

You absolutely don't *have* to use any of these programs or services to run eBay sales successfully. However, when you're running more than several listings a week, the addition of a "helper" makes things go ever so much smoother (especially if it's free or very low cost).

A large number of companies also offer online management services and offline programs. (Let's face it, as long as people will pay, they'll be happy to have something to sell you.) I can't cover each and every one — but the platforms that I mention in this chapter have been tried and tested. You may know of other effective (and economical) products — and I'd love to hear about them. I do know that these work and are good tools when you choose to expand your eBay sales.

Listed in this chapter are some options for handling various aspects of your sales. You find (at the end of the chapter) that eBay supplies some pretty robust tools that I use for my own eBay business. I mention some solid third-party alternatives, because lots of people prefer not to do everything exclusively on eBay. Your business is your own, and you may just want to list your items for sale on eBay and do the rest yourself. Your choice.

MARSHA SAYS

Be sure to check my website (www.coolebaytools.com) or my blog (http://mcollier.blogspot.com) for updates on services and articles on topics important to your business, as well as special discounts offered for free to my readers.

Seller Tools and Services

You're comfortable transacting your auctions online, so why not manage them online as well . . . with an extra level of privacy? The sites in this section offer useful services that save time in both posting your items and wrapping them up.

inkFrog

inkFrog, shown in Figure 20-1, is a web-based service helping eBay sellers since 1999. In 2006, inkFrog bought out another respected service, SpareDollar. They joined with eBay as a multi-channel selling solutions provider in 2016. In its present form, inkFrog represents a super bargain in a web-based management SaaS (Software as a Service).

You can manage every aspect of your eBay sales, including image hosting, ad design, automated email management, and report tracking. If you want to get fancy, you can design your item listing from any of its templates. Here are some of the basic features:

>> **Image hosting:** inkFrog hosts your images and has a handy uploader that allows you to insert your images with a click of your mouse.

>> **Template Builder:** Create your templates, using a simple form. Use one of their prebuilt themes and edit with their handy WYSIWYG editor.

>> **Integration with other ecommerce sites.**

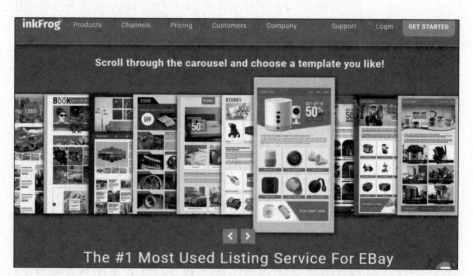

FIGURE 20-1:
inkFrog's super sauce is its Template Builder.

You can literally run your entire eBay account from inkFrog. You will have somewhat of a learning curve, so I suggest you learn the ropes of eBay on your own before you try this platform. You'd need to be an advanced seller to use all the benefits of inkFrog. A small business can get started on the site for $11 a month (after a 14-day free trial period). This covers 300 listings a month.

For more information, and even more features, visit the inkFrog website at www.inkfrog.com.

Sizely

If you're selling clothing on eBay, there's one platform you really need to know about and use. Sizely is an e-commerce tool for online sellers, which simplifies the process of illustrating your apparel-sizing information.

As you may know by now, clothing from different brands does not follow exact, consistent sizing — which makes online clothing purchases difficult for buyers who don't fit into the standard sizes. When you're selling used (gently used) clothing, often you'll find that sizes may vary due to wear or cleaning methods. (I blame the dryer.)

This platform was developed by an eBay seller who mostly sold clothing, to solve a problem of his own: how to implement garment measurements in order to give buyers a better understanding of how the garment would fit.

According to the folks at Sizely, including measurements in your listing description increases sales by 26 percent and decreases returns significantly. So instead of merely listing measurements in a bulleted list, you can include a graphic to help potential buyers picture the fit more clearly.

The website is insanely intuitive.

Go to templates and select the type of clothing you plan to list from the suggested items. Each type of clothing gives you a skeletal outline of the item and shows you where to measure it.

>> **On the image of the item you are selling, measure point to point at the indicated places.**

>> **Enter the size information in inches (or centimeters) in the spaces provided.**

>> **Click Generate Image and Sizely will give you alternatives to illustrate the sizing of your item (as shown in Figure 20-2).**

   You can use an HTML link to your illustrative graphic with the sizes embedded, copy and paste that code into eBay's HTML description area, or use the option to save the image to upload on your website or for your eBay Gallery images.

There's a free Starter plan that lets you start with 25 templates; each template represents a different item of clothing. The higher the plan you have, the more templates you have access to. Currently they have over 160!

Sign up to give it a whirl at www.size.ly.

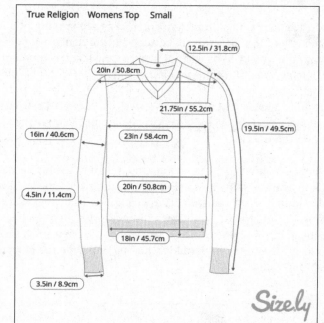

True Religion   Womens Top   Small

12.5in / 31.8cm

20in / 50.8cm

21.75in / 55.2cm

19.5in / 49.5cm

16in / 40.6cm

23in / 58.4cm

4.5in / 11.4cm

20in / 50.8cm

18in / 45.7cm

3.5in / 8.9cm

Sizely

FIGURE 20-2:
After you type in measurements, Sizely gives you a great visual to share in your listing.

Important Tools for Buyers and Sellers

One might think that everything is covered by eBay and the services listed up to this point, but there are a few other platforms to make your life easier on the site as a buyer . . . and as a seller.

Sniping with BidRobot

When it comes to buying fixed-price items on eBay, there's really no magic formula other than knowing how to use eBay's search. Using some of the tricks I teach on searching can help you ferret out the best of deals.

But what about auctions? There is very little more frustrating than losing an auction by a dollar, or so. When I first started writing about eBay, I began to use the word "snipe" — loosely (and generally) defined as "to shoot at individuals as opportunity offers from a concealed or distant position." So to snipe at an auction (metaphorically speaking), you lie in wait and catch the competition off-guard.

As you can tell by reading Chapter 7, I'm a big fan of sniping. It's my favorite way to win an auction. It makes the entire auction experience even more entertaining. When I have the time, I enjoy battling it out in the last few moments of an auction, bidding fiercely, even if (often) unsuccessfully.

There are quite a few auction sniping services on the web. I settled on the one I use now, BidRobot.com (shown in Figure 20-3), because I could quickly get responses to questions and queries.

When I find an auction that I'm serious about, I go to the BidRobot website, log in, and place my future snipe bids. All I have to do is type the item number and my high bid, and that's it. I can shut off my computer knowing that BidRobot will do my bidding for me. Nobody on eBay will know what item I'm desperate to have, because the magical BidRobot doesn't place my bid until a few seconds before the auction closes. If I'm the high bidder, no one will have the chance to bid against me! Bwah-ha-haaa!

FIGURE 20-3:
I use BidRobot whenever I need to absolutely, positively win an item!

It's easy to use BidRobot to snipe single auctions. For single auctions, just type the item number and bid by using only the yellow top section under the BidForm title. You can ignore the entry forms in all other sections.

But what happens when you find that a bunch of sellers have auctions for the same item at low bid amounts? You'd like to take a chance on each item — and only win one. That's where the *BidGroups* feature comes into play. It will allow you to bid on multiple eBay auctions for the same type of item. When you win any one auction that you've put into a BidGroup, BidRobot cancels the remaining bids in that specific group automatically.

BidRobot's services are reasonably priced, based on the amount of time that you want to use the service. As of this writing, BidRobot has placed bids for hundreds of thousands of eBay users since 1998! You pay a flat rate for all the snipes you can handle. You don't pay any extra charges for the service. For a free trial, visit BidRobot's website at this special URL for my readers: `www.bidrobot.com/cool`.

Find out what it's worth at Worthpoint

Have you ever watched a show on the History Channel, *American Pickers*? If you have, you've no doubt marveled at the stars' (pickers') talents to recognize value in the most common items. I wish I had their breadth of knowledge because so many great items appear at estate sales, but I never know which is the best to purchase for resale.

Enter the online collectible database Worthpoint (see Figure 20-4), the brainchild of William Seippel. After seeing his family members sell heirloom-quality antiques for a pittance, William decided to put his economics degree to work and develop a tool so that no one will (hopefully) be taken advantage of again.

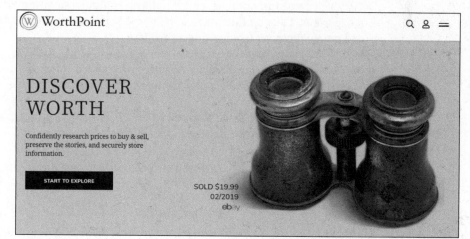

FIGURE 20-4:
Finding the worth of an item can save you a lot of time and money.

Will has been an avid collector since 1974, and dealer of just about all things antique since 1984. In 2006, he began to build what most consider to be the world's largest database of over 500 million items — and their sold prices online. This database, the *Worthopedia*, gives subscribers a chance to discover prices, descriptions, pictures, and sale dates from hundreds of auction houses. Genius, right?

Worthpoint also has a mobile app so you can check out items you might want to buy for resale directly from your smartphone at an estate sale or auction.

If you're going to buy or sell collectibles, the cost of a subscription will pay for itself many times over. There's so much value to this site that I could spend hours on it. You can go to the site for a 7-day trial (or seven price lookups) at www.worthpoint.com.

Buying a warranty through SquareTrade

The people who founded SquareTrade were friends of mine back in the day. They founded the company in 1999, selling a trust seal that would appear in eBay listings after they had vetted the seller. They performed online negotiation and dispute resolution long before eBay integrated these services into the site.

Perhaps they had bigger ideas. In 2006, they began selling consumer protection plans on electronics and devices. I've been buying SquareTrade warranties ever since. You can purchase their extended warranties for far less than retailers' warranties as well as warranties for eBay and online purchases.

They've covered my purchases for phones, computers, washers, dryers, and my refrigerator. The one time I actually needed service, they performed immediately and my washer was fixed within a few days.

In 2016, they were acquired by Allstate, who added other services to their site. They offer a Standard policy or a Standard Warranty that includes accidents.

The Standard SquareTrade Warranty (see Figure 20-5) protects eBay purchases from mechanical and electrical failures during normal use.

>> One to four years of coverage, as indicated at the time that you purchase your warranty

>> 100 percent parts and labor coverage

>> Item repairs, or the full item price paid back to you if SquareTrade can't fix it

>> Covers new, refurbished, and used items — even if there's no USA manufacturer's warranty on your item

Before you buy anything online (or in a brick and mortar store), visit `www.squaretrade.com` and check out the deals on warranties. For more information on SquareTrade and eBay, go to `https://pages.ebay.com/buyerprotection/squaretrade.html`.

eBay fee calculator: Salecalc

Prior to listing anything on eBay, I run the numbers through a fee calculator. Knowing your fees and expenses ahead of time is a best practice that leads to profitable sales. Air-balling your selling price may cost you money when the item sells.

eBay no longer has a calculator in the site. Knowing a pure picture of your bottom line in advance will help you price your items so that your profit is built in. (You can also estimate how low you can go with a Make Offer option on your listing.)

I've found a site that will do the calculations for you (not only for eBay sales but also for other online venues) with a few clicks of your mouse (or taps on an app). Simple to use, Salecalc allows you to run different pricing scenarios and will help you decide on the best format for your sale; `http://salecalc.com/ebay` is shown in Figure 20-6.

I like using this because I can work to figure out gross profits or just see the fee breakdowns. There are a lot of options here, and I've found it to be very reliable.

Salecalc also has an iOS mobile app, available in the iTunes app store.

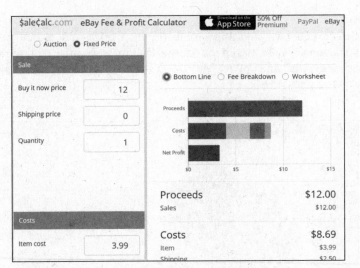

Kabbage: Working capital

Do you need cash to grow your online business? Since I'm a fan of bootstrapping a startup, I don't recommend you go into debt until you have a positive cash flow and know what you're doing with your online business.

So after you're up and rolling, you might come across a great deal on the latest hot-selling gizmos, but find yourself short of cash because they are sold only in lots of 50. All businesses need capital to grow. Kabbage provides working capital to online merchants through a short application process that can take under ten minutes (see Figure 20-7).

Kabbage provides funding only to online sellers. Online sellers are generally mis-understood by banks and financial services because traditional underwriting and funding criteria do not account for a virtual-commerce (e-commerce) business model or the value of recently sold inventory. When you apply, they look at many factors (other than your credit score) to determine how much they can advance, including your seller rating, time in business, transaction volume, and other feed-back measurements.

Visit their website at www.kabbage.com for more details.

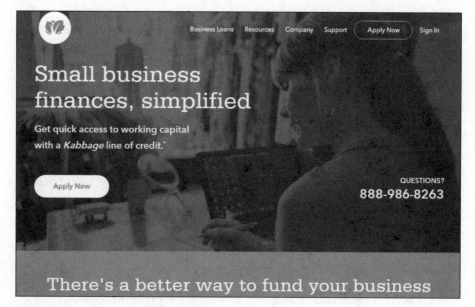

FIGURE 20-7: The Kabbage home page is your first step toward growing your business.

eBay's Software and Services

When the users call, eBay answers! As eBay grew, the need for additional services and software also grew. eBay answered the need with its Selling Manager products. Read on to see how these services tailored for the eBay user may benefit you.

Selling Manager, Selling Manager Pro, and Seller Hub

I have used Selling Manager Pro for my eBay sales for many years, and I find it to be a convenient and reliable way to quickly relist singly (or in bulk), track the progress of my sales, leave feedback, and keep track of what has and hasn't sold.

You also get a nice selection of reports to help you keep track of how your listings are performing. This way you can tell whether your sales are on target or not. Selling Manager (or Selling Manager Pro) replaces the Selling page of My eBay. This thorough data is updated automatically from eBay's servers and PayPal, so you have up-to-the-minute info.

Selling Manager is free to all sellers, and is embedded in the Seller Hub (if you're using it). The Pro version, which adds inventory management and reporting features, is tailored to high-volume sellers and costs $15.99 a month (as an add-on if you have a Basic or Starter store), but is free for Premium, Anchor, and Enterprise eBay Store subscribers. Information on both versions is available at

www.ebay.com/help/selling/selling-tools/selling-manager-selling-manager-pro?id=4098.

To try out Selling Manager Pro (there's a 30-day free trial).

1. **Go to your Account in My eBay and click Subscriptions.**

2. **Scroll down to Selling Manager or Selling Manager Pro and click Continue.**

3. **Read (and agree to) the user agreement; then click to Subscribe.**

Seller Hub (see Figure 20-8) is an advanced offering from eBay. It automates many of the tasks that large-volume sellers need. It also opens a window to new stats and trends for sales.

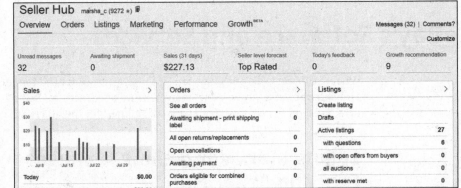

FIGURE 20-8:
eBay Seller Hub offers a solution for larger-volume sellers.

eBay PowerSellers

At one time, eBay offered an elite club for *PowerSellers*, sellers who sold larger quantities of merchandise (as rated by PowerSeller level) on the site. Anyone can qualify to become a PowerSeller, which includes levels of Bronze, Silver, Gold, Platinum, and Titanium, depending on the number of items you've sold or the dollar amount of your sales. The media still refers to the term PowerSeller, but the privileges of this program have been migrated into the Top Rated Program.

Top Rated Sellers

If you go to one of my listings, you'll notice the Top Rated Plus seal on them. A rating of Top Rated Seller is hard to attain, but it gives you distinct advantages over the competition. (I will admit that I've slipped in the past and fallen out of this status. But it's also been well worth reinstating.)

The advantages are clear; you receive

>> A ten percent discount on Final Value Fees (on item sale price only)

>> Unpaid item protection, which offers credit for certain listing upgrade fees on eligible listing formats

>> A snappy-looking seal on your listing pages and in search results (shown in Figure 20-9)

>> Improved search standing for fixed-price listings in Best Match search results

FIGURE 20-9:
The Top Rated Plus seal as it appears on my listings in searches.

NEW eBay YoYo Glossy Clear Red New Sealed in plastic

Brand New

$7.49
or Best Offer
Free Shipping
Free Returns
♡ Watch

🚚 FAST 'N FREE
Guaranteed by Fri, Aug. 9
Top Rated Plus

So how do you get Top Rated Seller status? You must meet the requirements. You may want to check your status in your Seller Standards Dashboard (mine is pictured in Figure 20-10). For the latest qualifications and benefits of this program, check here:

```
www.ebay.com/help/selling/seller-levels-performance-standards/
seller-levels-performance-standards?id=4080.
```

Read on for an overview of what it takes to get this status.

To become a Top Rated Seller, you must fulfill requirements in several areas: Sales, Shipping, Package Tracking, Returns, and transaction-related Defects.

>> A minimum of 100 transactions with buyers within the United States within the preceding twelve months.

>> Your sales in the preceding twelve months must reflect a minimum of $1,000.00.

>> Offer your buyers same-day or one-day handling time.

>> Accept returns for a minimum of 30 days after the item is delivered to the customer.

>> Upload valid tracking numbers directly on eBay — for your transactions with U.S. buyers, within your promised handling time, in the last three months.

>> If you offer 1-Day Handling time, you must upload the tracking number by 11:59 p.m. on the day after you receive the buyer's payment. (Weekends and holidays are considered days off and are not counted.)

>> You must have a maximum of a 0.5 percent defect rate; where *defects* mean Money Back Guarantee and PayPal Protection cases closed without seller resolution and seller-initiated transaction cancellations.

For more information, and any changes in the offerings or requirements, visit `http://pages.ebay.com/help/sell/top-rated.html`.

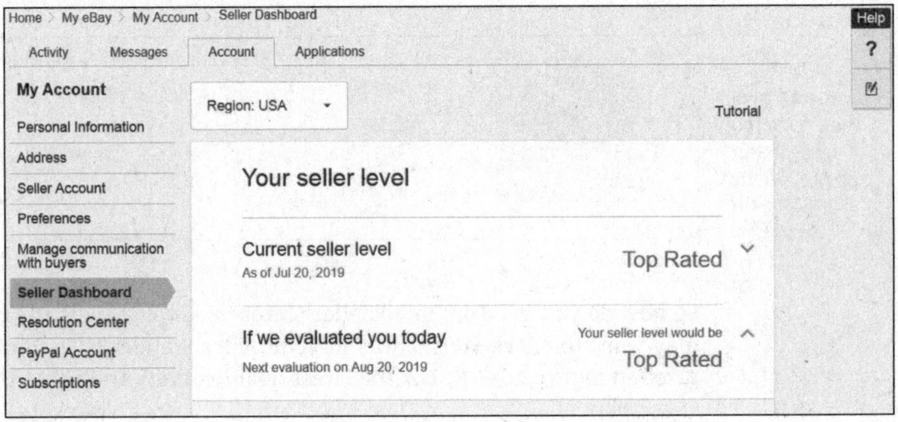

FIGURE 20-10: Click the link to your Seller Dashboard to see how you're doing.

Index

N

sales tax, 177

state incomes taxes, 178

television, impact on trends by, 208

Terapeak Research, 86

Terms of Service, 28

text-formatting features, on mobile app compared to laptop/desktop, 354

thank you (to buyer), 229–230

thermal label printer (for packaging), 246

third-party automation, 368

thrift stores, as source for inventory, 211

TIF (TIFF) image, 289

Time Left (on item page), 103

time-conversion chart, 103, 131, 195

timing (on selling), 157–159

title (Sell Your Item form), 183, 187–190, 363

token bid, 114, 131

Tools & apps link, 46–47

Top Rated Seller, 1, 57, 118, 144, 148, 379–380

Totally Bizarre subcategory, 46

tracking bugs, 299–300

tracking cookies, 299

tracking numbers, 145, 227, 230, 236, 364, 380

trademark and copyright protection, 167

trading cards, grading and authentication of, 332

transaction history, 228. *See also* Purchase History

transaction interference (bidding abuse), 319

transactions

blocking a customer, 257

compromise and communications as key to successful transactions, 334

cutting your losses when things go badly, 262–270

dealing with buyer who doesn't respond, 254–257

doing a little sleuthing, 256–257

editing fixed price listing, 264

ending listing early, 265–266

end-of-transaction emails, 65

getting children involved in, 155

going into nudge mode, 255–256

keeping track of, 65

making changes or canceling bids, 263–264

opening unpaid item case, 266–270

other possible auction problems, 257–262

Other Transactions and Notices preference, 55

PayPal transaction page, 140, 307

relisting your item, 270

requesting immediate payment, 254

Second Chance offer, 257–260

seller's remorse, 262

sending busted item, 261–262

setting buyer requirements, 254–255

troubleshooting of, 253–270

when a buyer backs out, 257–260

trending, 43, 207–209

tweets, 344–345

Twitter

Anita Nelson's account on, 343

author's account on, 6, 337, 346

connecting on, 344–346

for trending topics, 209

two-factor authentication, 305–307

U

Uline, 248

unclaimed freight, 214

under age (identity abuse), 321

underbidders, 82, 119

Un-Du, 246

UNICEF (online charity auction for), 352

unique, use of term in item title, 188

Unpaid Item Alert, 268

Unpaid Item Assistant, 267–268

Unpaid Item Case, 58, 120–121, 266–270

Unpaid Item Case form, 268

unpaid item claim, 259

unpaid item protection, 379

Unpaid Item report, 67

unwelcome bidder (bidding abuse), 319

UPC (Universal Product Code), 180, 185, 191

upgrade fees, 172

U-PIC, 233, 240, 261

UPS, as carrier option, 199, 231, 238–241

About the Author

Marsha Collier is the top-selling eBay author. Her name appears in the same breath as *e-commerce* and *customer service*. No surprise there. She's the author of the *For Dummies* series on eBay (*eBay For Dummies*, *eBay Business All-In-One For Dummies*), plus many other related, best-selling titles. She is one of the foremost e-commerce experts and educators in the world. Her books are published worldwide (special editions for the U.K., Germany, India, France, Canada, Australia, Russia, China — and an edition in Spanish). As of 2007, there were a million copies of her books in print, her first was published in 1997, and has been on multiple Best Seller lists. Marsha intermixes writing with her role as an experienced spokesperson. She makes regular appearances on television, radio, and in print to discuss business, technology, and customer service.

Marsha earned her eBay stripes as a longtime seller. She began her eBay career in 1996 to earn extra money for her daughter's education (and eventually paid for university with her eBay earnings). She was one of the first eBay PowerSellers. Now as a Top Rated Plus seller, you can find an interesting assortment of merchandise in her eBay Store. She also co-hosts Computer and Technology Radio on WSradio at http://bit.ly/tech-radio.

In 2004, Marsha began to blog at http://mcollier.blogspot.com to share timely topics for business and entrepreneurs.

As an early innovator in social media, Marsha penned several books; two of her favorites are *The Ultimate Online Customer Service Guide* and *Social Media Commerce For Dummies*. Her online brand has grown as she shares thoughts on how businesses can make the most of the Internet. She has been awarded many honors:

>> 2019 DigitalScoutings Top 50 Social Media Marketing Influencers

>> 2019 Browser Media Top 100 Digital Marketing Influencers

>> 2018 Brand24 Top 100 Digital Marketers

>> 2018 Onalytica Top 100 Digital Transformation Influencers

>> 2015, 2014 Brand Quarterly: 50 Marketing Thought Leaders Over 50

>> 2015 Inc. 25 Social Media Keynote Speakers You Need to Know

>> 2014 Huffington Post 100 Must Follow on Twitter

>> 2013, 2012, 2011 Forbes Top 20 Women Social Media Influencers

>> 2012 Small Business Book Awards: Startup Book Category, *Starting an eBay Business For Dummies*

Marsha currently resides in Los Angeles, California with her husband, Curt Buthman. You can contact Marsha via her website, coolebaytools.com.

Author's Acknowledgments

Thank you to everyone who has ever read one of my books and recommended one to someone else. Word of mouth is a powerful voice, and I appreciate all of you who spread the word. I couldn't have made it this long without your support.

This book couldn't have been written without the input from the hundreds of eBay sellers who share their successes and hard-knock stories with me.

Thank you to my husband, Curt Buthman, who understands how much I love writing these books and supports me in every way. Thanks also to my daughter, Susan Dickman, for being there when I need her for trending ideas.

My editor, Maureen Tullis, is beyond cool. Her comments and compliments made writing this book a pleasure. She's a real asset to the process, and this book wouldn't be as good as it is without her guidance. Patti Louise Ruby has been my tech editor (and friend) for longer than we'd both admit. She was one of eBay's first employees and stays up to date on the site — she double-checks my work!

Thanks also to Steve Hayes who's had faith in this series since edition one. Thank you for the 20 years of support.

Publisher's Acknowledgments

Executive Editor: Steve Hayes
Project Editor/Copy Editor: Scott Tullis
Technical Editor: Patti Louise Ruby
Editorial Assistant: Matthew Lowe

Production Editor: Magesh Elangovan
Project Manager: Maureen Tullis
Cover Image: Courtesy of Curt Buthman

Take dummies with you everywhere you go!

Whether you are excited about e-books, want more from the web, must have your mobile apps, or are swept up in social media, dummies makes everything easier.

Find us online!

dummies.com

PERSONAL ENRICHMENT

Staying Sharp
9781119187790
USA $26.00
CAN $31.99
UK £19.99

Facebook
9781119179030
USA $21.99
CAN $25.99
UK £16.99

Guitar
9781119293354
USA $24.99
CAN $29.99
UK £17.99

Investing
9781119293347
USA $22.99
CAN $27.99
UK £16.99

Beekeeping
9781119310068
USA $22.99
CAN $27.99
UK £16.99

Digital Photography
9781119235606
USA $24.99
CAN $29.99
UK £17.99

Meditation
9781119251163
USA $24.99
CAN $29.99
UK £17.99

Pregnancy
9781119235491
USA $26.99
CAN $31.99
UK £19.99

Samsung Galaxy S7
9781119279952
USA $24.99
CAN $29.99
UK £17.99

iPhone
9781119283133
USA $24.99
CAN $29.99
UK £17.99

Crocheting
9781119287117
USA $24.99
CAN $29.99
UK £16.99

Nutrition
9781119130246
USA $22.99
CAN $27.99
UK £16.99

PROFESSIONAL DEVELOPMENT

Windows 10
9781119311041
USA $24.99
CAN $29.99
UK £17.99

AutoCAD
9781119255796
USA $39.99
CAN $47.99
UK £27.99

Excel 2016
9781119293439
USA $26.99
CAN $31.99
UK £19.99

QuickBooks 2017
9781119281467
USA $26.99
CAN $31.99
UK £19.99

macOS Sierra
9781119280651
USA $29.99
CAN $35.99
UK £21.99

LinkedIn
9781119251132
USA $24.99
CAN $29.99
UK £17.99

Windows 10
9781119310563
USA $34.00
CAN $41.99
UK £24.99

SharePoint 2016
9781119181705
USA $29.99
CAN $35.99
UK £21.99

Fundamental Analysis
9781119263593
USA $26.99
CAN $31.99
UK £19.99

Networking
9781119257769
USA $29.99
CAN $35.99
UK £21.99

Office 2016
9781119293477
USA $26.99
CAN $31.99
UK £19.99

Office 365
9781119265313
USA $24.99
CAN $29.99
UK £17.99

Salesforce.com
9781119239314
USA $29.99
CAN $35.99
UK £21.99

Coding
9781119293323
USA $29.99
CAN $35.99
UK £21.99

dummies.com

dummies®
A Wiley Brand